PERFORMANCE BY DESIGN
Computer Capacity Planning by Example

W9-AWR-927

PERFORMANCE BY DESIGN
Computer Capacity Planning by Example

Daniel A. Menascé
Virgilio A.F. Almeida
Lawrence W. Dowdy

PRENTICE HALL PTR
UPPER SADDLE RIVER, NJ 07458
WWW.PHPTR.COM

Library of Congress Cataloging-in-Publication Data

A CIP catalog record for this book can be obtained from the Library of Congress)

Editorial/Production Supervision: Mary Sudul
Cover Design Director: Jerry Votta
Cover Design: Talar Boorujy
Art Director: Gail Cocker-Bogusz
Manufacturing Manager: Alexis R. Heydt-Long
Acquisitions Editor: Jeffrey Pepper
Editorial Assistant: Linda Ramagnano
Marketing Manager: Robin O'Brien

© 2004 Pearson Education, Inc.
Publishing as Prentice Hall Professional Technical Reference
Upper Saddle River, New Jersey 07458

Prentice Hall PTR offers excellent discounts on this book when ordered in quantity for bulk purchases or special sales.þ For more information, please contact: U.S. Corporate and Government Sales, 1-800-382-3419, corpsales@pearsontechgroup.com. For sales outside of the U.S., please contact: International Sales, 1-317-581-3793, international@pearsontechgroup.com.

Company and product names mentioned herein are the trademarks or registered trademarks of their respective owners.

All rights reserved. No part of this book may be reproduced, in any form or by any means, without permission in writing from the publisher.

Printed in the United States of America
First Printing

ISBN 0-13-090673-5

Pearson Education Ltd.
Pearson Education Australia Pty., Limited
Pearson Education Singapore, Pte. Ltd.
Pearson Education North Asia Ltd.
Pearson Education Canada, Ltd.
Pearson Educación de Mexico, S.A. de C.V.
Pearson Education—Japan
Pearson Education Malaysia, Pte. Ltd.

To my wife Gilda and to the beautiful family we built together. I am so glad we met in this world!

To my wife Rejane and my children Pedro and André.

To my parents, my wife Sharon, my son David and his wife Michelle, and my daughter Erin. You are the best!

. . . and to you, the reader. If something in these pages benefits your performance, then our design will have indeed succeeded.

Contents

Contents

Contents

Preface

Goal, Theme, and Approach

The idea of writing this book originated from our observation that some of the most fundamental concepts and methods related to performance modeling and analysis are largely unknown to most Information Technology (IT) practitioners. As a result, many IT systems are designed and built without sufficient consideration given to their non-functional requirements such as performance, availability, and reliability. More often than not, performance is an afterthought. Performance testing is done when a system is nearing completion. At that late stage, it may be necessary to conduct a major redesign to correct eventual performance problems. This approach is inefficient, expensive, time consuming, and professionally irresponsible.

A major goal of this book is to provide to those involved in designing and building computer systems a performance engineering framework to be applied throughout a computer system's life cycle. This framework is quantitative, rigorous, and based on the theory of queuing networks. Some of our readers may not be interested in the details behind the models. For that reason, we divided the book into two parts: the practice of performance engineering (Part I) and the theory of performance engineering (Part II).

Part I brings many examples and case studies supported by algorithms implemented in Visual Basic modules attached to the various MS Excel workbooks provided with the book. Five complete case studies are inspired in real-world problems: a database service sizing, a Web service capacity planning situation, a data center's cost and availability analysis, the sizing of an e-business service, and the performance engineering of a future help desk

1

application. After reading Part I, the reader should be able to 1) identify the sources of potential performance problems of a computer system and 2) build and solve performance models to answer what-if questions regarding competing hardware and software alternatives. The models that you build can be solved with the tools provided with the book.

Part II presents the theory of performance engineering in an intuitive, example-driven manner. Before the algorithms and methods are formalized, the basic ideas are derived from first principles applied to examples. The readers of part II are exposed to the most important techniques for solving 1) Markov models, 2) open and closed multiclass queuing networks using exact and approximate methods, and 3) non-product form queuing networks that represent software contention, blocking, high service time variability, priority scheduling, and fork and join systems.

Throughout Part I, references to specific techniques and methods of Part II provide a nice integration between the two components of this text.

Who Should Read This Book

Information technology professionals must ensure that the systems under their management provide an acceptable quality of service to their users. Managers must avoid the pitfalls of inadequate capacity and meet users' performance expectations in a cost-effective manner. Performance engineers, system administrators, software engineers, network administrators, capacity planners and analysts, managers, consultants, and other IT professionals will benefit from reading parts or the entire book. Its practical, yet sound and formal, approach provides the basis for understanding modern and complex networked environments.

This book can also be used as a textbook for senior undergraduate and graduate courses in Computer Science and Computer Engineering. Exercises are provided at the end of all fifteen chapters. At the undergraduate level, the book is a good starting point to motivate students to learn the important implications and solutions to performance problems. An undergraduate course would concentrate on the first part of the book, i.e., the practice of performance engineering. At the graduate level, it can be used in System Performance Evaluation courses. This book offers a theoretical and practical foundation in performance modeling. The book can also be used as a supplement for systems courses, including Operating Systems, Distributed Systems, and Networking, both at the undergraduate and graduate levels.

Book Organization

Part I: The Practice of Performance Engineering

Chapter 1 introduces several properties and metrics used to assess the quality of IT systems. Such metrics include response time, throughput, availability, reliability, security, scalability, and extensibility. The chapter also discusses the various phases of the life cycle of a computer system and shows the importance of addressing QoS issues early on in the design stage as opposed to after the system is deployed.

Chapter 2 presents the *qualitative* aspects of the performance engineering framework used in this book. The framework is based on queuing networks. The chapter uses examples of practical systems to introduce the various aspects of such queuing networks.

Chapter 3 focuses on the *quantitative* aspects of the queuing network framework and introduces the input parameters and performance metrics that can be obtained from these models. The notions of service times, arrival rates, service demands, utilization, queue lengths, response time, through-put, and waiting time are discussed. The chapter also introduces Operational Analysis, a set of basic quantitative relationships between performance quantities.

Chapter 4 presents a practical performance engineering methodology and describes its steps: specification of the system's performance goals, under-standing the current environment, characterization of the workload, development of a performance model, validation of the performance and workload models, workload forecasting, and cost $\times$ performance analysis of competing alternatives.

Chapter 5 uses a complete case study of a database service sizing to introduce the issue of obtaining input parameters to performance models from measurement data. The chapter also discusses various types of software monitors and their use in the data collection process.

Chapter 6 uses a Web server capacity planning case study to introduce several important concepts in performance engineering, including the determination of confidence intervals, the computation of service demands from the results of experiments, the use of linear regression, and comparison of alternatives through analytic modeling and through experimentation.

Chapter 7 applies performance modeling techniques to address the issue of properly sizing a data center. This sizing is part of the system design process and focuses on the number of machines and the number and skill level of maintenance personnel to achieve desired levels of availability.

Chapter 8 shows, through an online auction site case study, how performance models are used to analyze the scalability of multi-tiered e-business services. The workload of these services is characterized at the user level. User models are used to characterize the way customers navigate through the various e-business functions during a typical visit to an e-commerce site. This user-level characterization is mapped to a request-level characterization used by queuing network models. The models are used for capacity planning and performance prediction of various what-if scenarios.

Chapter 9 discusses Software Performance Engineering through a complete case study of the development and sizing of a new help desk application. The chapter explains how parameters for performance models can be estimated at various stages of a system's life cycle. The solutions of these models provide valuable feedback to developers at the early stages of a new application under development.

Part II: The Theory of Performance Engineering

Chapter 10 presents a basic, practical, and working knowledge of Markov models through easy-to-understand examples. Then, the general solution to birth-death Markov chains is presented.

Chapter 11 discusses the most important results in single queuing stations systems. The results presented include M/M/1, M/G/1, M/G/1 with server vacation, M/G/1 with non-preemptive priority, M/G/1 with preemptive resume priority, G/G/1 approximation, and G/G/c approximation. Computer and network related examples illustrate the use of the results.

Chapter 12 reconstructs single class Mean Value Analysis (MVA) from first principles and illustrates the use of the technique through a detailed example. The special case of balanced systems is discussed.

Chapter 13 generalizes the results of chapter 12 to the case of multi-class queuing networks. Results and algorithms for open, closed, and mixed queuing networks are presented. Both exact and approximate techniques are discussed.

Chapter 14 extends the results of chapter 13 for the case of load-dependent devices. These extended model address situations where a device's service rate varies with the queue size.

Chapter 15 discusses approximations to the Mean Value Analysis technique to deal with blocking, high variability of service times, priority scheduling, software contention, and fork and join.

Acknowledgments

Daniel Menascé would like to thank his students and colleagues at George Mason University for providing a stimulating work environment. He would also like to thank his mother and late father for their love and guidance in life. Special recognition goes to his wife, Gilda, a very special person, whose love and companionship makes all the difference in the world. His children Flavio and Juliana have tremendously enriched his life from the moment they were born.

Virgilio Almeida would like to thank his colleagues and students at UFMG. He would also like to thank CNPq (the Brazilian Council for Scientific Research and Development), which provided partial support for his research work. Virgilio would also like to express his gratitude to his family, parents (in memoriam), brothers, and many relatives and friends. His wife Rejane and sons Pedro and André have always been a source of continuous encouragement and inspiration.

Larry Dowdy would like to gratefully thank the students and faculty at the University of Leeds, England, particularly David Dubas-Fisher, Jonathan Galliano, Michael Harwood, and Gurpreet Sohal for their feedback, support, and insights. In addition, the Vanderbilt students in CS284 provided many constructive and insightful comments.

From the Same Authors

- *Capacity Planning for Web Services: Metrics, Models, and Methods*, D. A. Menascé and V. A. F. Almeida, Prentice Hall, Upper Saddle River, NJ, 2002.

- *Scaling for E-Business: Technologies, Models, Performance, and Capacity Planning*, D. A. Menascé and V. A. F. Almeida, Prentice Hall, Upper Saddle River, NJ, 2000.

- *Capacity Planning for Web Performance: Metrics, Models, and Methods*, D. A. Menascé and V. A. F. Almeida, Prentice Hall, Upper Saddle River, NJ, 1998.

- *Capacity Planning and Performance Modeling: From Mainframes to Client-Server Systems*, D. A. Menascé, V. A. F. Almeida, L. W. Dowdy, Prentice Hall, Upper Saddle River, NJ, 1994

Book's Web Site and Authors' Addresses

The Web site at www.cs.gmu.edu/~menasce/perfbyd/ will be used to keep the readers informed about new developments related to the book and to store the various Excel workbooks described in the book. Some of the Excel workbooks are password protected. The password is 2004.

The authors' e-mail, postal addresses, and Web sites are:

Professor Daniel A. Menascé
Department of Computer Science, MS 4A5
George Mason University
Fairfax, VA 22030-4444
United States
(703) 993-1537
menasce@cs.gmu.edu
www.cs.gmu.edu/faculty/menasce.html

Professor Virgilio A. F. Almeida
Department of Computer Science
Universidade Federal de Minas Gerais
P.O. Box 920
31270-010 Belo Horizonte, MG
Brazil
+55 31 3499-5887

virgilio@dcc.ufmg.br
www.dcc.ufmg.br/~virgilio

Professor Larry W. Dowdy
Department of Electrical Engineering and Computer Science
Vanderbilt University
Station B, Box 1679,
Nashville, TN 37235
(615) 322-3031
larry.dowdy@vanderbilt.edu
www.vuse.vanderbilt.edu/~dowdy/persinfo.html

We hope that you will enjoy reading this book as much as we enjoyed writing it!

Daniel Menascé,
Virgilio Almeida, and
Larry Dowdy

Part I
The Practice of Performance Engineering

Chapter 1

Computer System Lifecycle

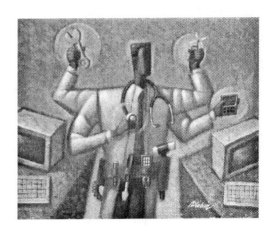

1.1 Introduction

IT systems are becoming increasingly ubiquitous and help support most aspects of everyday life. The Internet has helped accelerate the rate at which IT is integrated into most social systems. People rely on IT systems to address most of their major human and social concerns such as health, education, entertainment, access to communication services, access to customer support, finances, safety, privacy, access to government services, and travel. The various concerns of individuals and of the society as a whole may face major breakdowns and incur high costs if IT systems do not meet the Quality of Service (QoS) requirements of performance, availability, security, and maintainability that are expected from them.

For example, a call to 911—the emergency number in the U.S.—has to be answered by a dispatcher in a few seconds or human life may be endangered. When the stock market goes through periods of extreme ups and downs, a large number of online traders tend to flock to online trading sites, causing potential problems due to overloaded and non-responsive systems. The inability to trade in a timely manner may cause substantial financial losses. During health crises, such as the outbreak of new diseases, people need to get easy and fast access to health insurance companies to obtain authorization to be admitted to a hospital or to undergo a medical procedure.

In times of terrorism threats, major infrastructures, such as the telephone and cellular networks, may be targeted by terrorists or, in case of attacks to other structures, may become overloaded as their capacity to process calls is stretched thin, impairing the responsiveness of such systems. The operation of the military is becoming more and more dependent on an agile information and communications infrastructure to help locate, find, target, and destroy enemy forces. This infrastructure has to be properly designed and sized to handle the extraordinary demands of battlefield information exchanges.

Most people need to interact with automated or semi-automated customer support systems and expect near immediate response. Unfortunately, it is not uncommon for someone to be placed on hold for dozens of minutes before being connected to a human being who will take care of a problem or provide the needed information. These situations cause significant frustration and are a major cause for companies to lose customers.

The number of people signing up for access to a wide variety of communication services such as wireless and Internet access services is increasing at exponential rates. The growth in traffic has not been met by an adequate growth in system capacity. As a result, callers may hear the unpleasant recording "all circuits are busy, please try your call later," when trying to place a call. People have come to expect 24 / 7, instantaneous, and extremely reliable services.

1.2   QoS in IT Systems

IT systems touch people everywhere and every effort must be made to ensure that IT systems operate reliably and dependably so that they meet the needs of society and complement the capabilities of users [1].

This section discusses the following QoS attributes of an IT system: response time, throughput, availability, reliability, security, scalability, and extensibility.

1.2.1 Response Time

The time it takes a system to react to a human request is called the *response time*. An example is the time it takes for a page to appear in your browser with the results of a search of the catalog of your preferred online bookstore. The response time, usually measured in seconds, may be broken down into several components.

Figure 1.1 shows the three major components of the response time of a search request to an e-commerce site: browser time, network time, and server time. The browser time includes the processing and I/O time required to send the search request and display the result page. The network time component includes the time spent in the transmission from the browser to the user's Internet Service Provider (ISP), the time spent in the Internet, and the time spent in communication between the ISP at the e-commerce site and its server. The third component includes all the times involved in processing the request at the e-commerce site, all the I/O time, the networking time internal to the e-commerce site. Any of the three components include the time spent waiting to use various resources (processors, disks, and networks). This is called *congestion* time. The congestion time depends on the number of requests being processed by a system. The higher the number of requests in the system, the higher the congestion time. In this book we will learn how to compute the congestion time through the use of performance models.

1.2.2 Throughput

The rate at which requests are completed from a computer system is called *throughput* and is measured in operations per unit time. The nature of the operation depends on the computer system in question. Examples of systems

Browser Time		Network Time			E-commerce Server Time		
Processing	I/O	Browser to ISP Time	Internet Time	ISP to Server Time	Processing	I/O	Networking
·· **C O N G E S T I O N** ··							

Figure 1.1. Breakdown of response time.

and corresponding typical throughput metrics are given in Table 1.1. When considering a throughput metric, one has to make sure that the operation in question is well-defined. For example, in an Online Transaction Processing (OLTP) system, throughput is generally measured in transactions per second (tps). However, transactions may vary significantly in nature and in the amount of resources they require from the OLTP system. So, in order for the throughput value to be meaningful, one has to characterize the type of transaction considered when reporting the throughput. In some cases, this characterization is done by referring to a well established industry benchmark. For example, the Transaction Processing Performance Council (TPC) defines a benchmark for OLTP systems, called TPC-C, that specifies a mix of transactions typical of an order-entry system. The throughput metric defined by the benchmark measures the number of orders that can be fully processed per minute and is expressed in tpm-C [17].

Table 1.1. Examples of Throughput Metrics

System	Throughput Metric
OLTP System	Transactions per Second (tps)
	tpm-C [17]
Web Site	HTTP requests/sec
	Page Views per Second
	Bytes/sec
E-commerce Site	Web Interactions Per Second (WIPS) [18]
	Sessions per Second
	Searches per Second
Router	Packets per Second (PPS)
	MB transferred per Second
CPU	Millions of Instructions per Second (MIPS)
	Floating Point Operations per Second (FLOPS)
Disk	I/Os per Second
	KB transferred per Second
E-mail Server	Messages Sent Per Second

The throughput is a function of the load offered to a system and of the maximum capacity of a system to process work as illustrated in Example 1.1.

Example 1.1

Assume that an I/O operation at a disk in an OLTP system takes 10 msec on average. If the disk is constantly busy (i.e., its utilization is 100%), then it will be executing I/O operations continuously at a rate of one I/O operation every 10 msec or 0.01 sec. So, the maximum throughput of the disk is 100 (= 1 / .01) I/Os per second. But if the rate at which I/O requests are submitted to the disk is less than 100 requests/sec, then its throughput will be equal to the rate at which requests are submitted. This leads to the expression

$$\text{throughput} = \text{minimum} \quad [\text{servercapacity}, \text{offeredworkload}]. \quad (1.2.1)$$

This is expression has to be qualified by the assumption that arriving requests do not "change their mind" if the system is busy, as happens routinely in Web sites. ∎

As seen in the top curve of Fig. 1.2, throughput shows an almost linear increase at light loads and then saturates at its maximum value when one of the system resources achieves 100% utilization. However, in some cases, at high overall loads, throughput can actually decrease as the load increases further. This phenomenon is called *thrashing*, and its impact on throughput is depicted in the bottom curve of Fig. 1.2. An example of thrashing occurs when a computer system with insufficient main memory spends a significant amount of CPU cycles and I/O bandwidth to handle page faults as opposed to process the workload. This may occur because at high loads there are too many processes competing for a fixed amount of main memory. As each process gets less memory for its working set, the page fault rate increases significantly and the throughput decreases. The operating system continuously spends its time handling extra overhead operations (due to increased load), which diminishes the time the CPU can be allocated to processes. This increases the backlog even further, leading to a downward performance spiral that can cripple the system, in a way similar to a traffic jam.

An important consideration when evaluating computer systems is to determine the maximum effective throughput of that system and how to achieve it. More on this will be discussed in Chapter 3.

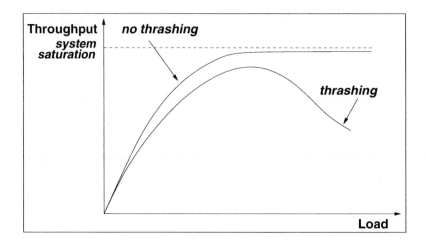

Figure 1.2. Throughput vs. load.

1.2.3   Availability

Imagine that you access an online bookstore and get as a result the page shown in Fig. 1.3. You are likely to become frustrated and may turn to another online bookstore to buy the book you are looking for. The consequences of system unavailability can be far more reaching than a loss of customers. The credibility and reputation of a company are vital. As mentioned by Schneider [15], service interruptions can even threaten lives and property.

Availability is defined as the fraction of time that a system is up and available to its customers. For example, a system with 99.99% availability over a period of thirty days would be unavailable for

$$(1 - 0.9999) \times 30 \text{ days} \times 24 \text{ hours/day} \times 60 \text{ min/hr} = 4.32 \text{ minutes.} \quad (1.2.2)$$

For many systems (e.g., an online bookstore), this level of unavailability would be considered excellent. However, for other systems (e.g., defense systems, 911 services), even 99.99% would be unacceptable.

The two main reasons for systems to be unavailable are failures and overloads. Failures may prevent users from accessing a computer system. For example, the network connection of a Web site may be down and no users may be able to send their requests for information. Alternatively,

Figure 1.3. Availability problems.

overloads occur when all components are operational but the system does not have enough resources to handle the magnitude of new incoming requests. This situation usually causes requests to be rejected. For instance, a Web server may refuse to open a new TCP connection if the maximum number of connections is reached.

Failures must be handled rapidly to avoid extended down times. The first step for failure handling is failure detection. Then, the causes of the failures must be found so that the proper resources (e.g., people and materiel) may be put in place to bring the system back to its normal operational state. Thus, failure handling comprises failure detection, failure diagnosis, and failure recovery.

One of the reasons for controlling and limiting the number of requests that are handled concurrently by an IT system is to guarantee good quality of service for the requests that are admitted. This is called *admission control* and is illustrated in Fig. 1.4, which shows two response time curves versus system load. If no admission control is used, response time tends to grow

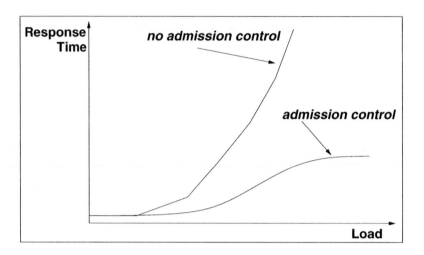

Figure 1.4. Impact of admission control on response time.

exponentially with the load. In the case of admission control, the number of requests within the system is limited so that response time does not exceed a certain threshold. This is accomplished at the expense of rejecting requests. Thus, while accepted requests experience an acceptable level of service, the reject ones may suffer very large delays to be admitted.

1.2.4   Reliability

The reliability of a system is the probability that it functions properly and continuously over a fixed period of time [8]. Reliability and availability are closely related concepts but are different. When the time period during which the reliability is computed becomes very large, the reliability tends to the availability.

1.2.5   Security

Security is a combination of three basic attributes:

- *Confidentiality*: only authorized individuals are allowed access to the relevant information.

- *Data Integrity*: information cannot be modified by unauthorized users.

- *Non-repudiation*: senders of a message are prevented from denying having sent the message.

To enforce these properties, systems need to implement *authentication* mechanisms [5] to guarantee that each side in a message exchange is assured that the other is indeed the person they say they are. Most authentication mechanisms used to provide system security are based on one or more forms of encryption. Some encryption operations may be very expensive from the computational standpoint. The tradeoffs between security and performance have been studied in [6, 7, 9, 14].

1.2.6   Scalability

A system is said to be *scalable* if its performance does not degrade significantly as the number of users, or equivalently, the load on the system increases. For example, the response time of system A in Fig. 1.5 increases in a non-linear fashion with the load, while that of system B exhibits a much more controlled growth. System A is not scalable while system B is.

1.2.7   Extensibility

Extensibility is the property of a system to easily evolve to cope with new functional and performance requirements. It is not uncommon for new functionalities to be required once a new system goes into production. Even a careful requirements analysis cannot necessarily uncover or anticipate all the needs of system users.

Changes in the environment in which the system has to operate (e.g., new laws and regulations, different business models) may require that the system evolve to adapt to new circumstances.

1.3   System Life Cycle

Addressing performance problems at the end of system development is a common industrial practice that can lead to using more expensive hardware than originally specified, time consuming performance-tuning procedures, and, in some extreme cases, to a complete system redesign [3]. It is therefore important to consider performance as an integral part of a computer system life cycle and not as an afterthought. The methods used to assure that that QoS requirements are met, once a system is developed, are part of the discipline called Performance Engineering (PE) [16].

This section discusses the seven phases of the life cyle of any IT system: requirements analysis and specification, design, development, testing, deployment, operation, and evolution as illustrated in Fig. 1.6. The inputs and outputs of each phase are discussed, the tasks involved in each phase are described, and QoS issues associated with each phase are addressed.

1.3.1 Requirements Analysis and Specification

During this phase of the life cycle of a computer system, the analysts, in conjunction with users, gather information about what they want the system to do. The result of this analysis is a requirements specifications document that is divided into two main parts:

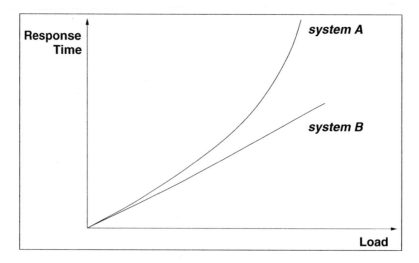

Figure 1.5. Scalability.

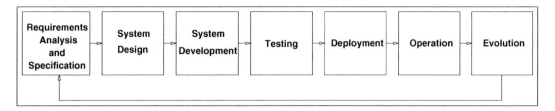

Figure 1.6. System life cycle.

- *Functional requirements:* The functional requirements specify the set of functions the system must provide with the corresponding inputs and outputs as well as the interaction patterns between the system and the outside world (users). For example, the functional requirements of an online bookstore could indicate that the site must provide a search function that allows users to search for books based on keywords, ISBN, title, and authors. The specification indicates how the results of a search are displayed back to the user. The functional requirements usually include information about the physical environment and technology to be used to design and implement the system. In the same example, the specification could say that the online bookstore site should use Web servers based on UNIX and Apache and that it should also provide access to wireless users using the Wireless Application Protocol (WAP) [19].

- *Non-functional requirements:* The non-functional requirements deal mainly with the QoS requirements expected from the system. Issues such as performance, availability, reliability, and security are specified as part of the non-functional requirements. A qualitative and quantitative characterization of the workload must be given so that the QoS requirements can be specified for specific workload types and levels. For example, a non-functional requirement could specify that "at peak periods, the online bookstore is expected to receive 50 search requests/sec and respond within 2 seconds to 95% of the requests."

Table 1.2. Online Trading Site Down Periods

Day	Start of Down Time	Duration of Down Time (min)
1	1:25 AM	12
1	7:01 AM	1
1	8:31 PM	5
2	2:15 AM	10
2	9:12 PM	6

Table 1.3. Online Trading Site Down Periods

Day	Start of Down Time	Duration of Down Time (min)
3	9:35 AM	15
3	1:13 PM	2
4	10:31AM	3
4	2:15 PM	8
4	3:12 PM	6

5. Re-evaluate a software development project you were involved in and list the non-functional requirements related to performance and availability specified for the project. Explain how these requirements were addressed in each phase of the system life cycle.

Bibliography

[1] Computer Science and Telecommunications Board, *Making IT Better: Expanding Information Technology Research to Meet Society's Needs*, National Academy Press, Washington, D.C., 2000.

[2] Y. Diao, N. Gandhi, J. L. Hellerstein, S. Parekh, and D. M. Tilbury, "Using MIMO Feedback control to enforce policies for interrelated metrics with application to the apache Web server," IBM Research TR RC22164, 2001.

[3] E. Dimitrov, A. Schmietendorf, and R. Dumke, "UML-based performance engineering possibilities and techniques," *IEEE Software*, January/February 2002, pp. 74–83.

[4] A. K. Ghosh, "Building software securely from the ground up," *IEEE Software*, January/February 2002, pp. 14–16.

[5] A. K. Ghosh, *E-Commerce Security: Weak Links Best Defenses*, John Wiley & Sons, New York, NY, 1998.

[6] A. Harbitter and D. A. Menascé, "The performance of public key enabled Kerberos authentication in mobile computing applications," *Proc. Eighth ACM Conference on Computer and Communications Security (CCS-8)*, Philadelphia, Pennsylvania, November 5-8, 2001.

[7] A. Harbitter and D. A. Menascé, "Performance of public key-enabled Kerberos authentication in large networks," *Proc. 2001 IEEE Symposium on Security and Privacy*, Oakland, California, May 13-16, 2001.

[8] D. E. Long, A. Muir, and R. Golding, "A longitudinal survey of internet host reliability," HP Labs, Technical Report HPL-CCD-95-4, February 1995.

[9] D. A. Menascé, "Security performance," *Internet Computing*, May/June 2003, vol. 7, no. 2, IEEE Computer Society.

[10] D. A. Menascé, "Load testing, benchmarking, and application Performance management," *Proc. 2002 Computer Measurement Group (CMG) Conf.*, Reno, NV, December 8-13, 2002, pp. 271–281.

[11] D. A. Menascé and V. A. F. Almeida, *Capacity Planning for Web Services: Metrics, Models, and Methods*, Prentice Hall, Upper Saddle River, New Jersey, 2002.

[12] D. A. Menascé, "Load testing of web sites," *Internet Computing*, July/August 2002, vol. 6, no. 4, IEEE Computer Society, pp. 70–74.

[13] D. A. Menascé, D. Barbará, and R. Dodge, "Preserving QoS of e-commerce sites through self-tuning: A performance model approach," *Proc. 2001 ACM Conference on E-commerce*, Tampa, Florida, October 14- 17, 2001.

[14] D. A. Menascé and V. A. F. Almeida, *Scaling for E-Business: Technologies, Metrics, Performance, and Capacity Planning*, Prentice Hall, Upper Saddle River, New Jersey, 2000.

[15] F. B. Schneider, "Toward trustworthy networked information systems," *Comm. ACM*, November 1998, vol. 40, no. 11, pp. 144.

[16] C. U. Smith, "Performance Engineering," in *Encyclopedia of Software Eng.*, J. J. Maciniak (ed.), John Wiley & Sons, New York, NY, 1994, pp. 794–810.

[17] Transaction Processing Performance Council, TPC-C: An Order-Entry Benchmark, www.tpc.org.

[18] Transaction Processing Performance Council, TPC-W: A Transactional Web E-commerce Benchmark, www.tpc.org.

[19] WAP Forum, www.wapforum.org.

Chapter 2

From Systems to Descriptive Models

2.1 Introduction

Performance and scalability are much easier to guarantee if they are taken
into account at the time of system design. Treating performance as an afterthought (i.e., as something that can be tested for compliance after a system
has been developed) usually leads to frustration. In this chapter, we start
to provide a useful framework that can be used by computer system designers to think about performance at design time. This framework is based
on the observation that computer systems, including software systems, are
composed of a collection of resources (e.g., processors, disks, communication
links, process threads, critical sections, database locks) that are shared by
various requests (e.g., transactions, Web requests, batch processes). Usually,
there are several requests running concurrently and many of them may want
to access the same resource at the same time. Since resources have a finite
capacity of performing work (e.g., a CPU can only execute a finite number
of instructions per second, a disk can only transfer a certain number of bytes
per second, and a communications link can only transmit a certain number

35

of bits per second) waiting lines often build up in front of these resources, in the same way queues form at bank tellers or at supermarket cashiers.

Thus, the framework used in this book is based on *queuing models* of computer systems. These models view a computer system as a collection of interconnected queues, or a *network of queues*. This chapter describes the qualitative aspect of the framework while the following chapters introduce more quantitative characteristics. A general discussion on modeling is presented before queuing models are introduced.

2.2   Modeling

A model is an abstraction or generalized overview of a real system. The level of detail of a model and the specific aspects of the real system that are considered in the model depend on the purpose of the model. A model should not be made more complex than is necessary to achieve its goals. For instance, if the purpose is to predict what would happen if more memory were added to the system, it may not be necessary to model (or even completely understand) the specific disk scheduling strategy. On the other hand, knowing the average number of jobs that can fit within an extra megabyte of memory would be necessary in the model.

The only completely reliable model of a system is itself (or a duplicate copy). However, it is often infeasible, too costly, or impossible to construct such a prototype model. Future designed systems are not yet available and physically altering existing systems is nontrivial. At the other extreme, intuitive models (i.e., relying on the "experience" or "gut instinct" of one's local "computer guru"), although quick and inexpensive, suffer from lack of accuracy and bias. More scientific methods to model building are then required.

There are two major types of more scientific models: *simulation* and *analytic* models. Simulation models are based on computer programs that emulate the different dynamic aspects of a system as well as their static structure. The workload is typically a set of customers (i.e., transactions, jobs, commands) that comes from a specified, often observed, trace script or benchmark. Alternatively, the customer workload is generated through a probabilistic process, using random number generators. The flow of customers through the system generates events such as customer arrivals at the waiting line of a server, beginning of service at any given server, end of service, and the selection of which device to visit next. The events are processed according to their order of occurrence in time. Counters accumulate statistics that are used at the end of a simulation to estimate the values of several important performance measures. For instance, the average response time, T, at a device (i.e., server) can be estimated as

$$T = \frac{\sum_{i=1}^{n_t} T_i}{n_t}$$

where T_i is the response time experienced by the ith transaction and n_t is the total number of transactions that visited the server during the simulation. The value of T obtained in a single simulation run must be viewed as a single point in a sample space. Thus, several simulation runs are required to generate a sample of adequate size to allow for a statistical analysis to be carried out.

Because of the level of detail generally necessary in simulation models, they are often too expensive to develop, validate, and run. On the other hand, once constructed, simulation models allow for the investigation of phenomena at a detailed level of study. The are good references on simulation techniques [3]-[5].

Analytic models are composed of a set of formulas and/or computational algorithms that provide the values of desired performance measures as a function of the set of input workload parameters. For analytic models to be mathematically tractable, they are generally less detailed than simulation models. Therefore, they tend to be less accurate but more efficient to run. For example, a single-server queue (under certain assumptions to be discussed in later chapters) can expect its average response time, T, to be

$$T = \frac{S}{1 - \lambda S}$$

where S is the average time spent by a typical request at the server (service time) and λ is the average arrival rate of customer requests to the server.

The primary advantages of analytic and simulation models are, respectively:

- Analytic models are less expensive to construct and tend to be computationally more efficient to run than simulation models.

- Because of their higher level of abstraction, obtaining the values of the input parameters in analytic models is simpler than in simulation models.

- Simulation models can be made as detailed as needed and can be more accurate than analytic models.

- There are some system behaviors that analytic models cannot (or very poorly) capture, thus necessitating the need for simulation.

The reader should be cautioned that simulation models that are not properly validated can produce useless and misleading results. As noted, in some situations exact analytic models are not available or are computationally inefficient. In these cases, one can resort to approximations that may render the model easier to solve or solvable in a more efficient manner. The price is one of fidelity and accuracy. It is difficult to gauge the accuracy of the approximation. Simulation models are quite useful in this regard, since one can always compare the results obtained from a detailed simulation model with those obtained by approximate analytic models. Once convinced that the approximation is reasonably accurate, the simulation model can be abandoned in favor of a simpler and more efficient analytic model.

In capacity planning, the analyst is generally interested in being able to quickly compare and evaluate different scenarios. Accuracies at the 10% to 30% level are often acceptable for this purpose. Because of their efficiency and flexibility, analytic models (exact or approximate) are generally preferable for capacity planning purposes. This is the approach taken in this book.

2.3 A Simple Database Server Example

Consider a database server that has one CPU and one disk. Database transactions arrive to the database server for execution at a certain rate (e.g., 1.5 transactions per second (tps)). During its execution, a transaction alternates using the processor and the disk, quite likely more than once. At any point in time, one transaction might be using the CPU and another using the disk, while yet other transactions are waiting to use the CPU or disk. Thus, the CPU and the disk can each be characterized as a *queue* with

a waiting line and a device that serves transactions. Figure 2.1 (a) shows
a graphical representation used to illustrate a queue with a single resource
server. Transactions arrive and wait if the resource is busy, otherwise they
start using the resource immediately. In some cases, there is a single waiting
line for multiple resources (e.g., a multiprocessor, a single line for multiple
tellers at the bank). This type of queue is represented in Fig. 2.1 (b). Here,
a transaction waits in line if all m resources are busy. As soon as a resource
becomes available, it starts serving one of the transactions waiting in the
queue.

The notation just described can be used to represent a simple database
server, as illustrated in Fig. 2.2. This figure depicts a network of queues,
or *Queuing Network (QN)*. Elements such as database transactions, HTTP
requests, and batch jobs, that receive service from each queue in the QN
are generically called *customers*. QNs are used throughout this book as a
framework to think about performance at all stages within a system's life
cycle.

Mapping an existing system into a QN is not trivial. Models are usually
built with a specific goal in mind. For instance, one may want to know how
the response time of database transactions varies with the rate at which
transactions are submitted to the database server. Or, one may want to know
the response time if the server is upgraded. Good models abstract out some
of the complexities of real systems while retaining what is essential to meet
the model goals. For example, the QN model for the database server example

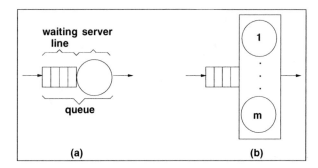

Figure 2.1. (a) Single queue with one resource server (b) Single queue with m resource
servers.

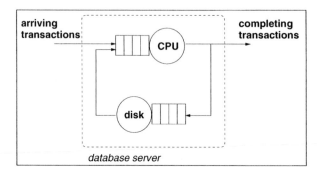

Figure 2.2. Queuing network for a simple database server.

abstracts the complexity of a rotating magnetic disk (e.g., disk controller, disk cache, rotating platter, arm) into a single resource characterized by a single parameter (i.e., the average number of I/Os that the disk can service per second). However, if one were interested in studying the effect of different disk architectures on performance, then the specific features of interest in the I/O architecture would have to be explicitly considered by the model.

In order to use a QN model of the database server to predict performance for a given transaction arrival rate (e.g., 1.5 tps) one needs to know how much time a typical transaction spends using the CPU and the disk (i.e., the total service time required by a transaction at the CPU and disk). The model is then used to compute the waiting time of a transaction at the CPU and at the disk. The total average service time of a transaction at a resource is called its *service demand*. This is an important notion that will be revisited many times in this book. Waiting times depend on service demands and on the system load (i.e., the average number of concurrent transactions in the system).

2.4   The Database Server Example: Multiple Classes

Suppose that an investigation of the database management system log reveals that individual transactions submitted to the database server have significantly different characteristics. However, also suppose that the analyst notes that these transactions can be grouped into three distinct groups of fairly similar transactions, as indicated in Table 2.1: trivial, medium, and

Table 2.1. Summary Statistics for the Database Server

Transaction Group	Percentage of Total	Average CPU Time (sec)	Avg. Number of I/Os
Trivial	45%	0.04	5.5
Medium	25%	0.18	28.9
Complex	30%	1.20	85.0

complex. These transaction groups differ in the average CPU time and average number of I/Os per transaction. Therefore, it would not be appropriate to characterize the transactions submitted to the database server as a single group. If they were combined into a single group the resulting model may be too approximate and with large errors. Thus, when describing a QN model, one has to also specify the *classes* of customers that use the resources of the QN, the workload intensity of each class, and the service demands at each resource per class.

A multiclass QN model should be used in the following cases:

- *Heterogeneous service demands.* The requests that form the workload can be clustered into groups that exhibit significantly different service demands on the system resources as is the case in Table 2.1.

- *Different types of workloads.* The types of requests in the workload are different in nature. For instance, a database server may be used for both: a) short online transactions and b) a batch workload to generate managerial reports.

- *Different service level objectives.* In this case, different classes of requests have different service level objectives. For example, the transaction groups of Table 2.1 may have 1.2 seconds, 2.5 seconds, and 8 seconds, as their acceptable limit on the average response time, respectively.

2.5 The Database Server Example: Open and Closed Classes

In the examples of the previous sections, the intensity of the workload was specified as the rate at which transactions arrive to the system. If the overall arrival rate of transactions is 1.5 tps, the arrival rates per class are 0.675 (= 1.5 × 0.45) tps, 0.375 (= 1.5 × 0.25) tps, and 0.45 (= 1.5 × 0.30) tps for trivial, medium, and complex transactions, respectively, according to Table 2.1. A customer class that corresponds to a workload specified in this way is called an *open class*. An open class has the following characteristics:

- *Workload intensity specified by an arrival rate.* For each open class, the intensity of the workload is represented by the average number of requests arriving per unit time. This arrival rate is usually independent of the system state (i.e., it does not depend on the number of other customers in the system).

- *Unbounded number of customers in the system.* As the arrival rate of customers increases, the number of customers in the system modeled by the QN tend to grow without bound.

- *Throughput is an input parameter.* In equilibrium, the throughput of an open class is equal to its arrival rate, and is therefore known. This results from observing that, in equilibrium, the flow into the system (i.e., the arrival rate) must equal the flow out of the system (i.e., the system throughput).

Consider now that at night, the database server of the previous sections is not available for the execution of online transactions. Instead, it is used to execute batch jobs that produce managerial reports. A customer class that represents this type of workload is called a *closed class*. The characteristics of a closed class are:

- *Workload intensity specified by the customer population.* For each closed class, the workload intensity is specified by the number of concurrent requests of that class that are in execution (i.e., the customer population for that class). For example, one may say that five batch jobs are being concurrently executed to produce reports. It is typically assumed that as soon as one job finishes, another job from the queue is ready to enter and take its place, thus maintaining a (near) constant number of customers in the system.

- *Bounded and known number of customers in the system.* The number of requests in the system is an input parameter and is therefore known and bounded.

- *Throughput is an output parameter.* The throughput of a closed class is obtained when solving the QN model and is a function (among other things) of the customer population for that class.

A QN model in which all classes are open is called an *open QN* model and a QN model in which all classes are closed is a *closed QN* model.

Figure 2.3 depicts a QN with a closed workload. and indicates that as soon as one job completes, another (equivalent) job is started. Thus, the number of jobs in the system remains constant.

2.6   The Database Server Example: a Mixed Model

Consider again the database server of the previous sections. Assume now that management has decided that the online transactions of Table 2.1 and the batch management reports should be allowed to execute at the same time at any time of day. However, before management commits to this decision, it needs to know if the database server will be able to support both these workloads while meeting the performance objectives for all of them,

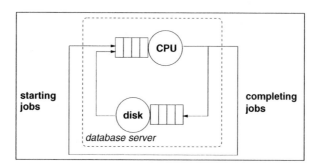

Figure 2.3. Queuing network for a database server with a closed workload.

as specified in Table 2.2. The performance goal for online transactions are specified in terms of an upper bound on the average response time. No limit on response time is set for the batch workload. However, a lower bound on throughput is specified for that class.

Such performance goals are also called *Service Level Agreements (SLAs)* since they represent an agreement between service providers and consumers of a service. SLAs and QoS objectives are related and sometimes used interchangeably. SLAs are specified for each class and may involve many different performance metrics such as response time, throughput, and availability. For example, one may have the following sets of SLAs for the services provided by a Web site:

- 99.99% availability during the 8:00 a.m.-11:00 p.m. interval, and 99.9% availability at other times.

- Maximum of four seconds of page download time for all requests submitted over non-secure connections and maximum of six seconds of page download time for requests submitted through secure connections.

- Minimum throughput of 2,000 page downloads per second.

The QN model required to answer the performance questions at the beginning of this section is a multiclass *mixed* QN model. It is mixed because some classes are open and some are closed. The representation of this model for the database server example is shown in Fig. 2.4.

Table 2.2. Service Level Agreements (SLAs) for the Database Server

Transaction Group	Maximum Average Response Time (sec)	Minimum Throughput
Trivial	1.2	-
Medium	2.5	-
Complex	8.0	-
Batch Reports	-	20 per hour

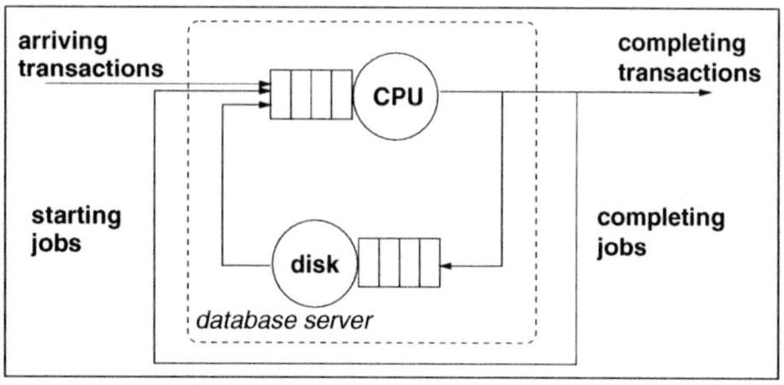

Figure 2.4. Mixed queuing network for a database server.

2.7   The Database Server Example: Types of Resources

Suppose that the database server of the previous sections is used to support a client/server application. Client workstations are connected to the database server through a local area network (LAN). Clients work independently and alternate between "thinking" (i.e., composing requests to be submitted to the database server) and "waiting" for a reply from the server. When a reply returns to a client workstation, another thinking/waiting cycle starts immediately. Therefore, we can represent the time spent at the client (i.e., the think time) as a resource that has no waiting line. This type of resource is called a *delay resource*, which we represent by a circle (without the rectangle that represents the queue).

The LAN that connects clients to servers is an Ethernet LAN, whose effective bandwidth decreases as the number of client workstations increases due to increased packet collisions. Thus, the LAN can be modeled as a resource that has a service rate that depends on its load. This type of resource is called a *load-dependent* resource and is represented graphically as a circle with an arrow plus a rectangle to represent the queue. Resources, such as the CPU and disk, that have a queue but have a constant service rate, are called *load-independent* resources. Figure 2.5 depicts the complete QN model with the clients represented as a delay resource, the LAN as a load dependent resource, and database server consisting of two load independent resources.

To summarize, three types of resources can be used in QN models:

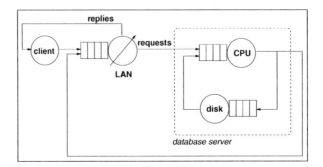

Figure 2.5. QN for database server with clients and LAN.

- *Load independent (LI).* These resources have a constant service rate that does not depend on the load (i.e., on the number of requests in the queue).

- *Load-dependent (LD).* The service rate of this type of resource is a function of the number of requests in the queue. This type of resource can be used, for example, to model a queue with m resources as in Fig. 2.1 (b). In this case, the service rate increases as the number of requests grows from 1 to m. Alternatively, as in the LAN example above, the service rate of a load dependent server may also decrease as the number of requests grows.

- *Delay (D).* There is no waiting line in this case. A request that arrives at a delay resource is served immediately. This type of resource is used to model dedicated resources (i.e., resources not shared with other requests) or situations in which there is an ample number of resources compared to the number of requests in the system.

2.8   The Database Server Example: Blocking

Suppose now that the IT managers of the database service want to provide a response time guarantee to their customers. In order to provide this guarantee, regardless of the arrival rate of requests, the number of concurrent database transactions has to be limited. In other words, some form of *admission control* has to be implemented (see Fig. 1.4). With an admission control, a limit, W, is set on the number of transactions allowed into the system. An arriving transaction that finds W transactions in the system is *blocked* (i.e., it is either rejected or placed in a queue waiting to enter the system). This is illustrated in Fig. 2.6, which shows the variation of the number of requests in the system versus time. Each arrow pointing upwards indicates an arrival. At arrival instants, when the load is less than W, the number in the system increases by one. Downward arrows indicate departures; at these instants, the number in the system decreases by one. The picture shows five requests arriving when the number of requests in the system is at its maximum value, W. These requests are blocked. Examples of mechanisms that limit the number of requests in a system include the maximum number of TCP connections handled by a Web server, the maximum number of database connections supported by a database server, and limits on multiprogramming level enforced by the operating system.

Limiting the total number of requests allowed in a computer system limits the amount of time spent by requests at the various queues and therefore guarantees that the response time will not grow unbounded. This is a type of congestion or admission control. Clearly, if requests are rejected, they will have to be resubmitted at a latter time. Figure 2.7 shows the QN for the database server with admission control indicating that transactions are rejected when the system is at its limit. It should be noted that in this case,

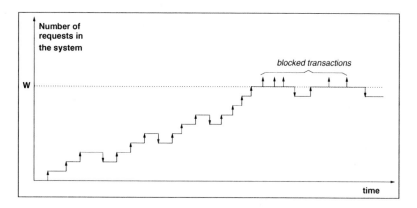

Figure 2.6. Number of transactions in the database server vs. time with admission control.

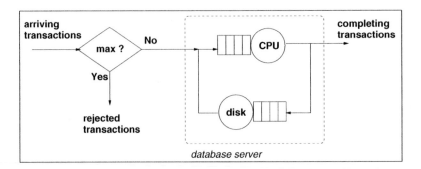

Figure 2.7. Database server QN with admission control.

the throughput is not necessarily equal to the arrival rate. In fact,

$$\text{Throughput} = \text{Arrival Rate} \times (1 - \text{Probability of Rejection}).$$

2.9   The Database Server Example: Software Contention

Suppose that the database server is now multithreaded. Each thread handles one transaction at a time and there is a maximum number of threads. If all threads are busy serving requests, incoming transactions must queue for an available thread. An important tuning decision is to determine the the optimal number of threads for a given arrival rate so that the system SLAs are met.

In this situation, there are two opposing effects. One, called *software contention*, represents the time that a transaction needs to wait for an available thread. The other, called *physical contention*, is the time spent by a transaction waiting to use physical resources (e.g., CPU and disk).

As the number of threads m increases, software contention decreases but physical contention increases because more transactions will be contending for the CPU and disk. Thus, response time may increase or decrease as a function of m, depending on which factor (software contention or physical contention) dominates, as illustrated in Fig. 2.8. The picture shows two graphs of response time vs. number of software threads for two values of the average arrival rate (λ_1 and λ_2) where $\lambda_1 < \lambda_2$. The curve for λ_1 shows the optimal value, m^*, for the number of threads that minimizes the average response time for λ_1.

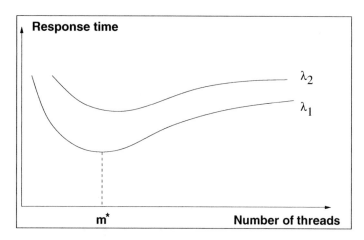

Figure 2.8. Response time vs. number of threads for two values of the average arrival rate (λ_1 and λ_2).

Figure 2.9 illustrates the queue for m software threads. The figure also indicates the QN that models the physical resources used by the busy threads. Methods for solving QNs that represent software contention are given in [6, 8] and are presented in Chap. 15.

2.10   Database Example: Simultaneous Resource Possession

Consider now that there is significant update activity in the database server and therefore, transactions need to acquire a database lock before they can update the database. Once a lock is acquired, a database transaction will either use the CPU or the disk while holding the database lock. Thus, two resources will be held by the transaction at the same time (i.e., a database lock and the CPU, or a database lock and the disk). This situation is called *simultaneous resource possession (SRP)*. In an SRP situation, a customer in a QN is allowed to hold one or more resources at the same time. A slightly different, yet equivalent, view is that a customer is executing in parallel, both at the database server lock and at the resource (i.e., CPU or disk) server. Figure 2.10 shows three time axes: one for the CPU, one for the database lock, and another for the disk. The picture shows how a transaction spends time waiting and holding each of these resources.

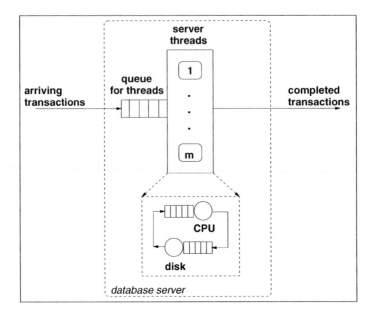

Figure 2.9. Database server with software contention.

Figure 2.11 illustrates the QN with a queue for database locks. Dashed arrows from the database locks to the CPU and disk indicate that database locks are held simultaneously with these two resources. The probability that a lock requested by a transaction is being held by another transaction increases with the system load. See [9] for analytic models with database locking mechanisms. Queuing networks with SRP can also be used to model

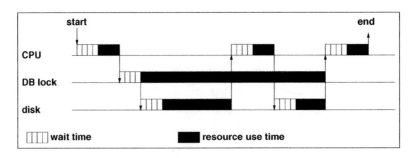

Figure 2.10. Time axes illustration of SRP.

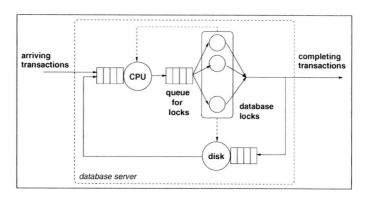

Figure 2.11. QN with simultaneous resource possession. Database locks are held simultaneously with the CPU and with the disk.

software contention. In this case, a software resource (e.g., a thread or a critical section) is being held simultaneously with another physical resource (e.g., a CPU or disk). Similarly, SRP can model other types of hardware contention (e.g., a bus in a shared-memory multiprocessor is held while a memory module is used).

2.11   Database Example: Class Switching

Consider now a situation in which a user is required to authenticate itself to the database server before a transaction is executed. Authentication protocols may use some form of cryptography, which is compute-intensive [7]. Thus, the service demand of a database transaction at the CPU varies significantly depending on whether the transaction is in the authentication phase or in the database access phase. Figure 2.12 illustrates the various phases of a transaction. When the service demands in each phase vary widely, one can use a modeling technique called *class switching*. Section 2.4 introduced the notion of multiple classes in a QN model; different classes can be used to model customers with very different service demands. In this case, a customer of the QN belongs to a single class. In class switching, a customer may switch from one class to another when moving between queues.

In the multiple class case, service demands are associated with a class and a queue. In addition, however, class switching probabilities, $p_{i,r;j,s}$, are used to indicated the probability that a class r customer switches to class

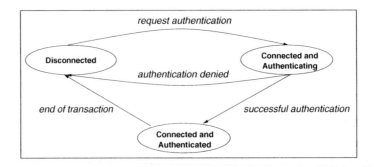

Figure 2.12. States of a database transaction.

s when moving from queue i to queue j. Class switching is used in [2] to analyze the performance of Kerberos-based authentication protocols.

2.12   Database Example: Queuing Disciplines

Suppose that the database server is serving both queries and update trans-actions and that the response time SLA of queries is more important than that of update transactions. In this case, queries should be given preferential treatment, such as a higher priority at the CPU, so that they execute faster than updates. Many different queuing disciplines can be considered in a QN:

- *First Come First Served (FCFS)*. Customers are served in the order of arrival at a queue, as in a supermarket cash register.

- *Priority Queuing*. When the server becomes available, the customer that has the highest priority is served next. If there is more than one customer with the same priority, FCFS is used to break the tie within each priority class. There are many possible variations of priority-based queuing disciplines: static priorities vs. dynamic priorities, preemptive vs. non-preemptive, preemptive resume vs. preemptive restart. In the static priority case, the priority of a customer does not change with time. With preemptive priority, arriving customers of higher priority are allowed to immediately seize a resource that is being used by a customer of lower priority. Preempted customers may continue from where they left off (the preemptive resume case) or they may have to to restart (preemptive restart). Chapter 11 present results for single queues with priorities and Chap. 15 discusses approximation results for QNs with queues that use priority-based queuing disciplines.

- *Round Robin (RR)*. In this case, each transaction is served for a short period of time, called a *quantum* or *timeslice*, after which the resource is switched to the next transaction in a circular fashion. Thus, if there are n transactions in a queue, the resource allocates a timeslice to transactions in the following order: $1, 2, \cdots, n, 1, 2, \cdots$. This type of scheduling discipline is commonly used by operating systems to schedule the CPU to the set of ready processes.

- *Processor Sharing (PS)*. This is the theoretical limit of RR as the timeslice approaches zero. Another way of thinking about PS when there are n transactions in a queue is that all n of them are served simultaneously, but each one sees a resources n times slower. It is typical to assume for modeling purposes that the context switch time for all queuing disciples is negligible.

Many other queuing disciples are possible and have been analyzed, including shortest job first, multi-level feedback, Last Come First Serve-Preemptive Resume (LCFS-PR), and random.

2.13   QN Models

A more formal and complete definition of a QN model is given here. A QN is a collection of K interconnected queues. A queue includes the waiting line and the resource that provides service to customers. Customers move from one queue to the other until they complete their execution and may be grouped into one or more customer classes. In some cases, customers may be allowed to switch to other classes when they move between queues.

A QN can be open, closed, or mixed depending on its customer classes: open if all classes are open, closed if all classes are closed, and mixed if some classes are open and some are closed. The solution of open, closed, and mixed QNs under certain assumptions was first presented in [1] and is discussed in more detail in Part II.

The input parameters to a QN model are divided into two groups:

- *Workload intensity.* These parameters provide an indication of the load of the system. It can be measured in terms of arrival rates for open classes or in terms of customer population for closed classes.

- *Service demands.* These parameters specify the total average service time provided by a specific resource to a given class of requests. Service demands do not generally depend on the load on the system. In some situations, however, there may be a dependence. An example is the service demand on the paging disk, which is a function of the page fault rate. In a poorly tuned system, the number of page faults may increase with the number of jobs.

Workload classes can also be characterized as *transaction*, *batch*, and *interactive*. A transaction workload is modeled as an open class with a workload intensity represented by an arrival rate (see the example of Section 2.3). A batch workload is modeled as a closed class whose workload intensity is represented by the number of customers of that class in the QN (see the example of a report generation class in Section 2.5). An interactive workload is a closed class used to model situations where requests are submitted by a fixed number, M, of terminals or client machines. The workload intensity in this case is represented by the number of terminals M and by the average think time, Z. The think time is defined as the time elapsed since a reply to a request is received until the next request is submitted by the same terminal or client (see the client/server example of Section 2.7). Table 2.3 summarizes the parameters that must be specified for each of these three types of workloads.

A queue in a QN is specified by the type of resource (i.e., LI, LD, or D) and the queuing discipline (e.g., FCFS, priority, RR, PS). The following basic notation is used throughout the rest of the book. Additional notation will be introduced as needed.

- K: number of queues in a QN.

- R: number of customer classes of a QN.

- $\vec{\lambda} = (\lambda_1, \cdots, \lambda_R)$: vector of arrival rates for an open multiclass QN; λ_r ($r = 1, \cdots, R$) is the average arrival rate of customers of class r.

Table 2.3. Parameters per Class Type

Parameter	Type of Class		
	Batch	Interactive	Transaction
Service demands	✓	✓	✓
Priority	✓	✓	✓
Customer population	✓		
Average arrival rate			✓
Number of terminals		✓	
Think time		✓	

- $\vec{N} = (N_1, \cdots, N_R)$: customer population vector for a closed multiclass QN; N_r $(r = 1, \cdots, R)$ is the number of customers of class r.

- $D_{i,r}$: service demand of class r $(r = 1, \cdots, R)$ customers at queue i $(i = 1, \cdots, K)$.

- Prior (r): priority of class r. Priorities are numbered from 1 to P with the highest priority numbered 1.

- $X_{0,r}$: throughput of class r customers.

- $R_{0,r}$: average response time of class r customers

QNs may also exhibit characteristics such as blocking, SRP, contention for software resources, and class-switching.

Example 2.1

Consider the example of Section 2.4 and the data in Table 2.1. Assume that the total arrival rate is 1.5 tps and that each I/O takes an average of 0.01 seconds. Thus, the service demand at the disk for each class is equal to the average number of I/Os multiplied by the average time per I/O. For example, the service demand at the disk for trivial transactions is 0.055 ($= 5.5 \times 0.01$) seconds. A complete description of the QN for the example of Section 2.4 is given in Table 2.4. By solving this QN using the methods and tools presented in later chapters of this book, the following response times are obtained: $R_{0,1} = 0.23$ sec, $R_{0,2} = 1.10$ sec, and $R_{0,3} = 5.08$ sec. ∎

Table 2.4. QN Specification for Example 2.1

$K = 2; R = 3$			Queue type/Sched. Discipline	
Open QN			LI/PS	LI/FCFS
Class (r)	Type	λ_r	$D_{\text{CPU},r}$	$D_{\text{disk},r}$
		(tps)	(sec)	(sec)
1 (Trivial)	open	0.675	0.04	0.055
2 (Medium)	open	0.375	0.18	0.289
3 (Complex)	open	0.450	1.20	0.850

Example 2.2

Consider now the QN shown in Fig. 2.3. Assume that two batch applications execute concurrently to generate management reports at night when no online activity is allowed. One of the applications generates sales reports and the other generates marketing reports. Both are multithreaded processes. The first application runs as a collection of five threads and the second as a collection of ten threads. Each thread generates one report. A complete description of the QN for the example of Section 2.4 is given in Table 2.5. By solving this QN using the methods and tools presented in later chapters of this book, one obtains the following throughputs: $X_{0,1} = 23.2$ reports/hour and $X_{0,2} = 24.6$ reports/hour. ∎

Table 2.5. QN Specification for Example 2.2

$K = 2; R = 2$			Queue type/Sched. Discipline	
Closed QN			LI/PS	LI/FCFS
Class (r)	Type	N_r	$D_{\text{CPU},r}$	$D_{\text{disk},r}$
			(sec)	(sec)
1 (Sales)	closed	5	45	50
2 (Marketing)	closed	10	80	96

2.14   Concluding Remarks

The exercise of modeling (i.e., abstracting a real system into some kind of representation) has many advantages. First, several properties of the real system can be elicited in the process of building a model. For example, sources of contention and the nature of the workload are better understood when a model is built. Second, a model is a useful guide on what type of measurements to take and what kind of data to collect. One should restrict the data collection effort to the data necessary to obtain input parameters for the model and to validate the model against the real system. Third, a number of interesting metrics can be readily computed from the input parameters even before the model is solved. For example, as it will be shown later in the book, one can obtain bounds on throughput and response time from service demands. Lastly, a model can be used to answer what-if questions about a real system, avoiding costly and time-consuming experiments.

The following chapters of this book provide the quantitative aspects necessary to use queuing models for capacity planning and performance prediction. Most of the models are implemented in MS Excel workbooks, which makes them easy to use.

2.15   Exercises

1. A 56 Kbps communication link is used to transmit 1500-byte long packets. What is the service demand of a packet on that link? Does the service demand of the packet change with the traffic on the link?

2. A 4-CPU machine is used to run a CPU-intensive benchmark that consists of several programs running concurrently. The programs in the benchmark are equivalent with respect to their use of CPU. What kind of QN model is most appropriate to model this situation? Specify the number of classes, their type (open or closed), the queues, and their types. Justify your answer.

3. A computer system supports a transaction workload submitting requests at a rate of 10 tps and a workload of requests submitted by 50 client workstations. What kind of QN should be used to model this situation: open, closed, or mixed?

4. A database server has two identical disks. The service demands of database transactions on these disks are 100 msec and 150 msec, respectively. Show how these service demands would change under the following scenarios:

   - Disk 1 is replaced by a disk that is 40% faster.
   - Enough main memory is installed so that the hit rate on the database server's cache is 30%.
   - The log option of the database management system is enabled. A log record is generated on disk 2 for each update transaction. Updates account for 30% of the transactions and recording a log record takes 15 msec.

5. The workload of a database server is decomposed into four types of transactions: trivial (TT), medium (MT), complex (CT), and update transactions (UT). Table 2.6 shows the arrival rates and service demands for each class.

   Capacity planners are interested in answering the following questions:

   - What is the effect on response time of TT transactions if their arrival rate increases by 50%?

Table 2.6. Parameters for a Four-Class Performance Model

	Class			
	TT	MT	CT	UT
Arrival rate (tps)	0.20	0.30	0.20	0.10
Service demand (sec)				
CPU	0.15	0.30	0.45	0.70
Disk 1	0.20	0.35	0.55	0.30
Disk 2	0.10	0.30	0.60	0.20

- What is the effect on response time of UT transactions if their arrival rate is increased by 25%?
- What is the effect on the response time of TT transactions if UT transactions are run on a different machine?

From this list of questions, it is clear that the model does not need to consider classes MT and CT separately. How would you aggregate these two classes into a single class? In other words, what is the arrival rate and what are the service demands of the new aggregated class?

6. A delay resource in a QN can be thought as a special case of a load-dependent resource. Give an expression for the service rate $\mu\ (n)$ as a function of the number, n, of customers in the resource and of the average service time, S, per customer.

Bibliography

[1] F. Baskett, K. Chandy, R. Muntz, and F. Palacios, "Open, closed, and mixed networks of queues with different classes of customers," *J. ACM*, vol. 22, no. 2, April 1975.

[2] A. Harbitter and D. A. Menascé, " A methodology for analyzing the performance of authentication protocols," *ACM Trans. Information Systems Security*, vol. 5, no. 4, November 2002, pp. 458-491.

[3] A. M. Law and W. D. Kelton, *Simulation Modeling and Techniques*, 3rd ed., McGraw-Hill, New York, 2000.

[4] M. H. MacDougall, *Simulating Computer Systems: Techniques and Tools*, MIT Press, Cambridge, Mass., 1987.

[5] S. M. Ross, *A Course in Simulation*, Macmillan, New York, 1990.

[6] D. A. Menascé, "Two-level iterative queuing modeling of software contention," *Proc. Tenth IEEE/ACM International Symposium on Modeling, Analysis and Simulation of Computer and Telecommunication Systems (MASCOTS 2002)*, Fort Worth, Texas, October 12-16, 2002, pp. 267–276.

[7] D. A. Menascé and V. A. F. Almeida, *Scaling for E-business: technologies, Models, Performance, and Capacity Planning*, Prentice Hall, Upper Saddle River, New Jersey, 2000.

[8] J. Rolia and K. C. Sevcik, "The method of layers," *IEEE Tr. Software Engineering*, vol. 21, no. 8, 1995, pp. 689–700.

[9] A. Thomasian, "Performance analysis of concurrency control methods," in *Performance Evaluation: Origins and Directions*, G. Haring, C. Lindemann, and M. Reiser (eds.), Springer, Berlin, 2000, pp. 329–354.

Chapter 3

Quantifying Performance Models

3.1 Introduction

Chapter 2 introduced the basic framework that will be used throughout the book to think about performance issues in computer systems: queuing networks. That chapter concentrated on the qualitative aspects of these models and looked at how a computer system can be mapped into a network of queues. This chapter focuses on the *quantitative* aspects of these models and introduce the input parameters and performance metrics that can be obtained from the QN models. The notions of service times, arrival rates, service demands, utilization, queue lengths, response time, throughput, and waiting time are discussed here in more precise terms. The chapter also introduces Operational Analysis, a set of basic quantitative relationships between performance quantities.

3.2 Basic Performance Results

This section presents the approach known as *operational analysis* [1], used to establish relationships among quantities based on measured or known data about computer systems. To see how the operational approach might be applied, consider the following motivating problem.

Motivating problem: *Suppose that during an observation period of 1 minute, a single resource (e.g., the CPU) is observed to be busy for 36 sec. A total of 1800 transactions are observed to arrive to the system. The total number of observed completions is 1800 transactions (i.e., as many completions as arrivals occurred in the observation period). What is the performance of the system (e.g., the mean service time per transaction, the utilization of the resource, the system throughput)?*

Prior to solving this problem, some commonly accepted operational analysis notation is required for the measured data. The following is a partial list of such measured quantities:

- T: length of time in the observation period

- K: number of resources in the system

- B_i: total busy time of resource i in the observation period T

- A_i: total number of service requests (i.e., arrivals) to resource i in the observation period T

- A_0: total number of requests submitted to the system in the observation period T

- C_i: total number of service completions from resource i in the observation period T

- C_0: total number of requests completed by the system in the observation period T

From these known measurable quantities, called *operational variables*, a set of derived quantities can be obtained. A partial list includes the following:

- S_i: mean service time per completion at resource i; $S_i = B_i/C_i$

- U_i: utilization of resource i; $U_i = B_i/T$

- X_i: throughput (i.e., completions per unit time) of resource i; $X_i = C_i/T$

- λ_i: arrival rate (i.e., arrivals per unit time) at resource i; $\lambda_i = A_i/T$

- X_0: system throughput; $X_0 = C_0/T$

- V_i: average number of visits (i.e., the visit count) per request to resource i; $V_i = C_i/C_0$

Using the notation above, the motivating problem can be formally stated and solved in a straightforward manner using operational analysis. The measured quantities are:

$$T = 60 \text{ sec}$$
$$K = 1 \text{ resource}$$
$$B_1 = 36 \text{ sec}$$
$$A_1 = A_0 = 1800 \text{ transactions}$$
$$C_1 = C_0 = 1800 \text{ transactions}$$

Thus, the derived quantities are

$$S_1 = \frac{B_1}{C_1} = \frac{36}{1800} = \frac{1}{50} \text{ second per transaction}$$
$$U_1 = \frac{B_1}{T} = \frac{36}{60} = 60\%$$
$$\lambda_1 = \frac{A_1}{T} = \frac{1800}{60} = 30 \text{ tps}$$
$$X_0 = \frac{C_0}{T} = \frac{1800}{60} = 30 \text{ tps}$$

Chapter 2 discussed the need to consider multiple class models to account for transactions with different demands on the various resources. The notation presented above can be easily extended to the multiple class case by considering that R is the number of classes and by adding the class number r ($r = 1, \cdots, R$) to the subscript. For example, $U_{i,r}$ is the utilization of resource i due to requests of class r and $X_{0,r}$ is the throughput of class r requests.

The subsections that follow discuss several useful relationships—called *operational laws*—between operational variables.

3.2.1   Utilization Law

As seen above, the utilization of a resource is defined as $U_i = B_i/T$. Dividing the numerator and denominator of this ratio by the number of completions from resource i, C_i, during the observation interval, yields

$$U_i = \frac{B_i}{T} = \frac{B_i/C_i}{T/C_i}. \tag{3.2.1}$$

The ratio B_i/C_i is simply the average time that the resource was busy for each completion from resource i, i.e., the average service time S_i per visit to the resource. The ratio T/C_i is just the inverse of the resource throughput X_i. Thus, the relation known as the Utilization Law can be written as:

$$U_i = S_i \times X_i. \tag{3.2.2}$$

If the number of completions from resource i during the observation interval T is equal to the number of arrivals in that interval, i.e., if $C_i = A_i$, then $X_i = \lambda_i$ and the relationship given by the Utilization Law becomes $U_i = S_i \times \lambda_i$.

If resource i has m servers, as in a multiprocessor, the Utilization Law becomes $U_i = (S_i \times X_i)/m$. The multiclass version of the Utilization Law is $U_{i,r} = S_{i,r} \times X_{i,r}$.

Example 3.1

The bandwidth of a communication link is 56,000 bps and it is used to transmit 1500-byte packets that flow through the link at a rate of 3 packets/second. What is the utilization of the link?

Start by identifying the operational variables provided or that can be obtained from the measured data. The link is the resource ($K = 1$) for which the utilization is to be computed. The throughput of that resource, X_1, is 3 packets/second. What is the average service time per packet? In other words, what is the average transmission time? Each packet has 1,500 bytes/packet $\times$ 8 bits/byte $= 12,000$ bits/packet. Thus, it takes $12,000$ bits/$56,000$ bits/sec $= 0.214$ sec to transmit a packet over this link. Therefore, $S_1 = 0.214$ sec/packet. Using the Utilization Law, we compute the utilization of the link as $S_1 \times X_1 = 0.214 \times 3 = 0.642 = 64.2\%$.   ∎

Example 3.2

Consider a computer system with one CPU and three disks used to support a database server. Assume that all database transactions have similar resource demands and that the database server is under a constant load of transactions. Thus, the system is modeled using a single-class closed QN, as indicated in Fig. 3.1. The CPU is resource 1 and the disks are numbered from 2 to 4. Measurements taken during one hour provide the number of transactions executed (13,680), the number of reads and writes per second on each disk and their utilization, as indicated in Table 3.1. What is the average service time per request on each disk? What is the database server's throughput?

The throughput of each disk, denoted by X_i ($i = 2, 3, 4$), is the total number of I/Os per second, i.e., the sum of the number of reads and writes per second. This value is indicated in the fourth column of the table. Using the Utilization Law, the average service time is computed as S_i as U_i/X_i. Thus, $S_2 = U_2/X_2 = 0.30/32 = 0.0094$ sec, $S_3 = U_3/X_3 = 0.41/36 = 0.0114$ sec, and $S_4 = U_4/X_4 = 0.54/50 = 0.0108$ sec.

The throughput, X_0, of the database server is given by $X_0 = C_0/T = 13,680$ transactions$/3,600$ seconds $= 3.8$ tps. ∎

3.2.2 Service Demand Law

Service demand is a fundamental concept in performance modeling. The notion of service demand is associated both with a resource and a set of requests using the resource. The *service demand*, denoted as D_i, is defined as the total average time spent by a typical request of a given type obtain-

Table 3.1. Data for Example 3.2

Disk	Reads Per Second	Writes Per Second	Total I/Os Per Second	Utilization
1	24	8	32	0.30
2	28	8	36	0.41
3	40	10	50	0.54

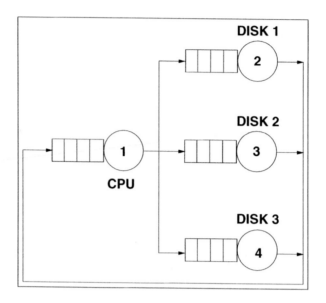

Figure 3.1. Closed QN model of a database server.

ing service from resource i. Throughout its existence, a request may visit several devices, possibly multiple times. However, for any given request, its service demand is the sum of all service times during all visits to a given resource. When considering various requests using the same resource, the service demand at the resource is computed as the average, for all requests, of the sum of the service times at that resource. Note that, by definition, service demand does not include queuing time since it is the sum of service times. If different requests have very different service times, using a multiclass model is more appropriate. In this case, define $D_{i,r}$, as the service demand of requests of class r at resource i.

To illustrate the concept of service demand, consider that six transactions perform three I/Os on a disk. The service time, in msec, for each I/O and each transaction is given in Table 3.2. The last line shows the sum of the service times over all I/Os for each transaction. The average of these sums is 36.2 msec. This is the service demand on this disk due to the workload generated by the six transactions.

Service demands are important because, along with workload intensity parameters, they are input parameters for QN models. Fortunately, there

Table 3.2. Service times in msec for six requests

I/O No.	Transaction No.					
	1	2	3	4	5	6
1	10	15	13	10	12	14
2	12	12	12	11	13	12
3	11	14	11	11	11	13
Sum	33	41	36	32	36	39

is an easy way to obtain service demands from resource utilizations and system throughput. By multiplying the utilization U_i of a resource by the measurement interval T one obtains the total time the resource was busy. If this time is divided by the total number of completed requests, C_0, the average amount of time that the resource was busy serving each request is derived. This is precisely the service demand. So,

$$D_i = \frac{U_i \times T}{C_0} = \frac{U_i}{C_0/T} = \frac{U_i}{X_0}. \qquad (3.2.3)$$

This relationship is called the Service Demand Law, which can also be written as $D_i = V_i \times S_i$, by definition of the service demand (and since $D_i = U_i/X_0 = (B_i/T)/(C_0/T) = B_i/C_0 = (C_i \times S_i)/C_0 = (C_i/C_0) \times S_i = V_i \times S_i$). In many cases, it is not easy to obtain the individual values of the visit counts and service times. However, Eq. (3.2.3) indicates that the service demand can be computed directly from the device utilization and system throughput. The multiclass version of the Service Demand Law is $D_{i,r} = U_{i,r}/X_{0,r} = V_{i,r} \times S_{i,r}$.

Example 3.3

A Web server is monitored for 10 minutes and its CPU is observed to be busy 90% of the monitoring period. The Web server log reveals that 30,000 requests are processed in that interval. What is the CPU service demand of requests to the Web server?

The observation period T is 600 (= 10×60) seconds. The Web server throughput, X_0, is equal to the number of completed requests C_0 divided by the observation interval; $X_0 = 30,000/600 = 50$ requests/sec. The CPU utilization is $U_{\text{CPU}} = 0.9$. Thus, the service demand at the CPU is $D_{\text{CPU}} = U_{\text{CPU}}/X_0 = 0.9/50 = 0.018$ seconds/request.   ∎

Example 3.4

What are the service demands at the CPU and the three disks for the database server of Example 3.2 assuming that the CPU utilization is 35% measured during the same one-hour interval?

Remember that the database server's throughput was computed to be 3.8 tps. Using the Service Demand Law and the utilization values for the three disks shown in Table 3.1, yields: $D_{\text{CPU}} = 0.35/3.8 = 0.092$ sec/transaction, $D_{\text{disk1}} = 0.30/3.8 = 0.079$ sec/transaction, $D_{\text{disk2}} = 0.41/3.8 = 0.108$ sec/transaction, and $D_{\text{disk3}} = 0.54/3.8 = 0.142$ sec/transaction.   ∎

3.2.3   The Forced Flow Law

There is an easy way to relate the throughput of resource i, X_i, to the system throughput, X_0. Assume for the moment that every transaction that completes from the database server of Example 3.2 performs an average of two I/Os on disk 1. That is, suppose that for every one visit that the transaction makes to the database server, it visits disk 1 an average of two times. What is the throughput of that disk in I/Os per second? Since 3.8 transactions complete per second (i.e., the system throughput, X_0) and each one performs two I/Os on average on disk 1, the throughput of disk 1 is 7.6 ($= 2.0 \times 3.8$) I/Os per second. In other words, the throughput of a resource (X_i) is equal to the average number of visits (V_i) made by a request to that resource multiplied by the system throughput (X_0). This relation is called the Forced Flow Law:

$$X_i = V_i \times X_0. \tag{3.2.4}$$

The multiclass version of the Forced Flow Law is $X_{i,r} = V_{i,r} \times X_{0,r}$.

Example 3.5

What is the average number of I/Os on each disk in Example 3.2?

The value of V_i for each disk i, according to the Forced Flow Law, can be obtained as X_i/X_0. The database server throughput is 3.8 tps and the throughput of each disk in I/Os per second is given in the fourth column of

Table 3.1. Thus, $V_1 = X_1/X_0 = 32/3.8 = 8.4$ visits to disk 1 per database transaction. Similarly, $V_2 = X_2/X_0 = 36/3.8 = 9.5$ and $V_3 = X_3/X_0 = 50/3.8 = 13.2$.   ■

3.2.4   Little's Law

Conceptually, Little's Law [2] is quite simple and intuitively appealing. We describe the result by way of an analogy. Consider a pub. Customers arrive at the pub, stay for a while, and leave. Little's result states that the average number of folks in the pub (i.e., the queue length) is equal to the departure rate of customers from the pub times the average time each customer stays in the pub (see Fig. 3.2).

This result applies across a wide range of assumptions. For instance, consider a deterministic situation where a new customer walks into the pub

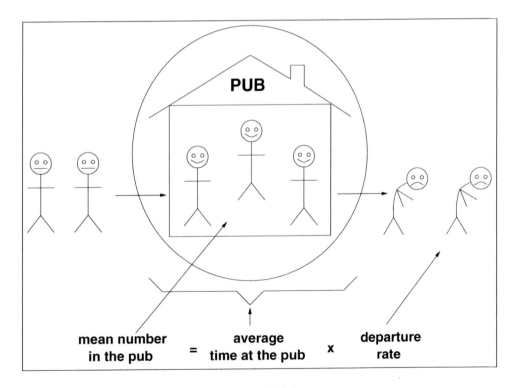

Figure 3.2. Little's Law.

every hour on the hour. Upon entering the pub, suppose that there are three
other customers in the pub. Suppose that the bartender regularly kicks out
the customer who has been there the longest, every hour at the half hour.
Thus, a new customer will enter at 9:00, 10:00, 11:00, ..., and the oldest
remaining customer will be booted out at 9:30, 10:30, 11:30, ... It is clear
that the average number of persons in the pub will be $3\frac{1}{2}$, since 4 customers
will be in the pub for the first half hour of every hour and only 3 customers
will be in the pub for the second half hour of every hour. The departure
rate of customers at the pub is one customer per hour. The time spent in
the pub by any customer is $3\frac{1}{2}$ hours. Thus, via Little's Law:

$$\text{avg. number in pub } = \text{ departure rate at pub } \times \text{ avg. time spent in pub}$$
$$3\frac{1}{2} = 1 \times 3\frac{1}{2}$$

Also, it does not matter which customer the bartender kicks out. For
instance, suppose that the bartender chooses a customer at random to kick
out. We leave it as an exercise to show that the average time spent in the
pub in this case would also be $3\frac{1}{2}$ hours. [Hint: the average time a customer
spends in the pub is one half hour with probability 0.25, one and a half
hours with probability $(0.75)(0.25) = 0.1875$ (i.e., the customer avoided the
bartender the first time around, but was chosen the second), two and a half
hours with probability $(0.75)(0.75)(0.25)$, and so on.]

Little's Law is quite general and requires few assumptions. In fact, Little's Law holds as long as customers are not destroyed or created. For example, if there is a fight in the pub and someone gets killed or a if a pregnant
woman goes into the pub and gives birth, Little's Law does not hold.

Little's Law applies to any "black box", which may contain an arbitrary
set of components. If the box contains a single resource (e.g., a single CPU,
a single pub) or if the box contains a complex system (e.g., the Internet, a
city full of pubs and shops), Little's Law holds. Thus, Little's Law can be
restated as

$$\begin{array}{c}\text{average number of}\\ \text{customers in a box}\end{array} = \begin{array}{c}\text{departure rate}\\ \text{from the box}\end{array} \times \begin{array}{c}\text{average time spent}\\ \text{in the box.}\end{array} \qquad (3.2.5)$$

For example, consider the single server queue of Fig. 3.3. Let the designated
box be the server only, excluding the queue. Applying Little's Law, the

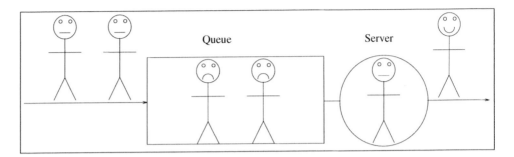

Figure 3.3. Single server.

average number of customers in the box is interpreted as the average number of customers in the server. The server will either have a single customer who is utilizing the server, or the server will have no customer present. The probability that a single customer is utilizing the server is equal to the server utilization. The probability that no customer is present is equal to the probability that the server is idle.

Thus, the *average* number of customers in the server equals

$$1 \times \text{Prob[single customer present]} + 0 \times \text{Prob[no customer present]}. \quad (3.2.6)$$

This simply equals the server's utilization. Therefore, the average number of customers in the server, N^s, equals the server's utilization. The departure rate at the server (i.e., the departure rate from the box) equals the server throughput. The average time spent by a customer at the server is simply the mean service time of the server. Thus, with this interpretation of Little's Law, $N_i^s = U_i = X_i \times S_i$. This result is simply the Utilization Law!

Now consider that the box includes both the waiting queue and the server. The average number of customers in the box (waiting queue + server), denoted by N_i, is equal, according to Little's Law, to the average time spent in the box, which is the response time R_i, times the throughput X_i. Thus, $N_i = R_i \times X_i$. Equivalently, by measuring the average number of customers in a box and measuring the output rate (i.e., the throughput) of the box, the response time can be calculated by taking the ratio of these two measurements.

Finally, by considering the box to include just the waiting line (i.e., the queue but not the server), Little's Law indicates that $N_i^w = W_i \times X_i$, where N_i^w is the average number of customers in the queue and W_i the average waiting time in the queue prior to receiving service.

Example 3.6

Consider the database server of Example 3.2 and assume that during the same measurement interval the average number of database transactions in execution was 16. What was the response time of database transactions during that measurement interval?

The throughput of the database server was already determined as being 3.8 tps. Apply Little's Law and consider the entire database server as the box. The average number in the box is the average number N of concurrent database transactions in execution (i.e., 16). The average time in the box is the average response time R desired. Thus, $R = N/X_0 = 16/3.8 = 4.2$ sec. ∎

3.2.5   Interactive Response Time Law

Consider an interactive system composed of M clients each sitting at their own workstation and interactively accessing a common database server system. Clients work independently and alternate between "thinking" (i.e., composing requests for the server) and waiting for a response from the server. The average think time is denoted by Z and the average response time is R. See Fig. 3.4. The think time is defined as the time elapsed since a customer receives a reply to a request until a subsequent request is submitted. The response time is the time elapsed between successive think times by a client.

Let $\overline{M}$ and $\overline{N}$ be the average number of clients thinking and the average number of clients waiting for a response, respectively. By viewing clients as moving between workstations and the database server, depending upon whether or not they are in the think state, $\overline{M}$ and $\overline{N}$ represent the average number of clients at the workstations and at the database server, respectively. Clearly, $\overline{M} + \overline{N} = M$ since a client is either in the think state or waiting for a reply to a submitted request. By applying Little's Law to the box containing just the workstations,

$$\overline{M} = X_0 \times Z \qquad\qquad (3.2.7)$$

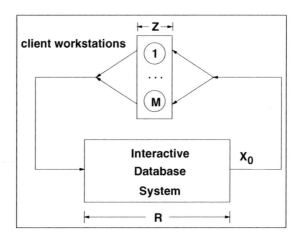

Figure 3.4. Interactive computer system.

since the average number of requests submitted per unit time (throughput of the set of clients) must equal the number of completed requests per unit time (system throughput X_0). Similarly, by applying Little's Law to the box containing just the database server,

$$\overline{N} = X_0 \times R \qquad (3.2.8)$$

where R is the average response time. By adding Eqs. (3.2.7) and (3.2.8),

$$\overline{M} + \overline{N} = M = X_0(Z + R). \qquad (3.2.9)$$

With a bit of algebra,

$$R = \frac{M}{X_0} - Z. \qquad (3.2.10)$$

This is an important formula known as the Interactive Response Time Law.

Example 3.7

If 7,200 requests are processed during one hour by an interactive computer system with 40 clients and an average think time of 15 sec, the average response time is

$$R = \frac{40}{7200/3600} - 15 = 5 \text{ sec.} \qquad (3.2.11)$$

■

Example 3.8

A client/server system is monitored for one hour. During this time, the utilization of a certain disk is measured to be 50%. Each request makes an average of two accesses to this disk, which has an average service time equal to 25 msec. Considering that there are 150 clients and that the average think time is 10 sec, what is the average response time?

The known quantities are: $U_{\text{disk}} = 0.5$, $V_{\text{disk}} = 2$, $S_{\text{disk}} = 0.025$ sec, $M = 150$, and $Z = 10$ sec. From the Utilization Law,

$$U_{\text{disk}} = S_{\text{disk}} \times X_{\text{disk}}.$$

Thus, $X_{\text{disk}} = 0.5/0.025 = 20$ requests/sec. From the Forced Flow Law,

$$X_0 = \frac{X_{\text{disk}}}{V_{\text{disk}}} = \frac{20}{2} = 10 \text{ requests/sec}.$$

Finally, from the Interactive Response Time Law,

$$R = \frac{M}{X_0} - Z = \frac{150}{10} - 10 = 5 \text{ sec}.$$

■

The multiclass version of the Interactive Response Time Law is $R_r = M_r/X_{0,r} - Z_r$. Figure 3.5 summarizes the main relationships discussed in the previous sections.

3.3   Bounds on Performance

Upper bounds on throughput and lower bounds on response time can be obtained by considering the service demands only (i.e., without solving any underlying model). This type of bounding analysis can be quite useful since it provides the analyst with the best possible performance one could hope from a system. The bounding behavior of a computer system is determined by its *bottleneck* resource. The bottleneck of a system is that resource with the highest utilization (or, equivalently, the resource with the largest service demand).

Utilization Law:
$$U_i = X_i \times S_i = \lambda_i \times S_i \qquad (3.2.12)$$

Forced Flow Law:
$$X_i = V_i \times X_0 \qquad (3.2.13)$$

Service Demand Law:
$$D_i = V_i \times S_i = U_i/X_0 \qquad (3.2.14)$$

Little's Law:
$$N = X \times R \qquad (3.2.15)$$

Interactive Response Time Law
$$R = \frac{M}{X_0} - Z \qquad (3.2.16)$$

Figure 3.5. Summary of Operational Laws.

Example 3.9

Consider again the database server of Example 3.2 and the service demands for the CPU and the three disks computed in Example 3.4. The service demands were computed to be: $D_{\text{CPU}} = 0.092$ sec, $D_{\text{disk1}} = 0.079$ sec, $D_{\text{disk2}} = 0.108$ sec, and $D_{\text{disk3}} = 0.142$ sec. Correspondingly, the utilization of these devices are 35%, 30%, 41%, and 54%, respectively (from Example 3.4 and Table 1.1). What is the maximum throughput X_0^{max} of the database server?

Using the Service Demand Law, it follows that $U_{\text{CPU}} = D_{\text{CPU}} \times X_0 = 0.092 \times X_0$, $U_{\text{disk1}} = D_{\text{disk1}} \times X_0 = 0.079 \times X_0$, $U_{\text{disk2}} = D_{\text{disk2}} \times X_0 = 0.108 \times X_0$, and $U_{\text{disk3}} = D_{\text{disk3}} \times X_0 = 0.142 \times X_0$. Since the service demands are constant (i.e., load-independent), they do not vary with the number of concurrent transactions in execution. The service demands do not include any queuing time, only the total service required by a transaction at the device. Therefore, as the load (i.e., as the throughput, X_0) increases on the database server, each of the device utilizations also increases linearly as a

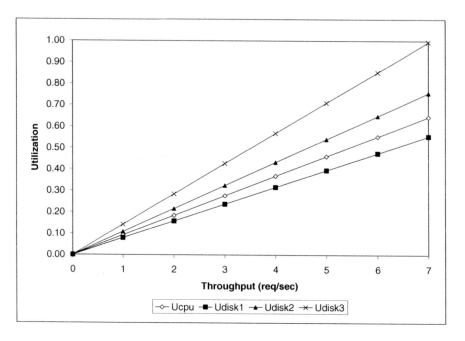

Figure 3.6. Utilization vs. throughput for Example 3.9.

function of their individual D_i's. See Fig. 3.6. As indicated in the figure, the utilization of disk 3 will reach 100% before any other resource, because the utilization of this disk is always greater than that of other resources. That is, disk3 is the system's bottleneck. When the system load increases to a point where disk 3's utilization reaches 100%, the throughput cannot be increased any further. Since $X_0 = U_{\text{disk3}}/D_{\text{disk3}}$, $X_0 \leq 1/D_{\text{disk3}}$. Therefore, the maximum throughput, $X_0^{\text{max}} = 1/D_{\text{disk3}} = 1/0.142 = 7.04$ tps. ∎

This example demonstrates that

$$X_0 = \frac{U_i}{D_i} \leq \frac{1}{D_i} \quad \text{for all resources i.} \qquad (3.3.17)$$

The resource with the largest service demand will have the highest utilization and is, therefore, the system's bottleneck. This bottleneck device yields the lowest (upper bound) value for the ratio $1/D_i$. Therefore,

$$X_0 \leq \frac{1}{\max \{D_i\}}. \qquad (3.3.18)$$

This relationship is known as the upper asymptotic bound on throughput under heavy load conditions [3].

Now consider Little's Law applied to the same database server and let N be the number of concurrent transactions in execution. Via Little's Law, $N = R \times X_0$. But, for a system with K resources, the response time R is at least equal to the sum of service demands, $\sum_{i=1}^{K} D_i$, when there is no queuing. Thus,

$$N = R \times X_0 \geq (\sum_{i=1}^{K} D_i) \times X_0, \qquad (3.3.19)$$

which can be rewritten as

$$X_0 \leq \frac{N}{\sum_{i=1}^{K} D_i}. \qquad (3.3.20)$$

This relationship is known as the upper asymptotic bound on throughput under light load conditions [3]. Combining Eqs. (3.3.18) and (3.3.20), the upper asymptotic bounds are:

$$X_0 \leq \min \left[\frac{1}{\max \{D_i\}}, \frac{N}{\sum_{i=1}^{K} D_i} \right]. \qquad (3.3.21)$$

To illustrate these bounds, consider the same database server in Examples 3.2 and 3.4. Consider the two lines (i.e., from Eq. (3.3.21)) that bound its throughput as shown in Fig. 3.7. The line that corresponds to the light load bound is the line N / 0.421 (solid line with solid diamonds). The horizontal line at 7.04 tps (solid line with unfilled diamonds) is the heavy load bound for this case. The actual throughput curve is shown in Fig. 3.7 as the dotted line with solid diamonds and lies below the two bounding lines. Consider now that the bottleneck resource, disk 3, is upgraded in such a way that its service demand is halved (i.e., by replacing it with a new disk that is twice as fast). Then, the sum of the service demands becomes 0.35 (= 0.092 + 0.079 + 0.108 + 0.071) sec. The maximum service demand is now that of disk 2, the new bottleneck, and the new heavy load bound (i.e., the inverse of the maximum service demand) is now 9.26 (= 1/0.108) tps. The solid lines with triangles show the bounds on throughput for the upgraded system. The actual throughput line (dashed line with triangles) is also shown.

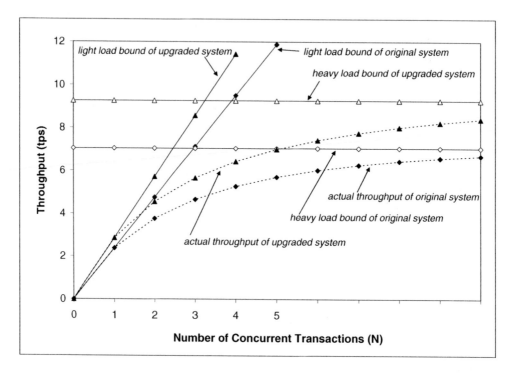

Figure 3.7. Bounds on throughput example.

Note that when the bottleneck resource was upgraded by a factor of two, the maximum throughput improved only by 32% (from 7.04 tps to 9.26 tps). This occurred because the upgrade to disk 3 was excessive. Disk 2 became the new bottleneck. It would have been sufficient to upgrade disk 3 by a factor of 1.32 (= 0.142/0.108) instead of 2 to make its service demand equal to that of disk 2. By using simple bottleneck analysis and performance bounds in this manner, performance can be improved for the least amount of cost.

Example 3.10

Consider the same database server of Examples 3.2 and 3.4. Let the service demand at the CPU be fixed at 0.092 sec. What should be the values of the service demands of the three disks to obtain the maximum possible throughput, while maintaining constant the sum of the service demands at the three disks? Note that this is a load balancing problem (i.e., the goal is to maximize the throughput by simply shifting the load among the three disks).

As demonstrated, the maximum service demand determines the maximum throughput. In this example, since the CPU is not the bottleneck, the maximum throughput is obtained when the service demands on all three disks is the same and equal to the average of the three original values. This is the balanced disk solution. In other words, the optimal solution occurs when $D_{\text{disk1}} = D_{\text{disk2}} = D_{\text{disk3}} = (0.079 + 0.108 + 0.142)/3 = 0.1097$ sec. In this case, the maximum throughput is 9.12 ($= 1/0.1097$) tps. Therefore, the maximum throughput can be expanded to increase 29.5% (i.e., from 7.04 tps to 9.12 tps) simply by balancing the load on the three existing disks.

To be convinced that the balanced disk solution is the optimal solution, assume that all disks have a service demand equal to D seconds. Now, increase the service demand of one of them by ϵ seconds, for $\epsilon > 0$. Since the sum of the service demands is to be kept constant, the service demand of at least one other disk has to be reduced in such a way that the sum remains the same. The disk that had its service demand increased will now have the largest service demand and becomes the bottleneck. The new maximum throughput would be $1/(D + \epsilon) < 1/D$. Thus, by increasing the service demand on one of the disks the maximum throughput decreases. Similarly, suppose that the service demand of one of the disks is decreased. Then, the service demand of at least one of the other disks will have to increase so that the sum remains constant. The service demand of the disk that has the largest increase limits the throughput. Let $D + \delta$, for $\delta > 0$, be the service demand for the disk with the new largest demand. Then, the maximum throughput is now equal to $1/(D + \delta) < 1/D$. Either way, the maximum throughput decreases as one departs from the balanced case. Said differently, the natural (and obvious) rule of thumb is to keep all devices equally utilized.
∎

Now consider a lower bound on the response time. According to Little's Law, the response time R is related to the throughput as $R = N/X_0$. By replacing X_0 by its upper bound given in Eq. (3.3.21), the following lower bounds for the response time can be obtained.

$$R = \frac{N}{X_0} \geq \frac{N}{\min\left[\frac{1}{\max\{D_i\}}, \frac{N}{\sum_{i=1}^{K} D_i}\right]} = \max\left[N \times \max\{D_i\}, \sum_{i=1}^{K} D_i\right].$$

(3.3.22)

Example 3.11

Consider the same database server as before. What is the lower bound on response time?

The sum of the service demands is 0.421 $(= 0.092 + 0.079 + 0.108 + 0.142)$ and the maximum service demand is 0.142 sec. Therefore, the response time bounds are given by

$$R \geq \max[0.142 \times N, 0.421].$$

(3.3.23)

These bounds are illustrated in Fig. 3.8, which also shows the actual response time curve. As seen, as the load on the system increases, the actual response time approaches the heavy load response time bound quickly. The actual values of the response time are obtained by solving a closed QN model (see Chapter 12) with the help of the enclosed `ClosedQN.XLS` MS Excel workbook. ∎

3.4   Using QN Models

One of the most important aspects in using QN models to predict performance is to understand what models to use and how to obtain the data for the model. In Chapter 2, different types and uses of QN models (open, closed, single class, or multiclass) were discussed. Numerical examples that illustrate the process are provided here.

Example 3.12

A Web server, composed of a single CPU and single disk, was monitored for one hour. The main workload of the server can be divided into HTML files and requests for image files. During the measurement interval 14,040 requests for HTML files and 1,034 requests for image files are processed. An analysis of the Web server log shows that HTML files are

3,000-bytes long and image files are 15,000-bytes long on average. The average disk service time is 12 msec for 1,000-byte blocks. The CPU demand, in seconds, per HTTP request, is given by the expression CPUDemand = $0.008 + 0.002 \times$ RequestSize, where RequestSize is given in the number of 1000-byte blocks processed. This expression for the CPU demand indicates that there is a constant time associated to processing a request (i.e., 0.008 seconds) regardless of the size of the file being requested. This constant time involves opening a TCP connection, analyzing the HTTP request, and opening the requested file. The second component of the CPU demand is proportional to the file size since the CPU is involved in each I/O operation. What is the response time for HTML and image file requests for the current load and for a load five times larger?

Since the workload is characterized as being composed of two types of requests, a two-class queuing network model is required. Should an open or closed model be used? The answer depends on how the workload intensity is specified. In this example, the load is specified by the number of requests

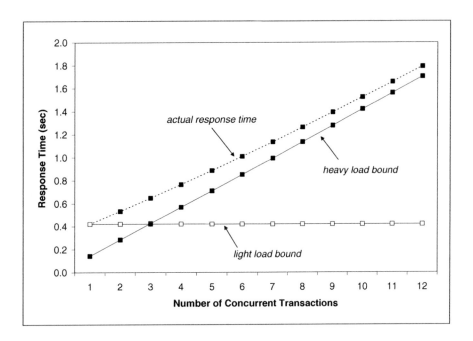

Figure 3.8. Bounds on response time example.

of each type processed during the measurement interval. In other words, the
arrival rate for each type of requests is:

$$\lambda_{\text{HTML}} = 14,040/3,600 = 3.9 \text{ requests/sec, and}$$
$$\lambda_{\text{image}} = 1,034/3,600 = 0.29 \text{ requests/sec.} \qquad (3.4.24)$$

This workload intensity is constant and does not depend on a fixed number
of customers. Therefore, an open QN model as described in Chapter 13
is chosen. The next step is to compute the service demands for the CPU
and disk for HTML and image file requests. Using the expression for CPU
time, the service demand for the CPU for HTML and image requests can
be computed by using the corresponding file sizes in 1,000-byte blocks for
each case as: $D_{\text{CPU,HTML}} = 0.008 + 0.002 \times 3 = 0.014$ sec and $D_{\text{CPU,image}} =$
$0.008 + 0.002 \times 15 = 0.038$ sec. The disk service demand is computed by
multiplying the number of blocks read for each type of request by the service
time per block. That is, $D_{\text{disk,HTML}} = 3 \times 0.012 = 0.036$ sec and $D_{\text{disk,image}} =$
$15 \times 0.012 = 0.18$ sec. By entering this data into the MS Excel `OpenQN.XLS`
workbook that comes with this book and solving the model, the results in
Table 3.3 are obtained.

Table 3.3. Service Demands, Arrival Rates, and Performance Metrics for Ex. 3.12

	HTML	Images
Arrival Rate (req/sec)	3.90	0.29
Service Demands (sec)		
CPU	0.014	0.038
Disk	0.036	0.180
Utilizations (%)		
CPU	5.5	1.1
Disk	14	5.2
Residence times (sec)		
CPU	0.015	0.041
Disk	0.045	0.223
Response times (sec)	0.060	0.264

In the case of open models, the throughput is equal to the arrival rate. Consider what happens under a five-fold increase in the load. The arrival rates become $\lambda_{\text{HTML}} = 5 \times 3.9 = 19.5$ requests/sec and $\lambda_{\text{image}} = 5 \times 0.29 = 1.45$ requests/sec. Solving the model with these values of the arrival rates, new response times of 0.93 sec for HTML and 4.61 sec for image requests are obtained. Thus, image file requests experience an increase in their response time by a factor of 17.5 and requests for HTML files experience a response time increased by a factor of 15.5. At the new load level, the disk utilization reaches 96% as indicated by the model, up from its previous 19.2% utilization (i.e., 14% + 5.2%). This indicates that the original system has excess capacity, but a five-fold load increase is nearing its maximum capacity.   ∎

Example 3.13

Reconsider the Web server of Example 3.12. What is the response time and throughput of HTML and image file requests when there is an average of 14 HTML requests and 6 image file requests being executed concurrently at all times?

In this case, the workload is specified by a number of concurrent requests in execution and not by an arrival rate. In this situation, a closed multi-class QN model (described in Chapter 13) is now appropriate. This model can be solved using the MS Excel workbook `ClosedQN.XLS`. The service demands are the same as in Example 3.12. Solving the model, $R_{\text{HTML}} = 0.72$ sec, $R_{\text{image}} = 3.57$ sec, $X_{\text{HTML}} = 19.3$ requests/sec, and $X_{\text{image}} = 1.7$ requests/sec. By comparing these results against these in Example 3.12, when the workload is increased five-fold, similar performance magnitudes are observed.   ∎

3.5 Concluding Remarks

Chapter 2 described the various types of performance models from a qualitative point of view. In this chapter, these models are quantified. A set of very important relationships between performance variables is introduced. These relationships, called Operational Laws, are quite general (i.e., robust) and are extremely useful because: i) they are very simple, ii) they are based on readily available measurement data, and iii) they can be used to obtain helpful performance metrics.

Simple bounding techniques were introduced and used to obtain upper bounds on throughput and lower bounds on response time from service demands. Examples were presented of applying QN models to various performance situations. In the following chapters of Part I the set of applications of performance models is expanded. The models used here are described in Part II and are implemented using the tools included.

3.6 Exercises

1. A computer system is monitored for one hour. During this period, 7,200 transactions were executed and the average multiprogramming level is measured to be equal to 5 jobs. What is the average time spent by a job in the system once it is in the multiprogramming mix (i.e., the average time spent by the job in the system once it is memory resident)?

2. Measurements taken during one hour from a Web server indicate that the utilization of the CPU and the two disks are: $U_{\text{CPU}} = 0.25$, $U_{\text{disk1}} = 0.35$, and $U_{\text{disk2}} = 0.30$. The Web server log shows that 21,600 requests were processed during the measurement interval. What are the service demands at the CPU and both disks, what is the maximum throughput, and what was the response time of the Web server during the measurement interval?

3. Consider the Web server of Exercise 3.2. Draw a graph of the Web server's throughput as a function of the number of concurrent requests. Comment on observations.

4. A computer system is measured for 30 minutes. During this time, 5,400 transactions are completed and 18,900 I/O operations are executed on a certain disk that is 40% utilized. What is the average number of I/O operations per transaction on this disk? What is the average service time per transaction on this disk?

5. A transaction processing system is monitored for one hour. During this period, 5,400 transactions are processed. What is the utilization

of a disk if its average service time is equal to 30 msec per visit and the disk is visited three times on average by every transaction?

6. The average delay experienced by a packet when traversing a computer network is 100 msec. The average number of packets that cross the network per second is 128 packets/sec. What is the average number of concurrent packets in transit in the network at any time?

7. A file server is monitored for 60 minutes, during which time 7,200 requests are completed. The disk utilization is measured to be 30%. The average service time at this disk is 30 msec per file operation request. What is the average number of accesses to this disk per file request?

8. Consider the database server of Example 3.2. Using `ClosedQN.XLS`, what is the throughput of the database server, its response time, and the utilization of the CPU and the three disks, when there are 5 concurrent transactions in execution?

9. A computer system has one CPU and two disks: disk 1 and disk 2. The system is monitored for one hour and the utilization of the CPU and of disk 1 are measured to be 32% and 60%, respectively. Each transaction makes 5 I/O requests to disk 1 and 8 to disk 2. The average service time at disk 1 is 30 msec and at disk 2 is 25 msec.

   - Find the system throughput.
   - Find the utilization of disk 2.
   - Find the average service demands at the CPU, disk 1, and disk 2.
   - Use `ClosedQN.XLS` to find the system throughput, response time, and average queue length at the CPU and the disks when the degree of multiprogramming is n, for $n = 0, ..., 4$.
   - Based on the above results, what is a good approximation for the average degree of multiprogramming during the measurement interval?

10. An interactive system has 50 terminals and the user's think time is equal to 5 seconds. The utilization of one of the system's disk was measured to be 60%. The average service time at the disk is equal to 30 msec. Each user interaction requires, on average, 4 I/Os on this disk. What is the average response time of the interactive system?

11. Obtain access to a UNIX or Linux machine and become acquainted with the command `iostat`, which displays information on disk and CPU activity. The data in Table 3.4 shows a typical output report from `iostat`. Each line displays values averaged over 5-second intervals. The first three columns show activity on disk sd0. The `kps` column reports KB transferred per second, the `tps` column shows the number of I/Os per second, and the `serv` column shows average disk service time in milliseconds. The next four columns display CPU activity. The `us` column shows the percent of time the CPU spent in user mode. The next column shows the percent of time the CPU was in system mode followed by the percent of time the CPU was waiting for I/O. The last column is the percent of time the CPU was idle. Compute the disk and CPU utilizations.

Table 3.4. Data for Exercise 3.9

sd0			cpu			
kps	tps	serv	us	sy	wt	id
25	3	6	19	3	0	78
32	4	7	13	4	0	83
28	2	7	20	3	0	77
18	2	8	24	2	0	74
29	3	9	18	5	0	77
33	4	12	23	3	0	74
35	4	8	25	5	0	70
25	4	10	32	4	0	64
26	3	11	28	4	0	68
34	4	12	22	6	0	72

12. You are planning a load testing experiment of an e-commerce site. During the experiment, virtual users (i.e., programs that behave like real users and submit requests to the site) send requests to the site with an average think time of 5 seconds. How many virtual users you should have in the experiment to achieve a throughput of 20 requests/sec with an average response time of 2 seconds?

Bibliography

[1] P. J. Denning and J. P. Buzen, "The Operational analysis of queueing network models," *Computing Surveys*, vol. 10, No. 3, September 1978, pp. 225-261.

[2] J. C. Little, "A Proof of the queueing formula $L = \lambda W$," *Operations Research*, vol. 9, 1961, pp. 383–387.

[3] R. R. Muntz and J. W. Wong, "Asymptotic properties of closed queuing network models," *Proc. 8th Princeton Conf. Information Sciences and Systems*, 1974.

Chapter 4

Performance Engineering Methodology

4.1 Introduction

Here is a central question: how can one plan, design, develop, deploy and operate IT services that meet the ever increasing demands for performance, availability, reliability, security, and cost? Or, being more specific, is a given IT system properly designed and sized for a given load condition? Can the insurance claims management system meet the performance requirement of subsecond response time? Is the infrastructure of a government agency scalable and can it cope with the new online security policies required for financial transactions? Can the security mechanisms be implemented without sacrificing user-perceived performance? Is the reservations system for cruise lines able to respond to the anticipated peak of consumer inquiries that occurs after a TV advertisement campaign?

By breaking down the complexity of an IT system, one can analyze the functionality of each component, evaluate service requirements, and design and operate systems that will meet user's expectations. In other words, the answer to the above questions requires a deep understanding of the system architecture and its infrastructure. This chapter presents the basic steps of a methodology for performance engineering that are needed to fulfill the major performance needs of IT services.

4.2 Performance Engineering

It has been a common practice in many systems projects to consider performance requirements only at the final stages of the software development process. As a consequence, many systems exhibit performance failures that lead to delays and financial losses to companies and users [25]. *Performance engineering* analyzes the expected performance characteristics of a system during the different phases of its lifecycle. Performance engineering 1) develops practical strategies that help predict the level of performance a system can achieve and 2) provides recommendations to realize the optimal performance level. Both tasks rely on the following activities that form the basis of a methodology.

- Understand the key factors that affect a system's performance.
- Measure the system and understand its workload.
- Develop and validate a workload model that captures the key characteristics of the actual workload.
- Develop and validate an analytical model that accurately predicts the performance of the system.
- Use the models to predict and optimize the performance of the system.

Performance engineering can be viewed as a collection of methods for the support of the development of performance-oriented systems throughout the entire lifecycle [7]. The phases of the system lifecycle define the workflow, procedures, actions, and techniques that are used by analysts to produce and maintain IT systems. Figure 4.1 provides an overview of a performance-based methodology for system design and analysis. This methodology is based on models that are used to provide QoS assurances to IT systems. These models are: workload model, performance model, availability model, reliability model, and cost model. At the early stages of a project, the information and data available to develop the models are approximate at best.

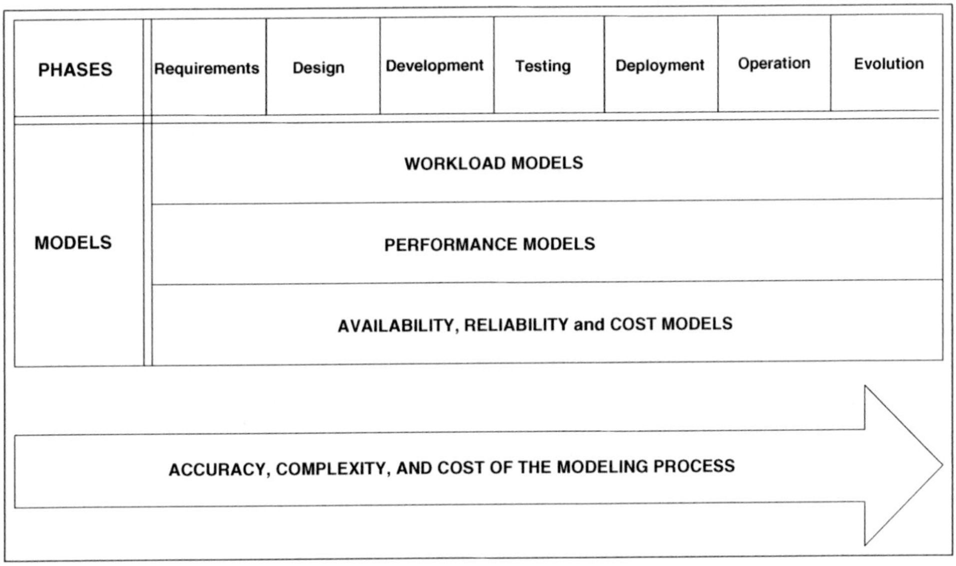

PHASES	Requirements	Design	Development	Testing	Deployment	Operation	Evolution
MODELS	WORKLOAD MODELS							
	PERFORMANCE MODELS							
	AVAILABILITY, RELIABILITY and COST MODELS							

ACCURACY, COMPLEXITY, AND COST OF THE MODELING PROCESS

Figure 4.1. Modeling process.

For instance, in the requirement analysis stage, it is difficult to construct a detailed workload model, specifying the demands placed by transactions on the system's resources. However, as the project evolves, more system information becomes available, reducing the error margin of the model's assumptions and increasing confidence in the estimated predictions of the future system's performance [23]. In summary, the workload and performance models evolve side by side with the system project throughout the stages of its lifecycle. Various types of workload and performance models can be used during the system lifecycle. Basically, they differ in three aspects: complexity, accuracy, and cost. Figure 4.1 illustrates the spectrum of the models for the different phases, ranked from least to most complex and costly. It is expected that as complexity and cost increase, the refined models becomes more accurate. At the low end of the figure, one may use back-of-the-envelope calculations as a simple, easy-to-use technique, with a relatively low level of accuracy. At the high end, detailed models of running systems are used that are accurate but, are also costly and complex.

4.3   Motivating Example

Facing sharp competition, consider an automotive parts distribution company that has decided to develop and implement a new call center. The goals of the new call center system are to: 1) foster better relationships with customers, creating customer loyalty and ensuring quality service, 2) improve efficiency and service performance, and 3) identify and explore new sales opportunities.

The information technology team has decided to create an integrated customer relationship management system. The proposed new architecture consists of computer telephony integration software that controls inbound calls and routes these calls to service representatives integrated with the application software. Figure 4.2 depicts an overview of the call center architecture.

The call center will be staffed by service representatives who handle customer orders, returns, queries by phone, fax, and e-mail. Basically, customers

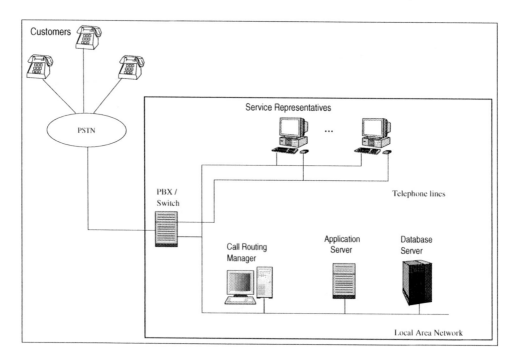

Figure 4.2. Architecture of the call center.

inquire about: 1) the status of an order, 2) the location of a shipment, and 3) problem resolution status. Each customer service representative will have immediate access to the following basic functions: 1) historical tracking of all customer contacts, 2) a single view of customer information, 3) records of resolution of past problems, and 4) help functions. Management realizes that customers are less tolerant of long calls. Thus, the system should meet sub-second response times on all functions and be operational 24 hours a day, 7 days a week.

The company wants to consider various scenarios when designing its call center. The IT team is planning to design, build, test, and deploy the new call center applications in 12 months. Before rollout, management wants assurances that the performance requirements are satisfied. Questions that project management asks include:

- Is the system design able to meet the subsecond response time for all functions?

- What will be the impact of doubling the number of system representatives in the next year?

- Can acceptable performance levels be maintained after integrating the system with the mainframe-based inventory application?

- Is the system capacity adequate to handle up to 1,000 calls in the busiest hour and yet preserve the subsecond response time goal?

- How do failures in the database server affect the 24×7 availability goal?

- What is the impact of starting to offer Web-based self-service to customers?

Example 4.1

Figure 4.2 shows illustrates the physical architecture of the call center system. During the *requirement analysis stage*, the analysts specify the type of system architecture and the resources that will support the QoS goals for the system. The analysts want an initial idea about the models that will be used in the performance engineering analysis phase.

Consider a first attempt for a workload model. Initially, one needs to define the workload to be characterized. There are multiple and different workloads in a system depending on the point of view from which one looks at the workload. The workload presented to the call center system consists of the rate of telephone calls into the call center. From the IT application standpoint, the workload consists of all functions it receives from the representatives during an observation period. A database server may receive queries from the application server, which in turn receives function execution requests from the representatives. The load of the local network is usually described in terms of its traffic characteristics, including the packet size distribution and the interpacket arrival time.

A second issue that must be about the workload model is the level of detail its description. A high-level description specifies the workload from the user's point of view. For instance, one could specify the load in terms of functions submitted by the users. On the other hand, a low-level characterization describing the user's requests in resource-oriented terms (e.g., average CPU time per function and number of I/O operations per function) is not available until the later stages of the system lifecycle.

At this stage of the project, the analysts have an overall view of the system's two-tier architecture, composed of an application server and a database server. Initially, the performance model is a simple black box. The desired output of the model includes throughput, response time, and availability. ∎

Example 4.2

Consider the call center system described in the motivating example. During the *system design stage*, the analyst needs to answer the following question: what should be the system throughput to meet the subsecond response time requirement? At this stage, the analyst makes assumptions such as: 1) the number of service representatives will be 200, and 2) during the busiest hour, 80% of the representatives are working simultaneously answering calls.

The conversation of a representative with a customer can be represented by a simple interaction model. The representative listens to the customer, selects a function, submits it to the system, waits for the system to respond, watches while the results appear, talks to the customer, terminates the call, and waits for another customer call. The think time corresponds to the period of time between a reply to a function execution request and the following submission. At this stage of the project, the analyst's view of the call center application is a black box, modeled by Fig. 4.3.

The analyst estimates an average think time of 30 sec, denoted by Z. The number of active representatives in the system, denoted by N, is equal to 200×0.80. The system throughput is denoted by X_0. If the response time, R, is not to exceed 1 second, it follows from the Interactive Response Time Law (see Chapter 3) that

$$R = N/X_0 - Z \leq 1 \text{ sec.}$$

Then,

$$X_0 \geq \frac{N}{(Z+R)} = \frac{N}{(Z+1)} = 5.16 \text{ functions/sec.}$$

∎

Example 4.3

During the *system development phase*, the various components of the system are implemented. Suppose that during this phase, the analysts determine that each function submitted by a representative demands 2.2 queries from the database server. Before developing the database component of the

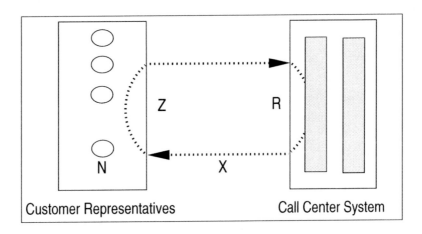

Figure 4.3. Model of the call center system.

system, they need to know the required capacity of the database server that is needed to meet the performance objectives.

The Forced Flow Law, discussed in Chapter 3, applied to the database server establishes a relationship between the database server throughput and the system throughput. That is,

$$X_{DB} = V_{DB} \times X_0, \tag{4.3.1}$$

where X_{DB} is the database server throughput, X_0 denotes the total system throughput, and V_{DB} is the average number of visits per function to the database server. The minimum database server throughput, in queries/sec, is obtained in Example 4.2 as $X_0 \geq 5.16$ functions/sec.

Considering that the minimum system throughput is 5.16 functions/sec and each function accesses the database server 2.2 times, the minimum database server throughput, measured in queries per second is

$$X_{DB} \geq 2.2 \times 5.16 = 11.32 \text{ transactions/sec}$$

■

Example 4.4

Measuring the performance of the call center applications is a key issue in the process of guaranteeing the quality of service objectives. It is also an essential step for performance engineering, because it collects data for performance analysis and modeling. These measurement data are used to calculate the model input parameters, which describe the system configuration, the software environment, and the workload of the call center system.

Let the average response time be denoted by R_{call}. The response time can be decomposed into three main components:

$$R_{call} = R_{Appl} + R_{LAN} + R_{DB},$$

where R_{Appl}, R_{LAN}, and R_{DB} represent the response time at the application server, the Local Area Network, and the database server, respectively.

The description of the motivating example provides a performance requirement that $R_{call} < 1$. In the *operation stage*, the system is constantly monitored to verify that performance objectives are being met. During the peak hour, the system shows signs of saturation, with average response times longer than one second. Management is considering upgrading the database server and wants to know what component of the server is most responsible for slowing down its response time. The relevant questions include: What is the average response time per query? What is the average throughput of the DB server? What are the utilizations of the CPU and disks?

For the sake of simplicity, consider that the database server services only one type of transaction: query. The DB server has one CPU and two disks. During the peak period, the DB server receives requests from the application server at a rate of 57,600 queries per hour. Based on measurements collected during the operation of the call center application, the analyst obtains the following data: on average, each query needs 50 msec of CPU and performs four I/Os on disk 1 and two I/Os on disk 2. Each I/O takes an average of 8 msec.

The throughput, X_0, is equal to the average arrival rate λ, given by: $57,600/3,600 = 16$ queries/sec. The service demand at the CPU, D_{CPU}, is 0.050 sec. The service demands at disks 1 and 2 are:

$$D_{\text{disk1}} = V_1 \times S_{\text{disk}} = 4 \times 0.008 = 0.032 \text{ sec, and}$$
$$D_{\text{disk2}} = V_2 \times S_{\text{disk}} = 2 \times 0.008 = 0.016 \text{ sec.}$$

From the Service Demand Law (see Chapter 3), $U_i = D_i \times X_0$. Therefore, the utilization of the CPU and the disks are given by $U_{\text{CPU}} = D_{\text{CPU}} \times X_0 = 0.05 \times 16 = 80\%$, $U_{\text{disk1}} = D_{\text{disk1}} \times X_0 = 0.032 \times 16 = 51.2\%$, and $U_{\text{disk2}} = D_{\text{disk2}} \times X_0 = 0.016 \times 16 = 25.6\%$, respectively. Using the residence time equation for open queuing networks of Chapter 13, the residence times at the CPU and disks are:

$$R'_{\text{CPU}} = \frac{D_{\text{CPU}}}{1 - U_{\text{CPU}}} = \frac{0.050}{1 - 0.8} = 0.250 \text{ sec}$$

$$R'_{\text{disk1}} = \frac{D_{\text{disk1}}}{1 - U_{\text{disk1}}} = \frac{0.032}{1 - 0.512} = 0.066 \text{ sec}$$

$$R'_{\text{disk2}} = \frac{D_{\text{disk2}}}{1 - U_{\text{disk2}}} = \frac{0.016}{1 - 0.256} = 0.022 \text{ sec.}$$

The total response time is the sum of all residence times. Thus, $R_{\text{DB}} = R'_{\text{CPU}} + R'_{\text{disk1}} + R'_{\text{disk2}} = 0.250 + 0.066 + 0.022 = 0.338$ sec. The CPU is the bottleneck since it has the largest service demand. As the load increases, the CPU utilization will reach 100% before any other device and will limit the throughput of the database server.   ■

Example 4.5

Now consider the *evolution stage* of the call center system. The company is considering to develop Web applications to allow customers access to the information they need without assistance from a customer representative. Web self-services reduce transaction costs and enhance the customer experience.

To let users directly access the call center database, management wants to make sure that security requirements will be met. Security depends on the context in which security issues are raised [4]. In the business context, the security emphasis is on the protection of assets. Management wants to minimize the risk of unauthorized modification of the information in the call center database. Thus, software engineers involved need to design a new type of transaction that satisfies the security requirements. The security requirement has implications on two areas of the system [4]: interface and internal architecture. The new interface should include authentication services that perform the mapping between the user's identity and the person using the system. New auditing features should be included to aid administrators discover the history of unauthorized access in the event of a security breach. In terms of the internal architecture, the designers plan to modify the access control mechanisms to the database information.

Before embarking on the developing and implementation of the Web application, management wants to assess the likely impact of the new application on the call center service. From the software model [25], the analyst is able to estimate the service demands for the new class of transactions, submitted via the Web. A new performance model for the database server is developed. The database server model is subject to two types of transactions: local queries and Web queries. The arrival rate of local queries transactions is 16 tps and the arrival rate of Web queries transactions is 1 tps. The service demands for the CPU, disks 1, and disk 2, are given in Table 4.1.

Table 4.1.   Service Demands and Arrival Rates of Database
Transactions for Ex. 4.5

	Local Queries	Web Queries
Arrival Rate (tps)	16	1
Service Demands (sec)		
CPU	0.050	0.150
Disk 1	0.032	0.200
Disk 2	0.016	0.100

Using the equations for the multiple-class case of open queuing networks
(see Chapter 13) and the `OpenQN.XLS` MS Excel workbook the model can be
solved and the results show management the impact of Web transactions on
call center applications. The response times for local queries and Web queries
at the database server are 1.14 sec and 3.85 sec, respectively. These numbers
provide management with a concrete sense of the impact of implementing
Web applications on the current infrastructure of the call center system. ∎

4.4   A Model-based Methodology

This section describes the basic steps used to design and analyze computer
systems with performance in mind. The methodology builds on workload
and performance models and can be used throughout the phases of the system lifecycle. Performance engineering provides a series of steps to be followed in a systematic way [2]. Figure 4.4 gives an overview of the main steps
of the quantitative approach to analyze the performance of a system.

The starting point of the methodology is to specify system performance
objectives. These objectives should be quantified as part of the system requirements. Performance objectives are used to establish service level goals.
Service level goals are defined, business metrics are established, and the performance goals of the system are documented. Once the system and its
quantitative objectives have been determined, one is able to go through the
quantitative analysis cycle. The various steps of the quantitative analysis
cycle are:

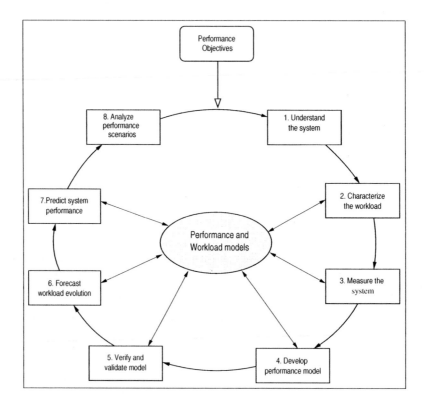

Figure 4.4. A model-based performance engineering methodology.

- *Understand the system.* The first step is to obtain an in-depth understanding of the system architecture and conduct an architecture-level
  review with emphasis on performance. This means answering questions
  such as: What are the system requirements of the business model?
  What type of software (i.e., operating system, transaction monitor,
  DBMS, application software) is going to be used in the system? This
  step yields a systematic description of the system architecture, its components, and goals. It is an opportunity to review the performance
  issues of the proposed architecture.

- *Characterize the workload.* In this step, the basic components that
  compose the workload are identified. The choice of components depends both on the nature of the system and the purpose of the characterization. The product of this step is a statement such as "The

workload under study consists of e-business transactions, e-mail messages, and data-mininig requests." The performance of a system with many clients, servers, and networks depends heavily on the characteristics of its load. Thus, it is vital in any performance engineering effort to understand clearly and characterize accurately the workload [8, 13]. The workload of a system can be defined as the set of all inputs that the system receives from its environment during any given period of time. For instance, if the system under study is a database server, then its workload consists of all transactions (e.g., query, update) processed by the server during an observation interval.

- *Measure the system and obtain workload parameters.* The third step involves measuring the performance of the system and obtaining values for the parameters of the workload model. Measurement is a key step to all tasks in performance engineering. It allows one to understand the parameters of the system and to establish a link between a system and its model. Performance measurements are collected from different reference points, carefully chosen to observe and monitor the environment under study. For example, consider that a database server is observed during 10 minutes and 100,000 transactions are completed. The workload of the database during that 10-minute period is the set of 100,000 transactions. The workload characteristics are represented by a set of information (e.g., arrival and completion time, CPU time, and number of I/O operations) for each of the 100,000 database transactions.

- *Develop performance models.* In the fourth step, quantitative techniques and analytical (or simulation or prototype) models are used to develop performance models of systems. Performance models are used to understand the behavior of complex systems. Models are used to predict performance when any aspect of the workload or the system architecture is changed. Simple models based on operational analysis discussed in Chapter 3 are accessible to software engineering practitioners. They offer insight into how software architectural decisions impact performance [11].

- *Verify and validate the models.* The fifth step aims at verifying the model specifications and validating the model's results. This step applies to both, performance and workload models. A performance model is said to be validated if the performance metrics (e.g., response time, resource utilizations, throughputs) calculated by the model match the measurements of the actual system within a certain acceptable margin of error. As a rule of thumb, resource utilizations within 10%, system throughput within 10%, and response time within 20% are considered acceptable [16]. A model is said to be verified if its results are an accurate reflection of the system performance [25]. Details of performance model calibration techniques are available [16]. In summary, this step answers questions such as: Is the right model for the system being considered? Does the model capture the behavior of the critical components of the system?

- *Forecast workload evolution.* Most systems suffer modifications and evolutions throughout their lifetime. As a system's demands change, so do workloads. Demands grow or shrink, depending on many factors, such as the functionalities offered to users, number of users, hardware upgrades, or changes to software components. The sixth step forecasts the expected workload for the system. Techniques and strategies for forecasting [12] workload changes should provide answers to questions such as: What will be the average size of e-mails by the end of next year? What will be the number of simultaneous users for the online banking system six months from now?

- *Predict system performance.* Performance guidance is needed at each stage of the system lifecycle, since every architectural decision can potentially create barriers in achieving the system performance goals. Thus, performance prediction is key to performance engineering work, because one needs to be able to determine how a system will react when changes in load levels and user behavior occur or when new software components are integrated into the system. This determination requires predictive models. Experimentation, is not usually viable because fixing performance defects may require structural changes that are expensive. In the seventh step, performance models are used to predict the performance of a system under many different scenarios.

- *Analyze performance scenarios.* Validated performance and workload models are used to predict the performance of a system under several different scenarios, such as upgraded servers, faster networks, changes in the system workload, changes to the user behavior, and changes to the software system. To help find the most cost-effective system architecture, different scenarios are analyzed in this step. Basically, each scenario consists of a future system feature and/or a workload forecast. Because every forecast item carries a certain degree of uncertainty, several possible future scenarios are considered. Different possible system architectures are analyzed. A selection of alternatives is generated so that system engineers may choose the most appropriate option, in terms of cost/benefit.

Two models are central components of the methodology: the workload model and the system performance model. Workload models are studied in detail in this chapter. Performance models were introduced in Chapter 3. Techniques for constructing models of different types of systems are developed in Chapters 10 through 15.

4.5 Workload Model

A workload model is a representation that mimics the real workload under study. It can be a set of programs written and implemented with the goal of artificially testing a system in a controlled environment. A workload model may also serve as input data for an analytical model of a system. It is not practical to have a model composed of thousands of basic components to mimic the real workload. Workload models should be compact and representative of the actual workload [14].

4.5.1 Types of Workload Models

Workload models can be classified into two main categories:

- *Natural models* are constructed either using basic components of the real workload as building blocks or using execution traces of the real workload. A natural benchmark consists of programs extracted from the real workload of a system. These programs are selected so that the benchmark represents the overall system load in given periods of time. Another natural model often used in performance studies is a workload trace. It consists of a chronological sequence of data representing specific events that occurred in the system during a measurement session. For example, in the case of a Web server, the log access contains one entry per HTTP request processed by the server. Among other information, each log entry specifies the name of the host making the request, the timestamp, and the name of the file requested. This type of log characterizes the real workload during a given period of time. Although traces exhibit reproducibility and representativeness features, they do have drawbacks. Usually, traces consist of huge amounts of data, which increases the complexity of using them in modeling exercises. It is usually difficult to modify a trace to represent different workload scenarios. Moreover, traces are suitable only for simulation or prototype models.

- *Artificial models* do not make use of any basic component of the real workload. Instead, these models are constructed out of special-purpose programs and descriptive parameters. Artificial models are partitioned into two classes: executable and non-executable models. Executable artificial models consist of a suite of programs especially written to experiment with particular aspects of a computer system. The class of executable models include workloads such as *instruction mixes, kernels, synthetic programs, artificial benchmarks*, and *drivers*. Instruction mixes are hardware demonstration programs intended to test the speed of a computer on simple computational and I/O operations. Program kernels are pieces of code selected from computationally intense parts of a real program. In general, kernels concentrate on measuring the performance of processors without considering the I/O system. Synthetic programs are specially devised codes that place demands on different resources of a computing system. Unlike benchmarks, synthetic programs do not resemble the real workload. Benchmarks, synthetic programs, and other forms of executable models are not adequate inputs for performance models. When the performance of a system is analyzed through the use of analytic or simulation models,

non executable representations for the workload are required. Because
the approach to performance engineering relies on the use of analytic
models for performance prediction, this book focuses on workload representations suitable for these kinds of models.

Non-executable workload models are described by a set of average parameter values that reproduce the same resource usage as the real workload.
Each parameter denotes an aspect of the execution behavior of the basic
component on the system under study. The basic inputs to analytical models are parameters that describe the service centers (i.e., hardware and software resources) and the customers (e.g., transactions and requests). Typical
parameters are:

- Component (e.g., transaction and request) interarrival times,
- Service demands,
- Component sizes, and
- Execution mixes (classes of components and their corresponding levels
  of multiprogramming).

Each type of system may be characterized by a different set of parameters. As an example, consider a parametric characterization of a workload of
a distributed system file server [5]. Several factors have a direct influence on
the performance of a file server: the system load, the device capability, and
the locality of file references. From these factors, the following parameters
are defined:

- Frequency distribution of the requests: describes the participation of
  each request (e.g., read, write, create, rename) on the total workload.
- Request interarrival time distribution: indicates the time between successive requests. It also indicates the intensity of the system load.
- File referencing behavior: describes the percentage of accesses made
  to each file in the disk subsystem.
- Size of reads and writes: indicates the I/O load. This parameter has
  a strong influence on the time needed to service a request.

The above parameters specify the workload model and are capable of driving synthetic programs that accurately represent real workloads.

Another study [22] looks at an I/O workload from a different perspective. The workload model for a storage device (i.e., queues, caches, controllers, disks) is specified by three classes of parameters: access time attributes, access type (i.e., fraction of reads and writes), and spatial locality attributes [1]. Access time attributes capture the time access pattern, which includes the arrival process (i.e., deterministic, Poisson, bursty), arrival rate, burst rate, burst count, and burst fraction. Spatial locality attributes specify the relationship between consecutive requests, such as sequential and random accesses. Due to "seek" delays, workloads with a larger fraction of sequential accesses typically exhibit better performance than those with random accesses. Thus, for a detailed model of an I/O device, it is important to include the spatial locality attributes of the workload.

4.5.2 Clustering Analysis

Consider a workload that consists of transactions that exhibit a large variability in terms of their CPU and I/O demands. Averaging the demands of all transactions would likely produce a workload model that is not representative of most of the transactions. Therefore, the transactions in the workload have to be grouped, or clustered, so that the variability within each group is relatively small when compared to the variability in the entire data set. These clusters correspond to different classes of a multiclass performance model.

The process of generating these rather homogeneous groups is called *clustering analysis*. While clustering analysis can be performed automatically by specific functions of software packages (e.g., SPSS, SAS, WEKA), a performance analyst should know the fundamentals of this technique.

A well-known clustering technique, called *k-means* clustering, is presented here. Assume that a workload is described by a set of p points $w_i = (D_{i_1}, D_{i_2}, \cdots, D_{i_M})$ in an M-dimensional space, where each point w_i represents a unit of work (e.g., transaction, request) executed by a computer system. The components of a point w_i describe specific properties of a transaction, such as the service demand at a particular device or any other value (e.g., I/O count, bytes transmitted) from which service demands can be obtained.

Many clustering algorithms, including k-means, require that a distance metric between points be defined. A common distance metric is the *Euclidean distance*, which defines the distance, $d_{i,j}$, between two points $w_i = (D_{i_1}, D_{i_2}, \cdots, D_{i_M})$ and $w_j = (D_{j_1}, D_{j_2}, \cdots, D_{j_M})$ as

$$d_{i,j} = \sqrt{\sum_{n=1}^{M} (D_{i_n} - D_{j_n})^2}. \qquad (4.5.2)$$

The use of raw data to compute Euclidean distances may lead to distortions if the components of a point have very different relative values and ranges. For instance, suppose that the workload of a Web server is described by points, each representing an HTTP request, of the type (f, c) where f is the size of the file retrieved by an HTTP request and c is the CPU time required to process the request. Consider the point $(25, 30)$ where f is measured in Kbytes and c in milliseconds. If f is now measured in Mbytes, the point $(25, 30)$ becomes $(0.025, 30)$. Such changes of units may result in the modification of the relative distances among groups of points [16]. Scaling techniques should be used to minimize problems that arise from the choice of units and from the different ranges of values of the parameters [16].

The k-means algorithm produces k clusters. Each cluster is represented by its *centroid*, which is a point whose coordinates are obtained by computing the average of all the coordinates of the points in the cluster. The algorithms starts by determining k points in the workload to act as initial estimates of the centroids of the k clusters. The remaining points are then allocated to the cluster with the nearest centroid. The allocation procedure iterates several times over the input points until no point switches cluster assignment or a maximum number of iterations is performed. Having as input data the p points $w_i = (D_{i1}, D_{i2}, \ldots, D_{iM})$, the steps required by the k-means algorithm are shown in Fig. 4.5.

Another distance-based clustering algorithm is the minimum spaning tree algorithm described in [16]. Fractal-based clustering of E-commerce workloads is discussed in [15].

---

1. Set the number of clusters to k.

2. Choose k starting points, to be used as initial estimates of cluster centroids. For example, one can select either the first k points of the sample or the k points mutually farthest apart. In this case, all the distances between the points need to be computed.

3. Examine each point of the workload and allocate it to the cluster whose centroid is nearest. The centroid's position is recalculated each time a new point is added to the cluster.

4. Repeat step 3 until no point changes its cluster assignment during a complete pass or a maximum number of passes is performed.

Figure 4.5. The k-means clustering algorithm.

4.6   Performance Models

Performance modeling is a key technique to understanding problems in IT systems. Because it is difficult to estimate performance, IT systems must be designed with service levels in mind. In other words, a designer of an IT service must know the limits of the system *a priori*. For instance, a designer must know the maximum number of transactions per second the system is capable of processing (i.e., an upper bound on throughput) or the minimum response time that can be achieved by a transaction processing system (i.e., a lower bound on response time).

Analytic performance models capture fundamental aspects of a computer system and relate them to each other by mathematical formulas and/or computational algorithms. Basically, analytic performance models require input information such as workload intensity (e.g., arrival rate, number of clients, and think time) and the service demand placed by the basic component of the workload on each resource of the system. Several queuing network-based algorithms for solving open and closed models with multiple classes are provided in Part II of this book and are implemented in MS Excel workbooks. The techniques include exact and approximate solutions. Many times, a relative or approximate performance estimate is all that is required. Simply knowing that the throughput is approximately 120 tps for one system alternative and approximately 300 tps for another alternative is sufficient information to select one option over another. These situations can be analyzed with simple performance bounding techniques presented in Chapter 3.

Detailed performance models require parameters, which can be grouped into the following categories.

- *System parameters.* Characteristics of a system that affect performance include, the number of processes in execution, the nature and intensity of intercomponent communication, buffer sizes, maximum number of supported threads, and network protocols.

- *Resource parameters.* Intrinsic features of a resource that affect performance include disk seek times, latency, transfer rates, network bandwidth, router latency, and CPU speeds.

- *Workload parameters.* These parameters are derived from the workload characterization and are divided into two subcategories.

  - *Workload intensity parameters.* provide a measure of the load placed on a system, indicated by the number of units of work that contend for system resources. Examples include the number of sessions started per day, number of transactions/day to an application server, number of operations requiring secure connections/sec, and number of database transactions executed per unit time.

  - *Workload service demand parameters.* specify the total amount of service time required by each basic component at each resource. Examples include the CPU time of transactions at the application server, the total transmission time of replies from the Web server back to the customer, and the total I/O time at the database server for a query function.

The critical goal of analyzing and designing IT systems is guaranteeing that performance objectives are satisfied. IT services are complex and can be very expensive. It is important to minimize the amount of guesswork when it comes to designing, implementing, and operating the systems that provide these services.

4.7   Specifying Performance Objectives

Users of IT services are generally not concerned with metrics such as CPU utilization, memory contention, network bandwidth, failure rates, router up-time, and other indicators of system performance. On the contrary, users tend to be more interested in metrics related to quality of the services (QoS) provided by a system. QoS is indicated by specific objectives. End-users want to know how well the system is performing and if they can get their work done on time. Users perceive system services through performance metrics such as *response time, availability, reliability, security,* and *cost.* Expected service levels govern the relationship between users and systems.

Performance objectives should be stated precisely. In the process of analyzing system requirements, one should avoid vague statements such as the following:

- The system response time should be satisfactory to end users.

- The system availability should be adequate.

- The system should be as reliable as possible.

In contrast, performance goals should be stated in a simple and precise manner, such as:

- The system throughput should be greater than 1,000 query transactions per second, with at least 90% of the transactions responding in less than 2 sec.

- The application server should have an availability of 99.9% during the business hours of weekdays.

- The response time of the patient information system should not exceed one second for local users.

- The mail server must be able to process at least 70,000 messages per day and 90% of the outgoing messages should not wait more than 2 minutes to be delivered.

4.7.1   Specifying a Service Level Agreement

Service Level Agreements (SLA) require IT to work with its end-users to define a list of services and their quality attributes, such as response time, availability, reliability, time-to-repair, and cost. The values of SLAs are specific to each organization and are determined by both management and users. As shown in Fig 4.6, an SLA is useful to manage IT services in various ways: 1) planning, by determining what the service levels need to be, and 2) assurance, by monitoring the service levels to ensure that they meet the specified requirements and by identifying problems when a service level is not met. Performance engineering is a methodology to support and manage service level agreements.

SLAs take different forms, depending on the nature of the IT service. For instance, SLAs can be divided into different performance levels, such as basic, enhanced, and premium. Each category typically incurs a different cost [10]. Users can then have a clear understanding of the resource and cost tradeoffs involved in designing, implementing, and operating an IT system [10].

Adequate capacity and infrastructure are provided so that acceptable or desirable values for performance metrics can be achieved. Before deciding on a particular service level for a system, one should assess the current level of service provided by the existing systems. After assessing the current level

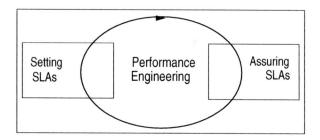

Figure 4.6. Performance Engineering process and SLAs.

of service, management faces the following question: Do the service levels need to be changed? If they are unsatisfactory or expensive to the users or if they have to be changed as a function of business goals, new service levels should be established. The following are some helpful criteria to establish new service levels.

- *Cost × benefit.* Service levels depend on both the workload and on the system configuration. Improving service levels usually implies an expansion of system capacity. This translates into cost. A trade-off analysis between benefits and cost should be carried out. For instance, response time is often reported to be inversely proportional to user productivity. The shorter the response time, the higher the productivity. However, it is reasonable to ask whether productivity gains compensate for the additional cost incurred to reduce response time. The better the service level, the higher the system cost. Managers and users should discuss performance goals in light of the cost of providing IT services.

- *Nature of the application.* To be acceptable to customers, service applications such as point-of-sale and airline reservation systems must provide fast response times. An airline reservation system may guarantee that 90% of the transactions should respond in 3 sec or less, with an average of 1.5 sec. An airline company may not afford to leave a reservation agent or an airport agent, who has to deal with passengers, waiting much longer than 3 sec [9]. Real-time applications that deal with customers, control manufacturing, and other critical systems must respond to requests within specified time limits.

- *Past performance goals.* Performance levels attained in the past can help IT management and users reach an agreement for future service levels. Users establish expectations based on their past experience about the time required to complete a given task.

4.7.2 Specifying Response Time

Response time is a critical factor to users of interactive systems. People interact so often with computer-based systems, everyone agrees that response time is an important determinant of personal productivity, error rates, and satisfaction [21]. It is evident that user satisfaction increases as response time shortens. Modest variations around the average response time are acceptable, but large variations may affect user behavior. A frequently asked question is: How should one set appropriate response time limits for a given system? The answer depends on how system response time affects user's performance. Adequate response time limits for a specific system and a user community can be determined by measuring the impact on user's productivity and by estimating the cost of providing improved response times. Guideline about computer response time and user behavior exist and the behavior of human-computer interactions have been studied extensively [17, 18]. Regarding the response time of a system:

- 0.1 second is about the limit when a user perceives that the system is reacting instantaneously.

- 1.0 second is about the limit when the flow of thought of a user is not interrupted, although the user may notice the delay.

- 10 seconds is about the limit when a user loses attention and the interaction with the system is disrupted.

4.7.3 Specifying Cost

The estimation of the cost of developing and delivering IT systems is an essential component of a performance engineering methodology. The system life cycle involves a number of design trade-offs with significant cost and performance implications. For example, the choice of thin clients versus fat clients to execute networked applications, the choice of the number of architectural layers of a system, and the choice of the number and capacity of servers of a datacenter affect both the performance and the cost of a system [3].

Without cost estimates, it is meaningless to discuss service level and performance objectives for a specific business. Managers need to calculate cost and estimate benefits to make good IT decisions. For example, to specify the availability goals for a credit card authorization system or a catalog sales center, one has to know the cost of a minute of downtime. Depending on the nature of the application, the average cost of one minute of downtime can be as high as $100,000 in the case of systems that support brokerage operations [19].

The Total Cost of Ownership (TCO) [20] model has been applied to evaluate the cost of a system. It means the total cost of owing a given system over some time horizon (e.g., five-year period). TCO intends to identify and measure elements of IT expenses beyond the initial cost of implementing a system. The most significant contributing items to TCO are:

- Hardware costs, including acquisition expenses or leasing expenses of equipment, such as servers, storage boxes, and connectivity components.

- Software costs, including personal productivity software, applications, database management, transaction monitors, intrusion detection, performance monitoring, and operating system software.

- Communication costs, including leased lines and communication services access.

- Management costs, including network management, systems storage, maintenance, and outsourced services.

- Support costs, including support services, support personnel training, end-user training, and help desk services.

- Facilities costs, including leasing of physical space, air conditioning, power, and physical security.

- Downtime costs, including both the cost of lost productivity of employees and the cost of lost income from missed business [19].

Measuring the Return on Investment (ROI) is also critical to evaluate the cost and benefits of a system. To measure the success of the investment of information technology two factors are considered: the improvement in the quality of service (e.g., user satisfaction and system use) and the return on investment (e.g., increased productivity and organizational impact). Thus, ROI methodologies are useful for analyzing the cost/benefits of IT projects.

Based on the requirement analysis of a system, one should develop a cost model to understand the cost/benefits of the system. When different system choices are evaluated, one needs to predict how much additional computing and communication resources will be needed for each choice and how much these elements cost now and in the future.

Example 4.6

Consider the call center system described in the motivating example. Management is planning to replace the database server with a powerful cluster of servers. Two brands of clusters are being compared, system Y and system Z. What factors should be considered in the process of choosing between the two systems?

First, IT management is considering the TCO model, instead of the pure purchase cost of the system. Thus, the basic cost of both systems includes hardware and software costs, hardware and software maintenance, operational personnel, and facilities costs for a three-year period. System Y costs $300,000 and system Z costs $350,000.

Second, IT management is looking at the performance attributes of both systems. Standard benchmarks indicate that the throughput of systems Y and Z are 220 tps and 230 tps with 90% of the transactions responding in less than 0.5 sec, respectively.

Third, IT management is evaluating other aspects of computing in their analysis. In addition to performance, management also consider the dependability of the systems [19]. Information obtained on the dependability of the two systems suggests an expected 38 hours of unavailability for system Y and 21 hours of downtime for system Z, over a period of three years.

The call center charges $5 per call from customers. The company estimates that in the next three years, the average rate of telephone calls into the call center will be 1,000/hour. Therefore, the estimated average cost per hour of downtime due to revenue loss is $5,000. The total cost of a system is calculated as:

$$\text{Total Cost} = \text{Basic Cost} + \text{Downtime Cost}$$

Using the above expression, the total cost for a three-year period for the two systems is:

- Cost of system Y = 300,000 + 38 × 1000 × 5 = \$490,000

- Cost of system Z = 350,000 + 21 × 1000 × 5 = \$455,000

The above methodology helps management justify selecting system Z. Although Z is more expensive initially, it is more dependable, which makes its total cost more attractive. ∎

4.8   Concluding Remarks

The principle concepts of performance engineering are presented in this chapter. A motivating example is described involving the planning, development, and implementation of a call center application. Five examples of how performance considerations should be included in the analysis, design, operation, and evolution of a system are presented. The main issue in performance engineering is how to guarantee that a system will meet its performance goals. The steps required to carry out a performance engineering effort are described. A central issue in the methodology are the models needed to represent workload and the performance of a system. The basic steps of a practical performance engineering methodology include the following.

- Specify the system performance goals.

- Understand the current environment.

- Perform a workload characterization and generate a workload model.

- Develop a performance model.

- Verify and validate the system model, which is composed of the workload and performance models.

- Forecast workload growth.

- Use the system model to analyze the performance of different system architectures and various workload scenarios.

- Select the best alternative (based on the performance model predictions) that presents the best cost-performance relation while satisfying the service levels specified.

4.9   Exercises

1. Consider the motivating example of Section 4.3. Describe the performance requirements of the system. Be as precise as possible.

2. Assume that the design phase of the call center application has been completed. Analysts are now working on the development phase. Describe the workload model for the two stages and comment on the additional information that could be added to the model during the development phase.

3. Consider the call center motivating example and the data provided in Example 4.4. What is the maximum throughput that can be achieved by the database server?

4. In the architecture of the motivating example, the application server receives and executes the functions submitted by the representatives. Suppose that the application server has 150 active processes that service the received functions. The analyst monitors the system and verifies that an application process executes for an average of 550 msec between database server requests. The database server handles 120 requests/sec. What is the average database response time?

5. In Example 4.4, the workload model consists of two classes of transactions. Aggregate these two classes into a single class. What is the bottleneck of the server? What is the maximum throughput achieved by the server, in terms of the aggregated transaction?

Bibliography

[1] V. A. F. Almeida, M. Crovella, A. Bestravos, and A. Oliveira "Characterizing reference locality in the WWW," *Proc. IEEE/ACM International Conference on Parallel and Distributed System (PDIS)*, December 1996, pp. 92–107.

[2] V. A. F. Almeida and D. A. Menascé, "Capacity planning: An essential tool for managing Web services," *IEEE IT Professional*, vol. 4, no. 4, July/August 2002.

[3] D. Ardagna and C. Francalanci, "A cost-oriented methodology for the design of Web-based IT architectures," *Proc. 17th ACM Symposium on Applied Computing*, Madrid, March 2002.

[4] M. Barbacci, T. Longstaff, M. Klein, and C. Weinstock, "Quality Attributes," Technical Report CMU/SEI-95-TR-021, Software Engineering Institute, December 1995.

[5] R. Bodnarchuk and R. Bunt, "A synthetic workload model for a distributed file system," *Proc. 1991 SIGMETRICS Conf. Measurement Comput. Syst.*, ACM, May 1991.

[6] M. Calzarossa and G. Serazzi, "Workload characterization," *Proc. IEEE*, vol. 81, no. 8, August 1993.

[7] R. Dumke, C. Rautenstrauch, A. Schmietendorf, and A. Scholz (eds.), *Performance Engineering: State of the Art and Current Trends*, LNCS, vol. 2047, Springer, 2001.

[8] D. Ferrari, G. Serazzi, and A. Zeigner, *Measurement and Tuning of Computer Systems*, Prentice Hall, Upper Saddle River, New Jersey, 1983.

[9] D. Gifford and A. Spector, "The TWA reservation system," *Comm. ACM*, vol. 27, no. 7, July 1984.

[10] C. Koch, "Put IT in Writing," *CIO Magazine*, November 15, 1998.

[11] M. Klein, "State of the Practice Report: Problems in the Practice of Performance Engineering," Technical Report CMU/SEI-95-TR-020, Software Engineering Institute, February 1996.

[12] D. Levine, P. Ramsey, and R. Smidt, *Applied Statistics for Engineers and Scientists: Using Microsoft Excel & MINITAB*, Prentice Hall, Upper Saddle River, New Jersey, 2001.

[13] D. A. Menascé, V. A. F. Almeida, R. Riedi, F. Pelegrinelli, R. Fonseca, and W. Meira Jr., "In search of invariants for E-business workloads," *Proc. 2000 ACM Conf. in E-commerce*, Minneapolis, Minnesota, October 17-20, 2000.

[14] D. A. Menascé and V. A. F. Almeida, *Capacity Planning for Web Services: Metrics, Models, and Methods*, Prentice Hall, Upper Saddle River, New Jersey, 2002.

[15] D. A. Menascé, B. Abrahão, D. Barbará, V. A. F. Almeida, and F. Ribeiro, "Characterizing E-Business Workloads Using Fractal Methods," *J. Web Engineering*, Rinton Press, vol. 1, no. 1, 2002, pp. 74–90.

[16] D. A. Menascé, V. A. F. Almeida, and L. W. Dowdy, *Capacity Planning and Performance Modeling: From Mainframes to Client-Server Systems*, Prentice Hall, Upper Saddle River, New Jersey, 1994.

[17] R. B. Miller, "Response time in man-computer conversational transactions," *Proc. AFIPS Fall Joint Comp. Conf.*, 33:267–277, December 1968.

[18] J. Nielsen, *Usability Engineering*, Morgan Kaufmann, San Francisco, California, 1994.

[19] D. Patterson, "A simple way to estimate the cost of downtime," *Proc. 16th Systems Administration Conference (LISA '02)*, USENIX, 2002.

[20] E. Schaider. "TCO in the Trenches," *Software Magazine*, December 1999.

[21] B. Schneiderman, "Response time and display rate in human performance with computers," *Computing Surveys*, ACM, vol. 16, no. 3, September 1984.

[22] E. Shriver, *Performance Modeling for Realistic Storage Devices*, Ph.D. dissertation, Computer Science Dept., New York Univ., May 1997.

[23] P. Singleton, "Performance modeling - what, why, when and how," *BT Technology Journal*, vol. 20, no. 3, July 2002.

[24] C. U. Smith, *Performance Engineering of Software Systems*, Addison-Wesley Publishing Company, Inc., 1990.

[25] C. U. Smith and L. G. Williams, *Performance Solutions: a Practical Guide to Creating Responsive, Scalable Software*, Addison-Wesley Publishing Company, Inc., 2002.

Chapter 5

Case Study I:
A Database
Service

5.1   Introduction

The remaining chapters of Part I present several case studies aimed at demonstrating important techniques used in performance analysis and capacity planning. Each case study has specific learning objectives. For example, in this chapter, a database service example is used to describe how service demands are obtained from different types of measurements and how a model is constructed and used to answer several "what-if" questions. (What if an extra disk is purchased? How much it improves user response time? Would adding a second processor be more cost effective?) The data, computations, and graphs presented in this chapter are easily generated from the provided MS Excel workbooks: DBServiceExample.xls, OpenQN-Chap5.xls, and k-means.xls.

5.2   Database Service Example

Consider a database service facility supported by a single CPU and two disks. Two measurement tools, a DBMS Performance Monitor and a OS

Performance Monitor provide the necessary workload characterization parameters. The DBMS Performance Monitor generates a log of the resource activity for every transaction as indicated in Table 5.1.

The CPU times measured by the DBMS Performance Monitor only account for time spent by transactions in user mode. The time spent by transactions executing in kernel mode (i.e., executing operating system code) is not accounted for by this monitor. The disk I/O count reflect the number of disk I/Os (i.e., hits, visits) that each transaction makes.

While the DBMS Performance Monitor provides measurement data at the user transaction level, the OS Performance Monitor provides measurement data at the system device level. Specifically, the OS Performance Monitor records the utilization of the CPU and of each disk as indicated in Table 5.2.

5.2.1 Preliminary Analysis of the Workload

The data provided in the DBMSLog worksheet of the DBServiceExample.xls MS Excel workbook contains an excerpt of the DBMS log for 200 transactions executed during a period of 150 seconds. Thus, the throughput of the database service facility during this interval is $X_0 = 200/150 = 1.33$ transactions per second (tps).

A preliminary analysis of the log data collected by the DBMS Performance Monitor is depicted in Fig. 5.1, which shows statistics of the CPU

Table 5.1. DBMS Performance Monitor Measurements

Transaction Id	CPU Time (msec)	Disk 1 I/O Count	Disk 2 I/O Count
.	.	.	.
.	.	.	.
005	25.4	12	21
006	32.8	18	15
007	107.6	36	10
.	.	.	.
.	.	.	.

Table 5.2. OS Performance Monitor Measurements

Resource	Utilization (%)
CPU	45
Disk 1	75
Disk 2	65

and disk usage by the transactions. The first section of the table in Fig. 5.1 shows basic statistics such as mean, standard deviation, sample variance, and coefficient of variation. The first three statistics are computed using Excel's Data Analysis tool. The coefficient of variation, CV, is defined as

$$CV = \frac{\text{standard deviation}}{\text{mean}}. \tag{5.2.1}$$

The CV is an important statistic and provides additional information of the variability within the data. The standard deviation provides an absolute measure of the variability, whereas the CV provides a relative measure of

	CPU Time (msec)	No. I/Os Disk 1	No. I/Os Disk 2
Mean	238.2	51.38	44.85
Standard Deviation	165.9	27.0	26.4
Sample Variance	27510.4	728.7	698.1
Coeff. of Variation	0.696	0.525	0.677
Minimum	23.6	5	7
First Quartile (Q1)	104.4	33	26
Median (Q2)	151.6	63	39
Third Quartile (Q3)	418.1	72	68
Maximum	507.5	85	92
Range	483.9	80	85
Largest	507.5	85	92
Smallest	23.60	5	7
Sum	47640.8	10275	8969

Figure 5.1. Basic statistics for the database service workload.

variability. As a small example, the data set {1, 4, 5} and the data set {1001, 1004, 1005} have the same standard deviation, but very different CVs. A higher coefficient of variation indicates that more variability exists in the data set. In the example of Fig. 5.1, the standard deviation of the CPU time is almost 70% of the mean (i.e., CV = 0.696). The CV is also a good "rule-of-tumb" indicator of the underlying distribution of the measurements within the data set. Without providing details here, data coming from an exponential distribution has a CV = 1. Hyperexponential distributions have a CV > 1 and hypoexponential distributions have a CV < 1.

The middle section of the table of Fig. 5.1 shows the minimum and maximum values, as well as quartile information of the data sets. The first quartile (Q1), is the 25th percentile (i.e., a value such that 25% of the data lies below that value). The second quartile (Q2), also called the *median*, is the 50th percentile. The third quartile (Q3) is the 75th percentile. For example, 25% of the CPU times are below 104.4 msec, 50% are below 151.6 msec, and 75% are below 418.1 msec. The fourth quartile follows from the maximum value, with 100An easy way to compute the p percentile of a data set using MS Excel is through the function `PERCENTILE` (e.g., the 25th percentile of an array of values is obtained as `PERCENTILE (<array>,0.25)`).

As a better indicator than the single CV statistic, minimum and maximum values along with the quartiles provide a good indication of the distribution of the data. A graphical depiction of this is given by the Box and Whisker plot [5]. This type of plot, illustrated in Fig. 5.2, shows the minimum and maximum values of a data set, as well as the three quartiles. Quartiles Q1 through Q3 are delimited by a box. A line corresponding to Q2 divides the box into two parts. Fifty percent of the data lies within the box. For instance, in the case of the total number of I/Os on disk 1, 50% of the transactions made between 33 and 72 I/Os on this disk. Of these transactions, half performed between 33 and 63 I/Os and the other half made between 63 and 72 I/Os on disk 1.

5.2.2 Workload Clustering

Another visualization of the data is depicted in Fig. 5.3 as an X-Y scatter plot showing the total number of I/Os by a transaction (i.e., at both disks) versus its CPU time. Thus, each transaction is represented by a dot in the

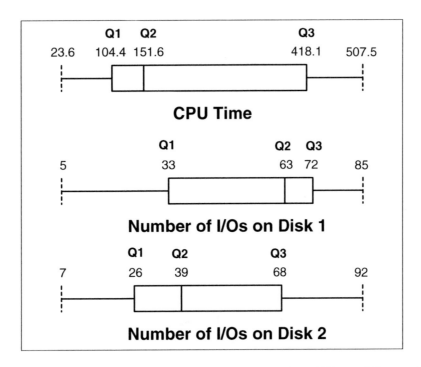

Figure 5.2. Box-and-Whisker plots for CPU time and number of I/Os on disks 1 and 2.

plot. The picture shows three clear "clouds" (i.e., clusters) of transactions, indicating that the transactions can be clustered in three groups labeled as low CPU/low disk (cluster 1), high CPU/high disk (cluster 2), and medium CPU/high disk (cluster 3). This example, though realistic and representative, is somewhat artificial. In many actual environments, data does not fall into such obvious clusters. Often, outlier points (i.e., transactions) are observed. Whether to ignore these points as renegades or to include them as special small clusters is a design decision. Determining the best number and the best clusters to most accurately represent the workload is far from a trivial task.

The means of the workload clusters are shown in Table 5.3, using the k-means clustering algorithm described in Chapter 4, and implemented in the k-means.xls MS Excel workbook.

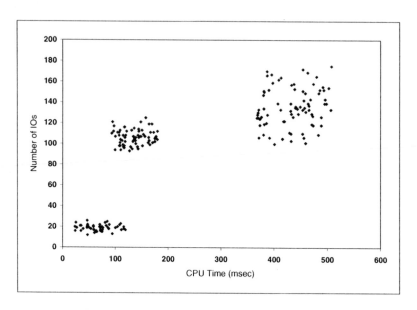

Figure 5.3. Total number of I/Os vs. CPU time (msec).

5.3   Building a Performance Model

A performance model for the database server is illustrated in Fig. 5.4. This is a multi-class open queuing network model. Three workload classes are modeled. Each class corresponds to one of the clusters indicated in Table 5.3. In order to obtain quantitative indicators for performance analysis and capacity planning, model parameters are required. As discussed in Chapter 2, these parameters include the workload intensity as well as service demands.

Table 5.3. Workload Clusters

Cluster Number	CPU Time (msec)	Number of I/Os		Number of Points
		Disk 1	Disk 2	
1	67.5	8.0	11.0	50
2	434.2	62.4	73.1	80
3	136.1	69.8	36.7	70

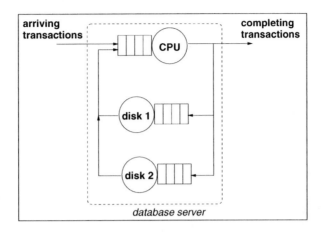

Figure 5.4. Queuing network model for the database server.

As indicated in Chapter 3, service demands can be obtained from the Service Demand Law as $D_{i,r} = U_{i,r}/X_{0,r}$. This equation requires the utilization, $U_{i,r}$, of each resource i by each class r. However, the measurements available from the OS Performance Monitor only provide total resource utilization, as indicated in Table 5.2. Therefore, a technique to obtain the per-class utilizations from the total utilization is needed. This is illustrated in the next subsection.

5.3.1   Apportioning Total Utilization to Individual Classes

The general method of apportioning the total utilization U_i of a resource i to a specific class r is represented by the relationship

$$U_{i,r} = U_i \times f_{i,r} \qquad (5.3.2)$$

where $f_{i,r}$ is a factor (i.e., a fraction) that depends on the type of device being apportioned.

Consider the CPU first. The total time required at the CPU by all classes (i.e., 47640.8 msec as indicated in Fig. 5.1) includes user time but does not include kernel time spent by transactions while executing OS code. In fact, if the CPU utilization is computed as the ratio of user mode CPU time to the length of the measurement interval (i.e., 150 sec or 150,000 msec), the CPU utilization would be 0.32. This value is smaller than the 0.45 value for the CPU utilization reported by the OS Performance Monitor (see Table 5.2). However, the percentage of kernel time attributed to each class is assumed to be in the same ratio as the user time attributed to each class. The apportionment factor for the CPU, $f_{CPU,r}$ is derived as follows.

$$f_{CPU,r} = \frac{\text{Total CPU time for class r}}{\text{Total CPU time for all classes}} \qquad (5.3.3)$$

Equation (5.3.3) makes the implicit assumption that a transaction's CPU time in kernel mode is proportional to the CPU time in user mode. The total CPU time for a given class is obtained from Table 5.3 by multiplying the average CPU time for the cluster (i.e., class) by the number of points in the cluster. The total CPU time for all classes comes directly from the statistics gathered from the DBMS Performance Monitor (see Fig. 5.2). Thus,

$$f_{CPU,1} = \frac{67.5 \times 50}{47640.8} = 0.071,$$

$$f_{CPU,2} = \frac{434.2 \times 80}{47640.8} = 0.729, \text{ and}$$

$$f_{CPU,3} = \frac{136.1 \times 70}{47640.8} = 0.200. \qquad (5.3.4)$$

(Note: These factors represent the percentage of the CPU's load attributed to each workload class. These factors sum to 1.0). The per-class CPU utilizations are computed using the apportionment factors and the total CPU utilization (i.e., 0.45 from Table 5.2) by using Eq. (5.3.2). Thus,

$$U_{CPU,1} = U_{CPU} \times f_{CPU,1} = 0.45 \times 0.071 = 0.032,$$

$$U_{CPU,2} = U_{CPU} \times f_{CPU,2} = 0.45 \times 0.729 = 0.328, \text{ and}$$

$$U_{CPU,3} = U_{CPU} \times f_{CPU,3} = 0.45 \times 0.200 = 0.090. \qquad (5.3.5)$$

Consider now the disks and the issue of apportioning total disk utilization values to the different classes. The same approach used for the CPU is used in this case. The difference lies in the way the apportionment factor of Eq. (5.3.2) is computed. Instead of using the percentage of time at the device, which is available at the CPU but not at the disks, the percentage of I/O counts is used as follows.

$$f_{\text{disk } i,r} = \frac{\text{Total no. I/Os on disk i by class r}}{\text{Total no. I/Os on disk i for all classes}} \qquad (5.3.6)$$

The total number of I/Os on disk 1 is 10,275 as indicated in Fig. 5.1. Using the clustering data in Table 5.3 to determine the number of I/Os per class, the appropriate apportionment factors for disk 1 are:

$$f_{\text{disk } 1,1} = \frac{8.0 \times 50}{10275} = 0.039,$$

$$f_{\text{disk } 1,2} = \frac{62.4 \times 80}{10275} = 0.486, \text{ and}$$

$$f_{\text{disk } 1,3} = \frac{69.8 \times 70}{10275} = 0.475. \tag{5.3.7}$$

Similarly for disk 2, the total number of I/Os on disk 2 (from Fig. 5.1) is 8,969. Thus, the apportionment factors for disk 2 are

$$f_{\text{disk } 2,1} = \frac{11.0 \times 50}{8969} = 0.061,$$

$$f_{\text{disk } 2,2} = \frac{73.1 \times 80}{8969} = 0.652, \text{ and}$$

$$f_{\text{disk } 2,3} = \frac{36.7 \times 70}{8969} = 0.287. \tag{5.3.8}$$

Using these factors and the disk utilizations found in Table 5.2, Eq. (5.3.2) provides the needed disk utilizations per class. The results are summarized in Table 5.4. This provides a per device, per class utilization breakdown of the OS Performance Monitor data found in Table 5.2.

5.3.2   Computing Service Demands

The model requires the per device, per class service demands, $D_{i,r}$. The Service Demand Law (see Chapter 3) states that $D_i = U_i/X_0$. Applied to the current multi-class example, $D_{i,r} = U_{i,r}/X_{0,r}$. The utilizations, $U_{i,r}$, are

Table 5.4. Utilization Values for All Classes

	Class 1	Class 2	Class 3	Total
CPU	0.032	0.328	0.090	0.45
Disk 1	0.029	0.365	0.356	0.75
Disk 2	0.040	0.423	0.187	0.65

available from Table 5.4. The throughput for each class, $X_{0,r}$, is obtained by dividing the number of transactions processed for each class by the duration of the measurement interval. The number of transactions processed per class is given in the last column of Table 5.3. Thus, recalling the measurement interval of 150 seconds,

$$X_{0,1} = 50/150 = 0.33 \text{ tps},$$
$$X_{0,2} = 80/150 = 0.53 \text{ tps, and}$$
$$X_{0,3} = 70/150 = 0.47 \text{ tps.} \tag{5.3.9}$$

Using the multi-class device utilizations from Table 5.4 and the multi-class throughputs from Eq. (5.3.9), the multi-class service demands at each device are easily computed from the Service Demand Law, $D_{i,r} = U_{i,r}/X_{0,r}$. The results are shown in Table 5.5.

5.4   Using the Model

The queuing network model of Fig. 5.4 is now completely parameterized using the service demands of Table 5.5 and the class arrival rates from Eq. (5.3.9). [Note: The transaction arrival rates must equal the transaction completion rates (i.e., $X_{0,1}$, $X_{0,2}$, and $X_{0,3}$) since this is a lossless system and the flow into the database server must equal the flow out of the database server.] The parameterized model is solved using `OpenQN-Chap5.xls`. The residence times for all classes and queues as well as the response time per class are shown in Table 5.6.

As indicated in Table 5.6, response times for classes 2 and 3 are relatively high. Moreover, disk 1 is the resource where all classes spend most of their time. This is not surprising since disk 1 has the highest overall utilization (see

Table 5.5. Service Demand Values for All Classes (in sec)

	Class 1	Class 2	Class 3
CPU	0.096	0.615	0.193
Disk 1	0.088	0.683	0.763
Disk 2	0.119	0.795	0.400

Table 5.6. Residence Times and Response Times for All Classes (in sec)

	Class 1	Class 2	Class 3
CPU	0.174	1.118	0.351
Disk 1	0.351	2.734	3.054
Disk 2	0.340	2.270	1.142
Response Time	0.865	6.122	4.546

Table 5.2). Thus disk 1 is the system bottleneck. From looking at Table 5.6, transactions from classes 1, 2, and 3 spend over 40%, 44%, and 67% of their time using or waiting to use disk 1, respectively. Note also that the ratios of the residence times at disk 1 to the corresponding service demand are quite high. These ratios are 4.0 ($\frac{0.351}{0.088}, \frac{2.734}{0.683}, \frac{3.054}{0.763}$) for each class on disk 1. In other words, the time a transaction spends on disk 1 is four times its total service time on that disk. Stated equivalently, a transaction's total waiting time at disk 1 is three times its total service time. In comparison, the corresponding waiting times at the CPU and disk 2 are only 0.8 and 1.9 times the class service times, respectively. Therefore, to improve performance (i.e., to reduce response times), the most effective strategy is to reduce the time spent on I/O and particularly at disk 1.

This baseline model can be used to evaluate relevant "what-if" scenarios. It has already been noted that performance would improve by upgrading the disk subsystem. Also, as the predicted workload intensity changes over time, an understanding of the predicted resulting performance is also important. For example, suppose that the workload intensity is predicted to change over the next ten months as indicated in Table 5.7. (Note that January's workload (i.e., $X_0 = 1.33$ tps) is the baseline workload intensity assumed up to this point.)

5.4.1 Adding a Third Disk

To cope with the increasing expected workload (i.e., Table 5.7) and to address the bottleneck, a new disk equivalent to the two existing disks is proposed to be added to the database server. The performance analyst also de-

Table 5.7. Workload Intensity Prediction

Month	Arrival Rate (tps)
January	1.33
February	1.45
March	1.68
April	2.26
May	2.68
June	3.25
July	3.98
August	4.78
September	5.74
October	6.76

cides that the I/O activity should be balanced on the three disks to further improve I/O performance. Balancing the load is achieved by distributing the file requests across the three disks so that the service demand of any class is the same at all three disks. Thus, the new values of the service demands for disks 1 through 3 are computed as

$$D_{\text{disk } i,r}^{\text{new}} = \frac{D_{\text{disk } 1,r}^{\text{old}} + D_{\text{disk } 2,r}^{\text{old}}}{3} \quad \text{for } i = 1, 2, 3. \tag{5.4.10}$$

These new values of the service demands are shown in Table 5.8.

The new response time values for the three classes are obtained with the help of `OpenQN-Chap5.xls` (Note: Remember to reinitialize the model to

Table 5.8. Service Demand Values With a Third Disk Added (in sec)

	Class 1	Class 2	Class 3
CPU	0.096	0.615	0.193
Disk 1	0.069	0.493	0.388
Disk 2	0.069	0.493	0.388
Disk 3	0.069	0.493	0.388

indicate that there are now four queues). The results are shown in the top part of Table 5.9 for the first five months (January-May) of the predicted new workload intensity levels. By looking at the first line in Table 5.9 (i.e., the January intensity of 1.33 tps) and comparing the class response times against the baseline metrics in Table 5.6, the effects of simply adding the third disk and balancing the I/O load across the disks results in over a 35% performance improvement (i.e., response time reduction). However, by May (i.e., workload intensity of 2.68 tps) the predicted performance is unacceptably poor, with class 2 anticipated response time exceeding 30 seconds.

By looking at the `ResidenceTimes` worksheet of `OpenQN-Chap5.xls`, it is seen that with the third disk, the CPU is the resource where class 1 and class 2 transactions spend most of their time. That is, for these classes, the disks are no longer the bottleneck, but rather it is the CPU that is the most limiting the performance. To maintain an acceptable response time from, say April (i.e., 2.26 tps) on, it is necessary to reduce contention on the CPU. One alternative is to replace the current CPU with a faster processor. Another alternative is to upgrade the system to a multiprocessor by adding a second CPU. This second scenario is considered in the next subsection.

5.4.2   Using a Dual CPU System

In order to maintain an acceptable QoS level past April, in addition to the extra disk and a balanced I/O load, an additional CPU is proposed in a dual CPU configuration. In order to analyze the effects of this change using `OpenQN-Chap5.xls`, the CPU queue is specified as `MP2` (i.e., a multiprocessor with two CPUs). The results are shown in the middle of Table 5.9 for the April and May workloads (i.e., 2.26 tps and 2.68 tps). The largest reduction in response time, as expected, is for classes 1 and 2, the ones that spend more time at the CPU. However, the improvements are relatively minor and the response times are still very high for classes 2 and 3 for an arrival rate of 2.68 tps (i.e., May's workload). An analysis of the residence time breakdown indicates that with the dual CPU, all three classes spend most of their time at the disks. That is, adding the second CPU shifted the system bottleneck back to the disks. The next step is to improve disk access performance further.

Table 5.9. Response Times (in sec) for Various Scenarios

Arrival Rate (tps)	Response Time (sec)		
	Class 1	Class 2	Class 3
Scenario: third disk added.			
1.33	0.56	3.89	2.53
1.45	0.61	4.21	2.75
1.68	0.73	5.02	3.28
2.26	1.39	9.65	6.37
2.68	4.34	30.28	20.78
Scenario: 3 disks and a dual CPU.			
2.26	1.11	7.86	5.81
2.68	3.47	24.71	19.03
Scenario: 3 disks 3× faster and a dual CPU.			
2.68	0.24	1.59	0.84
3.25	0.27	1.78	0.93
3.98	0.32	2.16	1.11
4.78	0.45	3.01	1.47
5.74	1.78	11.60	4.34
Scenario: 3 disks 3× faster and a quad CPU.			
5.74	0.33	2.25	1.41
6.76	0.45	3.15	2.09

5.4.3   Using Faster Disks

A more dramatic upgrade is considered here to hopefully cope with the increasing workload intensities. Each disk is replaced by one that is three times faster. This is reflected in the model parameters by simply dividing the service demands on all disks by a factor of three. Solving the model with these new disk speeds yields the results shown in the middle lower half of Table 5.9.

The results indicate that acceptable response times are obtained for an arrival rate up to 4.78 tps (i.e., through August). However, for 5.74 tps (i.e., September's workload), the response time for class 2 exceeds 10 seconds. A look at the residence times for class 2 reveals that 87% of its response time is being spent at the CPU. This indicates the need to further enhance the CPU.

5.4.4   Moving to a 4-CPU System

In order to reduce the response time of class 2 transactions at high arrival rates, the dual CPU is replaced by a quad CPU. This change is reflected in the model by specifying the type of the CPU as MP4. The results are shown in the lower portion of Table 5.9. With this final upgrade, the model indicates that the response times are at acceptable service levels for all classes throughout the ten months period of concern. Figure 5.5 illustrates how the response time varies for class 2 transactions (i.e., those transactions that have the highest CPU and I/O demands resulting in the highest response times) for each of the scenarios. If a 10-second service level is deemed "acceptable" then an appropriate capacity planning strategy becomes apparent: 1) in January purchase an additional disk and load balance the load across the three disks by moving files, 2) in May exchange the disks for ones that are three times faster and purchase an additional CPU, 3) in September, purchase two additional CPUs. Though the parameters and time frames may change, this case study illustrates the usefulness of a quantitative analysis using queuing network modeling approach.

The remaining sections of this chapter discuss the important issue of monitoring. Monitoring tools are used to obtain input parameters for performance models from measurement data. They are also used to validate performance predictions made by the models.

5.5   Monitoring Tools

Monitors are used for measuring the level of activity (i.e., workload intensities, device utilizations) of a computer system [2]. Ideally, monitors should affect as little as possible the operation of the system being measured in order to minimally degrade its performance. Monitors are characterized by their *type* and *mode*. There are three types of monitors depending upon their implementation: hardware, software, and hybrid. There are two different data colletion modes: event trace and sampling.

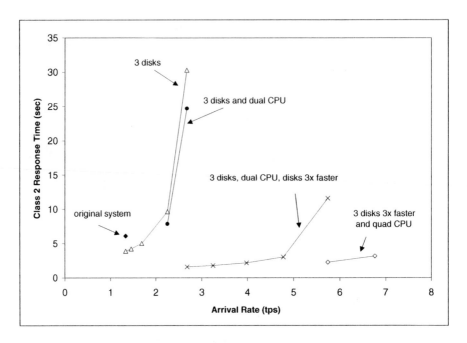

Figure 5.5. Class 2 response times for various scenarios.

5.5.1 Hardware Monitors

A *hardware monitor* is a specialized measurement tool that detects certain events (e.g., the setting of a register) within a computer system by sensing predefined signals (e.g., a high voltage at the register's control point). A hardware monitor captures the state of the computer system under study via electronic probes that are attached to its circuitry and records the measurements. The electronic probes sense the state of hardware components of the systems, such as registers, memory locations, and I/O channels. For example, a hardware monitor may detect a memory-read operation by sensing that the read probe to the memory module changes from the inactive to the active state [3, 4, 6].

The main advantages of hardware monitors are that they do not consume resources from the monitored system, they do not affect the operation or performance of the system, and they do not place any overhead on the system. One of the major problems of hardware monitors is that software features (e.g., the completion of a specific job) are difficult to detect, since these monitors do not have access to software-related information such as the identification of the process that triggered a given event. Thus, workload-specific data and the number of transactions executed by a given class are difficult to obtain using a hardware monitor.

5.5.2 Software Monitors

A *software monitor* consists of routines inserted into the software, either at the user level or (more often) at the kernel level, of a computer system with the aim of recording status information and events of the system [1, 4]. These routines gather performance data about the execution of programs and/or about the components of the hardware. Software monitoring is activated either by the occurrence of specific events (e.g., an interrupt signaling an I/O completion) or by timer interrupts (e.g., to see if a particular disk is active or not every 5 msec), depending on the monitoring mode.

Software monitors can basically record any information that is available to programs and operating systems. This feature, together with the flexibility to select and reduce performance data, makes software monitors a powerful tool for analyzing computer systems. The IBM Resource Management Facility (RMF) and Windows XP's Performance Monitor are examples of software monitors that provide performance information such as throughput, device utilizations, I/O counts, and network activity. A drawback of software monitors is that they use the the very resources that they measure. Therefore, software monitors may (and sometimes significantly) interfere with the system being measured. Depending on the level of overhead introduced, software monitors may yield results of minimal value.

Two special classes of software monitors are accounting systems and program analyzers. Each provides useful information that helps to parameterize QN models.

Accounting Systems. Accounting systems are tools primarily intended to apportion financial charges to users of a system [7, 8]. They are usually an integral part of most multiuser operating systems. The IBM/SMF (System Management Facility) is a standard feature of IBM's MVS operating system, which collects and records data related to job executions. UNIX's `sar` (System Activity Report) is another example of an accounting system.

Although their main purpose is billing, accounting tools can be used as a source for necessary model parameters in capacity planning studies. In general, accounting data include three groups of information.

- *Identification.* Specifies user, program, project, accounting number, and class of the monitored event.

- *Resource usage.* Indicates the resources (e.g., CPU times, I/O operations) consumed by programs.

- *Execution time.* Records the start and completion times of program execution.

Although accounting monitors provide useful data, there are often problems with their use in performance modeling. Accounting monitors typically do not capture the use of resources by operating systems. That is, they do not measure any unaccountable (i.e., non-user billable) system overhead. Another problem is the unique way that accounting systems view some special programs, such as database management systems (DBMS) and transaction monitors. These programs have transactions and processes that execute within them. Since accounting systems treat such special programs as single entities, they normally do not collect any information about what is executed inside these programs. However, in order to model transaction response time, information about individual transactions, such as arrival rates and service demands, are required. Thus, special monitors are required to examine the performance of some programs.

Program Analyzers. Program Analyzers are software tools that collect information about the execution of individual programs. These analyzers can be used to identify the parts of a program that consume significant computing resources [8]. They are capable of observing and recording events internal to the execution of specific programs. In the case of transaction oriented systems, program analyzers provide information such as transaction counts, average transaction response time, mean CPU time per transaction, mean number of I/O operations per transaction, and transaction mix. Examples of program analyzers include monitors for special programs such as

IBM's database products (i.e., DB2 and IMS) and transaction processing products (i.e., CICS).

5.5.3 Hybrid Monitors

The combination of hardware and software monitors results in a hybrid monitor, which shares the best features of both types. In a hybrid monitor, software routines are responsible for sensing events and storing this information in special "monitoring registers." The hardware component of the monitor records the data stored in these registers, avoiding interference in the normal I/O activities of the system. Thus, the advantage of capturing specific job related events (i.e., the primary benefit of software monitors), without placing significant overhead or altering the performance of the system (i.e., primary benefits of hardware monitors), is possible using hybrid monitors. The primary disadvantages associated with hybrid monitors are the requirements of special hardware (e.g., monitoring registers) and more specialized software routines (i.e., to record a more limited set of program events). Unless hybrid monitors are designed as an integral part of the system architecture, their practical use is limited.

5.5.4 Event-trace Monitoring

Any system interrupt, such as an I/O interrupt indicating the completion of a disk read/write operation, can be viewed as an *event* that changes the state of a computer system. At the operating system level, the state of the system is usually defined as the number of processes that are "at" each system device, either in the device's ready queue, blocked in the device's waiting queue, or executing in the device. Examples of events at this level are OS system calls that changes a process' status (e.g., an I/O request that moves a process from executing in the CPU to the waiting queue at a disk). At a higher level, where the number of transactions in memory represents the state of the system, the completion of a transaction (e.g., an interrupts to swap out a job) is an event. An *event trace monitor* collects information and chronicles the occurrence of specific events.

Usually, an event trace software monitor consists of special pieces of code inserted at specific points in the operating system, typically within interrupt service routines. Upon detection of an event, the special code generates a record containing information such as the date, time, and type of event. In addition, the record contains any relevant event-specific data. For instance, a record corresponding to the completion of a process might contain the CPU time used by the process, the number of page faults initiated, the number of I/O operations executed, and the amount of memory required. In general, event traces record changes in the active set of PCBs (process control blocks). These "change events" are later transferred to secondary storage.

When the event rate becomes very high, the monitor routines are executed frequently. This may introduce significant overhead in the measurement process. Depending on the events selected and the event rate, the overhead may reach levels as high as 30% or more. Overheads up to 5% are regarded as acceptable for measurement activities [8]. Since the event rate cannot be controlled or predicted by the monitor, the measurement overhead, likewise, becomes unpredictable. This is one of the major shortcomings of event trace monitors.

5.5.5   Sampling Monitoring

A *sampling monitor* collects information about a system (i.e., recorded state information) at specified time instants. Instead of being triggered by the occurrence of an internal event such as an I/O interrupt, the data collection routines of a sampling software monitor are triggered by an external timer event. Such events are activated at predetermined times, which are specified prior to the monitoring session. The sampling is driven by timer interrupts, based on a hardware clock.

The overhead introduced by a sampling monitor depends on two factors: the number of variables measured and the frequency of the sampling interval. With the ability to limit both factors, a sampling monitor is able to strictly control its overhead. However, long intervals result in low overhead. On the other hand, if the intervals are too long, the number of samples decreases and the confidence in the data collected, likewise, decreases. Thus, there exists a clear trade-off between overhead and quality of the measurements. Similarly, the higher the sampling rate, the higher the accuracy, and the higher the overhead. When compared to event trace monitoring, sampling provides a less detailed observation of a computer system but at a controllable overhead level. Errors may also be introduced because a certain percentage of potentially important interrupts are masked. For example, if some routines within the operating system cannot be interrupted by the timer, their contribution to the CPU utilization will not be accounted for by a sampling monitor [3].

Sampling monitors typically provide information that can be classified as system-level statistics: for example, the number of processes in execution and resource use, such as CPU and disk utilization. Process level statistics are better captured by event trace monitors, because it is easier to associate events to the start and completion of processes.

5.6   Measurements Techniques

As illustrated in Fig. 5.6, a measurement process involves three major steps: measurement specification, system instrumentation, and data analysis.

1. *Specify measurements.* In this step, the performance variables to be measured are selected. For example, suppose that the behavior of a specific virtual memory policy is of interest. In this case, performance variables such as the page fault rate, the throughput of paging disks,

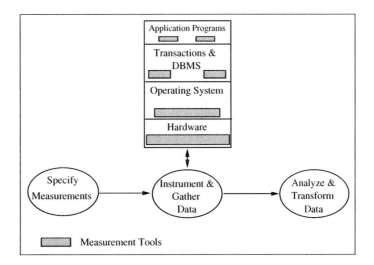

Figure 5.6. A representation of the measurement process.

and the average number of jobs competing for memory space, are required by the system model.

2. *Instrument and gather data.* After selecting the variables to be observed, the system is instrumented to gather the specified measurement data. This involves configuring the tools to measure the specified variables during the observation period and recording the required information. A computer system can be viewed as a series of layers that create an environment for the execution of application programs, as shown in Fig. 5.6. Depending upon the variables selected, several measurement tools may be required at various layers. For instance, if transaction service demands are required, measurement tools are needed at both the operating system level and at the transaction/DBMS level.

3. *Analyze and transform data.* Measurement tools gather potentially huge amounts of raw data, corresponding to a detailed observation log of system activities. Usually, raw data specify time intervals, event counts, transaction IDs, bytes transferred, and resources consumed. To be useful, these data items have to be mapped to their corresponding logical functions. That is, these bulky data items must be analyzed and transformed into meaningful information. For instance, information recorded by software measurement tools might include a record for each process that starts or completes during the observation period. These records must be manipulated to yield useful results, such as average execution time, number of processes executed, and device utilizations.

5.7   Obtaining Input Parameters

The representativeness and accuracy of a performance model depends directly on the quality of its input parameters. Two practical questions naturally arise when seeking to obtain the parameters needed for the system model:

- What are the information sources for obtaining the input parameters?

- What techniques are used to obtain the input parameters?

The most reliable and primary source of information is the performance measurements collected from direct observation of the system. Further information can be obtained from secondary sources such as product specifications provided by manufacturers. However, typical measurement data do not coincide directly with the input parameters required by performance models. For modeling purposes, typical measurement data need to be analyzed and transformed to become useful.

Typical input parameters required by performance models are service demands, arrival rates, think times, levels of multiprogramming, and the number of active terminals. Therefore, the basic question addressed in the remaining sections of this chapter is: How is typical measurement data obtained by performance monitors transformed into the input parameters required for performance models?

5.7.1 Measuring CPU Utilization

The services provided by the various software layers of a computer system may be abstracted and represented by the service demand parameters in an associated system model. Figure 5.7 exhibits various execution environments for application programs, ranging from the least complex environment, the bare machine, to sophisticated environments with multiple operating systems. From the definition of service demand, $D_i = U_i/X_0$. The system throughput, X_0, is the number of transactions processed by the system within the measurement interval and is a relatively easy parameter to obtain. However, the utilization of a device, U_i, is subject to different interpretations, according to the specific environment. The meaning of U_i is key to understanding the concept of service demand in different execution environments. Let U_i^t denote the total utilization of device i measured by a system monitor and $U_{i,r}$ represent the utilization of device i by class r.

Bare machine. The most basic environment in which to execute an application program is for the application program to run directly on top of the hardware resources. In this case, the program has complete control over the machine with no intervening operating system service, as shown in Fig. 5.7 (a). Consider the CPU. The total utilization U_{cpu}^t represents the fraction of time the CPU is busy doing only one type of activity: executing

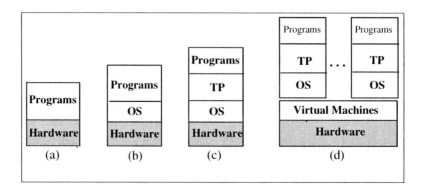

Figure 5.7. Execution environments for application programs.

program instructions. In this case,

$$U_{\text{cpu}}^t = U_{\text{cpu,prog}} \qquad (5.7.11)$$

where $U_{\text{cpu,prog}}$ refers to the fraction of actual CPU time consumed by application programs. In a bare machine, it is reasonable to assume that only one program is executing at a time. In other words, a single program of class r monopolizes the CPU, which means that

$$U_{\text{cpu},r} = U_{\text{cpu}}^t \qquad (5.7.12)$$

From the definition of service demand and from Eqs. (5.7.11) and (5.7.12), the CPU demand of the single class r program is given by

$$D_{\text{cpu},r} = \frac{U_{\text{cpu,prog}}}{X_{0,r}} \qquad (5.7.13)$$

In the case of a bare machine, Eq. (5.7.13) indicates that the CPU demand includes only the actual time a program spends executing at the CPU.

Example 5.1

Consider an early computer system with no operating system. The system executes one job at a time. During an observation period of 1,800 sec, a hardware monitor measures a utilization of 40% for the CPU and 100 batch job completions are recorded. Using Eq. (5.7.13), the average CPU demand for these jobs is computed as $0.4/(100/1800) = 7.2$ seconds per job. ∎

Operating system. Now consider an operating system that executes on top of the hardware resources and provides services (e.g., scheduling, I/O handling) to higher level applications. Application programs run on top of the operating system as illustrated in Fig. 5.7 (b). The total CPU utilization in this environment is composed of two parts:

$$U_{\text{cpu}}^t = U_{\text{cpu,os}} + U_{\text{cpu,prog}}, \qquad (5.7.14)$$

where $U_{\text{cpu,os}}$ corresponds to system overhead, (e.g., handling I/O operations, paging, and swapping).

Consider a system with R workload classes. The device utilization due to each class of the workload is a fraction of the total device utilization. Thus,

$$U_{\text{cpu},r} = U_{\text{cpu}}^t \times f_{\text{cpu},r}, \qquad (5.7.15)$$

where $f_{\text{cpu},r}$ is the relative fraction of the total utilization by class r. In the case of a single-class model $(R = 1)$, $f_{\text{cpu},1} = 1$. Various ways of calculating $f_{\text{cpu},r}$ are discussed later in this chapter. From Eqs. (5.7.14) and (5.7.15) it follows that the CPU demand is given by

$$D_{\text{cpu},r} = \frac{(U_{\text{cpu,os}} + U_{\text{cpu,prog}}) \times f_{\text{cpu},r}}{X_{0,r}}. \qquad (5.7.16)$$

Eq. (5.7.16) indicates that the effects of the OS on the performance is incorporated into the model implicitly through the way the service demand is calculated. For instance, the larger the overhead represented by $U_{\text{cpu,os}}$, the larger the CPU demand.

Example 5.2

Consider a computer system running batch programs and interactive commands. Suppose the system is monitored for 1,800 sec and a software monitor indicates a total CPU utilization of 60%. For the same period of time, the accounting log of the operating system records the CPU time for batch jobs and interactive commands separately. From the accounting data, the analyst obtains the CPU utilization by class: *batch* = 40% and *interactive* = 12%. The number of interactive commands is also observed to be 1,200. Note that since the accounting data do not capture the OS usage of the CPU, the two utilizations, 40% and 12%, do not add up to the total CPU utilization, 60%. The 8% difference is due to the OS. Using these measurement data, the CPU demand for the *interactive* class is given by

$$D_{cpu,interactive} = \frac{U^t_{cpu} \times f_{cpu,interactive}}{X_{0,interactive}}$$
$$= \frac{0.6 \times [0.12/(0.12 + 0.40)]}{1200/1800} = 0.208 \text{ sec}$$

■

Transaction processing monitor. A transaction processing system (TP) (e.g., IBM's CICS or BEA's Tuxedo) is an on-line real-time multiuser system that receives transaction requests, processes them, and returns responses to these requests [9]. The processing of a transaction request usually involves accessing a database. A key component of a transaction system is a *TP monitor*, which has the responsibility of managing and coordinating the flow of transactions through the system. The TP monitor provides a collection of services, such as communications control, terminal management, presentation services, program management, and authorization. Thus, a TP monitor provides a transaction execution environment on top of a conventional operating system, as illustrated in Fig. 5.7 (c). The total CPU utilization is viewed as a combination of three different components:

$$U^t_{cpu} = U_{cpu,os} + U_{cpu,tp} + U_{cpu,prog} \qquad (5.7.17)$$

where $U_{cpu,tp}$ indicates the CPU utilization by the TP monitor.

Consider now a system where multiple workload classes are executing on top of the transaction monitor. A portion of the total CPU utilization is allocated to the TP monitor. Of this allocation, a certain percentage is further allocated to the individual workload classes. Thus, the CPU utilization of a class r transaction running on top of the TP monitor is

$$U_{cpu,r} = U^t_{cpu} \times f_{os,tp} \times g_{tp,r} \qquad (5.7.18)$$

where U^t_{cpu} is the total CPU utilization, $f_{os,tp}$ is the fraction of the total CPU utilization allocated to the TP monitor servicing the class r transaction, and

$g_{\text{tp},r}$ is the fraction of the TP utilization used by class r transactions. The TP's fraction $f_{\text{os,tp}}$ is given by

$$f_{\text{os,tp}} = \frac{U^{\text{os}}_{\text{cpu,tp}}}{\sum_{\forall \text{ class } s} U^{\text{os}}_{\text{cpu},s}} \tag{5.7.19}$$

where $U^{\text{os}}_{\text{cpu},s}$ denotes the CPU utilization of a workload class s that runs on top of the OS, but may or may not run on top of the TP. $U^{\text{os}}_{\text{cpu,tp}}$ is the CPU utilization of the TP monitor measured by the accounting system of the OS. The fraction of the CPU allocated to transactions of class r running on top of the TP is given by

$$g_{\text{tp},r} = \frac{T^{\text{tp}}_{\text{cpu},r}}{\sum_{\forall \text{ class } t} T^{\text{tp}}_{\text{cpu},t}} \tag{5.7.20}$$

where $T^{\text{tp}}_{\text{cpu},r}$ is the within-TP CPU time of class r transactions, measured by a performance tool of the TP monitor. In Eq. (5.7.18), note that the total CPU utilization (U^t_{cpu}) is first apportioned via $f_{\text{os,tp}}$ in Eq. (5.7.19) to the class represented by the TP monitor. Using $g_{\text{tp},r}$ in Eq. (5.7.20), this value is then apportioned to class r within the TP monitor. From the Service Demand Law and from Eqs. (5.7.17) and (5.7.18), the CPU demand of class r transactions is expressed as

$$D_{\text{cpu},r} = \frac{(U_{\text{cpu,os}} + U_{\text{cpu,tp}} + U_{\text{cpu,prog}}) \times f_{\text{os,tp}} \times g_{\text{tp},r}}{X_{0,r}} \tag{5.7.21}$$

The terms $U_{\text{cpu,os}}$ and $U_{\text{cpu,tp}}$ of Eq. (5.7.21) indicate that OS and TP overheads are included as a part of the CPU demand of class r.

Example 5.3

Consider a mainframe that processes three classes of workload: *batch* (B), *interactive* (I), and *transactions* (T). Classes B and I run directly on top of the operating system, whereas user transactions, T, execute within the TP monitor. There are two distinct classes of T transactions: *query* and *update*. The performance analyst wants to know the CPU demand of the update transactions. Measurements collected by a system monitor for 1800 sec indicate a total CPU utilization of 72%. The accounting facility records CPU utilization on a per-class basis, giving the following: $U^{\text{os}}_{\text{cpu,B}} = 32\%$, $U^{\text{os}}_{\text{cpu,I}} = 10\%$, and $U^{\text{os}}_{\text{cpu,T}} = 28\%$. The program analyzer of the TP monitor provides the following statistics for the observation period: 1,200 query transactions and 400 update transactions are completed. They consumed 120 and 140 sec of CPU time, respectively. Using Eqs. (5.7.21), the CPU demand of update transactions is equal to

$$D_{cpu,update} = \frac{0.72 \times \frac{0.28}{0.32+0.10+0.28} \times \frac{140}{120+140}}{400/1800} = 0.698 \text{ sec}$$

[Note: If the total 140 sec of CPU time spent by the update transactions is divided by the number of such transactions executed (i.e., 400), an average of 0.35 sec per transaction results, representing half of the true service demand as computed above. This simplistic computation does not take into account the operating system overhead, which must be included.] ∎

Virtual machine: multiple operating systems. The ability to run multiple operating systems on a single processor has provided convenience and flexibility to users. By using processor scheduling and virtual memory mechanisms, an operating system is able to create the illusion of virtual machines, each executing on its own processor and own memory. Several virtual machines share an underlying common hardware (i.e., bare machine).

The usual mode of sharing within a virtual machine is multiplexing, which involves allocating time slices of the physical processor to several virtual machines that contend for processor cycles. Virtual machines enable the creation of various different execution environments all using a single processor. However, there is a price to pay for this additional flexibility: degraded performance. The larger the number of virtual machines, the higher the performance degradation.

VM is IBM's implementation of virtual machines on its mainframes. VM provides both interactive processing facilities and the capability to run *guest operating systems*. For instance, on a single mainframe, it is possible to have a situation where several versions of different guest operating systems (e.g., MVS and VSE) run simultaneously with interactive users (e.g., CMS) on top of a VM system. Fig. 5.7 (d) illustrates the existence of various execution environments on top of virtual machines that all share a common hardware complex. The point here is to answer the following question: How does the service demand reflect the existence of various virtual machines executing on top of a single real processor?

In a virtual machine environment, we view the CPU is shared by different layers of software, which can be expressed by the following:

$$U_{cpu}^t = U_{cpu,vm} + U_{cpu,os} + U_{cpu,tp} + U_{cpu,prog} \qquad (5.7.22)$$

where $U_{cpu,vm}$ represents the CPU utilization by the host operating system responsible for implementing virtual machines and supporting different guest operating systems. Thus, J different guest operating systems may coexist. On top of each of them, K different classes of workload may exist, some of them may run on top of a TP. Additionally, it is possible to have R different classes of transactions within the TP monitor. The CPU utilization by class r transactions running on top of a guest operating system can be written in a general form as

$$U_{cpu,r} = U_{cpu}^t \times f_{vm,os} \times g_{os,tp} \times h_{tp,r} \qquad (5.7.23)$$

Equation (5.7.23) can be viewed as a product of the total CPU utilization by three factors, each representing the *fraction* of CPU time received by each layer (i.e., VM, TP, and individual workload class) that makes up the execution environment. The total CPU utilization allocated to an individual guest operating, *os*, is represented by the fraction:

$$f_{vm,os} = \frac{U_{cpu,os}^{vm}}{\displaystyle\sum_{\forall \text{ OS } j} U_{cpu,j}^{vm}}. \qquad (5.7.24)$$

where $U_{cpu,j}^{vm}$ is the utilization of the CPU allocated to virtual machine j. The other fractions, $g_{os,tp}$ and $h_{tp,r}$, are defined analogously in Eqs. (5.7.19) and (5.7.20), respectively. As before (i.e., similar to Eq. (5.7.21)), the CPU demand of class r within a virtual machine environment is:

$$D_{cpu,r} = \frac{U_{cpu}^t \times f_{vm,os} \times g_{os,tp} \times h_{tp,r}}{X_{0,r}} \qquad (5.7.25)$$

where U_{cpu}^t is given in Eq. (5.7.22).

Example 5.4

Consider a virtual machine (VM) scheme that supports an execution environment with three guest operating systems: one for production (e.g.,

MVS1), one for development activities (e.g., MVS2), and one to handle a number of interactive users (e.g., CMS). The VM environment runs on top of a mainframe with a single processor. The production OS processes two workload classes: batch (B) and transaction (TP). The TP monitor supports the execution of two classes of transactions: *query* and *update*. The goal of this example is to calculate the average CPU demand for update transactions.

A system monitor observes the behavior of the mainframe for 1800 seconds. During this time it records a CPU utilization of 97%. For the same period, a software monitor of the VM system measures the following utilizations for the guest operating system: $U_{cpu,mvs1}^{vm} = 50\%$, $U_{cpu,mvs2}^{vm} = 14\%$, and $U_{cpu,cms}^{vm} = 20\%$. This last measurement indicates the total CPU utilization by all CMS users. The accounting system of MVS1 collects statistics per workload: $U_{cpu,B}^{os} = 30\%$ and $U_{cpu,TP}^{os} = 60\%$. Performance figures from the TP monitor show that 1,200 query transactions and 400 update transactions complete and consume 120 and 140 sec of CPU time, respectively. Using Eq. (5.7.25), the CPU demand of the update class is equal to

$$D_{cpu,update} = \frac{0.97 \times \frac{50}{50+14+20} \times \frac{60}{30+60} \times 140120 + 140}{400/1800} = 0.933 \text{ sec}$$

A similar calculation estimates the CPU demand for the batch jobs that run on the production system. Suppose that 80 production batch jobs complete during the observation period. Adapting Eq. (5.7.25) to this situation (i.e., considering only the CPU allocation to the production OS and the corresponding suballocation to the batch class), it follows that

$$D_{cpu,batch} = \frac{0.97 \times \frac{50}{50+14+20} \times \frac{30}{30+60}}{80/1800} = 4.33 \text{ sec.}$$

■

5.7.2   Overhead Representation

Overhead consists of resource usage by the operating system. Overhead has two components: a constant component and a variable component. The former corresponds to those activities performed by an OS that do not depend on the level of system load, such as the CPU time required to handle an I/O interrupt. The variable component of overhead corresponds to these activities that are dependent on the system load. For instance, as the number of jobs in memory increases, the work required by memory management routines also increases.

There are two approaches for representing overhead in performance models. One approach uses a special workload class of the model (i.e., an "overhead" class) for representing the overhead of the OS activities performed on behalf of application programs. There are problems associated with this approach. Because of its variable nature, the service demands of the special class must be made load-dependent. Thus, whenever the intensity parameters (e.g., multiprogramming level and arrival rate) of the application classes change, the service demands of the overhead class also have to be modified. The interdependency between overhead parameters and multiprogramming mix may make this approach difficult and error prone. For this reason, unless the operating system load is itself the subject of the performance analysis, representing overhead as an independent class of the model is typically avoided.

The second approach to representing overhead in performance models is to distribute overhead among the classes of application programs. That is, the overhead incurred on behalf of a class is incorporated within the class itself. This is the usual method for modeling overhead. As will be seen in the next section, the problem with this approach is the calculation of breakdown ratios for distributing overhead among the classes in correct proportions.

5.7.3 Arrival Rate

For relatively long measurement intervals, the arrival rate can be approximated by the throughput of the system. In other words, assuming that the system experiences an operational equilibrium (i.e., steady state); the difference between the number of arrivals and the number of completions is relatively small. Thus, the arrival rate, λ_r, of class r can be estimated by

$$\lambda_r = \frac{C_{0,r}}{T} \qquad (5.7.26)$$

where T is the length of the measurement interval and $C_{0,r}$ denotes the number of class r transactions (or programs) completed during T. Counts of completed transactions are usually provided by software monitors and program analyzers.

Example 5.5

A total of 5,140 order-entry transactions are processed by a system during the monitoring period of one hour. According to Eq. (5.7.26), the estimated arrival rate is $5,140/3,600 = 1.428$ tps.   ∎

The measurement interval should be long enough to minimize *initial effects* and *end effects*, which are represented by those transactions that are executed partially within and partially outside the measurement interval. In most cases it is impractical to avoid initial and end effects. Also, the impact of such effects on overall performance is typically minimal, especially when the number of observed transaction is large. Because the number of transactions processed is proportional to the length of the interval, initial and end effects for long intervals are less significant than those for short intervals.

5.7.4   Concurrency Level

The average number of jobs/requests being executed concurrently is an important parameter when modeling closed classes (e.g., batch jobs). The concurrency level is also called multiprogramming level in the context of multiprogrammed computer systems. There are several different methods for obtaining the multiprogramming level of a particular customer class. For instance, software monitors are able to measure and report the time-averaged number of jobs actually in execution in memory during a measurement interval [1]. If the elapsed times (i.e., memory residence times) of the n jobs executed during the measurement interval are available from the accounting logs, the average concurrency level, $\overline{N}_r$, of class r jobs can be estimated as follows:

$$\overline{N}_r = \frac{\sum_{i=1}^{n} e_{i,r}}{T} \tag{5.7.27}$$

where $e_{i,r}$ is the elapsed time of job i of class r.

Example 5.6

Consider the example of Fig. 5.8, which shows a timing diagram of the execution of four jobs (A, B, C, and D) and their respective elapsed times.

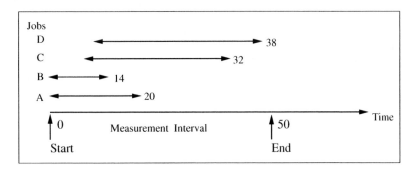

Figure 5.8. Average multiprogramming level.

Using Eq. (5.7.27), the average degree of multiprogramming is $(20 + 14 + 32 + 38)/50 = 2.08$.   ∎

[Note: Initial and end effects also impact the calculation of $\overline{N}_r$. The underlying assumption is that the initial state at the beginning of an observation period is approximately equal to the ending state at the end of the observation period. For example, if a job is $p\%$ completed when the observation period starts, it is assumed that a similarly sized job is $p\%$ completed at the end of the observation period. In this case, only one of the elapsed times of these jobs is included in the calculation of $\overline{N}_r$.]

Alternatively, if the average response time, R_r, for class r jobs and the arrival rate, λ_r, of class r are available, Little's Law can be used to calculate the average degree of multiprogramming as follows:

$$\overline{N}_r = \lambda_r R_r. \tag{5.7.28}$$

5.7.5 Number of Active Terminals and Think Time

Possible approaches to estimate the average number of active terminals $(\overline{M}_r)$ of class r include:

- Use information provided by software monitors concerning the average number of logged on users who performed some activity during the monitoring interval.

- Use measurement data provided by accounting logs to calculate the number of active terminals, as follows:

$$\overline{M}_r = \frac{\sum_{i=1}^{n} s_{i,r}}{T}, \qquad (5.7.29)$$

where $s_{i,r}$ is the measured length of terminal session i of class r users. To use Eq. (5.7.29), available records of all sessions performed during the monitoring period are required.

The average think time (Z_r) for users of class r can be obtained either from software monitors or from measurement data. The Interactive Response Time Law

$$Z_r = \frac{\overline{M}_r}{X_{0,r}} - R_r, \qquad (5.7.30)$$

can also be used when the average number of active terminals $(\overline{M}_r)$, the throughput $(X_{0,r})$, and average response time (R_r) of class r are known.

Example 5.7

Suppose that a time-sharing system supports the program development activities of 40 concurrently active programmers. The workload consists of commands entered by the programmers. During a monitoring period of 1 hour when the 40 programmers are logged on, the system executes 4,900 commands with an average measured response time of 2.5 sec. Applying Eq. (5.7.30), the average think time for this interactive workload is $40 \times 3600/4900 - 2.5 = 26.9$ sec. ∎

When using data from software monitors, special caution is required to assure that what is being reported is actually think time. There are different views for this parameter. Here, think time is defined as the time interval that elapses from the beginning of the previous command's response from the system until the next command by the user is submitted to the system.

5.7.6 CPU Service Demand

As seen in the example in Section 5.3, the basic formula for deriving the average CPU demand of class r is

$$D_{\text{cpu},r} = \frac{U_{\text{cpu},r}}{X_{0,r}}. \qquad (5.7.31)$$

Equation (5.7.31) requires the CPU utilization on a per-class basis (i.e, $U_{\text{cpu},r}$). In general, system monitors obtain total device utilizations but do not collect these statistics by class. Partial device utilizations by workload class are typically derived from accounting data. Since most accounting systems are intended primarily for billing purposes, they do not include any unaccountable system overhead. Consequently, it is usual to have the following relation:

$$\sum_{\forall \text{ class } r} U_{\text{cpu},r}^{\text{os}} < U_{\text{cpu}}^{t}, \tag{5.7.32}$$

where $U_{\text{cpu},r}^{\text{os}}$ is the CPU utilization of class r measured by an accounting software package. In other words, the resource usage of all programs does not add up to the global utilization observed by a software monitor. There are reasons for this inconsistency. First, some of the resources used by the operating system on behalf of application programs are not charged back to the application programs. For example, accounting software does not collect CPU time expended by the system in activities such as job initiation/termination, job scheduler, multiprogramming, context switching, and virtual storage support. Second, when a monitor operates on a sampling basis, the resource usage after the last sample before a program terminates is lost. The CPU time not collected by measurement tools is known as *uncaptured time*. The problem is how to distribute all unaccounted resource use among the classes of a workload in a fair manner. Most of the unattributed CPU time is likely to be overhead and must be apportioned among the workload classes.

The CPU utilization by each class can be written as

$$U_{\text{cpu},r} = U_{\text{cpu}}^{t} \times f_{\text{cpu},r} \tag{5.7.33}$$

where $f_{\text{cpu},r}$ is the relative fraction of the total CPU time used by class r. The apportionment factor $f_{\text{cpu},r}$ may be estimated in different ways, depending on the assumptions about the workload and the execution environment (hardware and operating system) [4].

- Assuming that the unaccounted CPU time is proportional to the number of programs executed in each class during the monitoring period, one viable definition of $f_{\text{cpu},r}$ is

$$f_{\text{cpu},r} = \frac{C_{0,r}}{\displaystyle\sum_{\forall \text{ class } s} C_{0,s}}. \tag{5.7.34}$$

where $C_{0,s}$ is the number of class s completions observed. In this case, the overhead is evenly distributed over all completing job. The shortcoming of this method is that the nature of programs being executed is not considered. That is, a 'heavyweight" program and a "lightweight" program are assumed to have equal overhead burdens.

- Based on the assumption that the amount of unaccounted time is proportional to the accounted CPU time, an alternative definition of $f_{cpu,r}$ is

$$f_{\text{cpu},r} = \frac{U_{\text{cpu},r}^{\text{os}}}{\sum_{\forall \text{ class } s} U_{\text{cpu},s}^{\text{os}}} \qquad (5.7.35)$$

where $U_{\text{cpu},s}^{\text{os}}$ is the CPU utilization of class s obtained from an OS software monitor. The problem with this approximation is that the unattributed CPU time may not be related to the accounted time. For instance, the amount of CPU time accumulated for interactive applications built on top of time-sharing systems (e.g., IBM's TSO) is considerably less than the same work done in batch mode [10].

- Assuming that most overhead is connected with the execution of I/O requests, a third apportionment factor for CPU time is given by

$$f_{\text{cpu},r} = \frac{\text{number of I/O operations by class } r}{\text{total number of I/O operations by all classes}}. \qquad (5.7.36)$$

Because of the uncertainties surrounding $f_{\text{cpu},r}$, the selected approximation is a design decision based on the particular problem and the particular workload. After solving the model, the results obtained can be used to validate the approximation selected. If the model does not match observed behavior, an alternative definition of $f_{\text{cpu},r}$ may be selected.

5.7.7   I/O Service Demands

The most commonly used approximation for deriving disk i service demands $(D_{i,r})$ for class r requests is

$$D_{i,r} = \frac{U_i^t}{X_{0,r}} \times f_{i,r}, \qquad (5.7.37)$$

where U_i^t is the total utilization of disk i, $X_{0,r}$ is the throughput of class r, and $f_{i,r}$ represents the fraction of the utilization of disk i due to workload class r. Software monitors do not usually provide statistics by class. Thus, inferences have to be made from measurement data to derive $f_{i,r}$. Four practical cases for estimating $f_{i,r}$ are presented.

Single-class disk. When the requests to a disk are all statistically similar, the disk can be modeled using a single class. In this case, disk i is dedicated to a single class r and there is no need to breakdown its total utilization. Thus,

$$f_{i,r} = 1. \tag{5.7.38}$$

User disk. When a disk contains only user data and is shared by several workload classes, the fraction apportioned to each class is approximately proportional to the number of I/O operations performed by each class. Thus,

$$f_{i,r} = \frac{\text{number of I/O operations to disk } i \text{ by class } r}{\text{total number of I/O operations to disk } i \text{ by all classes}}. \tag{5.7.39}$$

At this point, it is appropriate to consider the assumptions behind this estimate. To understand the I/O characteristics of an application, a distinction is made between two types of operations. *Logical I/O operations* refer to the requests made by application programs to access file records. *Physical I/O operations* correspond to actions performed by the I/O subsystem to access data blocks on specific I/O devices. There is rarely a one-to-one correspondence between logical and physical operations. At one extreme, when the data required by a logical operation are already in memory (e.g., I/O buffers), no physical I/O operations result. At the other extreme, operations such as a file open or a keyed access may require several physical operations to complete a single logical operation. In general, accounting systems record logical operations, whereas system monitors count physical operations. Because systems monitors do not collect statistics by class, the number of logical I/O operations reported by accounting systems is assumed in Eq. (5.7.39). Consequently, the proportion of physical I/O operations on disk i is assumed to equal the proportion of logical operations.

Swap disk. Swapping is a memory management mechanism that moves entire processes from main memory and from the swapping disk. In most operating systems, the majority of swapping is due to interactive users. To represent swapping in performance models, the service demand at each disk used for swapping purposes should be specified for each class. Swapping activity is measured by the number of swap I/O operations, which include swap-ins and swap-outs. The former refers to processes moved from disk to memory, whereas the latter corresponds to processes moved from memory to disk. The swapping requests can be apportioned among the classes proportionally to the number of swap operations attributed to each class. Thus,

$$f_{i,r} = \frac{\text{number of swap I/Os to disk } i \text{ by class } r}{\text{total number of swap I/Os to disk } i} \qquad (5.7.40)$$

where the number of swap I/O operations is obtained from accounting data.

Paging disk. Paging moves individual pages of processes from main memory to and from the paging disk. Paging activity generates significant I/O traffic and should be included in performance models of systems that have virtual memory. This activity is represented by the service demand of each class at the paging disks. The intensity of paging activities is measured by page-ins (i.e., pages moved from disk to memory) and and page-outs (i.e., pages moved from memory to disk). Page-ins cause delays to a program's progress, since the program has to wait until the page transfer completes. Thus, I/O operations due to page-ins should be considered as part of a program's demand for I/O service. Page-outs, on the other hand, cause no direct delay on a program's execution since page-outs occur when the program is either idle or when the program is concurrently executing elsewhere. Thus, page-outs are usually modeled as part of the system overhead [11, 12]. When disk i is used for paging, the fraction $f_{i,r}$ is approximately proportional to the number of page-ins generated by workload class r, as follows:

$$f_{i,r} = \frac{\text{number of page} - \text{in operations to disk } i \text{ by class } r}{\text{total number of page} - \text{in operations to disk } i}. \qquad (5.7.41)$$

5.8   Concluding Remarks

There are two key issues in the process of obtaining input parameters for performance models: parameter measurement and parameter estimation.

With regard to measurement, it is essential to understand what is being measured, how accurate the measurements are, and how reliable the resulting numbers are. In this chapter several aspects of the measurement process were discussed. In addition, several techniques used for monitoring the level of activity of a computer system were highlighted.

Parameter estimation deals with the determination of input parameters from secondary measurement data sources. Many times, monitors do not provide enough information for calculating the input parameters required by a performance model. Assumptions have to be made regarding the behavior of the system and inferences are made in order to derive the desired parameters.

Although this chapter does not focus on any particular product or manufacturer, it provides a set of general guidelines for transforming typical measurement data into the required input parameters for performance models. The guidelines can be applied to real problems in a straightforward manner. Because of the uncertainties associated with the process of estimating parameters, model validation is an indispensable step in the overall modeling process.

5.9 Exercises

1. Select from published literature or from product specification manuals two specific performance monitors. Briefly describe the two products and make a comprehensive list of the measurements provided by each monitor. Considering that the goal is to obtain input parameters for a performance model, discuss the positive and negative points of each of the two tools selected.

2. The MS Excel workbook `Ch05-Ex-MPG.xls` contains a list of elapsed times for 100 transactions that are executed during a period of 60 seconds. What is the average number of transactions concurrently executed?

3. The MS Excel workbook `Ch05-Ex-BW.xls` contains a list of transaction CPU times and their corresponding number of I/Os. Compute the basic statistics of Fig. 5.1 and draw the Box and Whisker plot for this data set. Draw an x-y scatter plot for the data using the CPU time as

the x-axis and the number of I/Os as the y-axis. Visually cluster the workload. What are the characteristics of the centroids of the clusters identified?

4. Suppose that the data in ChO5-Ex-BW.xls is obtained during a period of 15 seconds, that the CPU utilization is 35%, and that the disk utilization is 80%. Consider that each cluster found in the previous exercise corresponds to one class in a QN model. What is the overall throughput of the system in tps? What is the throughput for each class in tps? Compute the service demands at the CPU and disk for each of the classes.

5. Use OpenQN.xls to solve the QN model for the previous exercise assuming that the arrival rates are equal to the class throughputs obtained in the previous exercise.

6. A performance analyst monitored a computer system with one CPU and three disks (D1, D2, and D3) for 1 hour. The system workload consists of three different types of transactions: A, B, and C. Using data collected by the software monitor and the accounting facility, the analyst obtains the following measurements: $U_{cpu}^t = 82\%$, $U_{D1}^t = 28\%$, $U_{D2}^t = 20\%$, $U_{D3}^t = 35\%$, $C_{0,A} = 2200$, $C_{0,B} = 4000$, $C_{0,C} = 1000$. Determine the service demands for this workload and comment. Justify any assumptions by giving their pros and cons.

7. Consider a server dedicated to transactions generated by phone orders from customers. The server consists of a single processor and two disks (A and B). Disk A contains customer data and disk B is used for paging. The analyst responsible for studying the system performance decides to build an analytic model with 3 service centers (i.e., CPU, disk A, and disk B) and 2 classes (i.e., one for order-entry transactions and one representing the system overhead). The measurement data obtained from the system monitor are: $T = 900$ sec, $C_{0,trans} = 1800$, $U_{cpu} = 65\%$, $U_{disk\ A} = 20\%$, $U_{disk\ B} = 35\%$, page-ins = 22,500, and page-outs = 10,000. $C_{0,trans}$ is the number of user transactions completed during the monitoring period. The total CPU time for user

transactions recorded by the accounting system is 567 sec. Assume that:

- The CPU times required to handle a page-in and a page-out operation are 0.0015 and 0.0042 sec, respectively.
- Page-ins should be viewed as a part of the workload demand for I/O services and should be incorporated into the disk service demands. Page-out should be include in the system overhead.

Find the input parameters for the model.

8. Learn how to use the Windows XP or NT Performance Monitor. Write a program that generates a large number of I/Os to random blocks on a file. Add the `%Idle Time` counter for the `PhysicalDisk` object. This counter provides the percentage of disk idle time (i.e., 100 - disk utilization). From the Control Panel select the System icon and then select the Hardware tab. Click on the Device Manager and click on the hard drive under Disk drives. Select the Policies table and locate the "Enable write caching on the disk" option. Run your program with and without caching enabled. Observe what happens to the disk utilization. Comment on the results.

9. The workload of a database server is characterized by three types of transactions: trivial, medium, and complex. The database server, which consists of one CPU and one disk, is monitored during one hour. The CPU utilization is measured at 55% and the disk utilization is measured to be 85%. Additional measurements obtained during the observation period are shown in Table 5.10.

   - Find the service demands at the CPU and disk for trivial, medium, and complex transactions.
   - Assume that the arrival rates of medium and complex transactions are fixed at 1.6 tps and 0.6 tps, respectively. Using the QN solvers provided with the book, generate a graph with three av-

Table 5.10. Data for Exercise 5.9

	Trivial	Medium	Complex
No. of Physical I/Os	10	20	40
Total CPU Seconds	840	560	252
No. of Transactions Executed	10500	5600	2100

erage response time curves (one for each workload) as a function of the arrival rate of trivial transactions

- Repeat the item above for a situation where a new disk, identical to the existing disk, is installed in the database server in such a way that the I/O demand is balanced between the two disks.

Bibliography

[1] C. Rose, "A measurement procedure for queuing network models of computer systems," *ACM Computing Surveys*, vol. 10, no. 3, September 1978.

[2] D. Ferrari, G. Serazzi, and A. Zeigner, *Measurement and Tuning of Computer Systems*, Prentice Hall, Upper Saddle River, New Jersey, 1983.

[3] P. Heidelberger and S. Lavenberg, "Computer performance methodology," *IEEE Transactions on Computers*, vol. C-33, no. 12, December 1984.

[4] M. Kienzle, "Measurements of computers systems for queuing network models," *Technical Report CSRG-86*, Department of Computer Science, University of Toronto, Canada, October 1977.

[5] D. M. Levine, P. P. Ramsey, and R. K. Smidt, *Applied Statistics for Engineers and Scientists: Using Microsoft Excel & MINITAB*, Prentice Hall, Upper Saddle River, New Jersey, 2001.

[6] D. Lavery, "The design of a hardware monitor for the Cedar supercomputer," *CSRD Report no. 866*, University of Illinois at Urbana-Champaign, May 1989.

[7] I. Borovits and S. Neuman, *Computer System Performance Evaluation*, Lexington Books, Lexington, Massachusetts, 1979.

[8] J. Cady and B. Howarth, *Computer System Performance Management and Capacity Planning*, Prentice Hall, Brookvale, New South Wales, Australia, 1990.

[9] W. Highleyman, *Performance Analysis of Transaction Processing Systems*, Prentice Hall, Upper Saddle River, New Jersey, 1989.

[10] J. Cooper, "Capacity planning methodology," *IBM Systems Journal*, vol. 19, no. 1, 1980.

[11] J. P. Buzen, "A queuing network model of MVS," *ACM Computing Surveys*, vol. 10, no. 3, September 1978.

[12] J. Silvester and A. Thomasian, "Performance modeling of a large scale multiprogrammed computer using BEST/1," *Proceedings of the International Conference on Computer Capacity Mangement*, Chicago, 1981.

Chapter 6

Case Study II: A Web Server

6.1 Introduction

The case study presented in this chapter introduces several important concepts in performance engineering, including the determination of confidence intervals, the computation of service demands from the results of experiments, the usage of linear regression, and comparison of alternatives through analytic modeling and through experimentation. The examples discussed in this chapter are supported by the MS Excel workbooks `WSData.XLS`, `ClosedQN-Chap6.XLS`, `ClosedQN-Secure.XLS`, and `ServerComparison.XLS`.

6.2 The Web Server

Consider a large software company that uses an internal Web server to allow its programmers, testers, and documentation personnel to download two types of files: 1) PDF files containing documents and manuals, and 2) ZIP files containing software files (e.g., source code and executables). The Web server has one CPU and four identical disks. PDF files are stored on disks 1 and 2 in such a way that access to these files is evenly distributed between these two disks. Similarly, ZIP files are stored on disks 3 and 4 in a way that balances the load on these two disks. The main question of interest in this case study is: "What is the maximum number of concurrent PDF and ZIP file downloads that can be in progress in order to satisfy a certain prespecified SLA?"

The Web log contains one entry for each downloaded file, including its type and size. The worksheet Log of the MS Excel WSData.XLS workbook includes 1,000 entries for file downloads captured over 200 seconds during a peak hour. A sample of the first six entries in this worksheet is given below:

File Type	Size (KB)	Elapsed Time (sec)
PDF	303	1.43
ZIP	1233	5.81
ZIP	1077	5.08
PDF	315	1.48
ZIP	1240	5.84
PDF	413	1.95
.	.	.
.	.	.
.	.	.

The elapsed time column is the total time spent at the server to download the associated file. This time can be recorded in the HTTP log. For example, the elapsed time is captured in Microsoft's Internet Information Server (IIS) by selecting the "Time Taken" field in the Extended Logging Option.

6.3   Preliminary Analysis of the Workload

In order to obtain a first-cut analysis of the workload of this Web server, the entries in the Log worksheet are sorted by file type, then by file size, using Excel's Data → Sort facility. The result is recorded in the SortedLog worksheet of WSData.XLS. Then, the Descriptive Statistics facility of Excel (see Tools → Data Analysis) is separately applied to the set of PDF and ZIP file entries to obtain basic statistics for these types of files.

PDF Statistics: Figure 6.1 shows the basic statistics for the 411 PDF files in the log (i.e., 41.1% of all downloaded files). As seen, the average size

PDF File Size Statistics (in KB)	
Mean	377.6
Median	375.5
Standard Deviation	43.1
Sample Variance	1859.5
Range	149.2
Minimum	300.4
Maximum	449.6
Sum	155,183
Count	411
1/2 95% Confidence Interval	4.17

Figure 6.1. Basic statistics for PDF file sizes.

of a PDF file retrieved during the interval is 377.6 KB. The sample standard deviation is 43.1 KB. From these statistics, the coefficient of variation (i.e., the ratio between the standard deviation and the mean), C_{PDF}, is computed as

$$C_{\text{PDF}} = 43.1 \text{ KB}/377.6 \text{ KB} = 0.114.$$

This C_{PDF} is relatively small and indicates that the set of all PDF files can be modeled as a single class in the ensuing performance model. [Note: A good rule-of-thumb is that if the coefficient of variation in a data set is less than 0.25, it is safe to assume the data set forms a single class. For higher values of the coefficient of variation, further data clustering (e.g., see Chapter 4) may be required.]

Confidence Intervals: The last row of the table in Figure 6.1 indicates the 95% confidence interval for the mean size of downloaded PDF files. It is important understand the meaning of this number. This number indicates that one can say with a probability of 0.95 that the *actual* average of the size of PDF files is within 4.17 KB of the *sampled* average (i.e., 377.6 KB). That is, the actual average refers to the mean of the underlying distribution of downloaded file sizes, whereas the sampled average refers to the mean of only these particular 411 files downloaded in this sample. The actual average is unknown, since the true underlying distribution is also unknown. The sample average is known from 411 sampled files. Thus, in this example, the 95% *confidence interval* is 377.6 KB ± 4.17 KB, indicating that the unknown actual average is within this interval with probability 0.95. [Note: In Fig. 6.1, the "1/2" implies that 4.17 KB may be above or below the sample mean. The sample mean lies in the middle of the confidence interval.]

Understanding confidence intervals and their use is important for experimental performance engineering work because the sample mean (i.e., the average value obtained from a sample) by itself does not tell the complete story. Suppose that separate samples of file sizes are observed over a large number of days (e.g., one sample each day) and that the mean file size is computed for each day's sample. These sample means would not be all equal. Which sample mean should be chosen to correctly parameterize a QN model? Should the average value of the daily sample means be chosen? Should the average value of the total conglomerate number of file sizes be chosen?

Two important questions are: i) What is the relationship between the actual average value of a distribution and the observed average value of the sample mean? and ii) How is a confidence interval for the mean computed? These questions are answered in turn.

Let c be the half width of a confidence interval, μ be the expected value of a the underlying distribution, and $\bar{x}$ be the sample mean. Then,

$$Pr[\bar{x} - c \leq \mu \leq \bar{x} + c] = 1 - \alpha, \qquad (6.3.1)$$

for a $100\,(1-\alpha)\%$ confidence interval. The value $1-\alpha$ is called the confidence coefficient. Consider the PDF files again. The expression in Eq. (6.3.1) for a 95% confidence interval becomes

$$Pr[(377.6 - 4.17) \text{ KB} \leq \mu_{\text{PDF}} \leq (377.6 + 4.17) \text{ KB}] =$$
$$Pr[373.4 \text{ KB} \leq \mu_{\text{PDF}} \leq 381.8 \text{ KB}] = 0.95 \quad (6.3.2)$$

Thus, the confidence coefficient is 0.05 and the average size of retrieved PDF files is in the interval [373.4 KB, 381.8 KB] with a probability of 0.95.

The half width, c, of the confidence interval is obtained from the Central Limit Theorem [3] as

$$c = z_{1-\alpha/2}\, \frac{s}{\sqrt{n}} \qquad (6.3.3)$$

where s is the sample standard deviation, n is the sample size, and $z_{1-\alpha/2}$ is the $(1 - \alpha/2)$-percentile of a normal distribution with a mean of 0 and a standard deviation of 1. Practically speaking, c can be computed using MS Excel's `CONFIDENCE` function as

$$c = \text{CONFIDENCE}(\alpha, s, n). \qquad (6.3.4)$$

ZIP Statistics: Similar statistics for ZIP files are presented in Fig. 6.2. In this case, there are 589 downloaded ZIP files (i.e., 58.9% of the total). The average size of a downloaded ZIP file is in the interval [(1155.6 - 6.92) KB, (1155.6 + 6.92) KB] = [1148.7 KB, 1162.5 KB] with a probability of 0.95 (i.e., with 95% confidence). The coefficient of variation, C_{ZIP}, for the size of ZIP files can be easily computed (i.e., $C_{\text{ZIP}} = 85.7/1155.6 = 0.074$). Since C_{ZIP}, like C_{PDF}, is also very small, all ZIP files belong to the same class in the performance model.

6.4 Building a Performance Model

Recall that the main question in this case study is to determine the maximum number of PDF and ZIP files that can concurrently be downloaded while satisfying a given service level agreement. A closed multiclass QN model is used to answer this question.

As specified in Section 6.2, the Web server consists of one CPU and four identical disks. To complete the parameterization of the model, the

ZIP File Size Statistics (in KB)	
Mean	1155.6
Median	1157.9
Standard Deviation	85.7
Sample Variance	7350.0
Range	299.8
Minimum	1000.1
Maximum	1299.9
Sum	680,650
Count	589.0
1/2 95% Confidence Interval	6.92

Figure 6.2. Basic statistics for ZIP file sizes.

concurrency level for each class (i.e., file type) and the service demands at each device are needed.

6.4.1 Computing Concurrency Levels

From the preliminary workload analysis in Section 6.3, two types of classes are identified: downloads of PDF files and downloads of ZIP files.

The data from the log in Section 6.2 is used to estimate the mix of concurrent PDF versus ZIP file downloads. This mix represents the concurrency levels of the PDF and ZIP customer classes, respectively. The results from Section 5.7.4 are used here to compute the average concurrency level for each type of file. According to Eq. (5.7.27), the concurrency levels are computed as

$$\overline{N}_{\text{PDF}} = \frac{\sum_{i=1}^{411} e_{i,\text{PDF}}}{T} = \frac{731.5}{200} = 3.7 \qquad (6.4.5)$$

$$\overline{N}_{\text{ZIP}} = \frac{\sum_{i=1}^{589} e_{i,\text{ZIP}}}{T} = \frac{3,207.7}{200} = 16.1 \qquad (6.4.6)$$

where $e_{i,\text{PDF}}$ and $e_{i,\text{ZIP}}$ are the elapsed times of PDF and ZIP file downloads indicated in the `WSData.XLS` workbook, respectively. T is the measurement interval (i.e., 200 sec in the case of this log). Rounding the concurrency levels to the nearest integer yields 4 PDF downloads and 16 ZIP downloads. This ratio of 1:4 between these two types of files is used in the model to apportion the total customer population between these two classes.

6.4.2 Computing Service Demands

To complete the model parameterization, the service demands at the CPU and disk have to be computed for each customer class. The service demands are a function of the file sizes. In order to estimate these demands, the analyst conducts an experiment using a machine similar to the production Web server. A test server consisting of a single CPU and a single disk is sufficient. A set of n dummy files for each of six file sizes (e.g., 10 KB, 100 KB, 200 KB, 500 KB, 800 KB, and 1000 KB) are created and posted on the test server. Then, for each file size, the n files of that given size are downloaded from another machine while measuring the CPU and disk utilizations of the test server. The estimated service demands for the CPU and disk for a certain file size are then obtained from the Service Demand Law (see Chapter 3) as $U_{\text{CPU}}/(n/\mathcal{T})$ and $U_{\text{disk}}/(n/\mathcal{T})$, respectively, where $\mathcal{T}$ is the time taken to download all n files of the selected file size.

The results for the CPU times are plotted in Fig. 6.3, which shows, for each file size, the total CPU time (i.e., the CPU service demand) to download a file of a given size. The data points obtained in the experiment are shown in the graph by the dotted line. A trend line is added to these points using MS Excel (i.e., by right clicking on the dashed line and selecting `Add Trend Line`). A linear trend line is selected because visual inspection indicates a linear relationship between CPU time and file size. The linear regression (i.e., trend line) performed generates the relationship

$$\text{CPUTime} = 0.1046 \times \text{FileSize} - 0.0604 \qquad (6.4.7)$$

where CPUTime is in msec and FileSize is in KB. The R^2 value (i.e., the coefficient of determination provided by MS Excel) obtained in this linear regression is 0.9969. The closer to one this coefficient, the better the regression line fits the experimental data. As a rule of thumb, an R^2 value above 0.95 indicates that the regression line adequately models the observed data.

The same procedure is used to discover the relationship between the total I/O time (i.e., the disk demand) and the file size. The data points and trend line are shown in Fig. 6.4. The linear regression yields the equation

$$\text{IOTime} = 0.4078 \times \text{FileSize} + 0.2919 \qquad (6.4.8)$$

with a coefficient of determination equal to 0.9946.

The linear regression equations (i.e., Eqs. (6.4.7) and (6.4.8)) are used to compute the CPU and disk demands for each class for the production server as follows:

- PDF files: The average size of a downloaded PDF file is 377.6 KB (i.e., from Fig. 6.1). Using Eq. (6.4.7), the service demand at the CPU for this class is

$$D_{\text{CPU,PDF}} = 0.1046 \times 377.6 - 0.0604 = 39.4 \text{ msec.} \qquad (6.4.9)$$

  From the case study specification in Section 6.2, PDF files are stored on disks 1 and 2 and access to these files is evenly balanced between

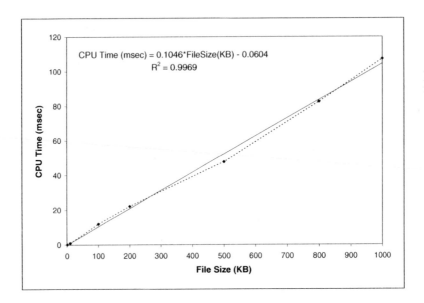

Figure 6.3. CPU Time (in msec) vs. file size (in KB).

these disks. As a result, the total I/O time is equally split between these disks. Thus, the service demands for PDF files at disks 1 and 2, using Eq. (6.4.8), are:

$$\begin{aligned} D_{\mathrm{disk1,PDF}} &= D_{\mathrm{disk2,PDF}} \\ &= 0.5 \times (0.4078 \times 377.6 + 0.2919) \\ &= 77.1 \text{ msec.} \end{aligned} \tag{6.4.10}$$

Since no PDF files are stored on disks 3 and 4,

$$D_{\mathrm{disk3,PDF}} = D_{\mathrm{disk4,PDF}} = 0. \tag{6.4.11}$$

- ZIP files: The average size of a downloaded PDF file is 1155.6 KB (i.e., from Fig. 6.2). Using Eq. (6.4.7), the service demand at the CPU for this class is

$$D_{\mathrm{CPU,ZIP}} = 0.1046 \times 1155.6 - 0.0604 = 120.8 \text{ msec.} \tag{6.4.12}$$

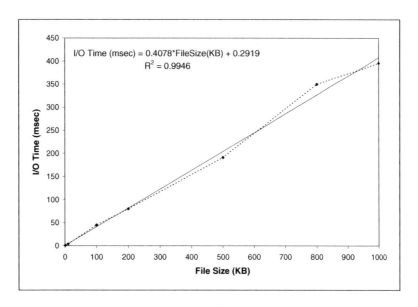

Figure 6.4. I/O Time (in msec) vs. file size (in KB).

ZIP files are stored evenly across disks 3 and 4. Thus, the service demands for ZIP files at disks 3 and 4 are:

$$
\begin{aligned}
D_{\text{disk3,ZIP}} &= D_{\text{disk4,ZIP}} \\
&= 0.5 \times (0.4078 \times 1155.6 + 0.2919) \\
&= 235.8 \text{ msec.}
\end{aligned}
\tag{6.4.13}
$$

Since no ZIP files are stored on disks 1 and 2,

$$
D_{\text{disk1,ZIP}} = D_{\text{disk2,ZIP}} = 0.
\tag{6.4.14}
$$

Thus, the service demands for the base QN model, referred to as the original configuration, are summarized in Table 6.1.

6.5 Using the Model

The MS Excel workbook `ClosedQN-chap6` can now be used to solve the model. The initial customer populations for classes PDF and ZIP are set at 4 and 16, respectively (see Section 6.4.1). The total Web server traffic intensity (i.e., the total customer population or the total number of concurrent

Table 6.1. Service Demands (in msec) for the Original Configuration

Resource	Class	
	PDF	ZIP
CPU	39.4	120.8
Disk 1	77.1	0.0
Disk 2	77.1	0.0
Disk 3	0.0	235.8
Disk 4	0.0	235.8

downloads) can be increased (or decreased) in the model by maintaining the 1:4 ratio between the PDF and ZIP downloads.

Suppose that the manager requests to see performance results of the original configuration against a balanced I/O configuration (i.e., one in which PDF and ZIP files are stored on disks 1 through 4 in such a way that access to each category of files is evenly distributed across all four disks). The new set of service demands for this balanced configuration is easily obtained. The CPU demands are the same as those in Table 6.1. The disk demands are computed by taking, for each class, the total disk demand (i.e., 154.2 msec and 471.6 msec for PDF and ZIP files, respectively) and, instead of dividing them evenly over two disks each, dividing them both over all four disks. Thus, for PDF files instead of 77.1 (= 154.2/2) msec for two disks, 38.6 (= 154.2/4) msec of service is required for each of four disks. Similarly, for ZIP files, the average per disk demand is 117.9 (= 471.6/4) msec. Table 6.2 shows the service demands for the balanced configuration.

The original and the balanced QN models are solved using Closed-QN-Chap6.XLS. A range of traffic intensities, varying from 20 to 180 total customers (i.e., maintaining the 1:4 ratio between PDF and ZIP customers), are considered. Figure 6.5 shows the throughput, measured in file downloads/sec, for PDF and ZIP files for both configurations. The corresponding download time results are shown in Fig. 6.6.

Observations from the throughput results (i.e., Fig. 6.5) indicate that:

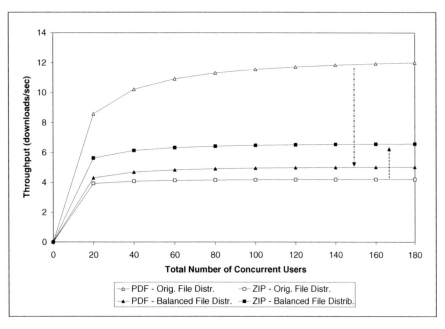

Figure 6.5. Throughput vs. number of concurrent users for the original file layout and for the balanced layout.

- After some point (i.e., after 20 users), the throughput saturates because the utilization of one of the Web server devices approaches 100%.

Table 6.2. Service Demands (in msec) for the Balanced Configuration

Resource	Class	
	PDF	ZIP
CPU	39.4	120.8
Disk 1	38.6	117.9
Disk 2	38.6	117.9
Disk 3	38.6	117.9
Disk 4	38.6	117.9

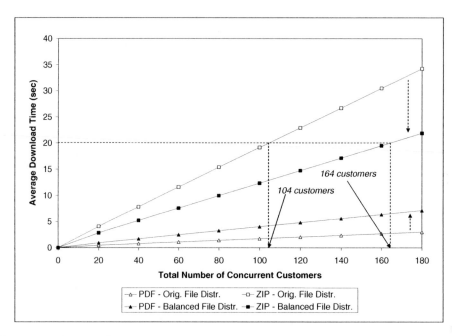

Figure 6.6. Average file download time vs. number of concurrent users for the original file layout and for the balanced layout.

- The maximum throughput for PDF files in the original configuration is 12 files/sec. However, for the balanced configuration, the maximum throughput for PDF files is reduced to 5 files/sec.

- The maximum throughput for ZIP files in the original configuration is 4.2 files/sec. However, for the balanced configuration, the maximum throughput for PDF files is increased to 6.6 files/sec.

- The throughput of ZIP files increases and the throughput for PDF files is reduced as the configuration is changed from the original to the balanced one. The total throughput measured in files per second (i.e., considering both PDF and ZIP files) is reduced by 28% by balancing the load across the disks (i.e., maximum throughput reduces from 16.2 (= 12 + 4.2) files/sec in the original configuration to 11.6 (= 5 + 6.6) files/sec in the balanced configuration). However, since ZIP files are significantly larger than PDF files (i.e., 1155.6 KB compared to 377.7 KB), the total throughput measured in bandwidth (i.e., KB/sec) increases by 1.4% (i.e., it increases from 9384.72 ($= 12 \times 377.6 + 4.2 \times$ 1155.6) KB/sec in the original configuration to 9514.96 ($= 5 \times 377.6 + 6.6 \times 1155.6$) KB/sec in the balanced configuration).

Suppose that the SLAs on download times for PDF and ZIP files are 7 seconds and 20 seconds, respectively (since ZIP files are roughly 3 times larger than PDF files, it is reasonable for the ZIP/PDF SLA ratio to be proportional). Observations from the download time results (i.e., Fig. 6.6) indicate that:

- After about 20 concurrent users, the throughput saturates for all classes (see Fig. 6.5) and, therefore, the download times increase linearly with the number of concurrent users (see Exercise 6.5).

- For 104 concurrent users, the average download time for ZIP files at the original configuration reaches its SLA of 20 seconds, while the download time for PDF files is well below its SLA of 7 seconds. Thus, the maximum number of concurrent downloads supported by the original configuration is 104.

- For the balanced configuration, the average download time for ZIP files reaches 20 seconds at 164 concurrent customers. At this point, the download times for PDF files is still below its 7-second SLA. Thus, the balanced configuration is superior to the original one and supports 58% more customers.

For 160 customers using the balanced configuration, the utilizations of all devices are nearly 100%. Specifically, the model indicates that $U_{\text{CPU}} = 0.98$, $U_{\text{disk1}} = U_{\text{disk2}} = 0.92$, and $U_{\text{disk3}} = U_{\text{disk4}} = 0.99$.

6.6 Secure Downloads

Management wants to add secure file downloads. However, before this option is implemented, it is important to assess the likely impact on performance of this change.

Transport Layer Security (TLS) [1], which is similar to Secure Sockets Layer (SSL) version 3.0, has been selected for user authentication and for secure file downloads. TLS has two phases. The first one, the handshake phase, is used by the browser and Web server to exchange secrets. These secrets are used to generate a confidential symmetric key that is subsequently used for data exchange in the second phase of the protocol. Public key encryption is used during the handshake phase to exchange the secrets and the symmetric encryption key is used for message exchange after the handshake is complete.

Public key encryption is computationally intensive and adds to the CPU service demand. Also, during file download, symmetric encryption is performed on the file before it is downloaded. This also adds to the service demand on the CPU. A quantitative description and analysis of TLS is given by Menascé and Almeida [4], which also provides the timings for the various encryption operations used here to estimate the additional demand on the CPU due to secure file downloads. Using the data in [4], the analyst builds a table of the CPU times needed for three security alternatives: low security, medium security, and high security. The security level alternative depends on the size of the key used in the handshake phase and on the strength of the encryption and message digest algorithms used in the data transfer phase. The required CPU times for the alternatives are shown in Table 6.3.

Column 2 of Table 6.3 represents the total CPU time required by the server for the handshake phase for each downloaded file. This time is added to the CPU service demand for each download, independent of file size. The third column of the table shows the amount of additional CPU time required for each KB downloaded. Thus, the total additional CPU time required is equal to the handshake time plus the average file size multiplied by the CPU processing time. Consider for example the low-security option and PDF

Table 6.3. CPU Times (msec) Required for Secure Download Options

	CPU Handshake Time per File (msec)	CPU Processing Time per KB (msec)
Low Security	10.2	0.104
Medium Security	23.8	0.268
High Security	48.0	0.609

files, whose average file size is 377.6 KB. The additional CPU time required for secure file downloads is 49.5 (= 10.2 + 0.104 × 377.6) msec. Table 6.4 summarizes the amount of time that has to be added to the CPU demands for both PDF and ZIP downloads for each of the three security options.

Using the new CPU service demands, the QN model is re-solved. Table 6.5 shows the throughputs (i.e., X_{PDF} and X_{ZIP}) and download times (i.e., R_{PDF} and R_{ZIP}) for PDF and ZIP files under the three security options for various concurrency levels. The model, ClosedQN-Secure.XLS, is used to obtain the results in this table. Under the low security option, the SLAs for both types of files are violated for 80 concurrent users. When medium security is used, the download times for PDF and ZIP files reach their SLAs for a load of 43 users. When the high-security option is used, no more than 22 concurrent downloads can be supported.

In all secure download options, the CPU is the bottleneck. Higher levels of concurrency can be supported by upgrading to a faster CPU (see Exercise 6.7).

6.7   Experimental Comparison of Two Servers

Performance engineering involves experimentation in addition to modeling. Different alternatives can be compared by designing experiments, conducting experiments, analyzing the results, and drawing conclusions.

Many factors may impact the performance of computer systems being compared and each factor may have several levels. Consider the issue of purchasing a new Web server. Several factors are relevant, which directly influence the performance of the Web Server. Such factors include: processor

Table 6.4. Additional CPU Service Demands (msec) Required for Secure Download

	PDF	ZIP
Low Security	49.5	130.4
Medium Security	125.0	333.5
High Security	278.0	751.8

Table 6.5. Download Times (in sec) for Three Security Options

No. Concurrent Downloads	X_{PDF} (files/sec)	X_{ZIP} (files/sec)	R_{PDF} (sec)	R_{ZIP} (sec)
Low Security				
20	2.25	3.15	1.78	5.09
40	2.26	3.17	3.55	10.08
60	2.25	3.18	5.32	15.10
80	2.25	3.18	7.10	20.12
Medium Security				
20	1.22	1.75	3.28	9.13
40	1.22	1.76	6.56	18.19
60	1.22	1.76	9.85	27.27
High Security				
20	0.63	0.91	6.34	17.49
40	0.63	0.92	12.69	34.93

speed, number of processors, and amount of main memory. Each of these factors may have more than one level as indicated in Table 6.6.

An exhaustive evaluation of all options considering all possible combinations of factors and levels, would require 48 ($= 4 \times 4 \times 3$) different experiments. This is called a *full factorial* design evaluation. The number of experiments in a full factorial design evaluation may be too large, making the experimental process time consuming and expensive. A significant reduction is the number of experiments is achieved by reducing the number of levels of each

Table 6.6. Example of Web Server Options

Factor	Levels
Processor Speed (GHz)	2.0, 2.4, 2.8, 3.1
Number of Processors	1, 2, 4, 8
Main Memory (GB)	1, 2, 4

factor and/or eliminating factors that do not make a significant contribution to overall performance.

A method for eliminating factors that are less relevant is a 2^k *factorial design*. The basic idea is to consider only two levels for each of the k factors. When factors affect performance monotonically (e.g., performance improves monotonically as the processor speed increases), the minimum and maximum levels of each factor are evaluated to determine whether or not the factor has a significant performance impact. For example, increasing the processor speed from 2.0 GHz to 3.1 GHz improves performance. By conducting experiments for two levels only, 2.0 GHz and 3.1 GHz, the effect of this factor can be determined.

An important aspect of an experiment is the workload and initial conditions used in the experiment. For example, selecting a representative workload and replaying it on the system under different configurations is effective. Care must be taken to ensure that different initial conditions, such as the contents of various caches and buffers, do not distort the results.

When analyzing the results of experiments there is always some degree of experimental error. This error contributes to variation within the measured results. Experimental error may come from non-controllable factors that may affect the results. Examples include extraneous load on the network, caching activity by file systems, garbage collection activities, paging activities, and other operating system background management activities. Thus, the variation in the results is due to: 1) different levels of the design factors involved, 2) interaction between factors, and 3) experimental error.

A technique known as ANOVA (Analysis of Variance) can be used to separate the observed variation into two main components: variation that can be attributed to assignable causes (e.g., amount of main memory or number of processors) and uncontrollable variation (e.g., network load, operating system background activities) [3]. A detailed description of ANOVA is outside the scope of this book. The interested reader may refer to [3]. However, it is useful to mention that single factor and two-factor ANOVA can be easily performed using MS Excel by using the `Tools` $\rightarrow$ `Data Analysis` facility.

Confidence intervals can be used as a simple method for comparing two alternatives [2] as explained via the following simple example. Suppose that management is interested in comparing the performance of their Web server with that of a new Web server. The performance analyst conducts an experiment to determine if the performance obtained from the two Web servers is different at a 95% confidence level.

The analyst carries out the following steps:

1. Select a representative workload, for example, a sample of 1,000 downloads of PDF and ZIP files at the peak period (see data in the `Log` worksheet of the MS Excel workbook `ServerComparison.XLS`).

2. Play the workload against the original and the new Web server. Record the download times for the files downloaded during the measurement interval (see measurement results in the `Log` worksheet of the MS Excel workbook `ServerComparison.XLS`).

3. Sort the results by file type (i.e., PDF and ZIP) and compute, for each file downloaded, the difference $\Delta_{new-orig}$ between the download time using the new server and the download time using the original server (see `SortedLog` worksheet of the `ServerComparison.XLS` MS Excel workbook).

4. Compute 95% confidence intervals for the mean of the differences $\Delta_{new-orig}$ for both PDF and ZIP file downloads. If the 95% confidence interval includes zero, then there is no significant difference between the two Web servers at a 95% confidence level. If zero falls outside the 95% confidence interval, the servers are deemed to be different at that confidence level (see results in the `SortedLog` worksheet of the `ServerComparison.XLS` MS Excel workbook).

The above four steps are performed to determine if the two Web servers give significantly different performance. A negative value of $\Delta_{new-orig}$ indicates the new server downloads files faster than the original server. The results of running the experiments are shown in Table 6.7. As indicated by the table, the 95% confidence interval for the mean of the difference in PDF file download times is [-0.0380, -0.0334], which does not include zero. Similarly, for ZIP files, the 95% confidence interval for the mean of the difference in download times is [-0.1160, -0.1058], which also does not include the zero.

Table 6.7. Results of Experimental Comparison of Two Web Servers

	PDF	ZIP
$\Delta_{\text{new}-\text{orig}}$	-0.0357	-0.1109
Lower bound 95% CI	-0.0380	-0.1160
Upper bound 95% CI	-0.0334	-0.1058

Thus, at the 95% confidence level, the new server outperforms the original server.

6.8   Concluding Remarks

The case study discussed in this chapter is used to illustrate how measurement data can be used to obtain performance parameters for a multiclass QN model. The model is used to evaluate various important scenarios, such as balancing disks, varying the concurrency level, selecting security levels, and purchasing new Web servers.

Experimentation is often used in lieu of analytic modeling. It is important to properly design experiments so that relevant factors and their levels may be used. There should be a balance between the number of options considered and the budget allocated to the experiments. Variations in the results of experiments due to errors and/or non-controlled variables are normal and expected. They are taken into account when analyzing the results of experiments.

Confidence intervals are shown to be quite useful. They are useful in determining the integrity of selected workload classes (e.g., Section 6.3). They are also useful in determining whether or not different configurations are significantly different (e.g., Section 6.7).

6.9   Exercises

1. Using the data in `WSData.XLS` workbook, compute the basic statistics for the file size for the set of all files downloaded (PDF and ZIP) taken together. Compute the coefficient of variation of the file size. Compare

the results obtained with the separate statistics for PDF and ZIP files shown in this chapter.

2. Use the results in the previous problem and construct a single class model (i.e., single file type). Calculate new service demands. Solve the new model and plot its throughput and average download times. Assess the "error" made by assuming this single class model when the actual system is multiclass. What is an appropriate SLA for this single class model?

3. Use the data in the WSData.XLS workbook and compute the 25th percentile and the 75th percentile of the PDF and ZIP file sizes. Draw a Box and Whisker plot for each data set.

4. Compute a 90% confidence interval for the size of PDF and ZIP files. Compare these intervals with the 95% confidence intervals shown in this chapter.

5. Show that when the throughput $X_0(n)$ saturates, the response time grows linearly with the number of customers n. (*Hint:* use Little's Law.)

6. Explain why the balanced configuration of Section 6.5 is better for ZIP files but worse for PDF files when compared with the original configuration.

7. Consider the three security options of Section 6.6. How much faster should the CPU be in order to support 164 concurrent downloads with same SLAs for each of the security options? (*Hint:* use the ClosedQN-Secure.XLS workbook.)

8. Reconsider the experimental comparison of the two servers in Section 6.7. At what confidence level would the new and the original Web servers be considered not to be significantly different?

Bibliography

[1] T. Dierks and C. Allen, "The TLS Protocol," Version 1.0, *The Internet Engineering Task Force (IETF)*, RFC 2246, January 1999.

[2] R. Jain, *The Art of Computer Systems Performance Analysis*, John Wiley & Sons, New York, 1991.

[3] R. L. Mason, R. F. Gunst, and J. L. Hess, *Statistical Design and Analysis of Experiments*, 2nd. ed., John Wiley & Sons, Hoboken, New Jersey, 2003.

[4] D. A. Menascé and V. A. F. Almeida, *Scaling for E-business: Technologies, Models, Performance, and Capacity Planning*, Prentice Hall, Upper Saddle River, New Jersey, 2000.

Chapter 7

Case Study III: A Data Center

7.1   Introduction

Shared data centers provide a wide variety of services to a large number of customers. The current trend toward service-based computing requires that services be deployed and configured on demand at geographically distributed virtual data centers [2]. There are several problems associated with the management of data center resources: compliance with service level agreements, energy management [1], thermal considerations [3], fault tolerance, security, privacy, and availability. Clearly, cost is the underlying constraint that makes these problems more challenging.

This chapter applies the modeling techniques described in Chapters 10 and 14 to address the issue of properly sizing a data center. This sizing is part of the system design process and focuses on the number of machines and the number and skill level of maintenance personnel to achieve desired levels of availability.

187

7.2   The Data Center

A data center has M machines and a staff of N people that maintain and service failed machines. The machines are functionally identical and share common networked file systems. A data center diagnostic system is used to: 1) automatically detect failures of the M machines, 2) maintain a queue of machines waiting to be repaired, 3) log the time a machine failed, and 4) record the times at which a repair person started and completed service on a machine. The diagnostic system uses a "heartbeat" mechanism to periodically ping the machines to determine if they are operational. As soon as a machine failure is detected, a trouble ticket is automatically generated and posted to the tracking database within the center's diagnostic system. Idle members of the repair staff continually monitor the tracking database and select the first machine in the queue of failed machines to be serviced next.

Each of the M machines in the data center is in one of two states: operational or failed. A failed machine may be waiting to be repaired by one of the N repair people or it may be in the process of being repaired. As indicated in Fig. 7.1, once a failed machine is repaired, it goes back to the pool of operational machines.

Management is interested in answering the following questions:

1. Given the rate at which machines fail, the number of machines, the number of repair people, and the average time it takes to repair a machine, what is the probability that exactly j $(j = 1, \cdots, M)$ machines are operational at any given time?

2. Given the rate at which machines fail, the number of machines, the number of repair people, and the average repair time, what is the probability that at least j $(j = 1, \cdots, M)$ machines are operational at any given time?

3. Given the failure rate of the machines, the number of machines, and the average repair time, how many repair people are necessary to guarantee that at least j $(j = 1, \cdots, M)$ machines are operational with a given probability?

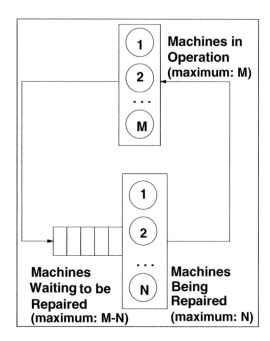

Figure 7.1. Failure-recovery model for the data center

4. What is the effect of the size of the repair team on the mean time to repair (MTTR) a machine? The MTTR is the time from which a machine fails until it becomes operational again. This includes the time spent waiting to repair a machine and the time needed to diagnose and fix the problem. Also, what is the effect of the size of the repair team on the percentage of machines that can be expected to be operational at any given time?

5. What is the effect of the average time it takes a member of the repair team to fix a machine (i.e., their skill level) on the overall MTTR (i.e., which includes the time waiting to repair)? Also, how does a repair person's skill level affect the percentage of operational machines? The average time required by a repair person to fix a machine can be reduced by either deploying better tools to the repair staff or providing better training to the repair staff.

7.3   Building a Model

An analytical model is built to answer the five questions posed in the previous section. The machine failure rate is denoted by λ and indicates the rate at which machines move from the operational state to the failed state. Thus, each machine stays in the operational state $1/\lambda$ time units, on average. This value is called the Mean Time to Failure (MTTF). It is assumed here that machines fail independently from one another and that all machines fail at the same average rate. (Note: If machines are observed to fail at different rates, a multiclass model can be constructed. In this case, machines in class r fail at rate λ_r. Multi-class models are considered in Chapters 13 and 14.) The machine repair rate is denoted by μ. That is, the average time it takes to service one machine is $1/\mu$ time units. It is assumed here that all repair personnel have the same skill level. (Note: if different repair people have different skill levels, a heterogeneous multi-server model can be constructed with each server (i.e., repair person) having their own personal repair rate.) As Fig. 7.1 indicates, if there are fewer repair technicians than the number of machines (i.e., $N < M$), then there may be a queue of machines waiting to be repaired (i.e., if more than N machines are in the failed state at any one time).

The system of Fig. 7.1 can be modeled by the Markov Chain (see Chapter 10) of Fig. 7.2, where state k represents the number of failed machines. A transition from state k to state $k + 1$ happens when a machine fails. A transition from state k to state $k - 1$ occurs when a machine is repaired. At state k, there are $M - k$ machines in operation and each has a failure rate of λ. Thus, the aggregate failure rate, λ_k, at state k, is given as

$$\lambda_k = (M - k)\,\lambda \qquad k = 0, \cdots, M - 1. \qquad (7.3.1)$$

The aggregate repair rate, μ_k, at state k depends on whether or not all N repair people are busy. Therefore,

$$\mu_k = \begin{cases} k\,\mu & k = 1, ..., N \\ N\,\mu & k = (N+1), ..., M \end{cases} \qquad (7.3.2)$$

Solving this Markov Chain means finding the steady state probabilities, p_k, of being in state k ($k = 0, \cdots, M$). This solution can be obtained using

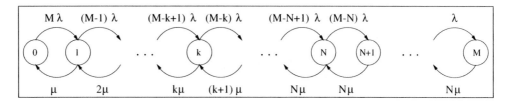

Figure 7.2. Markov chain model for the data center.

the Generalized Birth-Death (GBD) theorem of Chapter 10 given that the expressions for λ_k and μ_k are known. The GBD theorem states that

$$p_k = p_0 \prod_{i=0}^{k-1} \lambda_i / \mu_{i+1} \qquad \text{for } k = 0, 1, 2, \dots \qquad (7.3.3)$$

where p_0 is obtained by requiring that $\sum p_k = 1$.

The resulting expressions for the probability p_k that k machines are failed are given below (see Exercise 7.1).

$$p_k = \begin{cases} p_0 \left(\frac{\lambda}{\mu}\right)^k \begin{pmatrix} M \\ k \end{pmatrix} & k = 1, \dots, N \\[4mm] p_0 \left(\frac{\lambda}{\mu}\right)^k \begin{pmatrix} M \\ k \end{pmatrix} \frac{N^{N-k} \, k!}{N!} & k = (N+1), \dots, M \end{cases} \qquad (7.3.4)$$

where p_0 is obtained by requiring that $\sum_{k=0}^{M} p_k = 1$. Hence,

$$p_0 = \left[\sum_{k=0}^{N} \left(\frac{\lambda}{\mu}\right)^k \begin{pmatrix} M \\ k \end{pmatrix} + \sum_{k=N+1}^{M} \left(\frac{\lambda}{\mu}\right)^k \begin{pmatrix} M \\ k \end{pmatrix} \frac{N^{N-k} \, k!}{N!} \right]^{-1}. \qquad (7.3.5)$$

The average aggregate rate at which machines fail, $\bar{X}_f$, which is also equal to the average aggregate rate at which machines are repaired, can be computed from the probabilities p_k as

$$\bar{X}_f = \sum_{k=0}^{M-1} \lambda_k \times p_k = \sum_{k=0}^{M-1} (M - k) \, \lambda \, p_k. \qquad (7.3.6)$$

The Interactive Response Time Law (see Chapter 3) can be used to compute the MTTR (i.e., the average time spent by a machine from when it fails until it is back in operation). The analogy between Fig. 3.4 and Fig. 7.1 is as follows: client workstations correspond to machines in operation, the average think time Z corresponds to the MTTF $(1/\lambda)$, the average response time R corresponds to the MTTR, and the system throughput X_0 corresponds to the aggregate failure rate $\bar{X}_f$. Therefore,

$$\text{MTTR} = M/\bar{X}_f - \text{MTTF} = M/\bar{X}_f - 1/\lambda. \tag{7.3.7}$$

The average number of failed machines, N_f, can be obtained by applying Little's Law to the "black box" consisting of the queue of machines waiting to be repaired plus the set of all machines being repaired (i.e., the number of machines in the lower portion of Fig. 7.1). Hence,

$$N_f = \bar{X}_f \times \text{MTTR} = M - \bar{X}_f \times \text{MTTF} = M - \bar{X}_f/\lambda. \tag{7.3.8}$$

Similarly, the average number of operational machines, N_o, is

$$N_o = M - N_f = \bar{X}_f \times \text{MTTF} = \bar{X}_f/\lambda \tag{7.3.9}$$

which is Little's Law applied to the upper portion of Fig. 7.1. The Markov Chain model described in this section is implemented in the MS Excel workbook `Chap7-MarkovModel.XLS`.

7.4   Using the Model

In this section it is assumed that there are 120 machines in the data center and that the MTTF is equal to 500 minutes (i.e., $\lambda = 1/500 = 0.002$ failures per minute). The average time taken by a repair person to diagnose and repair a machine is assumed, unless stated otherwise, to be equal to 20 minutes (i.e., $\mu = 1/20 = 0.05$ repairs per minute).

The questions of Section 7.2 are now revisited and answered below.

1. Given the rate at which machines fail, the number of machines, the number of repair people, and the average time it takes to repair a machine, what is the probability that exacly j ($j = 1, \cdots, M$) machines are operational at any given time?

   The probability that j machines are operational at any given time is the probability that $M - j$ machines are failed. This probability,

p_{M-j}, is computed using Eqs. (7.3.4) and (7.3.5). Figure 7.3 shows this probability for three different values of the number of repair people ($N = 2$, 5, and 10). If only two repair people are used, the peak of the distribution occurs for about 50 machines and the probability that 50 machines are operational is about 5.6%. For $N = 2$, the probability that j machines are operational is negligible for $j \geq 67$. When five repair people are used, the situation improves dramatically. The peak of the distribution occurs for 116 machines. At that point, the probability that exactly 116 machines are operational is close to 10%. The bulk of the distribution is concentrated between 92 and 120 machines. Adding five more people to the repair staff (i.e., $N = 10$), improves the situation further: the probability that 116 machines are

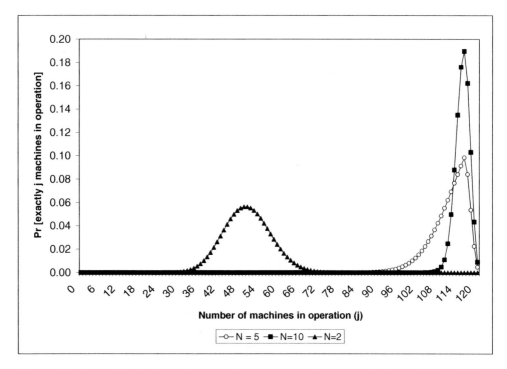

Figure 7.3. Probability that exactly j machines are operational vs. j for $M = 120, \lambda = 0.002$ and $\mu = 0.05$.

operational goes up to about 19% and the bulk of the distribution is concentrated between 108 and 120 machines.

2. Given the failure rate λ, the number of machines M, the number of repair people N, and the average repair time $1/\mu$, what is the probability P_j that at least j machines are operational at any given time?

   The probability P_j that at least j machines are operational can be computed as

$$P_j = \sum_{i=j}^{M} p_{M-i}. \qquad (7.4.10)$$

   Equations (7.3.4)-(7.3.5) provide the values of the probabilities p_{M-i} required in Eq. (7.4.10).

   The values of P_j are shown in Fig. 7.4 for $j = 1, \cdots, 120$ and for $N = 2, 3, 4, 5$, and 10. As expected, for low values of j the probability of j machines being operational is very close to 1. It is interesting to note the dramatic drop in each curve. This indicates that once the service personnel become overloaded, the entire system (i.e., nearly all the machines) tends toward failure. Having extra machines, beyond the number that the service personnel can maintain is pointless.

   For example, for $N = 2$, the probability that at least 40 machines are operational is 0.935 and the probability that at least 50 machines are operational is 0.52. The probability that at least 70 machines are in operation is virtually zero for $N = 2$. If the desired service level agreement is to have 110 machines operational, this SLA could not be met with a service staff size of 2 or 3. The SLA would only be met 14% of the time with a staff size of 4, 70% of the time with a staff size of 5, and 99% of the time with a staff size of 10.

3. Given the failure rate λ, the number of machines M, and the average repair time $1/\mu$, how many repair people are necessary to guarantee that at least two thirds of the machines (i.e., $j = 80$) are operational with a probability $P_j = 0.9$?

   Figure 7.4 shows that the horizontal dashed line for $P_j = 0.9$ intersects the $N = 4$ curve for $j = 88$ machines and the $N = 3$ curve for $j = 64$

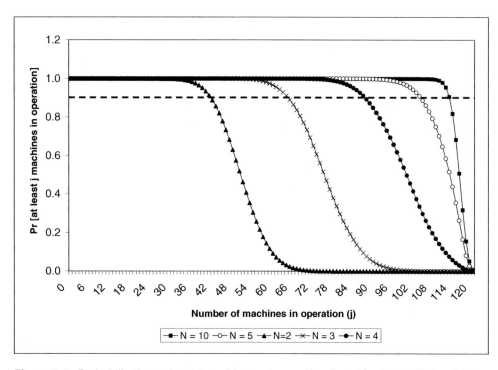

Figure 7.4. Probability that at least j machines are operational vs. j for $M = 120, \lambda = 0.002$ and $\mu = 0.05$.

machines. This indicates that at least four repair people are needed. Less than four would not guarantee that 80 machines are up and running with a probability of 0.9. A staff of four would guarantee that up to 88 machines are operational with a 0.9 probability.

4. What is the effect of the size of the repair team, N, on the mean time to repair (MTTR) a machine? Also, what is the effect of N on the percentage of machines that can be expected to be operational at any given time?

Using various values of N, the probabilities p_k are computed and the aggregate failure rate $\bar{X}_f$ is found according to Eq. (7.3.6). Then, the MTTR is obtained using Eq. (7.3.7). The results are shown in Table 7.1. The table shows a sharp decrease in MTTR as N varies

Table 7.1. Effect of Number of Repair People

N	N_o	N_f	MTTR (min)	$(N_o/M) \times 100$ (%)
1	25.0	95.0	1900.0	20.8
2	50.0	70.0	700.0	41.7
3	75.0	45.0	300.0	62.5
4	99.2	20.8	104.8	82.7
5	111.5	8.5	38.1	92.9
6	114.3	5.7	25.1	95.2
7	115.0	5.0	21.7	95.8
8	115.3	4.7	20.6	96.0
9	115.3	4.7	20.2	96.1
10	115.4	4.6	20.1	96.1
120	115.4	4.6	20.0	96.2

from 1 to 5. As the number of repair people is increased beyond 5, further decreases in the MTTR are minimal. With 5 repair people, the average time a machine is in failure mode (i.e., MTTR) is 38 minutes (i.e., 18 minutes waiting to be serviced and 20 minutes of service time). Also, with 5 repair people, an average of 111 (i.e., 93%) of the machines can be expected to be operational at any given time.

The last line of Table 7.1 shows the case in which $N = M = 120$ (i.e., where each machine has its own personal repair person). This is a degenerate case, but is helpful in illustrating the best possible performance for the system. In this case, machines never wait to be serviced. Thus, MTTR $= 1/\mu$. Applying Little's Law to the cycle composed of machines in operation and machines being repaired yields

$$M = \bar{X}_f \times (\text{MTTF} + \text{MTTR}) = \bar{X}_f \times (1/\lambda + 1/\mu). \qquad (7.4.11)$$

Thus,

$$\bar{X}_f = \frac{M}{1/\lambda + 1/\mu} = \frac{M \lambda \mu}{\lambda + \mu}. \qquad (7.4.12)$$

Applying Eq. (7.3.9) to find the average number of machines in operation, N_o, yields

$$N_o = \bar{X}_f \times \text{MTTF} = \frac{M \lambda \mu}{\lambda + \mu} \times \frac{1}{\lambda} = \frac{M \mu}{\lambda + \mu}. \qquad (7.4.13)$$

Substituting the values of $M = 120$, $\lambda = 0.002$ failures/min, and $\mu = 0.05$ repairs/min into Eq. (7.4.13) yields a value of $N_o = 115.4$ ($= (120 \times 0.05)/(0.002 + 0.05)$). This indicates that the upper limit on the number of machines that can be expected to be operational at any given time is 115.4. This assumes that each machine has its own repair person. However, as noted above, a repair staff size of 5 is expected to keep 111 machines operational. With an expected down time of 38 minutes per failed machine, this appears to be a prudent design decision.

5. What is the effect of a repair person's skill level (i.e., the average time $1/\mu$ required to fix a machine) on the overall down time (i.e., MTTR)? Also, how does the skill level affect the percentage of operational machines?

   Assuming, $N = 5$, the value of μ is varied so that the average time taken by a repair person to fix a machine varies from 10 min (i.e., $\mu = 1/10 = 0.10$) to 25 min (i.e., $\mu = 1/25 = 0.04$). The results are shown in Table 7.2. As expected , more skilled and faster repair people can improve the availability of the machines for the same number of people N and the same failure rate λ. For example, if $N = 5$ and each repair person is able to diagnose and fix a machine in 10 minutes on average, then the average down time is 10.4 min and 118 (i.e., 98%) of the machines remain operational. If $N = 5$ and if it takes an average of 25 minutes to repair a machine, Table 7.2 indicates that the average down time is 105 minutes and only 99 (i.e., 83%) of the machines are operational. From Table 7.1, this same level of performance can be achieved with $N = 4$, but with an average repair time of 20 minutes.

Table 7.2. Effect of the Repair Rate μ

Avg. time to repair a machine (min)	Repair Rate (μ) (1/min)	N_o	N_f	MTTR (min)	$(N_o/M) \times 100$ (%)
10	0.100	117.6	2.4	10.4	98.0
12	0.083	117.0	3.0	12.9	97.5
15	0.067	115.8	4.2	18.1	96.5
18	0.056	113.8	6.2	27.2	94.8
20	0.050	111.5	8.5	38.1	92.9
25	0.040	99.1	20.9	105.5	82.6

7.5   Another Modeling Approach

The system of Fig. 7.1 can be modeled equivalently by a two-device QN. One device is a delay server representing the machines in operation. The other device is a load-dependent server representing the repair people (See Fig. 7.5). The delay server is used to represent machines in operation. Once a machine is fixed, it goes into operation immediately without queuing. Moreover, the time a machine stays in operation does not depend on the behavior of other machines, but only upon its mean time to failure (i.e., $1/\lambda$).

Now consider the load dependent repair server. Given that there are N repair people, the collective rate at which machines are repaired depends on two things: 1) the number of failed machines, k, (including those waiting to be repaired and those being repaired) and 2) the number of repair people, N. If $k \leq N$, then all failed machines are being repaired and the collective rate at which machines become operational again is $k\mu$. However, if $k > N$, all repair people are busy and the collective repair rate is $N\mu$ (i.e., its maximum repair rate value). Thus, the service rate $\mu(k)$ of the load-dependent device is given by

$$\mu(k) = \begin{cases} k\,\mu & k = 1, ..., N \\ N\,\mu & k = (N+1), ..., M \end{cases}$$

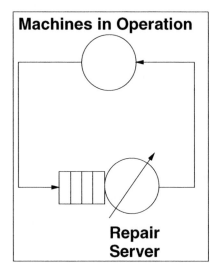

Figure 7.5. QN model of the data center.

To solve this model, the MVA method with load-dependent devices can be used. Load-dependent MVA is presented in Chapter 14. In particular, the single-class algorithm of Fig. 14.5 can be used.

Before solving the QN model, the service rate multipliers $\alpha(k)$ ($k = 1, \cdots, M$) are required. These multipliers are defined in Chapter 14 as $\alpha(k) = \mu(k)/\mu(1)$. Thus, from Eq. (7.5.14), it follows that

$$\alpha(k) \;=\; \begin{cases} (k\ \mu)/\mu = k & k = 1, ..., N \\ (N\ \mu)/\mu = N & k = (N+1), ..., M \end{cases} \qquad (7.5.14)$$

The solution of this MVA model with M customers (i.e., M machines circulating from being operational to being repaired) yields the average throughput $\bar{X}$ and the average residence time at each server. The average residence time at the load-dependent (LD) device, R'_{LD}, is the Mean Time to Repair (MTTR).

Applying Little's Law to the LD device (including its queue), the average number of failed machines, N_f, is computed as

$$N_f = \bar{X} \times R'_{\text{LD}}. \qquad (7.5.15)$$

Therefore, the average number of machines in operation, N_o, is just

$$N_o = M - N_f. \tag{7.5.16}$$

The solution of the MVA model also provides the probability distribution of the number of customers at the LD device (see Chapter 14). If desired, a multiclass MVA model with LD devices can be constructed and used to model situations in which the set of machines have different failure rates. In this case, the machines exhibiting different failure rates would be grouped into different customer classes in the model.

7.6   A Cost Analysis

A responsible cost and revenue analysis is crucial in any design process. Let C_p represent the annual personnel cost to the data center for each person on the repair staff. Let C_m represent the annual cost to the data center per machine. This cost includes annual hardware and software costs, software licenses, rental/lease space per machine, energy expenses/machine, and data center fixed costs pro-rated per machine. Thus, the total annual cost to the data center, C_a, is represented by

$$C_a = (N \times C_p) + (M \times C_m). \tag{7.6.17}$$

Let R_a be the annual revenue, represented by the expression

$$R_a = \beta(N_o - M_{\min}) \tag{7.6.18}$$

where $\beta > 0$ is a constant revenue multiplier, N_o is the average number of machines in operation, and $M_{\min}$ is the minimum number of machines that need to be in operation for the data center not to have to pay a penalty (indicated by a negative revenue) to its customers.

The annual profit P of the data center is the difference between the revenue and cost. Hence,

$$P = R_a - C_a = \beta(N_0 - M_{\min}) - ((N \times C_p + M \times C_m)). \tag{7.6.19}$$

The following values are used to generate the profit graph shown in Fig. 7.6: $M = 120, \lambda = 0.002/\text{min}, \mu = 0.05/\text{min}, M_{\min} = 10, C_p = \$100,000,$

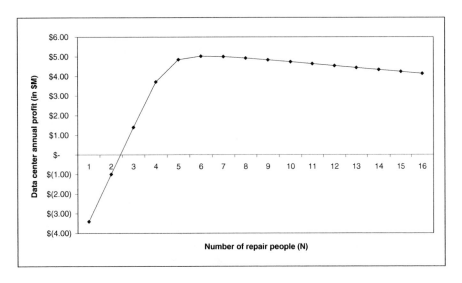

Figure 7.6. Annual profit vs. number of repair personnel for the data center.

$C_m = \$40,000$, and $\beta = \$100,000$. The curve indicates that for low numbers of service personnel (i.e., $N \leq 2$) the profit is negative because of low machine availability, implying penalties being paid to the customer. With additional personnel (i.e., $N > 2$), the availability increases and the profit becomes positive. The annual profit achieves its maximum value of $\$5.03$ million dollars with 6 service personnel. Beyond this point, the profit begins decreasing due to the increasing personnel cost and a slowly increasing value of the number N_o of operational (i.e., revenue generating) machines.

7.7 Concluding Remarks

This chapter demonstrates that the same type of analytic models used to investigate and predict performance issues are also useful to analyze availability considerations. In fact, availability and performance are important complementary aspects of the QoS of a computer system. The joint analysis of these two metrics leads to what is known as performability analysis.

This chapter illustrates the usefulness of Markov models and QNs as modeling approaches to investigate design issues of data centers. Capacity planning is conducted in terms of the number of machines and in terms of the quality and size of the maintenance staff in order to achieve certain availability goals.

7.8   Exercises

1. Use the Generalized Birth Death theorem of Chapter 10 to prove that Eqs. (7.3.4)-(7.3.5) are the solution to the Markov Chain of Section 7.3.

2. Suppose that the data center uses a load balancer to equally distribute the load among the M machines. Assume that the overall arrival rate of requests to the data center is γ requests/sec. If j machines are in operation, each sees an average arrival rate of γ/j requests/sec. Assume that the average response time of a request once at an operational machine is given by $S/(1-(\gamma/j).S)$ where S is the average service time of a request at a machine. Assume also that the load balancer does not route requests to failed machines. Assume further that if a machine fails, any requests in execution at that machine are lost and can be ignored for the purpose of this exercise. Give and expression for the average response time of a request at the data center.

3. Use the `Chap7-MarkovModel.XLS` MS Excel workbook to draw graphs of the probability that exactly P_j $(j = 0, \cdots, M)$ machines are operational as a function of the ratio λ/μ. Use $M = 120$ and draw curves for $N = 2, 5$, and 10.

4. Use the `Chap7-MarkovModel.XLS` MS Excel workbook to generate a table of MTTR for various values of the ratio λ/μ assuming $M = 120$ and $N = 5$.

Bibliography

[1] J. S. Chase, D. C. Anderson, P. N. Thakar, A. M. Vahdat, and R. P. Doyle, "Managing energy and server resources in hosting centers," *Proc. Eighteenth ACM Symposium on Operating Systems Principles*, Banff, Alberta, Canada, October 2001, ACM Press, 2001, pp. 103–116.

[2] S. Graupner, V. Kotov, and H. Trinks, "Resource-sharing and service deployment in virtual data centers," *Proc. 22nd International Conf. Distr. Comput. Systems Workshops (ICDCSW'02)*, July 2-5, 2002, IEEE Computer Society Press, pp. 666–671.

[3] C. D. Patel, R. Sharma, C. E. Bash, and A. Beitelmal, "Thermal considerations in cooling large scale high compute density data centers," *Proc. Eighth Intersociety Conf. Thermal and Thermomechanical Phenomena in Electronic Systems (ITHERM 2002)*, May 30-June 1, 2002, IEEE Press, pp. 767–776.

Chapter 8

Case Study IV: An E-Business Service

8.1 Introduction

The scalability of e-business sites is extremely important for the financial success of the business. When an e-business site becomes overloaded, customers become frustrated due. Customers take their business elsewhere and the corporation loses revenue [4]. To analyze the scalability of e-business sites one must characterize its workload at multiple levels, anticipating future user behavior and the increased request levels [3].

This chapter presents a case study of an online auction site. Open multiclass QN models are used to answer what-if questions about the site. The computations used in this chapter are supported by the `Chap8-CBMG.XLS`, `Chap8-OpenQN.XLS`, and `Chap8-OpenQN-TwoDisks.XLS` MS Excel workbooks.

8.2 The E-Business Service

Consider an online auction site that has a large number of registered customers. The overall architecture of the site is shown in Fig. 8.1. Users access the site from the Internet after passing through the necessary firewall. The

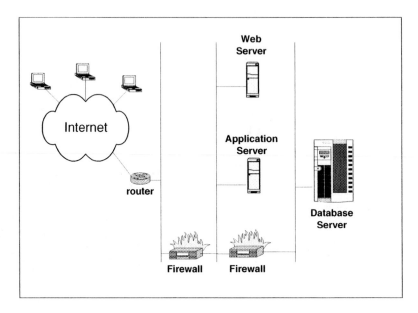

Figure 8.1. Online auction site architecture.

site itself consists of three servers: a Web server, an application server, and a database server. The Web server manages all the Web pages and handles all the direct interactions with the customers. The application server implements the core business logic of the site. The database server is used to store persistent data about auctions, bids, and registered customers. Each of these servers has one CPU and one disk. The generalization to the case of additional servers, servers with more than one CPU, and servers with multiple disks is straightforward and is discussed later in the chapter.

The online auction site offers the following services to its customers: create and broker auctions, search for auctions based on categories of items and keywords, monitor existing bids on open auctions, and place bids at strategic times on open auctions. In order to create an auction or to place a bid, customers are required to login to the site.

8.3   The E-Business Workload

The workload of the online auction site is characterized by its customer behavior using a Customer Behavior Model Graph (CBMG) [4]. This graph represents the behavior of a customer during a *session*, which is defined as a sequence of consecutive requests coming from the same customer during a single visit to a site. A CBMG has one node for each state in which a customer can be found during a session. Arcs between nodes indicate possible transitions between states. Figure 8.2 illustrates the CBMG for the auction site. The Entry state represents the customer before entering the site. Arc label $p_{i,j}$ represents the probability of transitioning directly from state i to state j. State x (not explicitly shown in Fig. 8.2) represents the Exit state. Once in the site, a customer can exit from any state i with probability $p_{i,x}$.

The CBMG of Fig. 8.2 has the following eight states: Entry (e), Home Page (h), Search (s), View Bids (v), Login (g), Create Auction (c), Place Bid (b), and Exit (x). The transitions between states are labeled by the probability that the transition occurs. For example, in Fig. 8.2, the probability that a customer will move to the Search (s) state after visiting the Home Page (h) is given by p_{hs}.

The CBMG can be used to compute the average number of visits, V_j, to each state j during a session. V_j can be computed from knowing the average number of visits to the other states and the transition probabilities. For

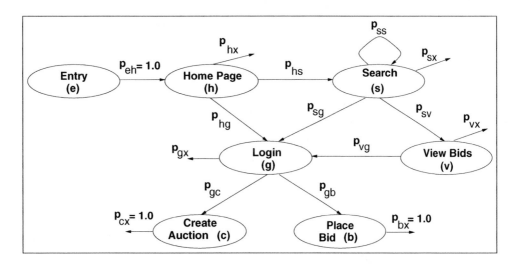

Figure 8.2. Customer Behavior Model Graph (CBMG) for the auction site.

instance, suppose state j can only be entered into from state i. Knowing V_i, V_j can be computed as $V_j = V_i \times p_{i,j}$. Said differently, V_j can be computed directly from the number of visits made to j's upstream neighbors and the probabilities of visiting j next. For example, Fig. 8.2, to compute V_g, one needs to know V_h, V_s, and V_v as well as the probabilities of going from states h, s, and v to state g. One can then write down the equation

$$V_g = V_h \times p_{hg} + V_s \times p_{sg} + V_v \times p_{vg}$$

This leads to a set of equations, one for every state. Applied to all states of the CBMG of Fig. 8.2, the following set of equations result.

$$V_e = 1 \tag{8.3.1}$$

$$V_h = V_e \times p_{eh} = 1 \tag{8.3.2}$$

$$V_s = V_h \times p_{hs} + V_s \times p_{ss} \tag{8.3.3}$$

$$V_v = V_s \times p_{sv} \tag{8.3.4}$$

$$V_g = V_h \times p_{hg} + V_s \times p_{sg} + V_v \times p_{vg} \tag{8.3.5}$$

$$V_c = V_g \times p_{gc} \tag{8.3.6}$$

$$V_b = V_g \times p_{gb} \tag{8.3.7}$$

Combining Eqs. (8.3.2) and (8.3.3) yields,

$$V_s = \frac{V_h \times p_{hs}}{1 - p_{ss}} = \frac{p_{hs}}{1 - p_{ss}} \tag{8.3.8}$$

The values of V_v, V_g, V_c, and V_b follow immediately from previously obtained values. In general, the set of equations derived from a CBMG is a system of linear equations (see Exercise 8.3) that can be easily solved using any statistical and/or mathematical software package.

Not all customer sessions of an e-commerce site are similar in terms of user navigational patterns. For example, some sessions may be characterized by a "window-shopping" type of behavior while others may reflect a navigational pattern of more serious buyers. Therefore, when characterizing the workload of an e-commerce site, one may find that the set of sessions can be clustered into groups of sessions that exhibit similar navigational patterns [5]. Each such cluster is represented by its own CBMG.

The characterization of the workload of the online auction site described in this case study yields two different types of sessions, session type A and session type B. A CBMG can be represented by an $n \times n$ matrix of transition probabilities between its n states. The transition probability matrices for the CBMGs of these two types of sessions are given in Tables 8.1 and 8.2. Twenty five percent of all sessions are of type A and the remaining are of type B.

Using Eqs. (8.3.1)-(8.3.7) on the CBMGs of Tables 8.1 and 8.2 yields the average number of visits to each state shown in Table 8.3. Sessions of type A are characterized by a higher number of visits to most states, in particular to states c and b (i.e., create auction and place bid) that tend to bring business to the auction site.

8.4   Building a Performance Model

Suppose that it is observed that there is a surge in the number of auctions created and the number of bids placed between 8 p.m. and 11 p.m. [1]. During that period, the average arrival rate of auction creation and bid placement requests is much higher than the average for the rest of the day. Management is interested in analyzing the performance of the various types of requests (i.e., home page hits, search executions, bid viewings, logins, auction creations, and bid placements) during the peak period, as the number

Table 8.1. Matrix of Transition Probabilities for the CBMG of Type A Sessions

	(e)	(h)	(s)	(v)	(g)	(c)	(b)	(x)
Entry (e)	0.00	1.00	0.00	0.00	0.00	0.00	0.00	0.00
Home (h)	0.00	0.00	0.70	0.00	0.10	0.00	0.00	0.20
Search (s)	0.00	0.00	0.40	0.20	0.15	0.00	0.00	0.25
View Bids (v)	0.00	0.00	0.00	0.00	0.65	0.00	0.00	0.35
Login (g)	0.00	0.00	0.00	0.00	0.00	0.30	0.60	0.10
Create Auction (c)	0.00	0.00	0.00	0.00	0.00	0.00	0.00	1.00
Place Bid (b)	0.00	0.00	0.00	0.00	0.00	0.00	0.00	1.00
Exit (x)	0.00	0.00	0.00	0.00	0.00	0.00	0.00	0.00

Table 8.2. Matrix of Transition Probabilities for the CBMG of Type B Sessions

	(e)	(h)	(s)	(v)	(g)	(c)	(b)	(x)
Entry (e)	0.00	1.00	0.00	0.00	0.00	0.00	0.00	0.00
Home (h)	0.00	0.00	0.70	0.00	0.10	0.00	0.00	0.20
Search (s)	0.00	0.00	0.45	0.15	0.10	0.00	0.00	0.30
View Bids (v)	0.00	0.00	0.00	0.00	0.40	0.00	0.00	0.60
Login (g)	0.00	0.00	0.00	0.00	0.00	0.30	0.55	0.15
Create Auction (c)	0.00	0.00	0.00	0.00	0.00	0.00	0.00	1.00
Place Bid (b)	0.00	0.00	0.00	0.00	0.00	0.00	0.00	1.00
Exit (x)	0.00	0.00	0.00	0.00	0.00	0.00	0.00	0.00

of session increases. They want to know the maximum capacity (measured as the maximum sustainable load of new sessions arriving per second) under the current SLA, stated as a maximum of 4 seconds average response time for creating new auctions and viewing bids.

The performance model required to answer the questions posed by management is a multiclass QN model with the following six classes: home (h), search (s), view (v), login (g), create (c), and bid (b). Given that requests arrive to the e-business site from a (hopefully) infinite population, an open multiclass QN model is used (see Chapter 13). The model is illustrated in

Table 8.3. Average Visits for Sessions of Type A and B

State	Session A	Session B
V_e	1.000	1.000
V_h	1.000	1.000
V_s	1.167	1.273
V_v	0.233	0.191
V_g	0.427	0.304
V_c	0.128	0.091
V_b	0.256	0.167

Fig. 8.3. There are two queues (i.e., devices) for the Web server (CPU and disk), two for the application server, and two for the database server. The parameters needed to solve an open QN multiclass model are: arrival rates of requests per class and service demands per request per class at each device.

Let γ be the total rate at which sessions are started, and let f_A and f_B be the fraction of type A and type B sessions, respectively. Thus, the arrival rate of requests for each of the eight classes is given by

$$\lambda_{\text{home}} = \gamma \left(f_A \times V_h^A + f_B \times V_h^B \right) \tag{8.4.9}$$

$$\lambda_{\text{search}} = \gamma \left(f_A \times V_s^A + f_B \times V_s^B \right) \tag{8.4.10}$$

$$\lambda_{\text{view}} = \gamma \left(f_A \times V_v^A + f_B \times V_v^B \right) \tag{8.4.11}$$

$$\lambda_{\text{login}} = \gamma \left(f_A \times V_g^A + f_B \times V_g^B \right) \tag{8.4.12}$$

$$\lambda_{\text{create}} = \gamma \left(f_A \times V_c^A + f_B \times V_c^B \right) \tag{8.4.13}$$

$$\lambda_{\text{bid}} = \gamma \left(f_A \times V_b^A + f_B \times V_b^B \right) \tag{8.4.14}$$

where V_r^T is the number of class r requests (i.e., visits) that session type T customers make to the site.

The transition probability matrices for sessions of types A and B, the visit ratio computations, and the arrival rate computations are implemented in the `Chap8-CBMG.XLS` MS Excel workbook. The service demands for the various types of requests are obtained by the analyst by recording and replaying scripts that submit a single type of request. Most load testing tools [2] allow for scripts to be captured, built, and parameterized to simulate loads

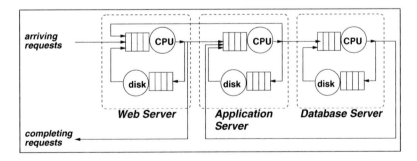

Figure 8.3. QN model for the online auction site.

imposed by *virtual users*. The service demand for a request of type r can be obtained by submitting a typically large number N of requests of that type to the site during a period of time T. Then, the utilization U_i of each device i of the site is measured during that period. The Service Demand Law is then used to compute the service demand $D_{i,r}$ of class r requests at device i as $U_i/(N/T)$. In this type of homogeneous experiments the entire utilization of device i, U_i, is attributed to the type of request that is being parameterized.

By running six controlled experiments, one per workload class, the values of the service demands for all six classes (i.e., h, s, v, g, c, and b) and for all devices (i.e., the CPU and disk at the Web, application, and database servers) are shown in Table 8.4. The first two rows correspond to the Web server devices, the next two correspond to the application server devices, and the last two to the database server devices.

8.5   Using the Performance Model

The response time, R_r, for class r requests in a multiclass open QN is given by (see Chapter 13)

$$R_r = \sum_{i=1}^{K} \frac{D_{i,r}}{1 - U_i} \qquad (8.5.15)$$

where $D_{i,r}$ is the service demand of class r requests at device i, U_i is the total utilization of device i, and K is the total number of devices, as shown in Chapter 13. Note that while $D_{i,r}$ is load-independent and does not change

Table 8.4. Service Demands (in sec) for Auction Site Queuing Model

Device	(h)	(s)	(v)	(g)	(c)	(b)
WS-CPU	0.008	0.009	0.011	0.060	0.012	0.015
WS-disk	0.030	0.010	0.010	0.010	0.010	0.010
AS-CPU	0.000	0.030	0.035	0.025	0.045	0.040
AS-disk	0.000	0.008	0.080	0.009	0.011	0.012
DS-CPU	0.000	0.010	0.009	0.015	0.070	0.045
DS-disk	0.000	0.035	0.018	0.050	0.080	0.090

as the system load varies, U_i is a function of the arrival rate of requests in each of the classes. Specifically,

$$U_i = \sum_{r=1}^{R} U_{i,r} = \sum_{r=1}^{R} \lambda_r \times D_{i,r} \qquad (8.5.16)$$

where R is the number of classes, $U_{i,r}$ is the utilization of device i due to class r requests, and λ_r is the arrival rate of requests of class r. The first summation in Eq. (8.5.16) simply states that the total utilization of a device is the sum of the utilizations due to all classes. The second summation uses the Service Demand Law to express the per class utilizations as a product of arrival rates and service demands. The computations for the multiclass open QN that solves the performance model for the auction site are in the `Chap8-OpenQN.XLS` MS Excel workbook.

To assess the effect on response time under various workload intensities (i.e., the original mandate posed by management), the value of the session start rate γ is varied from 8 sessions/sec to 11.1 sessions/sec. The response times are computed using `Chap8-OpenQN.XLS`. The results are plotted as a function of γ and are shown in Fig. 8.4. Values of γ higher than 11.1 sessions/sec cause the system to become unstable (i.e., the utilization of one of the devices, the database disk, reaches its maximum capacity of 100%). See Exercise 8.2. Thus, the database server disk is the system bottleneck in this case. The graphs of Fig. 8.4 indicate that, except for requests to display the home page, all other requests experience a sharp increase in response time when the rate of session starts exceeds 11 sessions/sec.

Management is interested in the value of γ that will make the average response time for requests to create auctions and place bids to exceed 4 seconds. These two request classes correspond to the upper two curves in Fig. 8.4. The response time curve for the bid requests is slightly above the curve for create auctions. At 10.9 session starts/sec, the maximum acceptable level of 4.0 sec for the average response time is exceeded.

As noted, the system bottleneck is the database server disk. The model shows that when $\gamma = 10.9$ session starts/sec more than 90% of the time is spent at that device. To improve system performance, a new disk could be installed at the database server in order to reduce the load on the bottleneck disk. The performance model can be easily used to analyze this situation.

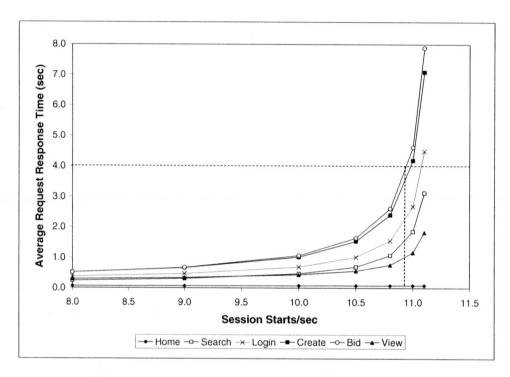

Figure 8.4. Response time at the auction site vs. session start rate.

Another device, representing the second disk at the database server, is added. The original service demand at the database server disk is divided between the two disks. The model is solved again. The results for two disks at the database server are in the `Chap8-OpenQNTwoDisks.XLS` MS Excel workbook. The upgrade causes the response times for the create auction and place bid requests to reduce to 0.489 sec and 0.458 sec, respectively, for a session start rate of 10.96 sessions/sec. This is a dramatic improvement. The addition of a new disk reduces the response time to about 11% of its original value.

8.6   Adding More Servers

The original online auction site assumes that there is a single Web server, a single application server, and a single database server. In general, there may be many identical servers in each tier. Consider a simple case of N_{ws} identical Web servers and a perfect load balancer that sends exactly $1/N_{ws}$ of the traffic to each Web server. Thus, the average arrival rate of requests at each Web server is equal to λ/N_{ws}, where λ is the overall arrival rate of requests to the site. In the following analysis, the application and database servers are ignored. Also, consider a single class of requests. The generalization to multiple classes is straightforward.

One way of modeling the N_{ws}-server situation is to replicate all queues that represent the devices (e.g., CPU, disks) of a Web server in the QN model so that there are N_{ws} of each device in the QN model. Given the assumption of identical Web servers and perfect load balancing, a simpler approach can be followed where all N_{ws} Web servers are represented in the QN model by a single equivalent Web server. The model is constructed so that the average response time of the set of N_{ws} servers is the same as that of the single equivalent server. Figure 8.5 illustrates this situation.

The response time of a request that goes through server j $(j = 1, \cdots, N_{ws})$ of Fig. 8.5-(a) is the same as the response time of the single equivalent Web server of Fig. 8.5-(b) with an arrival rate equal to λ/N_{ws}. (The two models have the same service demands at the CPU and disk devices.) The response time at the single equivalent server of Fig. 8.5-(b) is given by

$$R = \sum_{i=1}^{K} \frac{D_i}{1 - (\lambda/N_{ws})\, D_i} \tag{8.6.17}$$

where K is the number of devices (i.e., CPU ands disk) and D_i $(i = 1, \cdots, K)$ is the service demand of a request at device i. Note that the term $(\lambda/N_{ws})\, D_i$ is the utilization of device i according to the Service Demand Law. The generalization of Eq. (8.6.17) to multiple classes is

$$R_r = \sum_{i=1}^{K} \frac{D_{i,r}}{1 - U_i} = \sum_{i=1}^{K} \frac{D_{i,r}}{1 - \sum_{r=1}^{R}(\lambda_r/N_{ws})\, D_{i,r}} \tag{8.6.18}$$

where R_r is the average response time of class r requests, λ_r is the average arrival rate of requests of class r, and $U_i = \sum_{r=1}^{R}(\lambda_r/N_{ws})\, D_{i,r}$ is the total utilization of device i over all R classes.

As an example, consider the service demands of Table 8.4 and an overall session start rate γ of 11 sessions/sec. Then, consistent with the example in Section 8.3, assume 25% of type A customers and 75% of type customers. Then, the arrival rates for each type of request are given by $\lambda_{home} = 11.0$

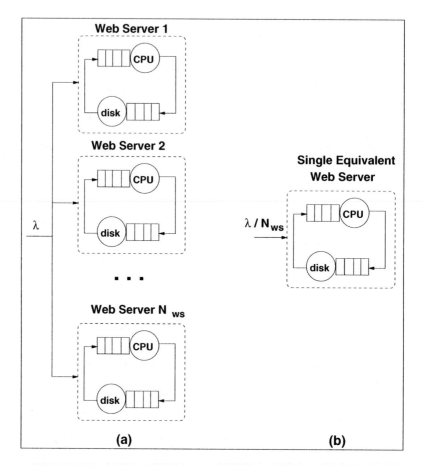

Figure 8.5. Single Web server equivalent to multiple Web servers.

requests/sec, $\lambda_{\text{search}} = 13.71$ requests/sec, $\lambda_{\text{view}} = 2.22$ requests/sec, $\lambda_{\text{login}} = 3.68$ requests/sec, $\lambda_{\text{create}} = 1.10$ requests/sec, and $\lambda_{\text{bid}} = 2.10$ requests/sec.

Consider three Web servers instead of one. The utilizations of the CPU and disk at the single equivalent Web server are given by

$$
\begin{aligned}
U_{\text{CPU}} &= \frac{\lambda_{\text{home}}}{3} \times 0.008 + \frac{\lambda_{\text{search}}}{3} \times 0.009 + \frac{\lambda_{\text{view}}}{3} \times 0.011 + \\
&\quad \frac{\lambda_{\text{login}}}{3} \times 0.060 + \frac{\lambda_{\text{create}}}{3} \times 0.012 + \frac{\lambda_{\text{bid}}}{3} \times 0.015 \\
&= \frac{11.0}{3} \times 0.008 + \frac{13.71}{3} \times 0.009 + \frac{2.22}{3} \times 0.011 +
\end{aligned}
$$

$$\frac{3.68}{3} \times 0.060 + \frac{1.10}{3} \times 0.012 + \frac{2.10}{3} \times 0.015 = 0.167$$

and

$$
\begin{aligned}
U_{\text{disk}} &= \frac{\lambda_{\text{home}}}{3} \times 0.030 + \frac{\lambda_{\text{search}}}{3} \times 0.010 + \frac{\lambda_{\text{view}}}{3} \times 0.010 + \\
&\quad \frac{\lambda_{\text{login}}}{3} \times 0.010 + \frac{\lambda_{\text{create}}}{3} \times 0.010 + \frac{\lambda_{\text{bid}}}{3} \times 0.010 \\
&= \frac{11.0}{3} \times 0.030 + \frac{13.71}{3} \times 0.010 + \frac{2.22}{3} \times 0.010 + \\
&\quad \frac{3.68}{3} \times 0.010 + \frac{1.10}{3} \times 0.010 + \frac{2.10}{3} \times 0.010 = 0.186
\end{aligned}
$$

Then, the response times of each of the six classes of requests at the Web server tier are computed using Eq. (8.6.18) as

$$R_{\text{home}} = \frac{0.008}{1 - 0.167} + \frac{0.030}{1 - 0.186} = 0.0465 \text{ sec}$$

$$R_{\text{search}} = \frac{0.009}{1 - 0.167} + \frac{0.010}{1 - 0.186} = 0.0231 \text{ sec}$$

$$R_{\text{view}} = \frac{0.011}{1 - 0.167} + \frac{0.010}{1 - 0.186} = 0.0255 \text{ sec}$$

$$R_{\text{login}} = \frac{0.060}{1 - 0.167} + \frac{0.010}{1 - 0.186} = 0.0843 \text{ sec}$$

$$R_{\text{create}} = \frac{0.012}{1 - 0.167} + \frac{0.010}{1 - 0.186} = 0.0267 \text{ sec}$$

$$R_{\text{bid}} = \frac{0.015}{1 - 0.167} + \frac{0.010}{1 - 0.186} = 0.0303 \text{ sec}$$

The same approach of replacing all servers of the Web tier by a single equivalent Web server can be applied to the application and database tiers.

8.7 Concluding Remarks

This chapter shows how multiclass open QN models can be used to analyze the scalability of multi-tiered e-business services. The workload of these services is characterized at the user level. User models such as the Customer Behavior Model Graph (CBMG) are used to characterize the way customers navigate through the various e-business functions during a typical visit to an e-commerce site. This user-level characterization can be mapped to a request-level characterization used by QN models. The models are used for capacity planning and performance prediction of various what-if scenarios.

8.8   Exercises

1. Assume that the mix of sessions of type A and B is changed to $f_A = 0.6$ and $f_B = 0.4$. Use Chap8-CBMG.XLS and Chap8-OpenQN.XLS to recompute the arrival rates for each class and solve the performance model again for a total arrival rate of sessions, γ, varying from 8 to 12 session starts/sec.

2. Provide an expression for the maximum theoretical value of the session start rate γ as a function of the service demands, the visit ratios at each state of the CBMGs, and the fraction of sessions of each type. Compute this maximum value of γ for the online auction site. (*Hints:* Remember that the utilization at each device cannot exceed 1. Use Eqs. (8.4.9)-(8.4.14) and Eq. (8.5.16).)

3. Find a system of linear equations whose solution provides the visit ratios for a general CBMG. Assume that the transition probabilities $p_{i,j}$ between states i and j are known for all states.

4. Assume the data of Table 8.3 and assume that 40% of the sessions are of type A and 60% of type B. What is the average number of auctions created per hour assuming that 11 sessions are started per second?

5. Assume that 2% of all auctions created have a winner (i.e., the auctioned item is successfully sold). Assume that an auction with a winner has an average of 50 bids. Also assume that the average price of a sold item is $50.00 and that the auction site receives a 2% commission on the sales price. Given the original configuration described in this chapter, find the maximum possible revenue throughput of the auction site (i.e., the maximum possible revenue generated by the auction site per second).

6. Repeat the previous exercise for the case of a new disk added to the database server.

7. Assume the average visit data of Table 8.3, the service demands of Table 8.4, and a mix of 45% of sessions of type A and 55% of type B. Assume there is only one Web server and one application server.

What is the minimum number of database servers required to support a session start rate of 15 sessions/sec?

8. The Customer Behavior Model Graph (CBMG) for an e-commerce site is shown in Fig. 8.6. As indicated in the figure, the site offers four e-business functions: access the home page (h), search the catalog (s), add to the shopping cart (a), and buy (b). The site functionality is implemented by a single machine that consists of one CPU and one disk. Table 8.5 shows the CPU and disk service demands for each of the four e-business functions offered by the site (i.e., h, s, a, and b). Assume that 10 new sessions are started at the site per second.

- Find the average number of visits per session to each of the four e-business functions.
- What is the arrival rate of requests to execute each of the four e-business functions?
- What is the total utilization of the CPU and of the disk?
- What are the residence times at the CPU and disk for each of the four e-business functions?
- What is the response time of each of the four e-business functions?

Bibliography

[1] D. A. Menascé and V. Akula, "Towards workload characterization of auction sites," *Proc. 6th Workshop Workload Characterization (WWC-6)*, Austin, Texas, October 27, 2003, pp. 12-20.

Table 8.5. Service Demands (in sec) for Exercise 8.8

	Home	Search	Add to Cart	Pay
CPU	0.010	0.015	0.010	0.020
Disk	0.015	0.025	0.015	0.010

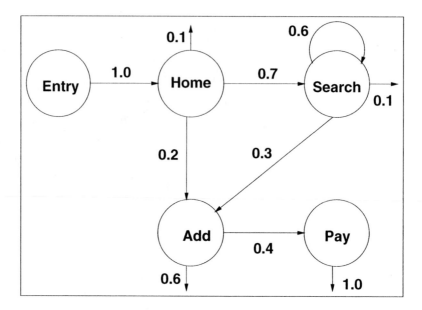

Figure 8.6. Customer Behavior Model Graph (CBMG) for Exercise 8.8.

[2] D. A. Menascé, "Load testing, benchmarking, and application performance management for the Web," *Proc. 2002 Computer Measurement Group Conference*, Reno, Nevada, December 2002, pp., 271–281.

[3] D. A. Menascé, V. A. F. Almeida, R. Riedi, F. Ribeiro, R. Fonseca, and W. Meira Jr., "A hierarchical and multiscale approach to analyze e-business workloads," *Performance Evaluation*, North-Holland, 54 (2003), pp. 33–57.

[4] D. A. Menascé and V. A. F. Almeida, *Scaling for E-Business: Technologies, Models, Performance, and Capacity Planning*, Prentice Hall, Upper Saddle River, New Jersey, 2000.

[5] D. A. Menascé, V. A. F. Almeida, R. Fonseca, and M. A. Mendes, "A methodology for workload characterization of e-commerce sites," *Proc. 1999 ACM Conference on Electronic Commerce*, Denver, Colorado, November 1999, pp. 119–128.

Chapter 9

Case Study V: A Help-Desk Service

9.1 Introduction

Several examples are presented in previous chapters to predict performance when changes occur in an existing system, either with respect to its workload or with respect to its hardware/software platform. Performance engineering involves building performance models for existing workloads and predicting the effects of possible upgrades. Measurements taken on existing workloads are used to obtain the service demands required by performance models, as indicated in Fig. 9.1.

However, in many performance engineering situations, one is confronted with the problem of predicting the performance of future *new* applications. Two types of new applications are considered here:

- *Internally developed products.* In this case, new applications are developed by a team of in-house programmers. This implies that the software structure and the target architecture are likely to be better understood. Parameters that characterize the new workload and hardware are known with higher confidence.

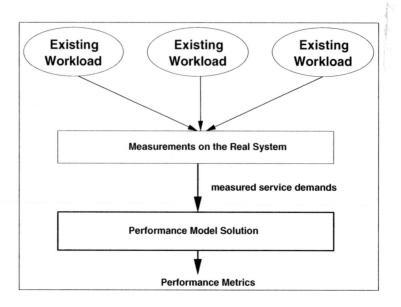

Figure 9.1. Capacity planning for existing workloads.

- *Externally developed products.* In this case, software products are developed by a third party. The software structure and the assumed target architecture are unpredictable. Model parameters are often intuitively estimated with a lower confidence in their accuracy.

Typically, the role of performance is seen as being of secondary importance in the development of new applications [16]. To their detriment, most applications are designed, implemented, and installed without prior or proper performance considerations. All too often, the pressure to release a new product as soon as possible takes precedence over a higher quality, better performing product. "We'll fix the performance problems in the next release" is the PWPF (i.e., penny-wise, pound-foolish) policy. Incorporating performance throughout the design of a new product is both financially beneficial and professionally responsible. As seen throughout this text, performance depends critically upon the particular combination of logical requirements, physical design, and the operating environment. The consequence of this neglect is that many applications are abandoned soon after (and sometimes before!) implementation. Often, such applications require expensive software rewrites and/or an increase in the current system's capacity.

Correct functionality of an application should not be its only requirement. New applications should also be required to meet certain specified
performance service levels. Analysts and designers should be concerned with
the performance requirements of new systems from the beginning stages of
the early design. This requires being able to construct useful performance
models from a relatively high level logical description of an application and
a relatively high level description of a target architecture. This is called
application sizing (AS).

Figure 9.2 depicts the role of application sizing in a typical performance
engineering study. If a new application is to augment existing applications, a
performance model can provide a performance assessment of the new application as well as an estimate of the impact (i.e., the *environmental impact*)
on already existing applications. Therefore, the inputs to the performance
model include the estimated service demands for the new application and
the measured service demands for the existing applications.

The process of constructing software systems that meet performance objectives is called *software performance engineering* (SPE). This term is cred-
ited to Connie Smith in her seminal paper published in 1981 [14]. SPE is

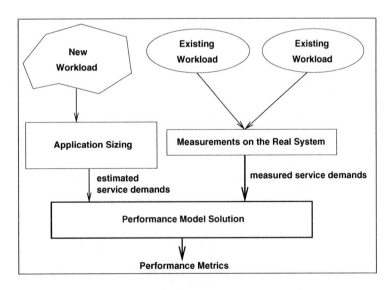

Figure 9.2. Application sizing for new workloads.

used to differentiate those designs that are likely to yield satisfactory performance from those that are likely to suffer serious performance problems. SPE is used to discard those designs that are likely to exhibit unacceptable performance. Such identifications are required before significant time is spent on the applications' development. This chapter illustrates how performance models are used in the SPE process. The presentation is motivated by the design of a new help desk application. The data and models used in the chapter can be found in the `Ch09-Data.XLS`, `Ch09-Data-Mod.XLS`, `Ch09-OpenQN.XLS`, and `Ch09-OpenQN.XLS` MS Excel workbooks.

9.2   The Help Desk Service

Consider a large high technology company with 21,600 employees who have access to a large variety of computing resources. A new help desk application is being designed to provide employees with assistance in solving problems related to their computing environments including operating systems, middleware, and applications. Three main functions of the new system have been identified:

- Access to a database of Frequently Asked Questions (FAQ) about common problems with the computing resources. About 10,000 questions and their detailed answers are stored in the database. These questions are indexed by roughly 500 different keywords. Users search for assistance based on keywords.

- Creation of a help ticket facility. This facility allows users who are not able to obtain satisfactory answers using the FAQ database to submit a description of their problem to a system support person. The problem description is entered into an automated pop up dialog box and is automatically entered into a database of open tickets. Thirty-five percent of the users who access the FAQ database cannot get their problems resolved and create help tickets. Fifteen percent of the users create help tickets every day without even accessing the FAQ database first. Information about a ticket is kept in a diary database for one year for statistical and quality control purposes.

- Tracking and verification of the status of open help tickets. Ten percent of the employees check the status of their open help tickets every day.

The anticipated architecture of the help desk system is depicted in Fig. 9.3. An application server implements the business logic for the FAQ, help tickets, and tracking system. A database server stores all persistent data. These two servers are connected by a 100-Mbps Ethernet LAN. Employees connect to the application server through the company's Intranet. Management is interested in appropriately sizing the database server, the most critical resource of the system, even before the application is fully developed.

9.2.1   Workload Characterization

Table 9.1 presents the data used to characterize the workload intensity of the new application. Daily and peak period activity are given for the three types of requests (i.e., FAQ access, ticket creation, and status inquiries). General

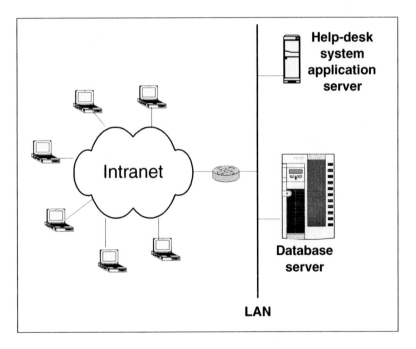

Figure 9.3. Help-desk system.

Table 9.1. Data for Application Sizing

Number of Employees (N_e)	21,600
Number of Questions (N_q)	10,000
Number of Keywords (N_k)	500
% Employees that Access the FAQ DB/day (f_{FAQ})	20%
% Access to FAQ DB During the Peak Period (P_{FAQ})	80%
Avg. Num. Queries to the FAQ DB per Access (N_q)	4
% Tickets Generated After Access to the FAQ DB (t_{FAQ})	35%
% Employees that Create Tickets/Day (f_t)	15%
% Tickets Created During the Peak Period (P_t)	54%
% Employees that Inquire About Ticket Status/Day (f_s)	10%
% Status Inquiries During the Peak Period (P_s)	90%
Peak Period Duration (in seconds) $(\mathcal{T})$	7,200

system activity is also given. The first three sections of the table are related to the three types of requests to be processed by the help desk system.

The average arrival rate of requests during the peak period can be computed for each type of request using the data of Table 9.1 as follows.

$$
\begin{aligned}
\lambda_{FAQ} &= \frac{N_e \times f_{FAQ} \times P_{FAQ} \times N_q}{\mathcal{T}} \\
&= \frac{21,600 \times 0.2 \times 0.8 \times 4}{7,200} = 1.92 \;\; \text{requests/sec} \\
\lambda_{ticket} &= \frac{N_e \times [(f_{FAQ} \times P_{FAQ} \times t_{FAQ}) + (f_t \times P_t)]}{\mathcal{T}} \\
&= \frac{21,600 \times [(0.2 \times 0.8 \times 0.35) + (0.15 \times 0.54)]}{7,200} = 0.41 \;\; \text{requests/sec} \\
\lambda_{status} &= \frac{N_e \times f_s \times P_s}{\mathcal{T}} = \frac{21,600 \times 0.1 \times 0.9}{7,200} = 0.27 \;\; \text{requests/sec} \quad (9.2.1)
\end{aligned}
$$

The arrival rate of new tickets, λ_{ticket}, has two components: one due to employees that access the FAQ database before generating ticket requests and the other due to employees who bypass the FAQ database.

9.2.2   Database Design

A high level conceptual design of the database that supports the new help desk system is shown in Fig. 9.4 using an Entity-Relationship (E-R) model. The are four entities: Question, Keyword, Employee, and Ticket. The Question entity has three attributes: QuestionId, Question, and Answer. QuestionId is the primary key (PK) attribute (i.e., the attribute that uniquely identifies a question). The Keyword entity has two attributes: KeywordId (the primary key) and Keyword. The Employee entity has six attributes: EmployeeId (the primary key), EmpName, EmpSSN, EmpEmail, EmpPhone, and EmpAddress. The Ticket entity has eight attributes: TicketNum (the primary key), EmployeeId, DateOpen, TimeOpen, Status, DateClosed, TimeClosed, and Description.

As shown in Fig. 9.4, these four entities interact with each other via the following relationships:

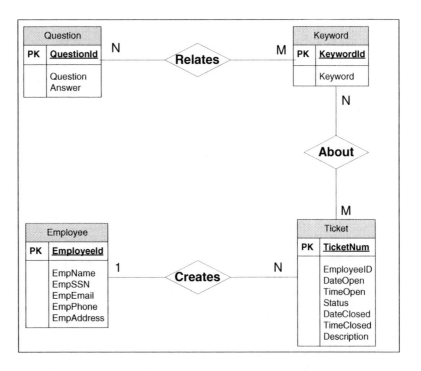

Figure 9.4. Entity-Relationship model for the database design.

- *Relates.* This is a many-to-many (N:M) relationship between Question and Keyword. That is, any specific question may be associated with several keywords. Likewise, any specific keyword may be associated with several questions.

- *About.* This is a many-to-many relationship between Keyword and Ticket. This relationship establishes an association between a ticket and the various keywords that describe a user's problems mentioned in the ticket.

- *Creates.* This is a one-to-many (1:N) relationship between Employee and Ticket. One employee may have several or none open tickets. However, a ticket is associated with only one employee.

The process of translating an E-R model into a relational database design is well-known [12]. Using this process, the E-R model of Fig. 9.4 is mapped into relational tables as indicated in Fig. 9.5. There are seven relational tables. Tables Question, Keyword, Employee, and Ticket have a direct correspondence to the entities of the same name in the E-R model. Tables KeywordQuestion, TicketEmployee, and TicketKeyword have a direct correspondence to the three relationships (i.e, Relates, About, and Creates).

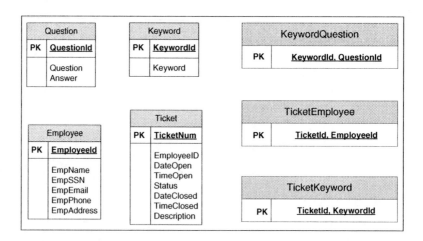

Figure 9.5. Database design for the help-desk system.

The database is a major component of the new help desk system. To appropriately size the database server, it is necessary to estimate the *cardinality* (i.e., the number of rows and row size) of each database table. The cardinality multiplied by the row size gives the total size of each table.

The cardinalities of the Question, Keyword, and Employee tables are easy to estimate. The number of questions in the system (i.e., 10,000), the number of keywords (i.e., 500), and the number of employees of the company (i.e., 21,600) come directly from Table 9.1.

The cardinality of the Ticket table is equal to the number of tickets generated during a typical year. (Recall that a ticket diary is kept in the database server of the previous year's activities.) Using the data of Table 9.1, the number of tickets created per day is equal to $N_e \times (f_{\mathrm{FAQ}} \times t_{\mathrm{FAQ}} + f_t) = 21600 \times (0.2 \times 0.35 + 0.15) = 4,752$. Therefore, 1,734,480 ($= 4,752 \times 365$) tickets are created during one year.

It is assumed that a question is associated with 10 keywords on average. Thus, the cardinality of the KeywordQuestion table has ten times the number of rows as the Question table (i.e., $10 \times 10,000 = 100,000$ rows).

The cardinality of the TicketEmployee table is the same as that of the Ticket table (i.e., 1,734,480 rows). This follows from the one-to-many "Creates" relationship in Fig. 9.4: every ticket corresponds to a single employee. The following additional assumptions are needed to estimate the cardinality of the two remaining tables.

It is also assumed that a ticket has an average of 5 keywords associated to it. Thus, the cardinality of the TicketKeyword table is five times that of the Ticket table (i.e., $5 \times 1,734,480 = 8,672,400$ rows).

The row size for each table is estimated based on the type of columns of each database table. For instance, questions are assumed to be within 1,000 characters and keywords are assumed to be 50 characters long. The row size estimates for all database tables as well as their cardinality is shown in Table 9.2. The last column of this table shows the total size of each table (i.e., the product of the cardinality by the row size).

9.2.3 Transaction Logic

A high-level description of the transaction logic (i.e., the software run on the application server and on the database server) is necessary for the purpose of

Table 9.2. Database Table Data

Database Table	Cardinality	Row Size (bytes)	Total Size (Kbytes)
Question	10,000	1000	10,000
Keyword	500	50	25
Employee	21,600	140	3,024
Ticket	1,734,480	260	450,965
KeywordQuestion	100,000	20	2,000
TicketEmployee	1,734,480	20	34,690
TicketKeyword	8,672,400	20	173,448

estimating service demands for the new help-desk application. The following description is annotated with enough information to allow for the estimation of service demands at each of the system devices (i.e., CPUs and disks). The basic approach for estimating service demands in an SPE study consists of estimating the number of I/Os per transaction. The CPU service demands are estimated as a function of the number of I/Os.

The description of the transaction logic for each of the three transaction types (i.e, FAQs, ticket, and status) is presented here using *Clisspe*, a language developed for the purpose of specifying systems for SPE studies [10]. The Clisspe language allows designers of client/server systems to describe different kinds of objects such as servers, clients, databases, relational database tables, transactions, and networks, as well as the relationships between them. The language also allows the designer to specify the actions executed by each transaction type. The process of computing service demands for each transaction type at each system device from a Clisspe specification is automated in a compiler for the language [10]. The compiler includes a detailed model of the database management system (including query optimization) and provides estimates on the number of I/Os and CPU time for SQL statements.

The transaction logic for a query to the FAQ database is shown in Fig. 9.6. The specification includes two types of Clisspe statements: `loop` and `select`. The `loop` statement indicates the average number of times a loop is executed. The `select` statement indicates the execution of a select statement on a certain database table. Clisspe allows for complex multi-join

```
01  loop #KeywordsPerQuery
02    ! obtain keyword id for a given a keyword
03    select from Keyword where Keyword;
04    ! obtain all question ids for a given keyword id
05    select from KeywordQuestion where KeywordId;
06    ! access the Question table to retrieve selected questions
07    loop #QuestionsPerKeyword
08      select from Question where QuestionId;
09    end_loop;
10  end_loop;
```

Figure 9.6. Transaction logic for query on FAQ database.

select statements. The names of constants are preceded in Clisspe by the "#" sign (e.g., #KeywordsPerQuery). Comments in Clisspe are preceded by the "!" sign. The transaction of Fig. 9.6 loops for a number of times equal to the number of keywords per query. For each keyword x, the corresponding keyword id, $id(x)$, is retrieved using the select statement of line 03. The where clause of a select statement indicates the names of the columns on which a search criteria is based. The select statement of line 05 retrieves question ids (i.e., a total number of #QuestionsPerKeyword) that correspond to the keyword id $id(x)$. For each of them, the actual question is retrieved using the select statement of line 08.

Similarly, the transaction logic for the creation of a new ticket is shown in Fig. 9.7. Two more Clisspe statements are used in this transaction: if-then and update. The if-then statement indicates a probability that the statements in the then clause are executed. The update statement indicates that an update or insertion is performed on a given table. The number of rows modified or inserted is indicated by the num_rows parameter. For example, line 05 inserts one extra row in the Ticket table. The logic of the creation of a new ticket starts by accessing the Employee table to verify the existence of the customer requesting the ticket. In the affirmative case, 1) a ticket is created in the Ticket table (line 05), 2) one row is added to the TicketEmployee

```
01  ! Access the employee table to the verify existence of an employee
02  select from Employee where EmployeeId;
03  if #ProbValidEmployee
04  then ! create ticket record
05        update Ticket num_rows= 1;
06        ! create a record in the TicketEmployee table
07        update TicketEmployee num_rows= 1;
08        ! create records in the TicketKeyword table
09        update TicketKeyword num_rows= #KeywordsPerTicket;
10  end_if;
```

Figure 9.7. Transaction logic for creation of a new ticket.

table (line 07), and 3) as many rows are created in the TicketKeyword table as there are keywords associated with the ticket (line 09).

Finally, and in a manner similar to the FAQ logic and the ticket logic, the transaction logic for a status inquiry transaction is shown in Fig. 9.8. The select statement in line 02 retrieves all ids of the tickets associated with a given employee. Then, the actual tickets are retrieved from the Ticket table by the select statement of line 05. Note that the where clause of this select statement specifies a selection based on both the TicketId and the Status.

```
01  ! Get all ticket ids for the employee
02  select from TicketEmployee where EmployeeId;
03  ! Retrieve all open tickets for the employee
04  loop #TicketsPerEmployee
05    select from Ticket where TicketId, Status
06  end_loop;
```

Figure 9.8. Transaction logic for viewing the status of open tickets.

The values of the various constants used in the specifications of the three types of transactions are assumed to be: #KeywordsPerQuery = 2, #QuestionsPerKeyword = 10,000 / 500 = 20, #ProbValidEmployee = 0.9, #KeywordsPerTicket = 5, and #TicketsPerEmployee = 1,734,480 / 21,600 = 80.3. These constants are used in the transaction's logic (i.e., Figs. 9.6-9.8) to provide the device demands in the ensuing performance model.

9.3   A Performance Model

In order to assess how this new help-desk application performs in a target architecture, a predictive performance model is constructed. Since the workload intensity is specified through arrival rates of the three types of transactions, an open multiclass model is used. The arrival rates are already available from Eq. (9.2.1). The next two sections estimate the number of I/Os and the service demands for each transaction class, respectively.

9.3.1   Estimating the Number of I/Os

The number of I/Os generated by a select statement depends on the type of indexes available for the tables accessed by the select statement. For example, take the Employee table. Assume that a select statement on this table is used to locate an employee with a given Social Security Number (SSN). If there is no index on SSN for this table, the database management system (DBMS) must scan all 21,600 rows of the table until such an employee is found. This is called a table scan, generates many I/Os, and can be quite expensive for large tables. If an index on SSN exists, the row for that employee can be typically located with a small number of I/Os.

An index on a database table T is a table with two columns. Each row is of the form (IndexKey, RowPointer), where the IndexKey is either a particular column value found in one or more rows of T or a concatenation of column values in a specified format. A RowPointer (called rowid in Oracle, rid in DB2, and tid in Ingres) uniquely identifies a row in T. Rows are stored in specific slots within database pages. Pages are stored within operating system files

One of the most common types of indexes, supported by virtually all commercial DBMSs, is the b-tree index [10, 12]. A b-tree has two types of nodes: index nodes and leaf nodes. Index nodes contain entries of the form (key value, pointer). A pointer points to either another index node or to a leaf node. Leaf nodes do not have any pointers. The number of pointers in an index node is called the fanout of the tree. A b-tree has a constant height (i.e., the number of nodes from the root of the tree to any leaf node is constant). Thus, the number of I/Os needed to locate a leaf node in a b-tree index is equal to the height h of the tree. Since the root of the tree will almost certainly be in the buffer pool, the number of I/Os is $h - 1$. The height of a b-tree with fanout k and L entries is given by

$$h = \lceil \log_k L \rceil. \tag{9.3.2}$$

In most cases of practical interest, the height of a b-tree is at most four.

Following the approach given in [10], it is possible to compute the fanout of a b-tree index. The format of a page of a b-tree index is [Header, $(\text{KeyValue}_1, \text{RowPointer}_1), \cdots, (\text{KeyValue}_k, \text{RowPointer}_k), \text{FreeSpace}]$. The fanout k for a b-tree index is computed as

$$k = \left\lfloor \frac{(\text{PageSize} - \text{HeaderSize}_i) \times f_i}{ks + rp} \right\rfloor \tag{9.3.3}$$

where

- PageSize: size in bytes of an index page.

- HeaderSize$_i$: size in bytes of the header field of an index page.

- f_i: percentage of the useful space of an index page that can be used to store keys and row pointers. In an active b-tree, this value is shown to be 71% on average for nodes below the root [11].

- ks: size in bytes of a key for the index.

- rp: size in bytes of a row pointer.

Table 9.3 shows the b-tree indexes assumed for all seven database tables. Tables KeywordQuestion and TicketEmployee have two indexes. The table shows the key size, the fanout computed according to Eq. (9.3.3), and the height of the b-tree computed according to Eq. (9.3.2). The values in the table assume that PageSize = 2048 bytes, HeaderSize = 20 bytes, $f_i = 0.71$, and $rp = 4$ bytes.

Table 9.3. Indexes for the Database Tables

Table	Index Key	Key Size (bytes)	Fanout	Height
Question	QuestionId	10	102	2
Keyword	KeywordId	10	102	2
Employee	EmployeeId	10	102	3
Ticket	TicketId	10	102	4
KeywordQuestion	(KeywordId,QuestionId)	20	59	3
KeywordQuestion	KeywordId	10	102	3
TicketEmployee	(TicketId,EmployeeId)	20	59	4
TicketEmployee	EmployeeId	10	102	4
TicketKeyword	(TicketId,KeywordId)	20	59	4

If a table scan is needed, the number of I/Os is equal to the number of data pages, ndp_T, needed to store a table T. This number is equal to

$$ndp_T = \left\lceil \frac{\text{NumRows}_T}{nrp_T} \right\rceil \qquad (9.3.4)$$

where NumRows_T is the cardinality of table T and nrp_T is the number of rows of table T that can be stored in a data page.

The value of nrp_T is computed as indicated in [10]. The layout of a data page is assumed to be: [Header, RowDirectory, FreeSpace, $\text{Row}_N, \cdots, \text{Row}_1$]. The row directory is a table with as many entries as the number of rows in the page. An entry in this directory contains the byte offset of the row within the page. The slot number of a row in a page is the number of its entry in the row directory. To allow for row size expansion, the free space on a data page is not fully used. A fill factor, f_d, is assumed that indicates the percentage of the page's useful space used to store rows. Thus, nrp_T can be computed as

$$nrp_T = \left\lfloor \frac{(\text{PageSize} - \text{HeaderSize}_d) \times f_d}{(rs_T + rd)} \right\rfloor \qquad (9.3.5)$$

where

- PageSize: size in bytes of a data page

- HeaderSize$_d$: size in bytes of the header field of a data page

- rs_T: size in bytes of a row of table T

- rd: size in bytes of an entry in the row directory

Eq. (9.3.5) assumes that a data page only stores information about a single table. The number of data pages needed to store each of the relational tables according to Eqs. (9.3.4) and (9.3.5) is shown in Table 9.4 assuming PageSize = 2048 bytes, HeaderSize$_d$ = 20 bytes, $f_d = 0.8$, and $rd = 2$ bytes.

The following approximation is used to estimate the number of I/Os due to a select statement:

- Case 1: No index is available. A table scan has to be used. It is assumed that all data pages have to be accessed. The number of data pages is given by Eq. (9.3.4) and shown in Table 9.4.

- Case 2: An index is available. In this case, the number of I/Os is given by the height of the b-tree, computed according to Eq. (9.3.2) and shown in Table 9.3. Since the root of the b-tree is typically in memory, one less I/O is required. The number of I/Os must also be increased by the number of rows retrieved by the select statement. Note that

Table 9.4. Database Table Sizes

Database Table	Row Size (bytes)	Rows per Page	No. of Data Pages
Question	1000	1	10,000
Keyword	50	31	17
Employee	140	11	1,964
Ticket	260	6	289,080
KeywordQuestion	20	73	1,370
TicketEmployee	20	73	23,760
TicketKeyword	20	73	118,800

a worst case scenario is assumed in which none of the selected rows share the same data page.

In the case of an update statement, the number of I/Os is equal to the number of rows updated plus the number of I/Os needed to update any table indexes. The number of I/Os necessary to update an index is assumed to be equal to the height of the b-tree minus 1 for the root being in memory.

Tables 9.5 through 9.7 indicate, for each of the three transactions types, the number of I/Os per select or update statement as well as the total number of I/Os for the transaction types. The first column of each table is the statement number in the specification of the transaction (see Figs. 9.6-9.8). The second column indicates the index that is used to perform the access in case of a select. In case of an update, the second column indicates which indexes have to be updated. The third column indicates the number of times, n_s, that the statement s is executed. This values can be obtained from the specification of the transaction logic in Clisspe. Consider for example the statement of line 08 in the FAQ transaction of Fig. 9.6. This statement is within two loops. The inner loop is executed #QuestionsPerKeyword (i.e., 20) times and the outer loop is executed #KeywordsPerQuery (i.e., 2) times. Thus, the statement in line 08 is executed 40 ($= 20 \times 2$) times. Column 4 indicates the probability, p_s, that the statement s is executed. Consider the statement in line 05 of the create ticket transaction of Fig. 9.7. This statement is executed if the statements in the **then** clause are executed. This happens with probability #ProbValidEmployee (i.e, 0.9). Column 5 indicates the number, ni, of I/Os on the index of column 2 per execution of statement s. This number is obtained as the height of the b-tree for the specific index minus one (because the root of the tree is assumed to be in memory). For example, consider the statement in line 05 of the FAQ transaction of Fig. 9.6. The select statement in that line is on table KeywordQuestion with a selection criterion based on column KeywordId. According to Table 9.3, this database table has an index on the column KeywordId with height 3. Thus, as indicated in Table 9.5, the number of I/Os on the index is 2 ($= 3 - 1$). Column 6 indicates the number, nd, of data page I/Os when statement s is executed. This number is determined based on the number of rows retrieved in each case. Consider again the statement in line 05 of

Table 9.5. Number of I/Os for a FAQ Transaction

Stmt no.	Index	No. of Exec.	Prob. Exec.	Index I/Os	Data I/Os	Total I/Os
3	none	2	1.0	0	17	34
5	KeywordId	2	1.0	2	20	44
8	QuestionId	40	1.0	1	1	80
					Total	158

Table 9.6. Number of I/Os for a New Ticket Transaction

Stmt no.	Index	No. of Exec.	Prob. Exec.	Index I/Os	Data I/Os	Total I/Os
2	EmployeeId	1	1.0	2	1	3.0
5	TicketId	1	0.9	3	1	3.6
7	(TicketId, EmployeeId)	1	0.9	3	1	3.6
7	EmployeeId	1	0.9	3	0	2.7
9	(TicketId, KeywordId)	1	0.9	15	5	18.0
					Total	30.9

the FAQ transaction of Fig. 9.6. The number of rows of the KeywordQuestion retrieved given a specific keyword id is equal to #QuestionsPerKeyword (i.e., 20). Finally, the last column of the table is the total number of I/Os computed as $(ni + nd) \times n_s \times p_s$.

Note that in Table 9.6 there are two rows for statement number 7, an update statement on table TicketEmployee (see Fig. 9.7). This double entry corresponds to the two indexes (one for the index key (TicketId, EmployeeId) and the other for the index key EmployeeId) that exist for the TicketEmployee database table (see Table 9.3). The update statement of line 07 requires one data I/O as reflected on the first line corresponding to statement 7.

All computations described in this section are shown on the Ch09-Data.XLS MS Excel workbook.

Table 9.7. Number of I/Os for a Status Viewing Transaction

Stmt no.	Index	No. of Exec.	Prob. Exec.	Index I/Os	Data I/Os	Total I/Os
2	EmployeeId	1.0	1.0	3	80.3	83.3
5	TicketId	80.3	1.0	3	1.0	321.2
					Total	404.5

9.3.2   Estimating Service Demands

Service demands can be estimated based on the number of I/Os shown in Tables 9.5-9.7. It is assumed that the average disk service time is equal to 8 msec. Measurements are taken at a test server to obtain the average CPU time per I/O. The value obtained in this test experiment is 1.5 msec of CPU time required per I/O.

Using these values one can obtain the matrix of service demands for the database server, assuming one CPU and one disk. For example, consider the FAQ transaction. From Table 9.5, each FAQ transaction requires a total 158 I/Os. Each of these I/Os requires 1.5 msec of CPU time and 8 msec of disk time. Thus, the service demand at the CPU for a typical FAQ transaction is 0.237 ($= 158 \times 0.0015$) seconds. The service demand at the disk is 1.264 ($= 158 \times 0.008$) seconds. The results are shown in Table 9.8, which also indicates the arrival rates per class from Eq. (9.2.1).

Table 9.8. Arrival rates and service demands per class

	FAQ	Create Ticket	Status Viewing
	Arrival rates (tps)		
	1.92	0.41	0.27
	Service Demands (sec)		
CPU	0.237	0.046	0.607
Disk	1.264	0.247	3.236

It can be quickly seen that a configuration with a single disk will not be able to support the new help desk application. The utilization of the disk is

$$
\begin{aligned}
U_{\text{disk}} &= U_{\text{disk,FAQ}} + U_{\text{disk,ticket}} + U_{\text{disk,status}} \\
&= \lambda_{\text{FAQ}} \times D_{\text{disk,FAQ}} + \lambda_{\text{ticket}} \times D_{\text{disk,ticket}} + \lambda_{\text{status}} \times D_{\text{disk,status}} \\
&= 1.92 \times 1.264 + 0.41 \times 0.247 + 0.27 \times 3.236 = 3.4 = 340\%. \, (9.3.6)
\end{aligned}
$$

(A similar calculation for the CPU indicates that the CPU utilization is 64%). Since the disk utilization exceeds 100% by more than a factor of 3, additional or faster disks are required by the database server. A balanced configuration with four disks is analyzed by assigning 25% of the service demand to each of four disks. The solution of the model is obtained with the help of the Ch09-OpenQN.XLS MS Excel workbook.

The results obtained with the model show that the response times for the three classes are: $R_{\text{FAQ}} = 9.1$ sec, $R_{\text{ticket}} = 1.8$ sec, and $R_{\text{status}} = 23$ sec. The model also shows that the utilization of each disk is 85% (i.e., 340% / 4) and the utilization of the CPU is 64%. The disks are still the bottleneck and are thus responsible for most of the response time. Management finds these response times to be high. In particular, a response time of 23 seconds for the view status of open tickets is considered to be unacceptable. An analysis of the number of I/Os for this transaction type shows that an average of 404.5 I/Os are required (see Table 9.7). An analysis of the transaction logic in Fig. 9.8 shows that the problem is that the TicketEmployee relation keeps all tickets, open and closed, for the past 365 days. From Table 9.2, this generates an average of 80.3 ($= 1,734,480/21,600$) tickets per employee stored in the Ticket table. However, the vast majority of these tickets are already closed and are of no interest to this transaction. Given these observations, the performance analyst suggests to the system designers that they create a new database table to archive the closed tickets. Then, the Ticket table would contain only open tickets. Given that tickets do not stay open for more than three days on average, this change in the database design and application logic would have a significant performance impact. The following results are obtained by redoing the computations, assuming that tickets are only kept active for three days: 1) the total number of I/Os to create a new ticket goes from 30.9 to 23.7 and 2) the total number of I/Os required to view the status of open tickets goes down from 404.5 to 4.64. The effect of this change in the overall response time is remarkable. The new response times are $R_{FAQ} = 3.91$ sec, $R_{ticket} = 0.6$ sec, and $R_{status} = 0.11$ sec. The results of the new computations for the service demands under the modified database design are shown in the `Ch09-Data-Mod.XLS` MS Excel workbook. The corresponding results from the open QN model are in `Ch09-OpenQN.XLS`.

9.4 Techniques for SPE

As the example discussed in the previous sections indicate, SPE techniques should be integrated into the software development life cycle. Several methodologies for software development have been proposed and used successfully in the software industry. Consider, for example, the waterfall model, introduced by Boehm [2], which decomposes the software development life cycle into five main phases: requirement analysis and specification, system design, program design, program coding, and system testing. Figure 9.9 illustrates these various phases and the relationships between each phase.

The requirement analysis and specification phase describes the problem to be solved by the new software. As a result of this phase, two types of requirements are generated: functional and non-functional requirements. The functional requirements describe the activities that the new system is supposed to perform. The non-functional requirements include SLAs on response times, throughputs, and availability, as well as a specification of the target hardware/software platform. This includes a specification of the processors, storage devices, operating system, database management system, transaction processing monitors, and middleware, of the target hardware/software platform.

The system design phase describes the solution to the problem specified in the previous requirements phase. The system is decomposed into modules and pseudo code for each module is generated. The relationship between modules is established and the type of data used by each module is specified. The number of invocations per module are derived from the system design. This allows a first approximation of the service demands. Performance predictions obtained with SPE data collected during this phase should be within 30% of the actual performance of the fully implemented application [16].

The third phase, program design, describes the mechanisms that best implement the solution. Algorithms and data structures are specified in this phase. Each of the modules resulting from the system design phase is mapped into one or more programs. A complete specification of each transaction is given in this phase. This specification is generally given in some form of pseudocode and is independent of the target programming language. Clisspe is appropriate in this phase. More precise estimates of the transaction service demands may be obtained in this phase since the number of I/O operations and/or DBMS calls can be derived from the transaction descriptions. The accuracy of the predictions obtained in this phase is expected to be in the range 15 to 20% [16].

The actual implementation occurs during the program coding phase. This phase is used to refine the I/O and CPU service demands for the various transactions as they are implemented. Test experiments of each transaction type on the target software/hardware platform are possible. These yield accurate values for I/O and CPU demands.

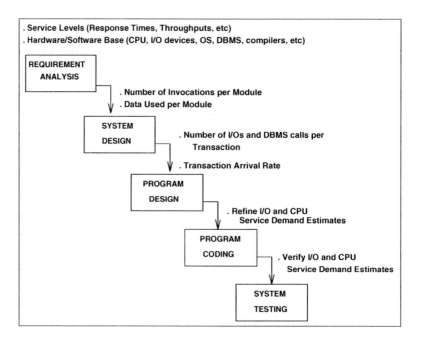

Figure 9.9. Waterfall model of software development.

The final phase is system testing. In this phase, an overall verification of I/O and service demand estimates is performed. Validation of performance predictions made by the models is possible.

Each phase of the software development life cycle increases the level of accuracy of the service demand estimates. The initial models developed during the early stages of the design can only be expected to provide gross order-of-magnitude performance predictions. Gunther indicates that progressively more accurate data can be captured in each phase of the software development life cycle using the spiral methodology for software development [6].

9.4.1 Obtaining Data for SPE

Application sizing involves cooperating with people from several departments, mainly the developers. This may pose problems of a managerial nature. Developers must appreciate and value the importance of SPE so that they assign it enough importance and give priority to it [16]. Numerous approaches can be used to obtain cooperation from people that should provide data for SPE [7] .

The primary difficulties in obtaining the proper data may arise from [16]:

- Inadequate communication between designers and performance engineers.

- Low priority given by designers to obtain and provide SPE data.

- Inadequate understanding by designers of the relevant SPE data. Some data parameters are more important than others and designers are not always aware of which parameters will affect performance most. For instance, the volume of physical I/O is an important factor in determining service demands at the peripherals and at the CPU.

It should also be realized that not all transactions will have a relevant impact on performance. In fact, as observed by practitioners [5, 15], more than 80% of user requests result in less than 20% of the transactions. This 80-20 rule of thumb calls for giving priority to obtaining SPE data for the 20% most frequent transactions.

Whenever there is a high degree of uncertainty over the value of a given service demand or workload intensity parameter, the use of best-case and worst-case analysis is appropriate [15]. In the process of refining the estimates, resources that have the greatest impact on performance should be identified. It is important to concentrate most of the effort in trying to obtain better estimates for the key parameters [15].

The service demand, $D_{i,r}$, of class r transactions at device i is estimated as follows in an SPE study:

$$D_{i,r} = \sum_{s \in \mathcal{S}_{i,r}} n_s \times p_s \times D_{i,r}^s \qquad (9.4.7)$$

where

- $\mathcal{S}_{i,r}$ is the set of all statements that contribute to the service demand of transactions of class r at device i

- n_s is the average number of times that statement s is executed

- p_s is the probability that statement s is executed

- $D_{i,r}^s$ is the average service demand at device i for class r due a single execution of statement s

The flow of control of each transaction or application determines the average number of times that a certain portion of the code is executed. For example, the analysis of a specification of a transaction in Clisspe allows for the easy computation of n_s and p_s through the nesting of loops and through branching statements [10]. $D_{i,r}^s$ can be obtained from simple experiments.

9.5 Concluding Remarks

It has been observed that minor modifications to the design of a transaction or to the physical database design can lead to performance improvements by factors of 5 to 10 [5, 6]. Modifications are much less costly during the system design phase than in the system testing phase. Performance problems found in the late phases of the software development life cycle may require major software rewrites to correct them.

As shown in this chapter, software performance engineering (SPE) techniques should be employed in any software development project to allow for alternative designs to be compared before any major implementation effort takes place. The main difficulty in applying SPE techniques lies in estimating service demands for nonexisting applications. Service demand estimates become increasingly accurate as the software development life cycle progresses. During early stages of development, even gross order-of-magnitude predictions are useful. To properly size an application, effort should be concentrated on the subset of transactions that will be most frequently invoked.

An analysis of why SPE is not yet fully integrated into software engineering practices can be found in [9]. This analysis raises five possible causes for the fact that software systems rarely meet their performance requirements: 1) lack of scientific models that must be used in software development, 2) little performance education in the vast majority of undergraduate Computer Science curricula, 3) shortage of Information Technology workers leading to poorly trained and performance naive software developers, 4) the "single-user" mindset of many programmers who ignore contention issues, and 5) the "small database" mindset that leads programmers to fail to consider the effects of queries to large databases. In an attempt to bridge the gap between the performance and software engineering communities, and between industry and academia, special purpose workshops are now appearing. Interested readers are encouraged to read the proceedings of these events to find out the latest on SPE theory and practice [1, 13, 17].

9.6 Exercises

1. Consider the flow of control given in the Clisspe specification of Fig. 9.10 where a, b, ...,e are statements. Give an expression for the service demand D_i at device i as a function of the service demands D_i^a through D_i^e.

2. A bank is considering the development of a new application to support a phone banking system. Customers will be allowed to dial into the bank and choose, from a touch-tone phone, one of two transactions: access balances and transfer funds. If a customer chooses to access balances, they can select from their checking or savings accounts. If a customer selects to transfer funds, they are asked to specify the type of account (checking or savings) from which to transfer funds

```
01  loop n
02     if p
03     then a;
04             loop m
05                 b; c;
06             end_loop;
07     else d;
08     end_if;
09     e;
10  end_loop;
```

Figure 9.10. Pseudo code for Exercise 9.1.

and the type of account into which the funds are to be transferred. Customers are then requested to enter the amount to be transferred. A transfer confirmation number is returned to the customer. Estimate the service demands for this new application and plot the response time as a function of the arrival rate. For which value of the arrival rate will the response time exceed 1 sec? Make the following assumptions:

- The computer system that will support the application consists of a CPU and two identical disks. The average service time on these disks is 8 msec.

- Every customer has an identification number (ID) and a pin number that must be entered before any transaction can take place.

- The following files will be managed by the application: CUSTOMERS (contains one record per customer, keyed by the customer ID), CHK_ACCOUNTS (for checking accounts, keyed by the customer ID), SAV_ACCOUNTS (for saving accounts, keyed by customer ID), HISTORY (contains an audit trail of all transactions executed, keyed by transaction date).

- Two physical I/O operations are needed on average to retrieve a record given a customer ID from the CUSTOMER, CHK_AC-COUNTS, or SAV_ACCOUNTS files.

- A total of 60% of the calls are expected to request only balance information on one account, 30% are expected to first request balance information on one account and then request a funds transfer involving this account and another account, and 10% are expected to request funds transfer without requesting balance information first.

- The CPU time per I/O is equal to 0.5 msec.

Make and justify any additional assumptions, including the file distributions on the two disks.

3. A university wants to develop a new application to allow students to register by phone at the beginning of each semester. Students dial a special number and are requested to enter their student identification number and the codes of the specific courses for which they wish to register. Conduct an application sizing to compare the following two alternatives:

- *Minimal consistency check.* In this alternative, the only consistency checks that are performed on-line involve verifying if the selected courses are indeed being offered. The student's registration request is recorded into a file in the order of arrival to be processed later in batch mode. No registration confirmation is issued by the on-line transaction.

- *Complete registration processing.* In this case, besides checking availability of the courses requested, the transaction should check whether the student has completed all prerequisites and whether the selected classes are still open. If any class is not open, the student should be placed on a waiting list. A registration confirmation number is given back to the student by the system.

Use the same assumptions about the hardware platform of Exercise 9.2. Make and justify any other assumptions necessary to determine the service demands of the new on-line registration application. Assume that the university has 25,000 students, that the system will be on-line for phone registration 24 hours a day for two weeks, and that each student requests enrollment in five courses on average. Determine the average response time for each of the two cases (i.e., minimal consistency check and complete registration processing).

4. Use the `Ch09-Data.XLS` MS Excel workbook to recompute the number of I/Os generated by the status viewing transaction if an index on EmployeeId is not available for the TicketEmployee table.

Bibliography

[1] S. Balsamo, P. Inverardi, and B. Selic, *Proceedings of the Third ACM Workshop on Software and Performance*, Italy, Rome, July 24-27, 2002.

[2] B. Boehm, "Software engineering," *IEEE Tr. Computers*, vol. C-25, no. 12, December 1976, pp. 1226-1241.

[3] H. Gomaa and D. A. Menascé, "Performance engineering of component-based distributed software systems," in *Performance Engineering: State of the art and current trends,* ed. A. Scholz, LNCS State of the Art Series, vol. 2047, Springer-Verlag, May 2001.

[4] H. Gomaa and D. A. Menascé, "Design and performance modeling of component interconnection patterns for distributed software architectures," *Proc. 2000 Workshop on Software and Performance*, Ottawa, Canada, September 17-20, 2000.

[5] A. Grummitt, "A performance engineer's view of systems development and trials," *Proc. Computer Measurement Group Conf.*, Nashville, Tennessee, December 9-13, 1991, pp. 455-463.

[6] J. Gunther, "Capacity planning for new applications throughout a typical development life cycle," *Proc. Computer Measurement Group Conf.*, Nashville, Tennessee, December 9-13, 1991.

[7] L. Lipner, "Sizing applications by cooperating: Mastering the unmeasurable," *Proc. Computer Measurement Group Conf.*, Nashville, Tennessee, December 9-13, 1991, pp. 977-985.

[8] D. A. Menascé, H. Ruan, and H. Gomaa, "A framework for QoS-aware software components," *Proc. 2004 ACM Workshop on Software and Performance,* San Francisco, California, January 14, 2004.

[9] D. A. Menascé, "Software, performance, or engineering?" *Proc. ACM 2002 Workshop on Software and Performance,* Rome, Italy, July, 2002.

[10] D. A. Menascé and H. Gomaa, "A method for design and performance modeling of client/server systems," *IEEE Tr. Software Eng.,* vol. 26, no. 11, November 2000, pp. 1066–1085.

[11] P. O'Neil, *Database Principles, Programming, Performance,* Morgan Kauffman, San Francisco, California, 1994.

[12] R. Ramakrishnan and J. Gehrke, *Database Management Systems,* 3rd ed., McGraw Hill, Boston, Massachusetts, 2003.

[13] C. U. Smith, P. Clements, and C. M. Woodside, *Proceedings of the First ACM Workshop on Software and Performance,* Santa Fe, New Mexico, October 12-16, 1998.

[14] C. U. Smith, "Increasing information systems productivity by software performance engineering," *Proc. CMG XII International Conf.,* December 1981.

[15] C. U. Smith, "Software performance engineering tutorial," *Proc. Computer Measurement Group Conf.,* Orlando, Florida, December 10-14, 1990, pp. 1311-1318.

[16] C. Wilson, "Performance engineering - better bred than dead," *Proc. Computer Measurement Group Conf.,* Nashville, Tennessee, December 9-13, 1991, pp. 464-470.

[17] C. M. Woodside, H. Gomaa, and D. A. Menascé, *Proceedings of the Second ACM Workshop on Software and Performance,* Ottawa, Canada, September 17-20, 2000.

Part II
The Theory of
Performance Engineering

Chapter 10

Markov
Models

10.1 Introduction

The goal of Part I of this text has been to provide a framework from which
system designers can reason about performance related concepts and apply
these concepts throughout the entire life cycle of IT systems. Performance
terms (e.g., response time, throughput, availability, reliability, security, scalability, extensibility) have been introduced. Performance results based on
the operational laws (e.g., Utilization Law, Service Demand Law, Forced
Flow Law, Little's Law, Interactive Response Time Law) have been defined
and applied to sample systems. Simple performance bounding techniques
and basic queuing network models have been established as tools to evaluate and predict system performance.

The goal of Part II is to motivate, establish, and explain the basic building blocks and underpinnings of the analytical techniques introduced in Part
I. It is one thing to be able to apply effectively any given performance tool.
This is an important and quite useful skill. However, the deeper level is to
be able to understand what is inside "the black box" and what comprises

the various tools. By understanding the inner workings and assumptions of the modeling techniques, they can be applied more reliably and with more confidence. The analogy with an automobile is appropriate. Learning the functionality of, and how to drive, an automobile is a useful skill that requires practice to improve. However, it is by learning how the engine operates, and the likely resulting consequences if not properly used, that makes one a truly effective (and safe!) driver. Part II provides such a basis.

This chapter describes Markov models. These models are the fundamental building blocks upon which most of the quantitative analytical performance techniques are built. Markov models themselves are based on state space diagrams. Such diagrams are powerful descriptive tools. They are both intuitive and natural, understandable by novices, yet rich enough to challenge experts. As will be seen, they can be applied across a wide range of applications. Markov models are often used to explain the current interactions between various system components. However, they can also be used for predictive purposes. Once a model is constructed, parameterized, and validated, it can be altered to predict (hopefully, accurately) what would happen if various aspects of the system's hardware or of the system's workload change. Thus, Markov models can be used for both descriptive and predictive purposes.

Basically, Markov models are relatively simple to create, solve, and use. To create such a model, the first step is to construct the state diagram by identifying all possible states that the modeled system may find itself. Second, the state connections (i.e., transitions) must be identified. Third, the model must be parameterized by specifying the length of time spent in each state once it is entered (or, equivalently, the probability of transitioning from one state to another within the next time period). After the model is constructed, it is "solved." This involves abstracting a set of linear "balance" equations from the state diagram and solving them for long term "steady state" probabilities of being in each system state. Once solved, the model can be validated and used for various performance prediction applications. Each of these aspects will be described and intuitively motivated via examples in this chapter.

The chapter outline is as follows. In Section 10.2, the overall context of system modeling is presented. In Section 10.3, two motivating examples are introduced which will be used throughout the chapter. Model construction is described in Section 10.4, followed by model solution techniques in Section 10.5. The interpretation and effective use of Markov models is the topic of Section 10.6. Section 10.7 provides the assumptions and limitations of Markov models. Topics that are somewhat beyond the basics are mentioned in Section 10.8. The chapter concludes by summarizing the primary points and suggesting several illuminating exercises.

10.2 Modeling Context

Consider the modeling paradigm described in Fig. 10.1. The initial step in evaluating the performance of a system is to construct a contextual model of the system being considered. The focus within this chapter is on basic Markov models. However, other models are also viable, including prototype models, simulation models, and analytical models. Prototype models involve the physical construction of a scaled version of the actual system and executing a typical workload on the prototype. The primary advantage is one of accuracy and the primary disadvantage is one of cost. Simulation models involve the writing of detailed software programs which (hopefully accurately) emulate the performance of the system. Trace driven simulations take a script from a typical workload (e.g., arrival times of requests, details of the request) and then mimic the behavior of the actual system. Simulations tend to be less accurate, yet much less costly than prototype models. Analytical models, which include Markov models, involve capturing the key relationships between the architecture and the workload components in mathematical expressions. For instance, instead of relying on a specific execution trace to provide the time between successive requests to a disk, a random variable from a representative distribution is used. The operational laws introduced in Chapter 3 are examples of mathematical relationships used by analytical models. The key advantages of such models are that they capture and provide insight into the interdependencies between the various system components. They are also flexible, inexpensive, and easily changed. The disadvantages are a lack of detail and they tend to be more difficult to validate. Thus, there are tradeoffs between the various modeling techniques.

Within the context of Markov models, model construction consists of three steps: state space enumeration, state transition identification, and pa-

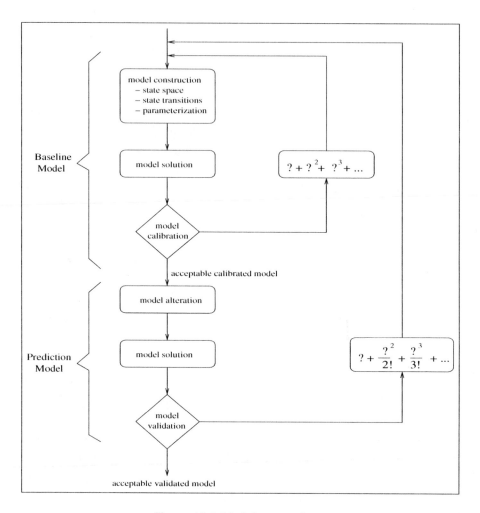

Figure 10.1. Modeling paradigm.

rameterization. State space enumeration involves specifying all reachable states that the system might enter. State transition identification indicates which states can be directly entered from any other given state. Parameterization involves making measurements and making assumptions of the original system. As will be seen with Markov models, model construction involves identifying not only all the states in which the system may find itself, but also how long one typically stays in each state and which states are immediately accessible from any given state. Measurements, intuition,

published results from the literature, and various assumptions are often used
to parameterize a model.

After model construction, the model must be "solved." With prototype
models, this involves running an experiment on the newly constructed hardware and monitoring its performance. With simulation models, this involves
running a software package (i.e., the simulator) and recording the emulated
performance results. With analytical models, this involves solving a set of
mathematical equations and interpreting the performance expressions correctly.

Once constructed and solved, the model must be calibrated. Calibration
involves comparing the performance results obtained from the model against
those observed in the actual system. Any discrepancies are resolved by
questioning each component and each assumption in the modeling process.
Often, one must return to a previous step since modeling errors may be
discovered during calibration. It is not atypical to cycle between the various
steps before an acceptable model is found. Because of this iterative process
of refining a model to match the actual system, the resulting model is an
acceptable calibrated model. It is calibrated to match the actual system on
a finite set of previously observed (i.e., baseline) performance measures.

Once calibrated, the baseline model can be used for the important purpose of prediction. As in a model of the weather, a model which only matches
previously observed weather patterns is of little use. One is much more interested in (and impressed by) a model that can predict what will happen
before it actually does. The same is true in computer modeling. By altering
the baseline model (e.g., adding in future growth rate parameters, changing
the hardware parameters to reflect anticipated upgrades) and then re-solving
the model, one can predict the future performance of a system prior to its
occurrence.

The final step is one of accountability – a validity check that the prediction is accurate. Too often, this step is ignored. It is more normal to
make a prediction, collect a consultant's fee, go on to another project (or
vacation!), and never return to see if one's prediction actually came true.
Time is usually the reason. Often there is a significant time lag of several
months between when a prediction is made and when the new system is
implemented. Also, it is common that assumptions change from when a pre-

diction is originally done. In either case, the performance prediction analyst rarely faces final accountability. However, it is only by completing this final check, by answering those harder series of questions when the predictions are incorrect, and by returning to a previous step in the modeling process, that the overall modeling paradigm is improved and the resulting prediction model is truly validated.

Markov models are described in the context of this overall modeling paradigm. They form an analytical modeling technique that is the basis of other analytical techniques (e.g., queuing network models, Petri net models). Emphasis will be placed on the model construction, solution, and prediction steps. Two motivating examples will be used to demonstrate the methodology.

10.3   Motivating Examples

Two motivating examples are presented. One is an analogy utilizing a situation outside the normal world of computing. The other is an extension of an earlier example in Chapter 3. The first uses finite probabilities as state transitions (i.e., the discrete state, discrete transition case), while the second uses flow rates as state transitions (i.e., the discrete state, continuous transition case).

Motivating Example #1: *Random Walk Through England*

As a graduation present by his mother, consider a lad who is given a year to spend in England. The only condition is that every day at 3:00 p.m., the lad must use his mobile phone to call his mother and simply let her know where he is and what he is doing. After only a couple of months, the mother deduces a definite pattern to her son's behavior. (See Fig. 10.2.)

- The lad is always doing something in one of four locations: drinking in a Leeds pub, sightseeing in London, kayaking in the Lake District, or hiking in the Yorkshire moors.

- If the lad is in a Leeds pub, he is either likely to go sightseeing in London the following day (60%), or he will still be found in a Leeds pub (40%).

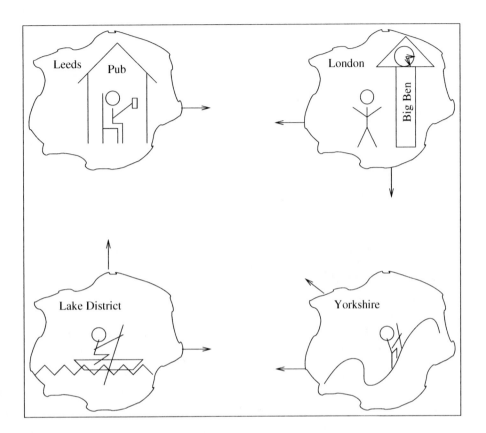

Figure 10.2. England example.

- If the lad is in London, he is likely to be found in a Leeds pub the following day (20%) or will decide to go hiking in the Yorkshire moors (80%).

- Once found in the Lake District, there is very good chance that the lad will still be found kayaking the following day (70%), but there is a possibility that he will next be found hiking the moors (20%) or back in a Leeds pub (10%).

- When found hiking in the moors, there is a good chance that he will still be hiking the following day (50%). However, he sometimes goes to a Leeds pub (30%) and sometimes decides to go kayaking in the Lake District (20%) the following day.

Simply knowing these patterns, the mother finds herself having to answer certain questions of others.

- *Father's question:* What percentage of days is the son actually not drinking in Leeds?

- *Lake District relatives' question:* Once the son finishes a day of kayaking in the Lake District, how long will it typically be before he returns?

- *Policeman's question:* How many days each month can the bobbies expect to see the son driving to London after drinking in Leeds?

- *Kayak renters' question:* How many visits each month does the son typically visit their shop and typically how long does the son keep their kayak out each visit?

Situations such as this are directly analogous to ones encountered when analyzing the performance of computer systems. For example, the workload characterization of a typical web user is very much like that of the lad. After visiting one web site (e.g., an online airline reservation site), the user is likely, with known probabilities, to visit certain other related web sites (e.g., a rental car site, a hotel reservation site). Knowing usage patterns can help answer a broad range of performance-related questions (e.g., throughput expectations, anticipated response time behavior, projections for capacity planning activities).

Motivating Example #2: *Database Server Support*

Consider a computer system with one CPU and two disks used to support a database server. (Note: This example is a slight modification of Example 3.2 given in Chapter 3.) Users remotely access the server and typically login, perform some database transactions, and logout. The following specifics are known about the system. (See Fig. 10.3.)

- To guarantee acceptable QoS levels, at most two users are allowed to be logged onto the database system at any one time. However, the demand for the system is sufficiently high so that it may be assumed that exactly two users are logged onto the system at all times. That

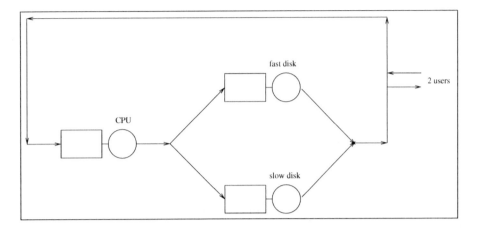

Figure 10.3. Database server example.

is, as soon as one user completes the requested transaction and exits the system, another eager user is waiting to log on.

- Each transaction alternates between using the CPU and using a disk. The particular disk required by a user depends on the transaction, since different transactions access different files, and different files reside on different disks.

- The two disks are of different speeds, with the faster disk being twice as fast as the slower disk.

- A typical transaction requires a total of 10 sec of CPU time.

- Transactions are equally likely to find the files they require on either disk.

- If a transaction's files are found on the fast disk, it takes an average of 15 seconds to access all the requested files.

- If a transaction's files are found on the slow disk, it takes an average of 30 seconds to access all the requested files.

From the above known observations, the system analyst is faced with answering various questions.

- *User's question:* What response time can the typical user expect?

- *System administrator's question:* How near capacity (i.e., what is the utilization) of each of the system resources?

- *Company president's question:* If I can capture Company X's clientele, which will likely double the number of users on my system, I will need to also double the number of active users on my system. What new performance levels should I spin in my speech to the newly acquired customers?

- *Company pessimist's question:* Since I know that the fast disk is about to fail and all the files will need to be moved to the slow disk, what will the new response time be?

Though both examples might appear at first glance to be somewhat dissimilar, they can be modeled and solved using the same Markov modeling approach.

10.4   Model Construction

As illustrated in Fig. 10.1, the first step when modeling a system is to construct the model. This involves enumerating the state space, identifying the state transitions, and parameterizing the model. These tasks are illustrated on both of the motivating examples.

Random Walk Through England: *Model Construction*
In order to construct the model, the first task is to enumerate all the possible states in which the system might find itself. This is the system's "state space." In this example, there are four possible states in which the mother may find the lad:

- Drinking in a Leeds pub (state 1)

- Sightseeing in London (state 2)

- Kayaking in the Lake District (state 3)

- Hiking in the Yorkshire moors (state 4)

This state space is mutually exclusive and collectively exhaustive. This means that it is not possible to be in more than one state at a time (i.e., mutually exclusive) and that it is not possible to be in any state other than in one of the identified states (i.e., collectively exhaustive).

The second task is to identify the state transitions. These are the "single step" transitions. That is, if the system (i.e., the lad) is in one state, identify those possible states that the system may find itself during the immediately following time step (i.e., the next day). In the current example, the following are the possible state transitions.

- If in state 1 (i.e., drinking in a Leeds pub), the lad may find himself next in state 1 or state 2 (i.e., still drinking in a Leeds pub or sightseeing in London).

- If in state 2 (i.e., sightseeing in London), the lad may find himself next in state 1 or state 4 (i.e., drinking in a Leeds pub or hiking in the Yorkshire moors).

- If in state 3 (i.e., kayaking in the Lake District), the lad may find himself next in states 1, 3, or 4 (i.e., drinking in a Leeds pub, still kayaking in the Lake District, or hiking in the Yorkshire moors).

- If in state 4 (i.e., hiking in the Yorkshire moors), the lad may find himself next in state 1, 3, or 4 (i.e., drinking in a Leeds pub, kayaking in the Lake District, or still hiking the Yorkshire moors).

The third task is to parameterize the model. This involves assigning weights to each of the state transitions. These weights indicate the flow rates (i.e., how likely it is to transition) from one state directly to another. In the example, these weights are given as probabilities.

- State 1 goes directly back to state 1 with probability 0.4 and to state 2 with probability 0.6.

- State 2 goes directly to states 1 or 4 with probabilities 0.2 and 0.8, respectively.

- State 3 goes directly to states 1, 3, or 4 with probabilities 0.1, 0.7, and 0.2, respectively.

- State 4 goes directly to states 1, 3, or 4 with probabilities 0.3, 0.2, and 0.5, respectively.

The complete model can be represented by the Markov state diagram shown in Fig. 10.4.

Database Server Support: *Model Construction*

(Refer to Fig. 10.3.) As in the England example (and in all Markov models), the first task is to enumerate all possible system states. In the England example, it was very straightforward. There was one user (i.e., the lad) who could be in one of four states. In this example, things are slightly more complex since there are two users, each of which could be at any of the three devices (i.e., CPU, fast disk, slow disk). However, by adopting the notation (X, Y, Z), where X denotes the number of users currently at the CPU, Y denotes the number of users at the fast disk, and Z denotes the number of users at the slow disk, the six possible states are:

- State $(2, 0, 0)$: both users are currently requesting CPU service.

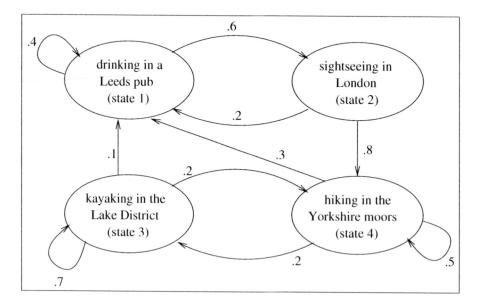

Figure 10.4. Markov model of the England example.

- State $(1, 1, 0)$: one user is requesting CPU service and the other is requesting service from the fast disk.

- State $(1, 0, 1)$: one user is requesting CPU service and the other is requesting service from the slow disk.

- State $(0, 2, 0)$: both users are requesting service from the fast disk.

- State $(0, 1, 1)$: one user is requesting service from the fast disk while the other user is requesting service from the slow disk.

- State $(0, 0, 2)$: both users are requesting service from the slow disk.

Often, a crucial part of the modeling process is to come up with good notation to describe each state. In this example, the tuple (X, Y, Z) is selected. Alternatively, the notation (A, B) could have been used, where A denotes the location of the first user (i.e., either at the CPU, fast disk (FD), or slow disk (SD)), and B denotes the location of the other user. This would lead to the following nine states: (CPU, CPU), (CPU, FD), (CPU, SD), (FD, CPU), (FD, FD), (FD, SD), (SD, CPU), (SD, FD), and (SD, SD). However, since both users are (statistically) identical, states such as (CPU, FD) and (FD, CPU) are equivalent and can be combined. Thus, although the resulting performance measures would be identical, the latter notation leads to a more complex model. Similarly, consider the notation $(I, J; K, L; M, N)$, where I denotes the user ID number (i.e., either -, 1, or 2) of the job, if any, which is waiting in the queue to use the CPU, and where J denotes the user ID number (i.e., either -, 1, or 2) of the job, if any, which is currently using the CPU. (Similarly, K and L denote the user ID number of any user waiting for and using the fast disk, respectively. M and N, likewise, represent the state at the slow disk.) This notation leads to 12 feasible states: $(2, 1; -, -; -, -)$, $(1, 2; -, -; -, -)$, $(-, 1; -, 2; -, -)$, $(-, 2; -, 1; -, -)$, $(-, 1; -, -; -, 2)$, $(-, 2; -, -; -, 1)$, $(-, -; 2, 1; -, -)$, $(-, -; 1, 2; -, -)$, $(-, -; -, 1; -, 2)$, $(-, -; -, 2; -, 1)$, $(-, -; -, -; 2, 1)$, and $(-, -; -, -; 1, 2)$. This notation not only distinguishes between user 1 and user 2 as in the previous notation, but also distinguishes between which user is getting service at a device and which user is waiting for service, if they are both at the same device. These latter two notations would be necessary in a multi-class model (see Chapter 12) where the characteristics of the users and the queues are different. However, such notations only add complexity here. The point of note is that the choice of notation to represent each state is important.

The second task is to identify the state transitions. These follow straight-forwardly.

- If both users are at the CPU (i.e., in state $(2,0,0)$), one of the users could complete service at the CPU and go to either the fast disk (i.e., to state $(1,1,0)$) or to the slow disk (i.e., to state $(1,0,1)$).

- If one of the users is at the CPU and the other is at the fast disk (i.e., in state $(1,1,0)$), either the user at the fast disk could finish and return to the CPU (i.e., back to state $(2,0,0)$), or the user at the CPU could finish and go to either the fast disk (i.e., to state $(0,2,0)$) or to the slow disk (i.e., to state $(0,1,1)$).

- Similarly, if one of the users is at the CPU and the other is at the slow disk (i.e., in state $(1,0,1)$), either the user at the slow disk could finish and return to the CPU (i.e., back to state $(2,0,0)$), or the user at the CPU could finish and go to either the fast disk (i.e., to state $(0,1,1)$) or to the slow disk (i.e., to state $(0,0,2)$).

- If both users are at the fast disk (i.e., in state $(0,2,0)$), one of the users could finish and return to the CPU (i.e., to state $(1,1,0)$).

- If one of the users is at the fast disk and the other is at the slow disk (i.e., in state $(0,1,1)$), either the user at the fast disk could finish and return to the CPU (i.e., to state $(1,0,1)$), or the user at the slow disk could finish and return to the CPU (i.e., to state $(1,1,0)$).

- If both users are at the slow disk (i.e., in state $(0,0,2)$), one of the users could finish and return to the CPU (i.e., to state $(1,0,1)$).

The third model construction task, parameterization, involves assigning weights to each of the state transitions. In the England example, these weights are given as simple transition probabilities. In the database server example, these are given as "flow rates," which is a generalization of transition probabilities. For example, suppose the system is in state $(2,0,0)$ where

both users are at the CPU. In this state, the CPU is actively working, satisfying user requests at a rate of 6 transactions per minute (since it takes an
average of 10 seconds to satisfy one typical user's CPU demand). Of the 6
transactions per minute that the CPU can fulfill, half of these transactions
next visit the fast disk (i.e., to state $(1, 1, 0)$) and half next visit the slow
disk (i.e., to state $(1, 0, 1)$). Therefore, the weight assigned to the $(2, 0, 0)$
$\rightarrow (1, 1, 0)$ transition is 3 and the weight assigned to the $(2, 0, 0) \rightarrow (1, 0, 1)$
transition is also 3.

As another example, consider state $(1, 1, 0)$ where one user is executing
at the CPU and the other user is using the fast disk. As before, the user
at the CPU leaves at rate 6, half the time going to the fast disk and half
the time going to the slow disk. Thus, the weight assigned to the $(1, 1, 0)$
$\rightarrow (0, 2, 0)$ transition is 3 and the weight assigned to the $(1, 1, 0) \rightarrow (0, 1, 1)$
transition is 3. Also, since the fast disk satisfies user requests at a rate of
4 transactions per minute (since it takes an average of 15 seconds to satisfy
one typical user's fast disk demand) and since all users at the fast disk next
visit the CPU, the weight assigned to the $(1, 1, 0) \rightarrow (2, 0, 0)$ transition is 4.

Using similar reasoning, it is relatively straightforward to parameterize
all possible state transitions. The complete model can be represented by the
Markov state diagram shown in Fig. 10.5.

10.5   Model Solution

The model solution step is surprisingly the most straightforward and easiest
aspect of the entire modeling paradigm. Robust software solution packages
based on the mean value analysis (MVA) technique (and provided with this
text) are available.

Given a parameterized Markov model, the definition of "model solution"
is to find the long term (i.e., the "steady state") probability of being in any
particular state. This refers to the probability of taking a random snapshot
(or checkpoint) of the system and finding the system in a particular state.
Steady state is independent of the initial starting state of the system. For
instance, consider the England example. If the lad starts out, say, kayaking
in the Lake District, there is a good chance (i.e., 70%) that if a snapshot is
taken one day later, he will be still be kayaking the following day. However,
this does not mean that on some given *random* day, say, two months from

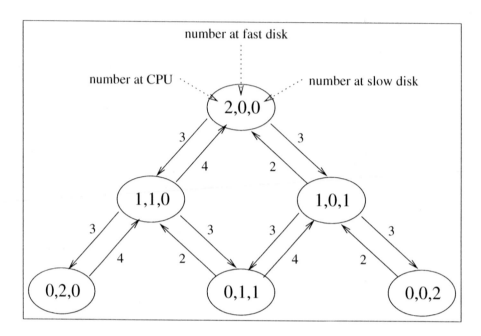

Figure 10.5. Markov Model of the database server example.

now, that the lad will be found kayaking with a probability of 70%. The steady state solution is the overall probability of being in each system state, independent of the starting state.

To find these steady state probabilities, a set of linear "balance" equations is formed. In general, there is one balance equation for each system state. Thus, given a Markov model with N states, there are N desired unknowns (i.e., the steady state probability of being in each state) along with N linear equations. The solution is a straightforward linear algebra math problem. This is illustrated on each of the two motivating examples.

Random Walk Through England: *Model Solution*

Reconsider Fig. 10.4. The balance equation for each system state is one that represents the fact that the overall "flow" into each state must equal the overall flow out of each state. That is, on average, the lad must walk out of the Leeds pub as many times as he walks in. (The consequences of any other result would reduce the system to one where the lad is either always or never in the pub.)

Let P_i represent the (steady state) probability of being in state i. Thus, P_1 represents the probability that the lad is in the Leeds pub, P_2 represents the probability that the lad is sightseeing in London, P_3 represents the probability that the lad is kayaking in the Lake District, and P_4 represents the probability that the lad is hiking in the Yorkshire moors.

Consider, for example, state 2 (i.e., sightseeing in London). The flow into state 2 is represented by the single incoming arc to state 2 in Fig. 10.4. That is, the only way to get to London is to first be in state 1 (i.e., in Leeds, which has a steady state probability of P_1) and then to select (with probability 0.6) to go the London the next day. Thus, the flow into state 2 is $0.6 \times P_1$. The flow out of state 2 is represented by the two outgoing arcs from state 2. That is, the only way to leave state 2 is to first be in state 2 (i.e., with probability P_2) and then to select (with probability $0.2 + 0.8$) to leave state 2 the next day. Thus, the flow out of state 2 is simply $(0.2 + 0.8) \times P_2 = P_2$. Therefore, the overall (flow in equals flow out) balance equation for state 2 is:

$$0.6 \times P_1 = P_2.$$

Similarly, consider state 1. The flow into state 1 is represented by the sum of the incoming arcs from the other three states, that is, $(0.2 \times P_2) + (0.1 \times P_3) + (0.3 \times P_4)$. The flow out of state 1 is represented by the single outgoing arc, $0.6 \times P_1$. Thus, the overall balance equation for state 1 is:

$$(0.2 \times P_2) + (0.1 \times P_3) + (0.3 \times P_4) = 0.6 \times P_1.$$

[Note: The self loop from state 1 back to itself represents the probability that the lad remains in Leeds on successive days. While important, this probability can be inferred from the other outgoing transition probabilities from state 1. That is, since the sum of the outgoing probabilities to other states is 0.6, the remaining 0.4 proportion must be a self-loop. The self loop does not directly exhibit itself in the state's balance equation. The reason is that, strictly speaking, it appears as both an incoming and outgoing arc on opposite sides of the state's balance equation, thereby cancelling each other out. Expressed differently, there are four incoming arcs to state 1, and two outgoing arcs, including the self loop. Therefore, the full balance equation for state 1 is:

$$(0.4 \times P_1) + (0.2 \times P_2) + (0.1 \times P_3) + (0.3 \times P_4) = (0.4 \times P_1) + (0.6 \times P_1).$$

which is equivalent to the previous equation. Thus, for simplicity and without loss of generality, self loops can be ignored when creating the balance equations.]

The balance equations for Fig. 10.4, for states 1, 2, 3, and 4, respectively, are:

$$(0.2 \times P_2) + (0.1 \times P_3) + (0.3 \times P_4) = 0.6 \times P_1$$
$$0.6 \times P_1 = P_2$$
$$0.2 \times P_4 = 0.3 \times P_3$$
$$(0.8 \times P_2) + (0.2 \times P_3) = 0.5 \times P_4.$$

Thus, there are four equations and four unknowns. At this point, it is tempting to infer that simple algebra can be used to uniquely solve for the desired results P_1, P_2, P_3, and P_4. However, there is one small issue. This set of equations (and, in general, any set of balance equations from a Markov model) is under-determined. This means that any three of the equations can be used to infer the fourth equation. (To verify this remark, simply add the left hand sides of the first three equations and set it equal to the sum of the right hand sides of the first three equations. By simplifying, the result is equal to the fourth equation. Thus, the fourth equation can be inferred from the first three.) This means that one of the equations is redundant, is unnecessary, and can be eliminated.

To find the unique solution, one of the equations is replaced by the "conservation of total probability equation" which states that the system must be in one of the system states. That is,

$$P_1 + P_2 + P_3 + P_4 = 1.0$$

By replacing, say, the fourth equation with this conservation equation, the resulting set of (now independent) four equations in four unknowns is:

$$(0.2 \times P_2) + (0.1 \times P_3) + (0.3 \times P_4) = 0.6 \times P_1$$

$$0.6 \times P_1 = P_2$$
$$0.2 \times P_4 = 0.3 \times P_3$$
$$P_1 + P_2 + P_3 + P_4 = 1.0$$

The linear algebraic solution to this set of equations is:

$$P_1 = \frac{55}{208} = 0.2644$$
$$P_2 = \frac{33}{208} = 0.1586$$
$$P_3 = \frac{48}{208} = 0.2308$$
$$P_4 = \frac{72}{208} = 0.3462$$

These represent the steady state probabilities of the lad being in each of the four states, 1 through 4, respectively.

Database Server Support: *Model Solution*

Reconsider Fig. 10.5. Mimicking the previous example, the "flow in = flow out" balance equation for each of the six states can be formed easily. The only difference is that, instead of arc weights being probabilities as in the previous example, the arc weights in the database server example are based on the service rates of the devices. [Note: Steady state probabilities do not depend on the *absolute* value of the arc weights, but rather on their *relative* values. That is, by multiplying all of the arc weights by any constant, the steady state values remain the same.] The balance equations for the six states, (2,0,0), (1,1,0), (1,0,1), (0,2,0), (0,1,1), and (0,0,2), are:

$$(4 \times P_{(1,1,0)}) + (2 \times P_{(1,0,1)}) = 6 \times P_{(2,0,0)}$$
$$(3 \times P_{(2,0,0)}) + (4 \times P_{(0,2,0)}) + (2 \times P_{(0,1,1)}) = 10 \times P_{(1,1,0)}$$
$$(3 \times P_{(2,0,0)}) + (4 \times P_{(0,1,1)}) + (2 \times P_{(0,0,2)}) = 8 \times P_{(1,0,1)}$$
$$3 \times P_{(1,1,0)} = 4 \times P_{(0,2,0)}$$
$$(3 \times P_{(1,1,0)}) + (3 \times P_{(1,0,1)}) = 6 \times P_{(0,1,1)}$$
$$3 \times P_{(1,0,1)} = 2 \times P_{(0,0,2)}$$

As before, one of the equations is "redundant." Therefore, by arbitrarily replacing the last equation by the conservation of total probability equation,

$$P_{(2,0,0)} + P_{(1,1,0)} + P_{(1,0,1)} + P_{(0,2,0)} + P_{(0,1,1)} + P_{(0,0,2)} = 1.0$$

the six equations in six unknowns can be uniquely solved to find the steady state probabilities for the six states:

$$P_{(2,0,0)} = \frac{16}{115} = 0.1391$$

$$P_{(1,1,0)} = \frac{12}{115} = 0.1043$$

$$P_{(1,0,1)} = \frac{24}{115} = 0.2087$$

$$P_{(0,2,0)} = \frac{9}{115} = 0.0783$$

$$P_{(0,1,1)} = \frac{18}{115} = 0.1565$$

$$P_{(0,0,2)} = \frac{36}{115} = 0.3131$$

10.6   Model Interpretation

Although knowing the steady state probabilities of being in each system state is technically "the solution" of the model, it is not especially helpful unless these probabilities can be properly interpreted and used to answer more practical questions. This is illustrated in the context of the two motivating examples.

Random Walk Through England: *Model Interpretation*

In Section 10.3, four motivating questions were posed that can now be answered.

- *Father's question:* What percentage of days is the son actually not drinking in Leeds?

  Answer: 74%. Since the steady state probability of being in state 1 (i.e., drinking in a Leeds pub)is 0.2644 (i.e., 26%), the rest of the time the lad is sightseeing, kayaking, or hiking.

- *Lake District relatives' question:* Once the son finishes a day of kayaking in the Lake District, how long will it typically be before he returns?

  Answer: 3.33 days. The mean time between entering a particular state (i.e., the state's "cycle time") is the inverse of the steady state probability of being in that state. Since the steady state probability of being in state 3 (i.e., kayaking in the Lake District) is 0.2308, the cycle time between successive entries into state 3 is $\frac{1}{0.2308} = 4.33$ days. Since it takes one day for the lad to kayak, the time from when he finishes a day of kayaking until he typically starts kayaking again is $4.33 - 1 = 3.33$ days. (Note: To grasp an intuitive sense of this relationship of cycle time being the inverse of the steady state probability, consider a hypothetical five state model where the lad cyclically visits each of the five states for one day each. Since each of the five states is equivalent, the lad is in each state 20% of his time. Thus, the cycle time between successive entries to each state is $\frac{1}{0.20} = 5$ days and the time between leaving a state until the state is reentered is $5 - 1 = 4$ days.)

- *Policeman's question:* How many days each month can the bobbies expect to see the son driving to London after drinking in Leeds?

  Answer: 4.76 days. Consider a 30 day month. The steady state probability of being found drinking in a Leeds pub (i.e., state 1) on any particular day is 0.2644. Thus, out of 30 days, $30 \times 0.2644 = 7.93$ days will find the lad drinking. However, since the lad decides to go to London with only probability 0.6 after a day of drinking in Leeds, the bobbys can expect to find the lad on the road to London $7.93 \times 0.6 = 4.76$ days each month.

- *Kayak renters' question:* How many visits each month does the son typically visit their shop and typically how long does the son keep their kayak out each visit?

  Answer: 2.08 visits per month, keeping the kayak an average of 3.33 days each visit. The only way to enter state 3 (i.e., kayaking) from another state is from state 4 (i.e., hiking). That is, the lad arrives to the Lake District only after hiking in the moors. The steady state probability of being found hiking on any particular day is 0.3462, or

$30 \times 0.3462 = 10.39$ days each month. However, after hiking for a day, the lad only decides to go kayaking the next day with probability 0.2. Therefore, the lad typically starts a new visit to the Lake District $10.39 \times 0.2 = 2.08$ times each month. This answers the first part of the question. To answer the second part, since the steady state probability of being found kayaking is 0.2308 on any particular day, the lad can be expected to be kayaking $30 \times 0.2308 = 6.92$ days out of each month. If he makes only 2.08 new visits each month, the duration of each visit is typically $\frac{6.92}{2.08} = 3.33$ days. An alternative, yet equivalent, approach to the solution is to note that the lad kayaks for only one day with probability 0.3. He kayaks for exactly two days with probability 0.7×0.3. He kayaks for exactly three days with probability $(0.7)^2 \times 0.3$ and, in general, he kayaks for exactly n days with probability $(0.7)^{n-1} \times 0.3$. The average time spent kayaking per visit is, thus, $\sum_{i=1}^{\infty} i(0.7)^{i-1}(0.3) = 3.33$ days. (It is only a numerical coincidence in this particular example that the answer to the Lake District relatives' question is the same as the answer to the second part of the kayak renters' question.)

Putting aside the analogy for a moment, the first question (i.e., the father's question) relates to the device utilization of the resources within the system being modeled. This is the probability of being in certain system states. The second question (i.e., the Lake District relatives' question) relates to the response time of the system. This is the time that it takes to return to a state after leaving the state. The third and fourth questions (i.e., the policeman's and the kayak renters' questions) relate to system throughput. This is the rate of traffic along certain arcs within the model.

Database Server Support: *Model Interpretation*

Also in Section 10.3, four motivating questions were posed relative to the database server example that can now be answered.

- *User's question:* What response time can the typical user expect?

  Answer: 44.24 seconds per user transaction. The response time can be found via application of the Interactive Response Time Law, $R =$

$\frac{M}{X_0} - Z$, introduced in Chapter 3. (See Fig. 3.4) With the think time Z being 0 (i.e., there is no think time component with the submitted user transactions in this example), the response time, R reduces to the simple ratio of the average number of users in the system, M, to the system throughput, X_0. In this example, the number of users in the system is fixed at two. The throughput of the system, measured at the CPU, is the product of its utilization and its service rate. The CPU is utilized in states $(2,0,0), (1,1,0)$, and $(1,0,1)$. Knowing the solution to the steady state probabilities of these states, the CPU utilization is $P_{(2,0,0)} + P_{(1,1,0)} + P_{(1,0,1)} = 0.1391 + 0.1043 + 0.2087 = 0.4521$. The service rate of the CPU is 6 transactions per minute. Therefore, the throughput measured at the CPU is $0.4521 \times 6 = 2.7126$ transactions per minute, resulting in an average response time of $\frac{2}{2.7126} = 0.7373$ minutes per transaction, which equals $0.7373 \times 60 = 44.24$ seconds per user transaction.

- *System administrator's question:* How near capacity (i.e., what is the utilization) of each of the system resources?

  Answer: The CPU's utilization is 0.4521, the fast disk's utilization is 0.3391, and the slow disk's utilization is 0.6783. These are found as direct sums of the relevant steady state probabilities. The CPU's utilization was calculated above. The fast disk is utilized in states $(1,1,0), (0,2,0)$, and $(0,1,1)$. Thus, the utilization of the fast disk is $P_{(1,1,0)} + P_{(0,2,0)} + P_{(0,1,1)} = 0.1043 + 0.0783 + 0.1565 = 0.3391$. In like manner, the utilization of the slow disk is $P_{(1,0,1)} + P_{(0,1,1)} + P_{(0,0,2)} = 0.2087 + 0.1565 + 0.3131 = 0.6783$.

- *Company president's question:* If I can capture Company X's clientele, which will likely double the number of users on my system, I will need to also double the number of active users on my system. What new performance levels should I spin in my speech to the newly acquired customers?

  Answer: The overall system throughput is predicted to go from 2.7126 transactions per minute to 3.4768 transactions per minute (i.e., up 28%). The user response time, however, is predicted to go from 44.24 seconds per transaction to 69.03 seconds per transaction (i.e., up 56%).

These numbers are the result of resolving the model with four active users instead of the original two. The original system had a state space diagram of six states. The new system model has 15 states. The precise model construction, solution, and interpretation is left as an exercise. However, these new performance predictions will help prepare the company president for what to expect.

- *Company pessimist's question:* Since I know that the fast disk is about to fail and all the files will need to be moved to the slow disk, what will the new response time be?

  Answer: 65.00 seconds per transaction (i.e., an increase of 47%). This number is a result of resolving the model with only two devices, the CPU and the slow disk. The resulting state diagram has only three states, one with both users at the CPU, one with a single user at both the CPU and the slow disk, and one with both users at the slow disk. By formulating and solving the balance equations, the resulting steady state probabilities are 0.0769, 0.2308, and 0.6923, respectively. This leads to a CPU utilization of 0.3077 and a system throughput of 1.8462 transactions per minute. By applying the Interactive Response Time Law, a resulting response time of 65.00 seconds per transactions is predicted. By anticipating such effects, the company can prepare for such possibilities.

The above two examples demonstrate how to use the knowledge of the steady state probabilities to arrive at more meaningful and more useful performance metrics. As seen, such models can be applied to predict the performance of anticipated new scenarios. Utilization of resources, system throughput, and user response times are the primary performance metrics of interest.

10.7   Model Assumptions and Limitations

Markov models are quite robust. However, there are key assumptions and resulting limitations. The primary ones are highlighted below.

- *Memoryless Assumption:* It is assumed that all the important system information is captured in the state descriptors of a Markov model. That is, simply knowing which state the system is in, uniquely defines all relevant information. This leads to subtleties. For instance, this implies that it doesn't matter how one arrives (i.e., by which path) to a particular state, only that one is currently in the particular state. Previous history of previous states visited is irrelevant when determining which state will be visited next. This assumption also implies that the length of time that the system is in a particular state, by continually taking self loops, is irrelevant. The only thing that is important in determining which state will be visited next is that the system is in a particular state at the current time. This places a nontrivial burden on choosing an appropriate notation for the state descriptor. For instance, if the jobs have different characteristics, this must be evident from the state descriptor. If the order in which jobs arrive to the systems makes a difference, this, too, must be captured in the state descriptor. Knowing the current state alone is sufficient. This is the defining Markov characteristic and any other information is unnecessary as it applies to the system's future behavior. That is, previous history can be forgotten. This explains the term "memoryless" as it applies to Markov models.

- *Resulting Limitation:* Because everything must be captured in the state descriptor, Markov models are susceptible to state space explosion. For example, if there are 10 customers at the CPU, each one unlike any other customer (i.e., a multi-class model) and the CPU is scheduled first-come-first-serve (i.e., where the order of customer arrivals is important), then the state descriptor of the CPU must contain which customer occupies which position in the queue. This leads to $10! = 3,628,800$ different possibilities/states for the CPU alone. However, if the customers behave similarly (i.e., a single class model) and the CPU is scheduled round robin with a short quanta (i.e., where the order of customer arrivals is not important), then the state descriptor of the CPU can be represented by a single number (i.e., the number of customers present). Having large state spaces implies additional complexity and a potential loss of accuracy.

- *Exponential Assumption:* Without going into depth, the exponential distribution is the only continuous distribution that is memoryless. For instance, suppose the average amount of CPU time required by a customer is 10 seconds. Knowing that the customer has already received 5 seconds worth of CPU time but not yet finished (i.e., previous history, which is irrelevant under the Markov memoryless assumption), the average amount of CPU time still needed is again 10 seconds. This is analogous to flipping a fair coin. The average number of flips to get a head is two. However, knowing that the first flip resulted in a tail, the average number of flips still needed to get a head is again two. Thus, Markov models assume that the time spent between relevant events, such as job arrival times and job service times, is exponentially distributed.

- *Resulting Limitation:* To mitigate the limitation imposed by exponential assumptions, the concept of phases (or stages) can be introduced. For example, again suppose that the average amount of CPU time required by a customer is 10 seconds. By partitioning the total service requirement into two phases of service (i.e., each phase being exponentially distributed with an average of five seconds), the CPU state for each customer can be decoupled into two states. That is, each customer can be in either its first stage of service or in its second stage of service. This technique opens up a whole host of other distributions (i.e., not simply exponential) that can be closely approximated. However, the price is again a potential state space explosion since the state descriptors must now contain this additional phase information.

Theoretically, Markov models can be constructed to any desired level of accuracy. The price is the complexity of the state descriptors and the resulting size of the state space. Practically, beyond a few thousand states, the computational complexity is limiting and any intuitive benefits are lost. Thus, the system analyst is faced with a tradeoff of determining an acceptable level of aggregation that affords both accuracy and efficiency.

10.8 Generalized Birth-Death Models

A class of Markov models, called *birth-death* models, is quite useful and exhibits a general solution. Given that the system is in a particular state k, indicating k customers in the system, one of two events can occur that can cause the system to leave state k. Either a *birth* occurs, where the arrival of another customer causes the system to enter state $k+1$, or a *death* occurs, where the departure of a customer causes the system to enter state $k-1$. Given that the current state is state k, assume that the arrival rate (i.e., the birth rate) of new customers is λ_k and that the completion rate (i.e., the death rate) of customers is μ_k. That is, the birth and death rates are state-dependent. See the state transition diagram of Fig. 10.6.

Following the solution approach of the previous sections, the system of flow balance equations is

$$\text{flow in} = \text{flow out}$$
$$\mu_1 P_1 = \lambda_0 P_0$$
$$\lambda_0 P_0 + \mu_2 P_2 = \lambda_1 P_1 + \mu_1 P_1$$
$$\vdots$$
$$\lambda_{k-1} P_{k-1} + \mu_{k+1} P_{k+1} = \lambda_k P_k + \mu_k P_k$$
$$\vdots$$

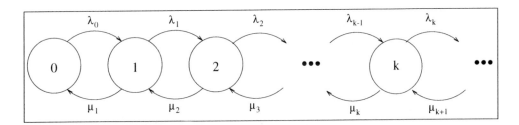

Figure 10.6. Generalized birth-death state-space diagram.

After some algebraic manipulation and using the conservation of total probability, $P_0 + P_1 + P_2 + \cdots = 1$, the solution is obtained as

$$P_0 = \left[\sum_{k=0}^{\infty} \prod_{i=0}^{k-1} \lambda_i / \mu_{i+1} \right]^{-1} \tag{10.8.1}$$

where the first term in the summation is defined to be 1. Therefore, the generalized steady-state solution, for any birth-death system, for being in any particular state k is:

$$P_k = \left[\sum_{k=0}^{\infty} \prod_{i=0}^{k-1} \lambda_i / \mu_{i+1} \right]^{-1} \prod_{i=0}^{k-1} \lambda_i / \mu_{i+1} \quad \text{for } k = 0, 1, 2, \ldots \tag{10.8.2}$$

From this generalized steady-state solution, obtaining expressions for other performance measures is straightforward:

$$\text{utilization} = P_1 + P_2 + \cdots = 1 - P_0 \tag{10.8.3}$$

$$\text{throughput} = \mu_1 P_1 + \mu_2 P_2 + \cdots = \sum_{k=1}^{\infty} \mu_k P_k \tag{10.8.4}$$

$$\text{queue length} = 0P_0 + 1P_1 + 2P_2 + \cdots = \sum_{k=1}^{\infty} k P_k \tag{10.8.5}$$

$$\text{response time} = \frac{\text{queue length}}{\text{throughput}} = \frac{\sum_{k=1}^{\infty} k P_k}{\sum_{k=1}^{\infty} \mu_k P_k} \tag{10.8.6}$$

10.9   Beyond the Basics

The approach adopted in this chapter has been to present Markov models in their simple, straightforward, and practical (i.e., vanilla) versions. The basics have been presented and applied via examples. There are many subtle points and extensions that are not addressed in depth here. To do so would require an entire text, developing and then expanding upon a richer set of basic definitions. To gain some perspective, the following definitions and facts are briefly presented. They are illustrated in the context of Fig. 10.7.

- *Recurrent state:* A recurrent state in a Markov model is a state that *can* always be revisited in the future after leaving the state, regardless of the subsequent states visited. In the figure, states A, B, C, F, G, H, and I are recurrent states.

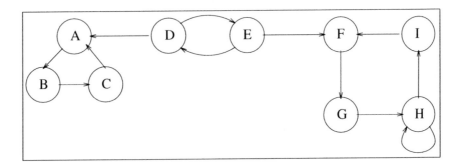

Figure 10.7. Generic Markov model.

- *Transient state:* A transient state in a Markov model is a state where, depending on the subsequent states visited, it *may not* be possible to return to the state after leaving it. States D and E are transient, since, say, after leaving state D, the system enters state A. It is then not possible to ever return to states D or E.

- *Fact:* Each state in the Markov model is either recurrent or transient. The set of recurrent states and the set of transient states is mutually exclusive and collectively exhaustive.

- *Fact:* All states reachable from a recurrent state are recurrent.

- *Fact:* All states that can reach a transient state are transient.

- *Periodic state:* A periodic state is a recurrent state where the system can only return to the periodic state in p, 2p, 3p, ..., steps, where p is the period, is as large as possible, and where $p > 1$. States A, B, and C are periodic with a period of 3. The self loop around state H prohibits it (and also states F, G, and I) from being periodic. For instance, state F can return to itself in 4, 5, 6, 7, 8, 9, ..., steps. Since p must be greater than 1, F is not periodic since it can return to itself in either 4 or 5 steps.

- *Fact:* All states reachable from a periodic state are periodic with the same period.

- *Chain:* A chain is a set of recurrent states that can all reach each other. The set is as large as possible. States A, B, and C form one chain. States F, G, H, and I form another chain. The diagram is, thus, a multi-chain Markov model.

- *Discrete state, discrete transition:* A Markov model is discrete state, discrete transition if the number of states is countable and the transitions between states can only take place at known intervals. The Markov model of the England example (i.e., Fig. 10.4) is an example of a discrete state, discrete transition Markov model. It has four states and transitions can only take place on known (i.e., day) boundaries. The arc weights in these models are probabilities.

- *Discrete state, continuous transition:* A Markov model is discrete state, continuous transition if the number of states is countable and the transitions between states can take place at any time, driven by an exponential distribution. The Markov model of the database server example (i.e., Fig. 10.5) is an example of a discrete state, continuous transition Markov model. It has six states and transitions can take place at any time. The transitions are governed by the speed of the devices, which are assumed (although unstated earlier) to be exponentially distributed. The arc weights in these models are flow rates.

- *Fact:* Discrete state, continuous transition Markov models do not have periodic states. This is since transitions can take place at any time. Therefore, it has been assumed implicitly that Fig. 10.7 is a discrete state, discrete transition model with (unstated) non-zero probabilities as arc weights.

- *Major fact:* Any finite Markov model, with no periodic states and whose recurrent states are all in the same chain, will have limiting state probabilities that are independent of the initial starting state. That is, such models will have steady state. The example in Fig. 10.7 does not have steady state that is independent of the initial starting state because it has two chains, not one. If the system starts in state A, the system will cycle between states A, B, and C and it will never enter the other states. Similarly, if the system starts in state F, the system will remain in states F, G, H, and I and will never enter the other states. Thus, in this example, the probability of being in a state is very much dependent on the starting state. Also, if the diagram only consisted of states A, B, and C, even though it would have a single chain, it still would not have steady state probabilities that are independent of the starting state because the states are periodic. For instance, if the system started in state A at time 0, it would be known exactly in which state the system would be in at any given time. For example, the probability that it would be in state B at time 3,000,001 would be 1.0 while the probability of being in state B at time 3,000,002 would be 0. Such systems are deterministic in nature.

- *Fact:* The steady state probability of being in a transient state is 0. For instance, suppose that states A, B, and C, were not in the model. Steady state would exist. Even if the system started in state D, the system may alternate between states D and E for some arbitrary length of time, but eventually the system will enter state F, never to return to states D or E. Thus, the long term (i.e., steady state) probability of being in states D or E is 0, and the probability of being in states F, G, H, and I would depend on their arc weights.

The Markov models of interest are those which have steady state behavior. The two motivating examples used throughout this chapter are representative (albeit small) illustrations.

10.10 Chapter Summary

This chapter presents a basic, practical, and working knowledge of Markov models. Markov models fit within the general modeling paradigm which involves model construction, solution, calibration, alteration, and validation. Markov models are useful for both descriptive as well as predictive purposes. They are versatile and can model a wide range of applications. Two quite diverse applications are considered in this chapter and each of the modeling steps is demonstrated in detail. The assumptions and limitations of Markov models are summarized. The basics, as well as building blocks for more advanced topics, are presented.

In general, the primary limitation of Markov models is that they are susceptible to state space explosion. This explosion poses a danger that the computational complexity of solving the balance equations is prohibitive.

Fortunately, there are subclasses of Markov models that lend themselves
to efficient, alternative solution techniques. One such subclass of models is
known as *separable* Markov models. (The database server example in this
chapter is one example of a separable Markov model.) Separable Markov
models can be solved using the Mean Value Analysis (MVA) technique, which
is the topic of the following chapter.

We believe that the best way to learn about and to understand the subtleties of system modeling is not a passive process, but rather an active
engagement. Arguably, the primary benefit of system modeling is the development of keen insights and intuition by the system analyst concerning
the interdependencies between various modeling parameters. To this end, a
rich set of exercises is provided. The reader is encouraged to participate by
attempting to solve these exercises. They are not trivial.

10.11   Exercises

1. Reconsider the first motivating example (i.e., the random walk through
   England). Instead of a single son, suppose there are twin sons. Both
   lads behave independently but statistically the same. That is, they do
   not necessarily travel together. One can be hiking the Yorkshire moors
   while the other is sightseeing in London, though the probabilities of
   where to go the following day are the same. If, by chance, both sons
   happen to be kayaking the same day, they share a kayak. Solve this
   new system and answer the following four questions.

   - *Father's question:* What percentage of days is neither son drink-
     ing in Leeds?
   - *Lake District relatives' question:* Once a son finishes a day of
     kayaking in the Lake District, how long will it typically be before
     one of the sons is next there?
   - *Policeman's question:* How many days each month can the bob-
     bies expect to see one or both of the sons driving to London after
     drinking in Leeds?
   - *Kayak renters' question:* How many days each month do they
     need to have a kayak available?

2. In Section 10.6, in the model interpretation of the database server support example, provide all the details to verify the answer to the company president's question.

3. Is the mean recurrence time for a periodic state always equal to its period? Justify your answer.

4. Reconsider Fig. 10.7. Suppose the probability of going from D to E is $\frac{1}{3}$, from D to A is $\frac{2}{3}$, from E to D is $\frac{3}{4}$, from E to F is $\frac{1}{4}$, from H to I is $\frac{1}{2}$, and from H back to itself is $\frac{1}{2}$. All other probabilities are 1. Give the mean recurrence time for each of the recurrent states.

5. Give a two state Markov model, where the mean recurrence time for state 1 is 1.75. What is the range of recurrence times that can be observed for state 2?

6. Consider a small store with a single worker. The store is only large enough to have at most two customers in the store. (If another customer walks up when two other customers occupy the store, the third customer does not enter the store and simply goes away.) Once a customer is in the store and the worker is available, the worker spends an average of 5 minutes serving the customer. The worker can only service one customer at a time. Suppose the acceptable service level is 7.5 minutes that an average customer spends in the store. What is the maximum allowable arrival rate of customers to the store to guarantee this level of service?

7. Give a two state Markov diagram, where the sum of the mean recurrence times of the two states is as small as possible.

8. Suppose that the actual workload on the system consists of two jobs, one completely CPU-bound and the other completely disk-bound. However, suppose that the system analyst decided to aggregate the two jobs into a single class. Thus, the assumed workload consists of two identical jobs, both of which spend half their time at the CPU and the other half at the disk. How much error is made in making this assumption? Justify your answer. You may choose to consider system throughput,

device utilization, response time, or some other important performance metric.

9. Consider the following "system." Students arrive at the weight room at the Rec Center with an inter-arrival time of 10 minutes, exponentially distributed. When a student enters the weight room he/she immediately proceeds to the treadmill. Assume that there is only one treadmill and only one student can use it at a time. Once a student finishes with the treadmill, she/he proceeds to one of the two stationary bikes. When finished with the bike, the student leaves and goes home. No loitering is allowed in the exercise room. That is, if someone arrives at a piece of equipment and they can't begin using the equipment immediately, they must leave the room and go home frustrated. Once someone starts exercising on a piece of equipment, he/she uses it for an average of 15 minutes (exponentially distributed).

   - Draw the appropriate Markov model. Label all arcs.
   - In steady state, what are the probabilities of being in each state?
   - Give the mean number of students using the stationary bikes.
   - What percentage of arriving students who come to the exercise room, wanting to use the treadmill, must leave frustrated because it's busy?
   - What is the "good" throughput of the exercise room (i.e., the rate at which students happily leave the Rec Center, having exercised on both pieces of equipment)?

10. Consider the following twist to the previous problem. In the weight room at the Rec Center the following equipment is present: one treadmill; two stationary bikes; and one rowing machine. After visiting the treadmill, students go to a bike with probability 0.3 and to the rowing machine with probability 0.7. After using a bike, students always go to the rowing machine. After using the rowing machine, students always go to the treadmill. Once someone starts exercising on a piece of equipment, he/she uses it for an average of 3 minutes (exponentially

distributed). There are exactly two students in the weight room at all times (i.e., when one student leaves the weight room, another student enters at the same time). Upon entering the weight room, a typical student will use the rowing machine 3 separate times (i.e., visits). If a student goes to a piece of equipment and he/she can't begin using it immediately because of the other athlete, he/she patiently wait their turn.

- Draw the Markov model of this system. Clearly label all the arcs.
- How many times does the typical student use the treadmill?
- How many times does the typical student use the rowing machine?
- What are the steady state probabilities of each state?
- What is the utilization of each piece of equipment?
- How many students leave the weight room per hour?
- How much time does the typical student stay in the weight room (i.e., what's the response time per student)?

11. An Internet Service Provider (ISP) has m dial-up ports. Connection requests arrive at a rate of λ requests/sec. An average session duration is equal to $1/\mu$ seconds (i.e., each session completes at a rate of μ req/sec).

- Draw a state transition diagram for the ISP showing the arrival and departure rates [*Hint:* the state k represents the number of active connections].
- Give an expression for the probability p_k ($k = 0, \cdots, m$) that k connections are active as a function of λ, μ, and m.
- Find an expression for the probability p_{busy} that a customer finds all dial-up ports busy as a function of the state probabilities p_k.

12. A Web server is subject to 10 load tests. The number, n, of requests processed by the server is kept constant during each test. There is only one request in execution at the server in test number 1. This number

is incremented by one at each subsequent test. The server's average response time, R, is measured for each load test. The results are shown in Table 10.1.

- Find the throughput of the Web server for each of the 10 tests.
- Assume the throughput characteristics of the Web server obtained in the previous item and assume also that the Web server is subject to a load of 2 request/sec. Suppose that requests are rejected when the number of requests at the server is equal to W. Find the fraction, f, of lost requests for $W = 1, \cdots, 10$. Plot a graph of f versus W.

Bibliography

[1] G. Bolch, S. Greiner, H. de Meer, and K. S. Trivedi, *Queueing Networks and Markov Chains: Modeling and Performance Evaluation with Computer Science Applications*, John Wiley & Sons, New York, 1998.

[2] P. J. Denning and J. P. Buzen, "The operational analysis of queueing network models," *Computing Surveys*, vol. 10, no. 3, September 1978, pp.

Table 10.1. Data for Exercise 10.12

n	R (in sec)
1	1.400
2	2.114
3	2.838
4	3.570
5	4.311
6	5.060
7	5.816
8	6.578
9	7.346
10	8.119

225–261.

[3] A. W. Drake, *Fundamentals of Applied Probability Theory*, McGraw-Hill Higher Education (Columbus), 1967.

[4] L. Kleinrock, *Queueing Systems, Volume I: Theory*, Wiley-Interscience, New York, 1975.

[5] E. D. Lazowska, J. Zahorjan, S. Graham, and K. C. Sevcik, *Quantitative System Performance: Computer System Analysis Using Queueing Network Models*, Prentice-Hall, Upper Saddle River, New Jersey, 1984.

Chapter 11

Single
Queue
Systems

11.1   Introduction

There are many examples of single queue systems in daily life. The ATM machine in the shopping mall is such an example. The ATM machine acts as a single server serving a single queue. A single line of people waiting to get money may form in front of the machine. If people are well-behaved, they will use the ATM machine on a First Come First Serve (FCFS) basis, patiently waiting in line to receive service. This is an example of a single server, single queue system, with a FCFS *queuing discipline*.

This chapter explores some important classical analytic results for single queue systems. These results are shown to be useful in modern computer system situations. The term *queuing station* is used broadly here to indicate a collection of one or more waiting lines along with a server or collection of servers that provide service to these waiting lines. Examples of queuing stations discussed in this chapter include: 1) a single waiting line and a single server, 2) multiple waiting lines (arranged by priority) and a single server, and 3) a single waiting line and multiple servers. When the context is clear, the terms "queue" and "queuing station" are used interchangeably. All results presented in this chapter assume that FCFS is the queuing discipline in all waiting lines. The following chapters deal with situations in which queuing stations are connected to one another to form a Queuing Network.

The results discussed in this chapter are implemented in the Ch11-SingleQueues.XLS MS Excel workbook. This chapter is not intended to provide a comprehensive treatment of single queue systems. More comprehensive surveys and results appear elsewhere [1, 2, 3, 4]. The goal here is to summarize and apply the key results of single queue systems to performance design issues.

11.2   Single Queue Single Server Systems

Figure 11.1 depicts a single-line single-server queue. The system of Fig. 11.1 is also known as a G/G/1 queue. The first "G" indicates that the distribution of interarrival times of customers arriving to the system can be any generic distribution. The second "G" indicates that the service time distribution of the single server is also generic. The "1" indicates that there is a single server.

Customers arrive, join a waiting line if the server is not idle, wait their turn to use the server according to a FCFS queuing discipline, and depart after having received service. The average arrival rate of customers is denoted by λ, the average time spent waiting in the queue is denoted by W, the average service is denoted by $E[S]$, and the response time (i.e., the sum

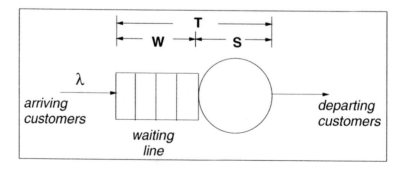

Figure 11.1. A single-line single-server system.

of the average waiting time plus the average service time) is denoted by T. Thus,

$$T = W + E[S]. \tag{11.2.1}$$

Sometimes, the inverse of the average response time (i.e., $1/E[S]$) is denoted by μ and represents the speed, or service rate, of the server. Likewise, the inverse of the arrival rate (i.e., $1/\lambda$) represents the average time between successive arrivals.

The following relationships are obtained by applying Little's Law (see Chapter 3) to the waiting line, to the entire queue, and to the server

$$N_w = \lambda \times W \tag{11.2.2}$$

$$N = \lambda \times T \tag{11.2.3}$$

$$N_s = \lambda \times E[S] \tag{11.2.4}$$

where N_w, N, and N_s denote the average number of customers in the waiting line, in the entire queuing station, and at the server, respectively. The average number of customers in the server is also the fraction of time that the server is busy (i.e., its utilization). See Exercise 11.1.

In this chapter, ρ is used to denote the utilization of a server instead of the notation U used in other chapters. This choice is made because there is a rich literature on single queues and ρ is more widely used to express utilization. By using the same notation, readers are able to recognize the formulas discussed here to be equivalent to results presented in other publications. Hence,

$$\rho = \lambda \times E[S] = N_s. \tag{11.2.5}$$

Since the utilization of the server is the probability that the server is busy, the probability that the server is idle is equal to the probability p_0 that there are no customers in the queuing station. Hence,

$$p_0 = 1 - \rho = 1 - \lambda \times E[S]. \tag{11.2.6}$$

Example 11.1

The average interarrival time of packets to a communication link is equal to 5 msec and each packet takes 3 msec on average to be transmitted through the link. What is the utilization of the link?

The average interarrival time is the inverse of the average arrival rate. Therefore, $\lambda = 1/5 = 0.2$ packets/msec. Thus, the utilization of the link is, according to Eq. (11.2.5), equal to $\rho = 0.2$ packets/msec $\times 3$ msec/packet $= 0.6 = 60\%$.   ∎

Unfortunately, the result of Eq. (11.2.6) is the only known exact result for G/G/1. However, by imposing additional assumptions about the distributions of the interarrival time and/or service time, a number of other interesting results are possible as discussed in the sections that follow. An approximate result for G/G/1 is given in Section 11.7.

11.3   The M/M/1 Queue

The most well-studied special case of the G/G/1 queue occurs when the interarrival times are exponentially distributed and the service times are also exponentially distributed. This queue is referred to as an M/M/1 queue. The "M" stands for Markovian or memoryless. The memoryless property applied to the arrival process means that if the distribution of the time between consecutive arrivals is exponentially distributed with parameter λ, then the distribution of the residual time until the next arrival is also exponentially distributed with the same parameter λ. Applied to the service time process, the memoryless property indicates that the distribution of the residual service time is the same as that of the service time. The exponential distribution is the only continuous distribution with the memoryless property. Additional important properties of the exponential distribution are:

- The cumulative distribution function (CDF) of an exponentially distributed random variable X with parameter λ is given by

$$F_X(x) = \Pr[X \leq x] = 1 - e^{-\lambda x}. \tag{11.3.7}$$

- The average and the standard deviation of an exponentially distributed random variable with parameter λ are both equal to $1/\lambda$. Therefore, the coefficient of variation of an exponentially distributed random variable is equal to 1. The exponential is the only continuous distribution with coefficient of variation equal to 1.

- If interarrival times are exponentially distributed with parameter λ, then the probability of observing exactly k arrivals in a given time period from time 0 to time t is:

$$\Pr\left[k \text{ arrivals in } (0, t)\right] = \frac{(\lambda\, t)\, e^{-\lambda t}}{k!}. \qquad (11.3.8)$$

This is a Poisson distribution with parameter λ. A Poisson distribution arises when arrivals come from a large number of independent sources.

- Poisson arrivals imply that interarrival times are exponentially distributed.

Because in the M/M/1 queue both the arrival and service processes are Markovian, a simple Markov model (see Chapter 10) can be constructed where the state k is the number of customers in the queuing station. Using the Generalized Birth-Death theorem (see Chapter 10) with $\lambda_i = \lambda$ and $\mu_i = \mu = 1/E[S]$ the probability p_k that there are k customers in the queuing station can be computed as

$$p_k = (1 - \rho)\rho^k \quad k = 0, 1, \cdots \qquad (11.3.9)$$

where $\rho = \lambda E[S]$. See Exercise 11.2. The following results for M/M/1 can be obtained from the probabilities p_k and from Little's Law:

$$N = \frac{\rho}{1 - \rho} \qquad (11.3.10)$$

$$T = N/\lambda = \frac{E[S]}{1 - \rho} \qquad (11.3.11)$$

$$W = T - E[S] = \frac{\rho E[S]}{1 - \rho} \qquad (11.3.12)$$

$$N_w = \lambda W = \frac{\rho^2}{1 - \rho} \qquad (11.3.13)$$

Example 11.2

A file server receives requests from a Poisson process at a rate of 30 requests/sec. Measurement data indicate that the coefficient of variation of the service time of a request at the file server is very close to 1 and that the average service time of a request is 15 msec. What is the average response time of a request at the file server? What would be the average response time if the arrival rate of requests were to double?

Because the coefficient of variation of the service time is equal to 1, the service time is exponentially distributed. Thus, the M/M/1 results can be used to answer the question. The utilization of the file server is $\rho = \lambda E[S] = 30 \times 0.015 = 0.45$. The average response time is $T = E[S]/(1 - \rho) = 0.015/(1 - 0.45) = 0.027$ seconds. If the arrival rate increases to 60 requests/sec, the utilization becomes $\rho = 60 \times 0.015 = 0.90$ and the average response time increases to $T = 0.015/(1 - 0.90) = 0.15$ seconds. Note that a two-fold increase in the arrival rate produces an increase in the average response time by a factor of 5.6.   ∎

11.4   The M/G/1 Queue

A well-studied special case of the G/G/1 queue occurs when the interarrival times are exponentially distributed but the service time distribution is any arbitrary (i.e., general) distribution. This queue is called an M/G/1 queue. The basic result for an M/G/1 queue, known as the Pollaczek-Khintchine (P-K) formula [2] for the average waiting time W, is

$$W = \frac{\rho \, E[S] \, (1 + C_s^2)}{2 \, (1 - \rho)} \qquad (11.4.14)$$

where C_s^2 is the square of the coefficient of variation of the service time distribution. [Note: if $C_s = 1$, the system is an M/M/1 queue.]

The other equations for M/G/1 follow directly from Eqs. (11.2.1)-(11.2.3):

$$T = E[S] + \frac{\rho \, E[S] \, (1 + C_s^2)}{2 \, (1 - \rho)} \qquad (11.4.15)$$

$$N_w = \frac{\rho^2 \, (1 + C_s^2)}{2 \, (1 - \rho)} \qquad (11.4.16)$$

$$N = \rho + \frac{\rho^2 \, (1 + C_s^2)}{2 \, (1 - \rho)} \qquad (11.4.17)$$

Example 11.3

Suppose that e-mail messages arrive at an e-mail server from a Poisson process at a rate of 1.2 messages per second. Also suppose that 30% of the messages are processed in 0.1 sec, 50% in 0.3 sec, and 20% in 2 sec. What is the average time $E[S]$ it takes to process a message? What is the average time W a message waits in the queue to be processed? What is the average response time T of an e-mail message? What is the average number of messages N_w waiting in the queue? What is the average number of messages N in the e-mail server?

The average time to process a message is

$$E[S] = 0.3 \times 0.1 + 0.5 \times 0.3 + 0.2 \times 2 = 0.58 \text{ seconds}$$

The utilization of the e-mail server is $\rho = \lambda \times E[S] = 1.2$ messages/sec $\times$ 0.58 seconds/message $= 0.696$. The coefficient of variation of the processing time, C_s, is the ratio between the standard deviation, σ_s, and the average processing time $E[S]$. The standard deviation is the square root of the variance σ_s^2, which is obtained as $\sigma_s^2 = E[S^2] - (E[S])^2$, where $E[S^2]$ is the second moment of the processing time. In this case,

$$E[S^2] = 0.3 \times 0.1^2 + 0.5 \times 0.3^2 + 0.2 \times 2^2 = 0.848 \text{ seconds}^2$$

Thus, the standard deviation σ_s is

$$\begin{aligned}
\sigma_s &= \sqrt{\sigma_s^2} = \sqrt{E[S^2] - (E[S])^2} \\
&= \sqrt{0.848 - 0.58^2} = \sqrt{0.848 - 0.336} = 0.715 \text{ seconds.}
\end{aligned}$$

The coefficient of variation C_s is then $C_s = \sigma_s/E[S] = 0.715/0.58 = 1.233$. From Eqs. (11.4.14)-(11.4.17):

$$\begin{aligned}
W &= \frac{\rho \, E[S] \, (1 + C_s^2)}{2 \, (1 - \rho)} = \frac{0.696 \times 0.58 \times (1 + 1.233^2)}{2 \, (1 - 0.696)} = 1.673 \text{ seconds} \\
T &= E[S] + W = 0.58 + 1.673 = 2.253 \text{ seconds} \\
N_w &= \lambda \times W = 1.2 \times 1.673 = 2.008 \text{ messages} \\
N &= N_w + \rho = 2.008 + 0.696 = 2.704 \text{ messages}
\end{aligned}$$

■

Example 11.4

What is the ratio between the average waiting time of an M/G/1 queue with exponentially distributed service times and the waiting time of an M/G/1 queue with constant service times?

The coefficient of variation C_s of a server with an exponentially distributed service time is 1. When the service times are constant, the variance, and therefore the coefficient of variation, is zero. Thus,

$$W_{\text{exp}} = \frac{\rho \, E[S] \, (1 + 1^2)}{2 \, (1 - \rho)} = \frac{\rho \, E[S]}{1 - \rho}$$

$$W_{\text{constant}} = \frac{\rho \, E[S] \, (1 + 0)}{2 \, (1 - \rho)} = \frac{\rho \, E[S]}{2(1 - \rho)} = \frac{1}{2} W_{\text{exp}}.$$

Thus, the time spent in the waiting line at an exponential server is on average twice the time spent in the waiting line of a constant speed server.   ∎

Figure 11.2 shows various curves of the average response time versus utilization for an M/G/1 queue with $E[S] = 1$ and for four values of C_s: 0, 0.5, 1, and 2. When $C_s = 0$, the M/G/1 queue is also referred to as an M/D/1 queue because service times are deterministic. When $C_s = 1$ service times are exponentially distributed and the resulting queue is an M/M/1 queue. As illustrated in Fig. 11.2 and from Eq. (11.4.15), the average response time increases as a function of the square of the coefficient of variation of the service time. This result indicates that performance degrades as the variability in the server increases. Thus, reducing the uncertainty (i.e., the standard deviation) of the service times placed on devices improves performance.

11.5 M/G/1 with Vacations

The previous analysis of an M/G/1 queue assumes that the server works non-stop as long as there are customers in the system. This property is also referred to as being "work conserving." In some situations, the server may decide to take a break (say to get coffee) when the system is empty. There are several natural cases where this type of situation occurs. For example, a storage subsystem may use idle periods to commit to disk all writes that are in the buffer. In this case, a newly arriving I/O request will have to wait until the buffer is flushed before it is served. As another example, a server may start a preventive maintenance procedure as soon as it becomes idle. Another example arises in enterprise grid environments, where idle processors (e.g., workstations) are claimed by remote applications. When the owner of the workstation returns, an extra delay is experienced while

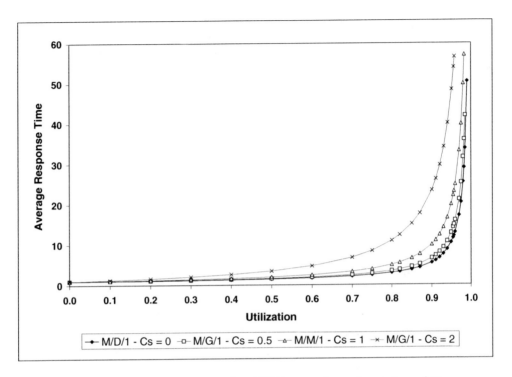

Figure 11.2. Response time of an M/G/1 queue for various values of C_s.

the remote application is checkpointed, preempted by the returning owner, and migrated back to the remote client.

The following results for an M/G/1 queue with vacations assumes that:

- The server goes on vacation for a time V as soon as the server becomes idle. The vacation time V is a random variable with any arbitrary distribution with average $E[V]$ and second moment $E[V^2]$.

- A customer that arrives to an empty system and finds the server on vacation has to wait until the server returns from vacation.

- The server goes back to vacation if it returns from vacation to an empty system.

The average waiting time for an M/G/1 system with vacations is given in Eq. (11.5.18). The first term is the regular M/G/1 expression of Eq. (11.4.14).

The second term is the average residual vacation time (i.e., the average time an arriving customer has to wait for the server to return from vacation).

$$W = \frac{\rho\ E[S]\ (1 + C_s^2)}{2\ (1 - \rho)} + \frac{E[V^2]}{2\ E[V]} \tag{11.5.18}$$

Example 11.5

A computer system serves requests that arrive from a Poisson process at a rate of 0.2 requests/sec. The processing time characteristics of a request are $E[S] = 3.5$ sec and $C_s = 0.3$. When there are no requests to be processed, the system performs a preventive maintenance procedure that lasts one second, on average, and has a coefficient of variation equal to 2. When the maintenance procedure is complete, the system resumes to serve requests if there are any in the queue. Otherwise, the system starts another maintenance procedure. What is the average waiting time of a request?

The value of ρ is 0.7 ($= 0.2 \times 3.5$). In order to use Eq. (11.5.18), the second moment of the vacation time is required. Since, $\sigma_V^2 = E[V^2] - (E[V])^2$ it follows that

$$\frac{\sigma_V^2}{(E[V])^2} = \frac{E[V^2]}{E[V]\ E[V]} - 1$$

$$C_V^2 = \frac{E[V^2]}{E[V]\ E[V]} - 1$$

$$1 + C_V^2 = \frac{E[V^2]}{E[V]\ E[V]}$$

$$\frac{(1 + C_V^2)\ E[V]}{2} = \frac{E[V^2]}{2\ E[V]} \tag{11.5.19}$$

Using Eqs. (11.5.18) and (11.5.19) with the numerical values given in the example, W can be computed as:

$$W = \frac{0.7 \times 3.5 \times (1 + 0.3^2)}{2\ (1 - 0.7)} + \frac{(1 + 2^2) \times 1}{2} = 6.95 \text{ seconds.}$$

Table 11.1 gives a comparison of two M/G/1 queues: one with vacations and one without. The average vacation time is varied. As it can be seen, the average waiting time is tripled when the average vacation (i.e., maintenance)

Table 11.1. Variation of Waiting Time vs. Maintenance Time for Example 11.5

$E[V]$	M/G/1 no vacation	M/G/1 with vacation
0.0	4.45	4.45
0.5	4.45	5.70
1.0	4.45	6.95
1.5	4.45	8.20
2.0	4.45	9.45
2.5	4.45	10.70
3.0	4.45	11.95
3.5	4.45	13.20
4.0	4.45	14.45
4.5	4.45	15.70
5.0	4.45	16.95
5.5	4.45	18.20
6.0	4.45	19.45

time is equal to the average service time (i.e., when $E[V] = E[S] = 3.5$ sec). Thus, having an otherwise idle processor begin service immediately (i.e., with no vacation time) on an arriving customer improves performance nontrivially. ■

11.6 M/G/1 with Priorities

Many computer systems (e.g., operating systems and communication systems) assign different priorities to the incoming requests. Figure 11.3 illustrates a situation with different waiting lines and one server. The different waiting lines are used by requests of different priorities. The priority of an arriving customer determines which priority waiting line is entered. Thus, customers are classified into P different static priorities before arriving into the system. Upon arrival, customers join the waiting line that corresponds to their priority class. Priority classes are numbered from 1 to P with P being the highest priority class and 1 being the lowest. The arrival rate of

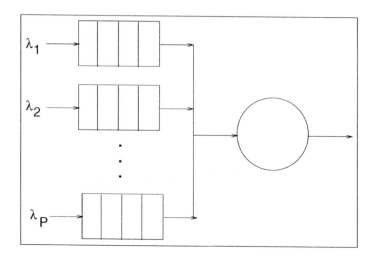

Figure 11.3. A single server system with priority classes.

requests of priority p $(p = 1, \cdots, P)$ is denoted by λ_p. The average service time and second moment of class p requests are denoted by $E[S_p]$ and $E[S_p^2]$, respectively.

The server processes the customer of highest priority according to either a non-preemptive strategy or with a preemptive resume strategy [3]:

- *Non-preemptive.* In this case, when the server becomes idle it takes the first request from the highest priority queue to serve. Once service begins on a request it is not interrupted until the request is completed, even if a request of higher priority than the one in service arrives. In other words, requests cannot be *preempted* once service begins.

- *Preemptive resume.* If a request of priority p arrives and finds a request of priority q $(q < p)$ being served, the higher priority request seizes the server (i.e., preempts the server by interrupting service of the priority q request). Once there are no more requests of priority higher than q, the preempted request resumes its processing from the point at which it was interrupted.

11.6.1 Non-Preemptive Priorities

The waiting time W_p of requests of priority p $(p = 1, \cdots, P)$ is computed as [3]:

$$W_p = \frac{W_0}{(1 - \pi_p)\,(1 - \pi_{p+1})} \tag{11.6.20}$$

where

$$W_0 = \frac{1}{2} \sum_{j=1}^{P} \lambda_j\, E[S_j^2], \text{ and} \tag{11.6.21}$$

$$\pi_p = \sum_{j=p}^{P} \lambda_j\, E[S_j]. \tag{11.6.22}$$

W_0 represents the average time an arriving request has to wait for the server to complete processing the current request in service. The product $\lambda_j\, E[S_j]$ is the utilization ρ_j due to priority j requests. The total utilization ρ is then

$$\rho = \sum_{p=1}^{P} \rho_p = \sum_{p=1}^{P} \lambda_p\, E[S_p]. \tag{11.6.23}$$

The average response time of priority class p requests is $T_p = W_p + E[S_p]$.

Example 11.6

A router receives packets at a rate of 1.2 packets/msec from a Poisson process. All packets are transmitted through the same outgoing link. Assume that 50% percent of the packets are of priority 1, 30% percent are of priority 2, and 20% percent are of priority 3. Assume that the mean and second moment of the packet transmission times are as shown in Table 11.2. What is the average waiting time per packet class?

Table 11.2. Data for Example 11.5

Priority (p)	$E[S_p]$ (msec)	$E[S_p^2]$ (msec^2)
1	0.5	0.375
2	0.4	0.400
3	0.3	0.180

The arrival rates per class are: $\lambda_1 = 1.2 \times 0.50 = 0.6$ packets/msec, $\lambda_2 = 1.2 \times 0.3 = 0.36$ packets/msec, and $\lambda_3 = 1.2 \times 0.2 = 0.24$ packets/msec. Then, from Eq. (11.6.22):

$$
\begin{aligned}
\pi_1 &= \lambda_1 \times E[S_1] + \lambda_2 \times E[S_2] + \lambda_3 \times E[S_3] \\
&= 0.6 \times 0.5 + 0.36 \times 0.4 + 0.24 \times 0.3 = 0.516 \\
\pi_2 &= \lambda_2 \times E[S_2] + \lambda_3 \times E[S_3] = 0.36 \times 0.4 + 0.24 \times 0.3 = 0.216 \\
\pi_3 &= \lambda_3 \times E[S_3] = 0.24 \times 0.3 = 0.072
\end{aligned}
$$

From Eq. (11.6.21):

$$
\begin{aligned}
W_0 &= 0.5 \times (\lambda_1 \times E[S_1^2] + \lambda_2 \times E[S_2^2] + \lambda_3 \times E[S_3^2]) \\
&= 0.5 \times (0.6 \times 0.375 + 0.36 \times 0.400 + 0.24 \times 0.180) = 0.206 \text{ msec}
\end{aligned}
$$

Finally, from Eq. (11.6.20):

$$
\begin{aligned}
W_1 &= \frac{W_0}{(1 - \pi_1)\,(1 - \pi_2)} = \frac{0.206}{(1 - 0.516)\,(1 - 0.216)} = 0.543 \text{ msec} \\
W_2 &= \frac{W_0}{(1 - \pi_2)\,(1 - \pi_3)} = \frac{0.206}{(1 - 0.216)\,(1 - 0.072)} = 0.283 \text{ msec} \\
W_3 &= \frac{W_0}{(1 - \pi_3)} = \frac{0.206}{1 - 0.072} = 0.222 \text{ msec}
\end{aligned}
$$

The average response times for each priority class are $T_1 = W_1 + E[S_1] = 0.543 + 0.5 = 1.043$ msec, $T_2 = W_2 + E[S_2] = 0.283 + 0.4 = 0.683$ msec, and $T_3 = W_3 + E[S_3] = 0.222 + 0.3 = 0.522$ msec. ∎

11.6.2 Preemptive Resume Priorities

The average response time T_p in this case is given by [3]:

$$
T_p = \frac{E[S_p]\,(1 - \pi_p) + \sum_{i=p}^{P} \lambda_i\, E[S_i^2]/2}{(1 - \pi_p)\,(1 - \pi_{p+1})}. \tag{11.6.24}
$$

Note that classes of priority lower than p are not represented in Eq. (11.6.24) because of preemption. That is, because of preemptions, requests of a lower priority have no impact on higher priority requests.

Example 11.7

Assume the same data of the previous example and assume a preemptive resume server. What are the average response times of each customer class?

Equation (11.6.24) yields,

$$T_1 = \frac{E[S_1]\,(1 - \pi_1) + \sum_{i=1}^{3} \lambda_i\, E[S_i^2]/2}{(1 - \pi_1)\,(1 - \pi_2)}$$

$$= \frac{0.5 \times (1 - 0.516) + \sum_{i=1}^{3} \lambda_i\, E[S_i^2]/2}{(1 - 0.516)\,(1 - 0.216)} = 1.181 \text{ msec}$$

$$T_2 = \frac{E[S_2]\,(1 - \pi_2) + \sum_{i=2}^{3} \lambda_i\, E[S_i^2]/2}{(1 - \pi_2)\,(1 - \pi_3)}$$

$$= \frac{0.4 \times (1 - 0.216) + \sum_{i=2}^{3} \lambda_i\, E[S_i^2]/2}{(1 - 0.216)\,(1 - 0.072)} = 0.560 \text{ msec}$$

$$T_3 = \frac{E[S_3]\,(1 - \pi_3) + \sum_{i=3}^{3} \lambda_i\, E[S_i^2]/2}{(1 - \pi_3)}$$

$$= \frac{0.3 \times (1 - 0.072) + \sum_{i=3}^{3} \lambda_i\, E[S_i^2]/2}{(1 - 0.072)} = 0.323 \text{ msec}$$

Note that class 3 receives improved response time in the preemptive case than in the non-preemptive case (i.e., 0.323 vs. 0.522 msec of response time). This is due to the fact that class 3 is not affected by classes 1 and 2. Class 1 receives degraded performance in the preemptive case (i.e., 1.181 vs. 1.043 msec of response time) since it only uses the server when there are no requests of classes 2 and 3 present in the system. The behavior of class 2 depends on the specific parameters of the problem. In the preemptive case, class 2 requests do not have to wait for class 1 requests to complete service but can be preempted by class 3 requests.   ∎

11.7   Approximation Results

M/G/1 results cannot be used when the interarrival time distribution is not exponentially distributed. However, the approximation

$$W_{G/G/1} \approx \frac{C_a^2 + \rho^2\, C_s^2}{1 + \rho^2\, C_s^2} \times \frac{\rho\, E[S]\,(1 + C_s^2)}{2\,(1 - \rho)} \tag{11.7.25}$$

where C_a is the coefficient of variation of the interarrival time is useful [2].

This approximation is exact for M/G/1. To verify this, note that in the M/G/1 case, $C_a = 1$ since interarrival times are exponentially distributed. Thus, the first term of the equation becomes one and the second term is the M/G/1 result of Eq. (11.4.14). The approximation of Eq. (11.7.25) is good for G/M/1 queues. It is "fair" for G/G/1 queues and improves as ρ increases.

Example 11.8

Measurements taken from a storage device used by a database server indicate that I/O requests arrive at an average rate of 80 requests/sec. The standard deviation of the interarrival time is measured as 0.025 sec. The average I/O time is measured as 0.009 sec with a standard deviation of 0.003 sec. What is the approximate waiting time of an I/O request at the storage device?

The average interarrival time $\bar{t}$ is the inverse of the average arrival rate. Thus, $\bar{t} = 1/80 = 0.0125$ sec. The coefficient of variation of the interarrival time is $C_a = \sigma_a/\bar{t} = 0.025/0.0125 = 2$. The utilization of the storage device is $\rho = \lambda \times E[S] = 80 \times 0.009 = 0.72$. The coefficient of variation of the service time is $C_s = \sigma_s/E[S] = 0.003/0.009 = 1/3$. Equation (11.7.25) can be used to approximate the average waiting time at the storage device:

$$W \approx \frac{2^2 + 0.72^2 \times (1/3)^2}{1 + 0.72^2 \times (1/3)^2} \times \frac{0.72 \times 0.009 \times [1 + (1/3)^2]}{2 \times (1 - 0.72)} = 0.0493 \text{ seconds.}$$

$$(11.7.26)$$

If C_a were equal to one, the average waiting time would be 0.0129 sec according to the M/G/1 result (i.e., Eq. (11.4.14)). This example further demonstrates the rule of thumb that increased variability (as indicated by the coefficient of variation) hurts performance).   ∎

Consider now the queue of Fig. 11.4 which has c identical servers and a single waiting line. This is known as the G/G/c queue and its utilization is

$$\rho = \frac{\lambda \, E[S]}{c}.$$

$$(11.7.27)$$

The exact solution for G/G/c is not known but its average waiting time can be approximated by

$$W_{\text{G/G/c}} \approx \frac{C\,(\rho, c)}{c\,(1 - \rho)/E[S]} \times \frac{C_a^2 + C_s^2}{2}$$

$$(11.7.28)$$

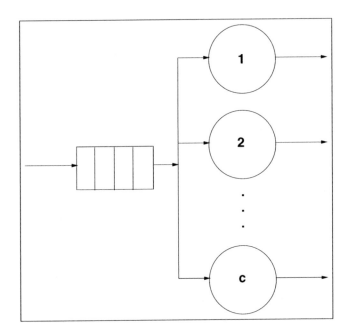

Figure 11.4. A single waiting line with multiple servers.

where
$$C(\rho, c) = \frac{(c\,\rho)^c/c!}{(1-\rho)\sum_{n=0}^{c-1}(c\,\rho)^n/n! + (c\,\rho)^c/c!}.\qquad(11.7.29)$$

This equation is Erlang's C formula [2]. The error in the approximation of Eq. (11.7.28) increases with C_a and with C_s. In the case of an M/M/c system (i.e., exponentially distributed interarrival times and exponentially distributed service times), the approximation of Eq. (11.7.28) is an exact solution and becomes

$$W_{\mathrm{M/M/c}} = \frac{C\,(\rho, c)}{c\,(1-\rho)/E[S]}\qquad(11.7.30)$$

because $C_a = 1$ and $C_s = 1$ for this case.

Example 11.9

A computer system receives requests that require an average of 2 seconds of service time. The coefficient of variation of the service time is 0.5 and the coefficient of variation of the interarrival time is 0.8. What is the minimum number of processors that should be used to keep the average response time below 2.5 seconds when the utilization of the system is 80%.

The question can be answered by using the G/G/c approximation of Eq. (11.7.28). The required parameters are: $\rho = 0.80, C_a = 0.8, C_s = 0.5$, and $E[S] = 2$ sec. The number of processors, c, is varied from 1 to 8. The results are presented in Table 11.3, which shows that at least 5 processors are needed.   ■

11.8   Concluding Remarks

Single queue systems provide useful information when estimating waiting times due to contention for shared resources. The M/G/1 queue is one of the most studied queuing systems. A large number of results are available, including vacationing servers and different priority scheduling schemes. Approximate results for G/G/1 and G/G/c are also given. The following chapters consider networks of queues, where individual queues are interconnected.

11.9   Exercises

1. Show that in a G/G/1 queue, the average number of customers at the server is equal to the utilization of the server.

Table 11.3. Response Time (sec) vs. No. Processors

No. Processors	Avg. Response Time (sec)
1	5.56
2	3.58
3	2.96
4	2.66
5	2.49
6	2.38
7	2.31
8	2.25

2. Derive Eqs. (11.3.9) and (11.3.11) using the Generalized Birth-Death theorem.

3. Derive the average waiting time for M/M/1 from Eq. (11.7.30).

4. Consider two Web clusters, A and B. Cluster A has n servers and cluster B has m $(m > n)$ servers. Requests arrive at each cluster at a rate of λ requests/sec. A load balancer in front of each cluster evenly distributes the requests to each server in the cluster. The average service time of a request in cluster A is x seconds and the average service time of a request in cluster B is $k \times x$ where $k > 1$. The service time of a request in either cluster has an arbitrary distribution. Derive an expression for the value of m so that the average response of a request in cluster A is the same as in cluster B.

5. A computer system receives requests from a Poisson process at a rate of 10 requests/sec. Assume that 30% of the requests are of type a and the remaining are of type b. The average service times and the coefficients of variation of the service times for these two types of requests are: $E[S_a] = 0.1$ seconds, $C_s^a = 1.5$, $E[S_b] = 0.08$ seconds, and $C_s^b = 1.2$. Compute the average response time for each type of request under each of the following scenarios: 1) requests of type a and b have equal priorities, 2) requests of type a have non-preemptive priority over requests of type b, 3) requests of type b have non-preemptive priority over requests of type a, 4) requests of type a have preemptive priority over requests of type b, and 5) requests of type b have preemptive priority over requests of type a.

6. Consider the class 3 requests in Example 11.7 when the server uses a preemptive resume scheduling policy (see Section 11.6.2). It is stated the performance (i.e., the waiting time) of the highest priority requests (i.e., class 3 in this case) is not affected by the lower priority requests. Prove this statement by computing the waiting time of class 3 requests using vanilla M/G/1 results (i.e., from Section 11.4). Compare the result to the value computed in Section 11.6.2.

Bibliography

[1] D. Gross and C. M. Harris, *Fundamentals of Queueing Theory*, 3rd ed., Wiley-Interscience, 1998.

[2] L. Kleinrock, *Queueing Systems, Vol I: Theory*, John Wiley & Sons, New York, 1975.

[3] L. Kleinrock, *Queueing Systems, Vol II: Computer Applications*, John Wiley & Sons, New York, 1976.

[4] R. Nelson, *Probability, Stochastic Processes, and Queuing Theory: The Mathematics of Computer Performance Modelling*, Springer Verlag, New York, 1995.

Chapter 12

Single
Class
MVA

12.1 Introduction

The Achilles' heel of Markov models is their susceptibility to state space explosion. Even in simple models, where there are a fixed number of customers, where all customers are identical, and where the demands placed by each customer on each device are exponentially distributed, the number of states is given by the expression

$$\binom{N + K - 1}{K - 1}$$

where N is the number of customers and K is the number of devices. For small systems, such as the database server example in the previous chapter with $N = 2$ and $K = 3$, the number of states is 6. However, in a moderate sized office network with, say, 25 users and 25 workstations, the number of states is more than 63 trillion. With 50 users and 50 workstations, the number of states is over 5×10^{28}. Since there is one linear equation (i.e., equating flow into the state to the flow out of the state) for every state, solving such a large number of simultaneous equations is infeasible.

However, the good news is that clever algorithms have been developed for a broad class of useful Markov models that do not require the explicit solution to a large number of simultaneous equations. One such technique is Mean Value Analysis (MVA). Instead of solving a set of simultaneous linear equations to find the steady state probability of being in each system state, from which performance metrics (e.g., system throughput, device utilizations, user response times) can be derived, MVA is a simple recursion. MVA calculates the performance metrics directly for a given number of customers, knowing only the performance metrics when the number of customers is reduced by one. The recursion is intuitive, efficient, and elegant. The majority of commercially viable performance evaluation packages owe their success to MVA. Its impact on the field of analytical performance evaluation has been huge.

In this chapter, MVA is reconstructed from first principles and presented in its simplest form. All of the N customers are assumed to be (statistically) identical, forming a single class of customers. Each of the K devices is assumed to be load independent, meaning that the device neither speeds up nor slows down depending upon the number of customers at the device. Finally, the demand that a customer places on a device (i.e., the service required by a customer at a particular device) is assumed to be exponentially distributed. There are enhancements to MVA that remove each of these restrictions (i.e., allowing multi-class customers, allowing load dependent servers, and allowing non-exponential service), but presenting such extensions is not the purpose of this chapter. Rather, the desire is for an appreciation of and an intuitive, working understanding of MVA.

This chapter is example based. In Section 12.2, the database server example from previous chapters is extended and used to develop and illustrate the basic MVA algorithm. A concise, algorithmic description of MVA is given in Section 12.3. The special case of balanced systems is presented in Section 12.4. Section 12.5 describes extensions and limitations associated with MVA. The chapter concludes with a summary and relevant exercises.

12.2   MVA Development

Previous Paradigm Revisited: Reconsider the database server example from the previous chapter, whose high-level diagram is reproduced in Figure 12.1.

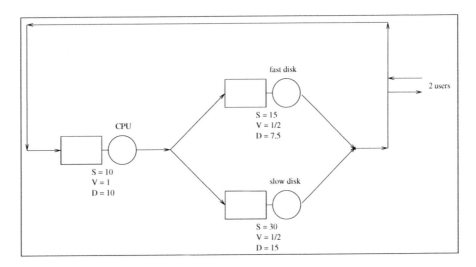

Figure 12.1. Database server example revisited.

The mean service time (S) per visit, the average number of visits (V) per transaction, and the total demand $(D = S \times V)$ per transaction is indicated for each device. The underlying Markov model is reproduced in Figure 12.2. By solving the six balance equations, the steady state probabilities were found to be:

$$P_{(2,0,0)} = \frac{16}{115} = 0.1391$$

$$P_{(1,1,0)} = \frac{12}{115} = 0.1043$$

$$P_{(1,0,1)} = \frac{24}{115} = 0.2087$$

$$P_{(0,2,0)} = \frac{9}{115} = 0.0783$$

$$P_{(0,1,1)} = \frac{18}{115} = 0.1565$$

$$P_{(0,0,2)} = \frac{36}{115} = 0.3131$$

From these probabilities, other useful performance metrics can be easily derived. For example, the average number of customers at the CPU is a simple weighted sum of the above probabilities. That is, there are two

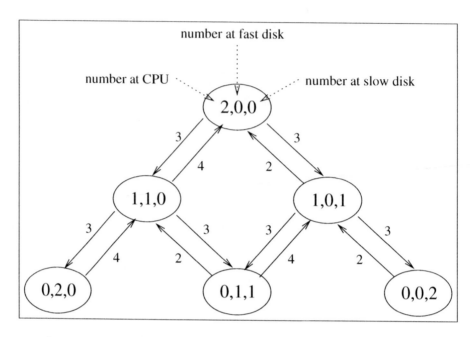

Figure 12.2. Markov model of the database server example (2 customers).

customers at the CPU in state $(2,0,0)$ with probability $\frac{16}{115}$, one customer at the CPU in state $(1,1,0)$ with probability $\frac{12}{115}$, one customer at the CPU in state $(1,0,1)$ with probability $\frac{24}{115}$, and no customers at the CPU in the remaining three states. Therefore, the average number of customers at the CPU is:

$$2 \times P_{(2,0,0)} + 1 \times P_{(1,1,0)} + 1 \times P_{(1,0,1)} = \frac{68}{115} = 0.5913 \text{ customers.}$$

Similarly, the average number of customers at the fast disk is:

$$1 \times P_{(1,1,0)} + 2 \times P_{(0,2,0)} + 1 \times P_{(0,1,1)} = \frac{48}{115} = 0.4174 \text{ customers}$$

and the average number of customers at the slow disk is:

$$1 \times P_{(1,0,1)} + 1 \times P_{(0,1,1)} + 2 \times P_{(0,0,2)} = \frac{114}{115} = 0.9913 \text{ customers.}$$

The sum of these three numbers, $0.5913+0.4174+0.9913 = 2.0000$, accounts for the two customers in the system.

The utilization of each device can also be easily calculated knowing the steady state probabilities. For instance, the CPU is utilized in states $P_{(2,0,0)}$, $P_{(1,1,0)}$, and $P_{(1,0,1)}$ and is not utilized (i.e., is idle) in the remaining three states, where no customers are at the CPU. Therefore, the utilization of the CPU is:

$$P_{(2,0,0)} + P_{(1,1,0)} + P_{(1,0,1)} = \frac{16}{115} + \frac{12}{115} + \frac{24}{115} = \frac{52}{115} = 0.4522.$$

Likewise, the utilization of the fast disk is:

$$P_{(1,1,0)} + P_{(0,2,0)} + P_{(0,1,1)} = \frac{12}{115} + \frac{9}{115} + \frac{18}{115} = \frac{39}{115} = 0.3391$$

and the utilization of the slow disk is:

$$P_{(1,0,1)} + P_{(0,1,1)} + P_{(0,0,2)} = \frac{24}{115} + \frac{18}{115} + \frac{36}{115} = \frac{78}{115} = 0.6783.$$

[**Important sidenote:** Since the slow disk is half as fast as the fast disk and since it is equally likely to find the required files on either disk, the demand (i.e., D) placed on the slow disk (i.e., 15 seconds) is twice as much as on the fast disk (i.e., 7.5 seconds). That is, a typical customer spends twice as much time in service at the slow disk than it does at the fast disk. It is no coincidence, therefore, that the utilization of the slow disk is twice that of the fast disk. Similarly, a typical customer spends $(\frac{2}{3})^{\text{rds}}$ the amount of time (i.e., $D = 10$ seconds) at the CPU than it does at the slow disk (i.e., $D = 15$ seconds). The speed of the CPU is three times faster than the slow disk (i.e., a typical visit to the CPU lasts for 10 seconds as opposed to 30 seconds per visit at the slow disk), but the CPU gets twice as many visits as the slow disk because the files are equally spread over the two disks. Since the demand at the CPU is $(\frac{2}{3})^{\text{rds}}$ that of the slow disk, its utilization, 0.4522 is, likewise, $(\frac{2}{3})^{\text{rds}}$ that of the slow disk, 0.6783. *Device utilizations are in the same ratio as their service demands, regardless of number of customers in the system (i.e., the system load).*]

Once device utilizations are known, device throughputs follow directly from the Utilization Law presented in Chapter 3. Device i's throughput, X_i, is its utilization, U_i, divided by its service time, S_i. Thus, the throughput of the CPU is $\frac{0.4522}{10} = 0.0452$ customers per second, or 2.7130 customers per minute. Likewise, the throughput of each disk is 1.3565 customers per minute. This is consistent since the throughput of the CPU is split evenly between the two disks.

Knowing the average number of customers, n_i, at each device and the throughput, X_i, of each device, the response time, R_i, per visit to each device is, via Little's Law, the simple ratio of the two, $\frac{n_i}{X_i}$. Thus, the response times of the CPU, the fast disk, and the slow disk are 13.08 seconds, 18.46 seconds, and 43.85 seconds, respectively.

Since a typical customer's transaction visits the CPU once and only one of the disks (with equal likelihood), the overall response time of a transaction is a weighted sum of the individual device residence times. Thus, a transaction's response time is $1 \times 13.08 + \frac{1}{2} \times 18.46 + \frac{1}{2} \times 43.85 = 44.24$ seconds. A summary of the relevant performance measures is presented in Table 12.1.

Now consider the same database server example, but with three customers instead of two. The associated Markov model is an extension of Figure 12.2 and is illustrated in Figure 12.3. The ten balance equations (plus the conservation of total probability equation) are shown in Table 12.2, the steady state solution to the balance equations is shown in Table 12.3, and the associated performance metrics are given in Table 12.4. These are straightforward extensions of the case with two customers and are left as exercises for the reader.

[**Sidenote**: As a consistency check on the performance metrics given in Table 12.4, the sum of the average number of customers at the devices equals the total number of customers in the system (i.e., three). Also, the utilization of the CPU is $(\frac{2}{3})^{\text{rds}}$ that of the slow disk, and the utilization of the slow disk is twice that of the fast disk (i.e., the utilizations remain in the same ratio as their service demands). The throughputs of the disks are identical and sum to that of the CPU.]

The Need for a New Paradigm: This technique of going from the two customer case to the three customer case (i.e., state space extension, balance equation derivation, solution of the linear equations, interpretation of the

Table 12.1. Performance Metrics for the Database Server Example (2 customers)

Average Number of Customers	
CPU	0.5913
fast disk	0.4174
slow disk	0.9913
Utilizations (%)	
CPU	45.22%
fast disk	33.91%
slow disk	67.83%
Throughputs (customers per minute)	
CPU	2.7130
fast disk	1.3565
slow disk	1.3565
Residence Times (seconds)	
CPU	13.08
fast disk	9.23
slow disk	21.93
Response Time (seconds)	44.24

performance metrics) does not scale as the number of devices and the number of customers increases. A new paradigm of analyzing the *relationships* between the performance metrics is required.

As an example, consider the relationship between the residence time at the CPU with three customers (i.e., 15.91 seconds) to the average number of customers at the CPU with two customers (i.e., 0.5913). Given that there are three customers in the network, at the instant when a customer arrives at the CPU, the average number of customers that the arriving customer sees already at the CPU is precisely the average number of customers at the CPU with two customers in the network. (This is an important result known as the "Arrival Theorem".) Therefore, in a network with three customers, an arriving customer at the CPU will expect to see 0.5913 customers already there. Thus, the time it will take for the newly arriving customer to complete

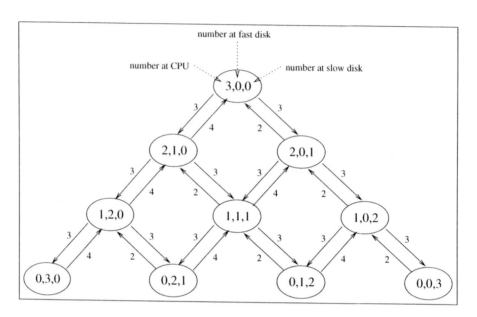

Figure 12.3. Markov model of the database server example (3 customers).

service and leave the CPU (i.e., its residence time) will be the time it takes to service those customers already at the CPU plus the time it takes to service the arriving customer. Since the average service time per customer at the CPU is 10 seconds, it will take an average of 10×0.5913 seconds to service those customers already at the CPU, plus an additional 10 seconds to service the arriving customer. Therefore, the residence time is $10(1+0.5913) = 15.91$ seconds.

This "discovered" relationship can be generalized. Letting $R_i(n)$ represent the average response time per visit to device i when there are n customers in the network, letting S_i represent the average service time of a customer at device i, and letting $\bar{n}_i(n-1)$ represent the average number of customers at device i when there are a total of $n-1$ customers in the entire system, the above relationship is represented as:

$$R_i(n) = S_i\left[1 + \bar{n}_i(n-1)\right].$$

Thus, knowing the average number of customers at a device when a total of $n-1$ customers are in the system, the response time at the device with n

Table 12.2. Balance Equations for the Database Server Example (3 customers)

$$(4 \times P_{(2,1,0)}) + (2 \times P_{(2,0,1)}) = 6 \times P_{(3,0,0)}$$

$$(3 \times P_{(3,0,0)}) + (4 \times P_{(1,2,0)}) + (2 \times P_{(1,1,1)}) = 10 \times P_{(2,1,0)}$$

$$(3 \times P_{(3,0,0)}) + (4 \times P_{(1,1,1)}) + (2 \times P_{(1,0,2)}) = 8 \times P_{(2,0,1)}$$

$$(3 \times P_{(2,1,0)}) + (4 \times P_{(0,3,0)}) + (2 \times P_{(0,2,1)}) = 10 \times P_{(1,2,0)}$$

$$(3 \times P_{(2,1,0)}) + (3 \times P_{(2,0,1)}) + (4 \times P_{(0,2,1)}) + (2 \times P_{(0,1,2)}) = 12 \times P_{(1,1,1)}$$

$$(3 \times P_{(2,0,1)}) + (4 \times P_{(0,1,2)}) + (2 \times P_{(0,0,3)}) = 8 \times P_{(1,0,2)}$$

$$3 \times P_{(1,2,0)} = 4 \times P_{(0,3,0)}$$

$$(3 \times P_{(1,2,0)}) + (3 \times P_{(1,2,1)}) = 6 \times P_{(0,2,1)}$$

$$(3 \times P_{(1,1,1)}) + (3 \times P_{(1,0,2)}) = 6 \times P_{(0,1,2)}$$

$$3 \times P_{(1,0,2)} = 2 \times P_{(0,0,3)}$$

$$P_{(3,0,0)} + P_{(2,1,0)} + P_{(2,0,1)} + P_{(1,2,0)} + P_{(1,1,1)}$$
$$+ P_{(1,0,2)} + P_{(0,3,0)} + P_{(0,2,1)} + P_{(0,1,2)} + P_{(0,0,3)} = 1.0$$

Table 12.3. Solution for the Database Server Example (3 customers)

$P_{(3,0,0)}$	=	$\frac{64}{865}$	= 0.0740
$P_{(2,1,0)}$	=	$\frac{48}{865}$	= 0.0555
$P_{(2,0,1)}$	=	$\frac{96}{865}$	= 0.1110
$P_{(1,2,0)}$	=	$\frac{36}{865}$	= 0.0416
$P_{(1,1,1)}$	=	$\frac{72}{865}$	= 0.0832
$P_{(1,0,2)}$	=	$\frac{144}{865}$	= 0.1665
$P_{(0,3,0)}$	=	$\frac{27}{865}$	= 0.0312
$P_{(0,2,1)}$	=	$\frac{54}{865}$	= 0.0624
$P_{(0,1,2)}$	=	$\frac{108}{865}$	= 0.1249
$P_{(0,0,3)}$	=	$\frac{216}{865}$	= 0.2497

customers is a simple (i.e., one addition and one multiplication) calculation. Therefore, the response time at the fast disk, when there are three customers in the network, is the product of its service time (i.e., 15 seconds) and the number of customers at the disk (i.e., the arriving customer, 1, plus the number of customers at the disk when there are only two customers in the

Table 12.4. Performance Metrics for the Database Server Example (3 customers)

Average Number of Customers	
CPU	0.8462
fast disk	0.5653
slow disk	1.5885
Utilizations (%)	
CPU	53.18%
fast disk	39.88%
slow disk	79.77%
Throughputs (customers per minute)	
CPU	3.1908
fast disk	1.5954
slow disk	1.5954
Residence Times (seconds)	
CPU	15.91
fast disk	10.63
slow disk	29.87
Response Time (seconds)	56.41

network, 0.4174), namely $15(1 + 0.4174) = 21.36$ seconds. Likewise, the residence time at the slow disk is $30(1 + 0.9913) = 59.74$ seconds.

Now consider overall system response time. For a given number of customers in the network (i.e., n) and a given number of devices (i.e., K), then knowing the average number of visits that each customer makes to each device (i.e., the V_i's) and the average time spent at each device per visit (i.e., $R_i(n)$), the overall response time, $R_0(n)$, is simply the sum of the residence times (i.e., $R_i'(n)$):

$$R_0(n) = \sum_{i=1}^{K} R_i'(n) = \sum_{i=1}^{K} [V_i \times R_i(n)].$$

In the database server example, with three customers, the residence times at the three devices (i.e., CPU, fast disk, and slow disk) are 15.91, 21.26, and

59.74 seconds, respectively. The number of visits to each of these devices per transaction is 1.0, 0.5, and 0.5, respectively. Thus, the overall response time is $(1.0 \times 15.91) + (0.5 \times 21.26) + (0.5 \times 59.74) = 56.41$ seconds.

To summarize so far, knowing only the average number of customers at each device with two customers, the device residence times when there are three customers in the network can be quickly derived. Knowing these residence times leads directly to the overall response time.

Now consider overall system throughput. Little's Law indicates that the average number of customers in the system (i.e., n) is the simple product of system throughput, $X_0(n)$, and system response time, $R_0(n)$. Thus,

$$X_0(n) = \frac{n}{R_0(n)}$$

from which the individual device throughputs can be found using the Forced Flow Law,

$$X_i(n) = V_i \times X_0(n).$$

Thus, in the database server example, with three customers, overall system throughput is $X_0(3) = \frac{3}{R(3)} = \frac{3}{56.41} = 0.0532$ customers per second, or 3.1908 customers per minute. With the V_i's being 1.0, 0.5, and 0.5 for the CPU, fast disk, and slow disk, respectively, their individual device throughputs are 3.1908, 1.5954, and 1.5954 customers per minute.

To update the summary to this point, knowing only the average number of customers at each device with $n - 1$ customers, the device residence times when there are n customers in the network can be quickly derived. Knowing these residence times leads directly to the overall response time, which, in turn, leads directly to the system and individual device throughputs.

From here, the device utilizations follow from the device throughputs via the Utilization Law,

$$U_i(n) = S_i \times X_i(n).$$

The final piece is to find the average number of customers at each device when there are n customers in the system (i.e., $\bar{n}_i(n)$). However, knowing the individual device throughputs, $X_i(n)$, and the individual device response times, $R_i(n)$, this again follows directly from Little's Law applied to each individual device,

$$\bar{n}_i(n) = X_i(n) \times R_i(n).$$

But, from the Forced Flow Law, $X_i(n) = V_i \times X_0(n)$. Thus,

$$\bar{n}_i(n) = X_0(n) \times V_i \times R_i(n) = X_0(n) \times R'_i(n).$$

In the database server example, this implies that the average number of customers at the CPU when there are three customers in the system is the simple product of the CPU's throughput (i.e., 3.1908 customers per minute, or 0.0532 customers per second) and its response time (i.e., 15.91 seconds) which yields 0.8462 customers. Similarly, the average number of customers at the fast disk when there are three customers in the system is $0.0266 \times 21.26 = 0.5653$ customers. At the slow disk, there are $0.0266 \times 59.74 = 1.5885$ customers.

The development of the MVA iteration is now complete. Given the average number of customers at each device with $n - 1$ customers in the system, the device residence times when there are n customers in the network can be derived. Knowing these residence times leads to the overall response time, which, in turn, leads to the system and individual device throughputs. The device throughputs lead to the device utilizations and to the average number of customers at each device with n customers in the system. Knowing these, the iteration continues to derive the performance metrics with $n + 1$ customers in the system, and, in general, to any desired number of customers ... all without formulating and solving any of the underlying steady state balance equations. Elegant!

One small detail is the initialization of the iterative process. However, this is resolved by simply noting that when no customers are in the system, the average number of customers at each device is, likewise, zero. Thus, when $n = 0$, $\bar{n}_i(0) = 0$ for all devices i.

12.3 The MVA Algorithm

The MVA algorithm is given concisely in Table 12.5. This is for any single class network with N customers and K devices. The average service time of a customer at device i is S_i and the average number of visits that a customer makes to device i is V_i. For all customer populations n $(1 \leq n \leq N)$, the algorithm finds the following performance metrics: the average residence time at each device, the overall system response time, the overall system throughput, the individual device throughputs, the device utilizations, and the average number of customers at each device.

Applied to the database server example, where the average service times are 10 seconds, 15 seconds, and 30 seconds, respectively, for the CPU (cp), fast disk (fd), and slow disk (sd), and where the average number of visits to each device are 1.0, 0.5, and 0.5, the MVA iteration proceeds as follows:

Initialize the average number of customers at each device i: $(\bar{n}_i(0) = 0)$.

Table 12.5. The MVA Algorithm

Initialize the average number of customers at each device i:
$$\bar{n}_i(0) = 0.$$
For each customer population $n = 1, 2, \ldots N$,
    calculate the average residence time for each device i:
$$R'_i(n) = V_i\ S_i\ [1 + \bar{n}_i(n-1)] = D_i\ [1 + \bar{n}_i(n-1)]$$
    calculate the overall system response time:
$$R_0(n) = \sum_{i=1}^{K} [V_i \times R_i(n)] = \sum_{i=1}^{K} R'_i(n)$$
    calculate the overall system throughput:
$$X_0(n) = \frac{n}{R_0(n)}$$
    calculate the throughput for each device i:
$$X_i(n) = V_i \times X_0(n)$$
    calculate the utilization for each device i:
$$U_i(n) = S_i \times X_i(n)$$
    calculate the average number of customers at each device i:
$$\bar{n}_i(n) = X_0(n) \times R'_i(n).$$

$$\bar{n}_{cp}(0) = 0.0000 \text{ customers}$$
$$\bar{n}_{fd}(0) = 0.0000 \text{ customers}$$
$$\bar{n}_{sd}(0) = 0.0000 \text{ customers}$$

For customer population $n = 1$, calculate the average residence time for each device i: $(R_i'(n) = V_i \ S_i \ [1 + \bar{n}_i(n-1)]) = D_i \ [1 + \bar{n}_i(n-1)].)$

$$R_{cp}'(1) = 10 \times 1 \ (1 + 0.0000) = 10.00 \text{ seconds}$$
$$R_{fd}'(1) = 15 \times 0.5 \ (1 + 0.0000) = 7.50 \text{ seconds}$$
$$R_{sd}'(1) = 30 \times 0.5 \ (1 + 0.0000) = 15.00 \text{ seconds}$$

Calculate the overall system response time: $(R_0(n) = \sum_{i=1}^{K} R_i'(n)).$

$$R_0(1) = 10.00 + 7.50 + 15.00 = 32.50 \text{ seconds}$$

Calculate the overall system throughput: $(X_0(n) = \frac{n}{R(n)}).$

$$X_0(1) = \frac{1}{32.50} = 0.0308 \text{ customers per second}$$

Calculate the throughput for each device i: $(X_i(n) = V_i \times X_0(n)).$

$$X_{cp}(1) = 1.0(0.0308) = 0.0308 \text{ customers per second}$$
$$X_{fd}(1) = 0.5(0.0308) = 0.0154 \text{ customers per second}$$
$$X_{sd}(1) = 0.5(0.0308) = 0.0154 \text{ customers per second}$$

Calculate the utilization for each device i: $(U_i(n) = S_i \times X_i(n)).$

$$U_{cp}(1) = 10.00(0.0308) = 0.3077 = 30.77\%$$
$$U_{fd}(1) = 15.00(0.0154) = 0.2308 = 23.08\%$$
$$U_{sd}(1) = 30.00(0.0154) = 0.4615 = 46.15\%$$

Calculate the average number of customers at each device i: ($\bar{n}_i(n) = X_0(n) \times R'_i(n)$).

$$\bar{n}_{cp}(1) = 0.0308(10.00) = 0.3077 \text{ customers}$$
$$\bar{n}_{fd}(1) = 0.0308(7.50) = 0.2310 \text{ customers}$$
$$\bar{n}_{sd}(1) = 0.0308(15.00) = 0.4620 \text{ customers}$$

For customer population n = 2, calculate the average residence time for each device i: ($R'_i(n) = D_i[1 + \bar{n}_i(n-1)]$).

$$R'_{cp}(2) = 10(1 + 0.3077) = 13.08 \text{ seconds}$$
$$R'_{fd}(2) = 7.5(1 + 0.2308) = 9.23 \text{ seconds}$$
$$R'_{sd}(2) = 15(1 + 0.4615) = 21.93 \text{ seconds}$$

Calculate the overall system response time: ($R_0(n) = \sum_{i=1}^{K} R'_i(n)$).

$$R_0(2) = 13.08 + 9.23 + 21.93 = 44.24 \text{ seconds}$$

Calculate the overall system throughput: ($X_0(n) = \frac{n}{R(n)}$).

$$X_0(2) = \frac{2}{44.24} = 0.0452 \text{ customers per second}$$

Calculate the throughput for each device i: ($X_i(n) = V_i \times X_0(n)$).

$$X_{cp}(2) = 1.0(0.0452) = 0.0452 \text{ customers per second}$$
$$X_{fd}(2) = 0.5(0.0452) = 0.0226 \text{ customers per second}$$
$$X_{sd}(2) = 0.5(0.0452) = 0.0226 \text{ customers per second}$$

Calculate the utilization for each device i: ($U_i(n) = S_i \times X_i(n)$).

$$U_{cp}(2) = 10.00(0.0452) = 0.4522 = 45.22\%$$
$$U_{fd}(2) = 15.00(0.0226) = 0.3391 = 33.91\%$$
$$U_{sd}(2) = 30.00(0.0226) = 0.6783 = 67.83\%$$

Calculate the average number of customers at each device i: $(\bar{n}_i(n) = X_0(n) \times R'_i(n))$.

$$\bar{n}_{cp}(2) = 0.0452(13.08) = 0.5913 \text{ customers}$$
$$\bar{n}_{fd}(2) = 0.0452(9.23) = 0.4174 \text{ customers}$$
$$\bar{n}_{sd}(2) = 0.0452(21.93) = 0.9913 \text{ customers}$$

For customer population n = 3, calculate the average residence time for each device i: $(R'_i(n) = D_i [1 + \bar{n}_i(n - 1)])$.

$$R'_{cp}(3) = 10(1 + 0.5913) = 15.91 \text{ seconds}$$
$$R'_{fd}(3) = 7.5(1 + 0.4174) = 10.63 \text{ seconds}$$
$$R'_{sd}(3) = 15(1 + 0.9913) = 29.87 \text{ seconds}$$

Calculate the overall system response time: $(R_0(n) = \sum_{i=1}^{K} R'_i(n))$.

$$R_0(3) = 15.91 + 10.63 + 29.87 = 56.41 \text{ seconds}$$

Calculate the overall system throughput: $(X_0(n) = \frac{n}{R_0(n)})$.

$$X_0(3) = \frac{3}{56.41} = 0.0532 \text{ customers per second}$$

Calculate the throughput for each device i: $(X_i(n) = V_i \times X_0(n))$.

$$X_{cp}(3) = 1.0(0.0532) = 0.0532 \text{ customers per second}$$
$$X_{fd}(3) = 0.5(0.0532) = 0.0266 \text{ customers per second}$$
$$X_{sd}(3) = 0.5(0.0532) = 0.0266 \text{ customers per second}$$

Calculate the utilization for each device i: $(U_i(n) = S_i \times X_i(n))$.

$$U_{cp}(3) = 10.00(0.0532) = 0.5318 = 53.18\%$$
$$U_{fd}(3) = 15.00(0.0266) = 0.3988 = 39.88\%$$
$$U_{sd}(3) = 30.00(0.0266) = 0.7977 = 79.77\%$$

Calculate the average number of customers at each device i: $(\bar{n}_i(n) = X_0(n) \times R'_i(n))$.

$$\bar{n}_{cp}(3) = 0.0532(15.91) = 0.8462 \text{ customers}$$
$$\bar{n}_{fd}(3) = 0.0532(10.63) = 0.5653 \text{ customers}$$
$$\bar{n}_{sd}(3) = 0.0532(29.87) = 1.5885 \text{ customers}$$

These performance metrics found via MVA for two and three customers (i.e., when $n = 2$ and when $n = 3$) correspond directly to those found from first principles (i.e., by constructing the Markov model, forming the balance equations, solving the balance equations, and interpreting the results) as demonstrated in Section 12.2 and shown in Tables 12.1 and 12.4. The significant difference is that the amount of computation required using MVA is negligible. MVA easily scales to a high number of devices and a high number of customers.

12.4 Balanced Systems

The MVA iteration starts once the customer distribution among the devices is known. That is, knowing how $n - 1$ customers are distributed among the devices, (i.e., the $\bar{n}_i(n - 1)$'s), the performance measures when there are n customers in the system follow directly, as seen from the MVA algorithm given in Table 12.5.

Now consider a *balanced* system. A system is considered to be balanced if a typical customer places the same average load (i.e., demand D) on each of the devices. This implies that all devices are equally utilized. A balanced system is not one where all devices are the same speed, only that the faster devices are either visited more often or the demand per visit to them is higher. A balanced system implies that there is no single bottleneck in the system, where improvements to that one device (i.e., the bottleneck device) would have a greater positive impact on overall performance than improvements made to any other device. In some sense, balanced systems are the ideal, with no particular device or resource single-handedly limiting performance. Balanced systems are important to consider, since they provide an upper bound on performance, a gold standard toward which to aspire.

For example, reconsider the database server example. From Tables 12.1 and 12.4 (and indeed for any number of customers in the network), the slow disk has the highest utilization. It is the system bottleneck and the system is not balanced. Because the slow disk is over-utilized compared to the other devices, one way to improve performance would be to move some of the files from the slow disk to the fast disk. This has the effect of reducing the load (and utilization) of the slow disk and increasing the load (and utilization) of the fast disk. (Another way to achieve balance between the two disks would be to replace the slower disk by another fast disk. This would further improve performance, but would be more expensive than simply moving files between the disks.)

By moving disk files so that the fast disk is visited twice as often as the slow disk, the overall system becomes balanced. Now consider this balanced system with ten customers in the system, as shown in Figure 12.4. Notice now that all device demands (i.e., the D's) are equal. The normal way to solve this system would be to run ten iterations of MVA, one for every customer level. However, because the system is balanced, only one MVA step is required.

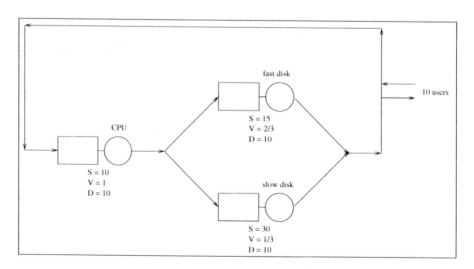

Figure 12.4. Balanced database server example (10 customers).

To see this, recall that the only thing necessary (i.e., the iteration basis) for finding the performance measures for ten customers is for MVA to know the average number of customers at each device when there are only nine customers in the system (i.e., $\bar{n}_i(9)$ for each device i). Since the system is balanced, the nine customers are equally distributed among the devices with three customers being at each of the three devices. Knowing that $\bar{n}_i(9) = 3$ for each i, from the MVA algorithm in Table 12.5, it follows quickly that the average residence time for each device i (i.e., $R_i'(n) = D_i\,[1 + \bar{n}_i(n-1)]$) is:

$$R_{cp}'(10) = 10(1 + 3.0000) = 40.00 \text{ seconds}$$
$$R_{fd}'(10) = (2/3)\,15(1 + 3.0000) = 40.00 \text{ seconds}$$
$$R_{sd}'(10) = (1/3)\,30(1 + 3.0000) = 40.00 \text{ seconds}$$

The overall system response time (i.e., $R_0(n) = \sum_{i=1}^{K} R_i'(n)$) is:

$$R_0(10) = 40.00 + 40.00 + 40.00 = 120.00 \text{ seconds}$$

The overall system throughput (i.e., $X_0(n) = \frac{n}{R_0(n)}$) is:

$$X_0(10) = \frac{10}{120.00} = 0.0833 \text{ customers per second}$$

The throughput for each device i (i.e., $X_i(n) = V_i \times X_0(n)$) is:

$$X_{cp}(10) = 1.0(0.0833) = 0.0833 \text{ customers per second}$$
$$X_{fd}(10) = \frac{2}{3}(0.0833) = 0.0556 \text{ customers per second}$$
$$X_{sd}(10) = \frac{1}{3}(0.0833) = 0.0278 \text{ customers per second}$$

The utilization for each device i (i.e., $U_i(n) = S_i \times X_i(n)$) is:

$$U_{cp}(10) = 10.00(0.0833) = 0.8333 = 83.33\%$$
$$U_{fd}(10) = 15.00(0.0556) = 0.8333 = 83.33\%$$
$$U_{sd}(10) = 30.00(0.0278) = 0.8333 = 83.33\%$$

And, finally, the average number of customers at each device i (i.e., $\bar{n}_i(n) = X_0(n) \times R_i'(n)$) is:

$$\bar{n}_{cp}(10) = 0.0833(40.00) = 3.3333 \text{ customers}$$
$$\bar{n}_{fd}(10) = 0.0833(40.00) = 3.3333 \text{ customers}$$
$$\bar{n}_{sd}(10) = 0.0833(40.00) = 3.3333 \text{ customers}$$

In balanced systems, all the device demands (i.e., the D_i's) are equivalent. Let this common device demand be D. Therefore, finding the overall system response time can be simplified to:

$$
\begin{aligned}
R_0(n) &= \sum_{i=1}^{K} \left[V_i \times R_i'(n) \right] \\
&= \sum_{i=1}^{K} \left[V_i S_i \left[1 + \bar{n}_i(n-1) \right] \right] \\
&= \sum_{i=1}^{K} \left[D_i \left[1 + \bar{n}_i(n-1) \right] \right] \\
&= \sum_{i=1}^{K} \left[D \left[1 + \frac{n-1}{K} \right] \right] \\
&= KD \left[1 + \frac{n-1}{K} \right] \\
&= KD + Dn - D \\
&= D(K + n - 1)
\end{aligned}
$$

and overall system throughput is simply:

$$X_0(n) = \frac{n}{R_0(n)} = \frac{n}{D(K + n - 1)}.$$

As a verification in the balanced database server example, where $n = 10$, $D = 10$, and $K = 3$, the overall system response time is $R_0(10) = 10(3 + 10 - 1) = 120$ seconds and the overall system throughput is $X_0(10) = \frac{10}{120} = 0.0833$ customers per second. Thus, performance metrics for balanced systems, which follow directly from the MVA formulae, are extremely easy to compute. Overall response time requires one addition, one subtraction, and one multiplication. Overall system throughput requires one extra division.

12.5   MVA Extensions and Limitations

The basic MVA algorithm is quite powerful and elegant. It is applicable across a wide set of performance models. It has been the focus of much research and several extensions have been developed. These include:

- Multi-class networks
- Networks with load dependent servers
- Networks with open and closed classes of customers

Several approximation techniques have also be adapted to MVA to model systems having non-product form features, including first-come-first-serve and priority multi-class networks. The extension of MVA to product form, load-independent, multi-class networks is the topic of the following chapter. Chapter 14 extends MVA and the treatment of multiclass open QNs to the load-dependent case. Several approximations to deal with non-product form QNs are presented in Chapter 15.

However, even with its widespread applicability, there are limitations and shortcomings surrounding MVA. For example:

- MVA does not provide the steady state probabilities of individual system states. Thus, if it were important to know the probability that there were, say, less than five customers at a device in order to meet some QoS criteria, MVA would not be helpful. It would be necessary to revert to solving the global balance equations. As its name implies, MVA only provides the *mean values* of various performance metrics, not the associated distributions.

- MVA does not provide transient analysis information. For instance, if it were necessary to know how long it would take the system to recover from a temporary overload in one sector of the system and return to "steady state" behavior, MVA would be inadequate.

- MVA does not model state dependent behavior. For example, consider the modeling of a simple routing protocol, with two paths between a particular source and destination, where the customers (i.e., message packets) select the path least busy (i.e., dependent on the particular system state). Although a Markovian model can be easily constructed and solved for this situation, MVA is of little use.

- MVA solves product form networks. As a result, MVA is not directly applicable to non-product form situations. These restrictions exclude certain device service distributions (e.g., Gaussian, uniform, constant), certain device queuing disciplines (e.g., priority, multi-class FCFS), and certain device loading strategies (e.g., shortest queue routing, deterministic routing). In some of these cases, approximate MVA techniques have been developed as discussed in Chapter 15.

12.6　Chapter Summary

The Mean Value Analysis technique is arguably one of the most significant contributions to the field of performance evaluation within the past 25 years. It is the primary solution engine behind the large majority of state-of-the-art analytical solution packages currently in use. MVA is intuitive, elegant, and simple.

This chapter first motivates, then develops, then summarizes, then applies, and finally qualifies MVA. Examples from the database server example introduced in previous chapters are used to demonstrate MVA. The following exercises are intended to reinforce and to broaden the reader's understanding and range of applicability of MVA.

12.7　Exercises

1. From the balance equations given in Table 12.2: a) give the details to verify the solution given in Table 12.3 and b) give the details to verify the associated performance metrics shown in Table 12.4.

2. Consider the following "system." Eight students are always in the weight room at the Rec Center. As soon as one student exits, another enters. Upon entering, a student goes to treadmill, then to the station-

ary bike, and then to the rowing machine. There is a single treadmill, stationary bike, and rowing machine. A student exercises for an average of 5 minutes on the treadmill, 8 minutes on the stationary bike, and 4 minutes on the rowing machine. A typical student makes two cycles through the three pieces of equipment before leaving. If a particular piece of equipment happens to be busy when a student wants to use it, he/she patiently waits until it becomes free.

- Use MVA to find the average number of students leaving the weight room per hour and also the average amount of time that each student stays in the weight room.

- Plot the average amount of time that each student stays in the weight room as a function of the number of students allowed in the weight room. Vary the number of students allowed in the weight room from 1 to 15.

- Suppose that it is desired to place a cap on the maximum utilization that any piece of equipment should be used (i.e., to allow for equipment maintenance time). If this cap is set at 80%, what is the maximum number of students that should be allowed in the room?

- Which piece of equipment is the system bottleneck? If a certain percentage of students were allowed to bypass this particular piece of equipment, what percentage of students should be allowed to bypass it so that it is no longer the system bottleneck?

- If an additional stationary bike were purchased and students were randomly assigned (i.e., equally likely) to use either bike, by how much would the average time be reduced that a student spends in the weight room?

3. In Section 12.4, the database server example was balanced by moving files from the slow disk to the fast disk. Another way to achieve balance would be to speed up both the slow disk and the CPU. By how much would the speed of these devices need to be improved to achieve a

balanced system? How much would these upgrades improve overall system performance (e.g., throughput and response time)?

4. In the original database server example with two customers, the files are evenly distributed over the two disks. That is, after leaving the CPU, customers are equally likely to visit either disk. Use MVA and vary the proportion of time that the fast disk is visited as opposed to the slow disk. (This models the movement of files from one disk to the other.) Find the optimal proportion of files that should to stored on the fast disk in order to maximize overall system throughput.

5. Repeat the previous problem six times, varying the number of customers in the system to be 1, 2, 3, 5, 10, and 15. Plot the results. Provide an hypothesis of why this optimal proportion changes as a function of the number of customers in the system. Hypothesize what the optimal proportion would be if the number of customers in the system grows toward infinity. Justify your hypotheses.

6. A Web server has one CPU and one disk and was monitored during one hour. The utilization of the CPU was measured at 30%. During this period, 10,800 HTTP requests were processed. Each request requires, on average, 3 I/Os on the server's disk. The average service time at the disk is 20 msec.

- What are the service demands of an HTTP request at the CPU and at the disk?
- Find the throughput, $X_0(n)$, of the Web server for $n = 0, 1, 2$, and 3, where n is the number of concurrent HTTP requests in execution at the Web server.
- Assume that the Web server receives requests at a rate of $\lambda = 5$ requests/sec. At most three HTTP requests can be in execution at any point in time. Requests that arrive and find 3 requests being processed will be placed in a processing queue, which is assumed to have an infinite size. Find the average response time of an HTTP request. This time includes the time spent by a request in the processing queue plus the time required to process

the request. [*Hint:* use the Generalized Birth-Death theorem of Chapter 10 together with the results of the previous item.]

Bibliography

[1] F. Baskett, K. M. Chandy, R. R. Muntz, and F. G. Palacios, F.G., "Open, closed, and mixed networks of queues with different classes of customers," *J. ACM 22,* 2, April 1975, pp. 248–260.

[2] S. C. Bruell and G. Balbo, *Computational Algorithms for Closed Queueing Networks,* North Holland, New York, 1980.

[3] E. D. Lazowska, J. Zahorjan, S. Graham, and K. C. Sevcik, *Quantitative System Performance: Computer System Analysis Using Queueing Network Models,* Prentice-Hall, Upper Saddle River, New Jersey, 1984.

[4] D. A. Menascé, V. A. F. Almeida, and L. W. Dowdy, *Capacity Planning and Performance Modeling: From Mainframes to Client-Server Systems,* Prentice-Hall, Upper Saddle River, New Jersey, 1994.

[5] M. Reiser and S. Lavenberg, "Mean value analysis of closed multichain queueing networks," *J. ACM 27,* 2, April 1980, pp. 313–322.

[6] K. C. Sevcik and I. Mitrani, "The distribution of queueing network states at input and output instants," *J. ACM 28,* 2, April 1981, pp. 358–371.

[7] W. Wang and K. C. Sevcik, "Experiments with improved approximate mean value analysis algorithms, " *Performance Evaluation 39,* 1, February 2000, pp. 189–206.

[8] J. Zahorjan, K. C. Sevcik, D. L. Eager, and B. I. Galler, "Balanced job bound analysis of queueing networks," *Comm. ACM 25,* 2, February 1982, pp. 134–141.

Chapter 13

Queuing Models with Multiple Classes

13.1 Introduction

The real power of performance models becomes evident when they are used for predictive purposes. In performance engineering, models are essential because of their ability to predict adequately the performance of a particular system under different workloads. Real-life systems experience a wide variety of customers (e.g., experienced heavy users, novices, web surfers, e-mail users, bank transactions) with different resource usage profiles. Actual workloads do not tend to be a single class of homogeneous customers. Typically, each customer differs from every other customer. However, it is impractical to model each customer's individual idiosyncrasies exactly. Rather, customers are grouped into classes of similar behaviors, which are then represented in the model as the average behavior of the class and the customer population of the class. Therefore, techniques are needed that solve multiple-class performance models. This chapter provides MVA-based algorithms for solving open and closed product-form queuing network models with multiple classes. The techniques include exact and approximate solutions. The MS Excel workbooks `OpenQN.XLS` and `ClosedQN.XLS` implement the open and closed multiclass QN solution techniques described in this chapter, respectively.

13.2   The Need for Multiple-Class Models

There are various motivations for constructing multiple-class models to capture the features of heterogeneous workloads. These models can be used to represent different QoS and SLA requirements for the different workload classes. Multi-class models capture the priorities and special services that each workload class requires.

As a more detailed example, consider the widespread use of electronic mail for personal communication. The need to provide reliable and high-quality mail service motivates providers to conduct comprehensive capacity planning analysis for their mail servers. A mail server can be viewed as a collection several underlying subsystems, including storage buffers, network routers, and processing servers. A typical problem faced by service providers is how to properly size (i.e., amount of storage capacity, number of network ports, processor speed) a mail servers in the most cost-effective way. Profiles of e-mail clients exhibit dramatic differences in their resource demands by factors of 50 and more between light and heavy e-mail users [5, 20]. Representing the workload of such disparate profiles by a single workload class does injustice to both light and heavy users. For example, approximating one heavy user and one light user by two medium users results in an inaccurate workload representation. The identities of the heavy user and the light user are lost, being replaced by two non-existent medium users. Hence, such mail server performance models call for different classes of requests to provide meaningful results.

The choice of the workload abstraction and the corresponding number of classes are key steps in performance modeling. For example, different Service Level Agreements (SLA) are usually imposed on different workload classes [14]. SLAs represent guarantees regarding the quality of service provided by a system. An SLA for one workload class could state that 90% of all messages to local users get delivered to the target mailbox within 60 sec. Another SLA for a different workload class could be that 98% of messages sent to remote mail servers are received by the remote server within 90 seconds.

The accuracy of the system model is strongly influenced by the number of workload classes chosen. Too few classes can lead to inaccurate generalizations whereas too many classes lead to excessive detail and complexity. As an example, consider the case of a Web-based shopping system. In the performance analysis of the system, three workload classes are considered: cacheable transactions, noncacheable transactions, and search transactions [2]. The transaction requests are grouped into classes based on the impact of their performance on the system. Cacheable requests have their responses stored in an application server cache and consequently demand less processor and disk time than noncacheable requests. Processing a noncacheable request requires approximately 100 times more CPU time than required if the request were in cache [2]. Thus, it is obvious that each class of transactions uses the system resources differently and experiences very different response times. Single-class models are unable to answer important performance questions related to specific workload classes, because they cannot single out differences among groups of transactions. Single-class models are effective in capturing global behavior but are limited in their predictive capability of individual group (and often important) behavior.

Although multiple-class models are more useful and natural for describing workloads of real systems, they present problems to the modeler. For instance, it is difficult to obtain parameters (e.g., multiclass service demands and multiclass visit ratios) for models with multiple classes. Usually, monitoring tools do not provide measurements on a per-class basis. Inferences (sometimes wild guesses) have to be made to parameterize each workload class and to apportion the system overhead among the classes. As a result, it is more difficult to obtain accurate parameters for multiple class models than for single-class ones.

Example 13.1

An explicit SLA defines the expectations between application clients and service providers. Increased expectations are associated with increased costs for meeting those expectations. Thus, an SLA expresses a direct relationship between a class of customers and the service demands (and the related costs) of their applications. Some customers require very short response time for critical applications and are willing to pay more for these specific transactions. Suppose that the manager of a data center service provider is negotiating an SLA with a client representing a financial company for three types of applications: risk portfolio analysis, purchase transactions, and browsing transactions. The initial proposal states that the average response time for risk portfolio analysis is to be 3 hours and the client is willing to pay 15 dollars for this service per execution. Purchase transactions are to have an average system response time (i.e., from when a client submits a purchase request until a purchase verification message is returned) of less than 1 sec and each transaction will cost 50 cents. Browsing transactions are to have an average response time of less than 2 sec and will cost 10 cents each. Before agreeing to the SLA, the data center manager needs to know whether the currently installed capacity can accommodate the proposed new services for the financial company client. This is an important step of the process because the SLA may also specify financial penalties if the response times are not met. How should the data center's performance analyst specify the workload? A single-class workload description does not provide adequate detail for analyzing the SLA. Instead, the performance analyst specifies a multiple-class workload model as follows.

- Class 1: The risk portfolio analysis is modeled by a closed class, consisting of a set of background processes, defined by the service demands (i.e., processor and disks) and the number of processes in execution during "the peak hour."

- Class 2: The online purchase transactions are modeled by an open class, defined by the service demands (i.e., processor and disks) and the average arrival rate during "a peak minute."

- Class 3: The browsing transactions are modeled by an open class, defined by service demands (i.e., processor and disks) and an average arrival rate during "a peak minute."

The three-class model is solved using the techniques presented in this chapter and the response times obtained. Based on the predicted response times, the data center manager will know if the currently installed capacity is sufficient for the contract. If not, in order to meet the new performance objectives, the data center will have to increase its capacity before agreeing to the SLA contract. In this case, management will incur new hardware acquisition costs, which will have to be prorated against the revenue generated by the new transactions.   ■

13.3   Simple Two-Class Model

Consider a transaction processing server with a single processor and two disks. The load on the system consists of two types of transactions: queries and updates. During the peak hours, the system is under heavy load, such that four transactions are in execution almost all the time. The analyst knows that if more than four transactions are allowed to be in execution concurrently, the system is susceptible to thrashing due to limited memory, disk, and processing capacity. After monitoring the system for a given period of time, the system administrator observes that the most common execution mix during the peak hours is a combination of three query transactions and one update transaction.

The performance analyst wants to improve system performance by investigating different system scenarios. Because of the workload type (i.e., transaction oriented), it is natural to represent the system as an open model with a maximum number of four concurrent transactions. To avoid thrashing, if a transaction arrives at the system and finds four other transactions already in execution, it is required to wait in the system entry queue. Thus, it is necessary to represent the effects of blocking, which makes the model non product-form (i.e., much more difficult to solve analytically). An alternative view is that of a closed model with a constant number of four transactions in execution. This view is both a good representation for the system during peak hours and does not violate product-form assumptions, allowing the model to be solved more easily. The drawback is that the model represents only the time a transaction spends in execution. Blocking effects are not captured by this model. Chapter 15 presents techniques for modeling blocking effects.

The choice between the open and closed representations for modeling a system is influenced by several factors, including the difficulty in solving the model and the difficulty in obtaining the parameters required by each type of model. In this example, an open model includes the parameterization of blocking queues to represent more realistic behavior. Solving the model is more complex and may require the use of approximation techniques. In contrast, a closed model is more approximate, but easier to solve since it requires only one additional parameter, the average number of transactions in execution.

The two types of transactions differ in both function and resource usage. Update transactions impose significant write traffic to the disks, while query transactions can often be satisfied by the cache and impose less load on the disks. Consistent with observed ACID [11] transaction properties, the model assumes that update transactions demand more resources than query transactions. Thus, the analyst represents the system as a two-class model, as illustrated in Fig. 13.1. Resource demands by each class (i.e., query transactions and update transactions) at each device are shown.

Suppose the transaction processing server is monitored for 30 minutes (i.e., 1800 sec) and the measurement data shown in Table 13.1 is collected. From Table 13.1, the two classes are characterized by different service demands. For example, while update transactions divide their I/O load across the two disks, query transactions do not make use of disk 2 (i.e., the service demand at disk 2 is equal to 0). Since the transactions of both classes share the same devices, it is reasonable to assume that the service time per disk

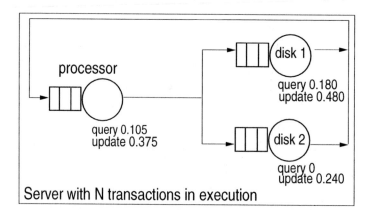

Figure 13.1. Two-class queuing model.

Table 13.1. Measurement Data for the Transaction Processing System

Class	Service Demand (sec)			Transactions in the System	Transactions Completed
	Processor	Disk 1	Disk 2		
Query	0.105	0.180	0.000	3	7368
Update	0.375	0.480	0.240	1	736

visit is roughly the same across the two classes. However, updates require more disk accesses than do queries. Thus, the differences in service demands at a given device stem from the number of visits that a transaction makes to the device. In this example, the service demands show that an update transaction performs many more I/O operations than does a query transaction (i.e., updates require more visits to the disks). By viewing the measurement data in Table 13.1, update transactions visit disk 1 twice as much as disk 2. Query transactions do not visit disk 2 and visit disk 1 3/8 (i.e., $0.180/0.480$) as often as update transactions.

In a single-class model, customers are assumed to be statistically identical in terms of their resource requirements. As a result, customers are undistinguishable in single-class models and the order in which transactions are serviced at a device is irrelevant. This observation, however, is not valid for multiclass models, because customers of different classes are often treated differently (i.e., writers may be given priority over readers at the disk to ensure the most up-to-date information available). Therefore, the issue of scheduling is relevant in models of multiple classes. Suppose that at a given instant of time, the four example transactions are contending for processor time (i.e., all transactions are contending for CPU service). Which transaction (query or update) should be serviced next? The goal of a scheduling policy is to assign customers to be executed by a server to optimize some system objective, such as minimizing average response time, maximizing throughput, meeting a real-time deadline, or satisfying an SLA commitment. For instance, by specifying a priority scheduling policy, a processor spends most of its time on classes of customers that are considered most critical. In the same way, a scheduling discipline can give priority to lightweight transactions over heavyweight transactions, in an attempt to minimizing the average response time of short (i.e., lightweight) requests.

Modern operating systems implement various versions of well-known scheduling disciplines such as *first come first served (FCFS), round robin (RR), shortest job next (SJN), shortest remaining time (SRT), earliest dead-line (ED),* and *least laxity (LL).* For example, SJN scheduling policy could be used to model disk scheduling, where the "job size" is based on the number of tracks that the disk head must move [12]. This is analogous to the *shortest seek time first (SSTF)* disk scheduling policy. In short, the performance of a multiclass model depends on both the service demands per class and on the scheduling policies of each device.

Once an appropriate multiclass model is selected and parameterized, an appropriate solution technique is needed. That is, a solution technique is required that calculates performance measures for each workload class in the model. Making use of methods learned so far, a first approach to solving a multiclass model is to construct an equivalent single-class model. To do this, it is necessary to aggregate the performance parameters of the multiple classes into a single class. The service demand of the aggregate class at any server is the average of the individual class demands weighted by the relative class throughputs. The number of transactions of the aggregate class corresponds to the sum of the number of transactions in the system due to each individual class. If the measured throughputs of the two classes are $7,368/1800 = 4.093$ tps and $736/1,800 = 0.409$ tps, respectively, then the processor service demand of the aggregate class is calculated as

$$D_{\text{processor,aggr}} = \frac{0.105 \times 4.093 + 0.375 \times 0.409}{4.093 + 0.409} = 0.130 \text{ sec.}$$

The aggregate class demands at the two disks can be similarly calculated. Table 13.2 summarizes the parameters obtained for the aggregate class. The single-class model defined by the parameters of Table 13.2 can then be solved by using single class MVA (see Chapter 12). The calculated throughput for this single-class model equals 4.49 tps, which, in this example, is an excellent approximation to its multiclass counterpart, 4.50 tps.

Dowdy et al. [9] have shown that a single-class model of an actual multi-class system pessimistically bounds the performance of the multiclass system. These bounds help the analyst to identify the magnitude of possible errors

Table 13.2. Parameters for the Aggregate Class

Class	Service Demand (sec)			Number of Transactions in the System
	Processor	Disk 1	Disk 2	
Aggregate	0.130	0.207	0.023	4

that come from an incorrect workload characterization of a multiclass system. Using operational relationships ($U_i = X_0 \times D_i$ and $R = n/X_0$), the following results for the single-class model are calculated: $U_{cpu} = 4.49 \times 0.130 = 58\%$, $U_{disk\ 1} = 4.49 \times 0.207 = 93\%$, $U_{disk\ 2} = 4.49 \times 0.02310\%$, and $R = 4/4.49 = 0.89$ sec.

Once the equivalent single-class model has been constructed and solved, the analyst often wants to investigate the effects of possible future modifications to the system. Examples include:

- What is the predicted increase in the throughput of query transactions if the load of the update class is moved to off-peak hours?

- Realizing that disk 1 is the bottleneck (i.e., the device with the highest utilization) and disk 2 is lightly loaded, what is the predicted response time if the total I/O load of query transactions is moved to disk 2?

The aggregate single-class model is not able to answer these questions, because it does not provide performance results on an individual class basis. Therefore, techniques to calculate the performance of models with multiple classes are needed.

13.4   Notation and Assumptions

When customers in a queuing network model exhibit different routing patterns, different service time requirements, and/or different scheduling disciplines, the model is said to have multiple classes of customers. Consider a local area network with P client workstations and Q servers. Each client workstation may have its own local storage, but it may also require additional storage capacity from the servers. After executing at a workstation, a process sends a request across the network to acquire service from one of the storage servers. Each client workstation process places one request at a time on the network. A queuing model of this system is proposed in [22]. If all client processes have identical workload requirements and balance their service requests across all file servers, the system can be modeled by a single-class workload with P processes. However, if each client process restricts its requests to a subset of servers, with each client visiting a different set of servers, performance can be significantly improved. By judiciously segregating clients on the servers, potential queuing delays are reduced and average response time is likewise reduced. In this alternative model, each client process has a different routing probability (i.e., each process visits a different set of servers) and a separate workload class is required to represent each client workstation. Thus the system is modeled with P classes, each with exactly one process in each class.

In general, the queuing networks considered here consist of K devices (or service centers) and R different classes of customers. A central concept in the analysis and solution of queuing networks is the state of the network. The state represents a distribution of customers over classes and devices. The network state is denoted by a vector $\vec{n} = (\vec{n}_1, \vec{n}_2, \ldots, \vec{n}_K)$, where component $\vec{n}_i$ ($i = 1, \ldots, K$) is a vector that represents the number of customers of each class at server i. That is, $\vec{n}_i = (n_{i,1}, n_{i,2}, \ldots, n_{i,R})$ where $n_{i,r}$ represents the number of class r customers at server i. For instance, returning to the example in Fig. 13.1 the state of the system is defined as $(\vec{n}_1, \vec{n}_2, \vec{n}_3)$, where $\vec{n}_i$ is a tuple specifying the number of update and query transactions at device i. Two possible states in this example include $((1,3), (0,0), (0,0))$ and $((0,1), (0,2), (1,0))$. The former state indicates that all transactions (i.e., one update and three query transactions) are at the processor. The latter state represents the situation where one query transaction is executing at the processor, two queries are at disk 1, and the update transaction is being serviced at disk 2.

The BCMP theorem [3], developed by Baskett, Chandy, Muntz, and Palacios, specifies a combination of service time distributions and scheduling disciplines that yield multiclass product-form queuing networks that lend themselves to efficient model solution techniques. Open, closed, or mixed networks are allowed. A closed network consists of only closed classes with a constant number of customers in each class at all times. In contrast, an open network allows customers in each class to enter or leave the network. A mixed network is closed with respect to some classes and open with respect to other classes. Basically, the set of assumptions required by the BCMP theorem for a product-form solution is as follows.

- *Service centers with a FCFS discipline.* In this case, customers are serviced in the order in which they arrive. The service time distributions are required to be exponential with the same mean for all classes. Although all classes must have the same mean service time at any given device, they may have different visit ratios, which allows the possibility of different service demands for each class at any given device. The service rate is allowed to be load dependent, but it can be dependent only on the total number of customers at the server and not on the number of customers of any particular class. For instance, requests from clients to a file server can be normally modeled by a FCFS load-independent server. Disks are usually modeled as FCFS service centers, with load-dependent service rates to represent reduced service times as the load at the disk increases (i.e., effectively modeling shortest seek time first or SCAN scheduling policies).

- *Service centers with a PS discipline.* When there are n customers at a server with a processor sharing (PS) discipline, each customer receives service at a rate of $1/n$ of their normal service rate. Each class may have a distinct service time distribution. The *round robin* (RR) scheduling discipline allows customers to receive a fixed quantum of service. If the customer does not finish execution within its allocated quantum, it returns to the end of the queue, awaiting further service. In the limiting case, when the quantum approaches zero, the RR discipline becomes the PS discipline. Operating systems normally employ the RR discipline. Thus PS is a reasonable approximation to represent processor scheduling disciplines of modern operating systems.

- *Service centers with infinite servers (IS).* When there is an infinite supply of servers in a service center, there is never any waiting for a server. This situation is known as IS, delay server, or no queuing. For instance, think time at terminals in an interactive system is usually modeled by delay servers. In a lightly loaded LAN, the time needed to send a request from a client workstation to a server can also be approximated by a delay server. Basically, any component of a system where there is a constant delay that is independent of the overall load (i.e., arrive rate, multiprogramming level) can be modeling by an IS server.

- *Service centers with a LCFS-PR discipline.* Under last-come-first-served-preemptive-resume (LCFS-PR), whenever a new customer arrives, the server preempts servicing the previous customer (if any) and is allocated to the newly arriving customer. When a customer completes, the server resumes executing its previously preempted job. Each class may have a distinct service time distribution. High priority interrupts that require immediate but small amounts of service are adequately modeled by LCFS-PR servers.

In open networks, the time between successive arrivals is assumed to be exponentially distributed. Bulk arrivals are not allowed. Multi-class product-form networks have efficient computational algorithms for their solution. The two major algorithms are convolution [6] and MVA [16]. Because of their simplicity and intuitive appeal, this chapter presents MVA-based algorithms for exact and approximate solutions of models with multiple classes. (Also see [13] for MVA-based algorithms of QNs and [8] for solution algorithms based on decomposition and aggregation techniques.) The following notation is used for the multiclass models presented here.

- K: number of devices or service centers of the model
- R: number of classes of customers
- M_r: number of terminals of class r
- Z_r: think time of class r
- N_r: class r population
- λ_r: arrival rate of class r
- $S_{i,r}$: average service time of class r customers at device i

- $V_{i,r}$: average visit ratio of class r customers at device i
- $D_{i,r}$: average service demand of class r customers at device i; $D_{i,r} = V_{i,r}S_{i,r}$:
- $R_{i,r}$: average response time per visit of class r customers at device i
- $R'_{i,r}$: average residence time of class r customers at device i (i.e., the total time spent by class r customers at device i over all visits to the device); $R'_{i,r} = V_{i,r}R_{i,r}$
- $\bar{n}_{i,r}$: average number of class r customers at device i
- $\bar{n}_i$: average number of customers at device i
- $X_{i,r}$: class r throughput at device i
- $X_{0,r}$: class r system throughput
- R_r: class r response time

13.5 Closed Models

The load intensity of a multiclass model with R classes and K devices is represented by the vector $\vec{N} = (N_1, N_2, \ldots, N_R)$, where N_r indicates the number of class r customers in the system. The goal of multiclass algorithms is to calculate the performance measures of the network as a function of $\vec{N}$. In the transaction system example (i.e., Fig. 13.1), the performance measures are calculated for each class (update and query) for the population $\vec{N} = (1, 3)$ (i.e., for one update transaction and three query transactions).

The two types of processing that are usually modeled as closed classes are background batch jobs and interactive jobs. The key feature is that the total load placed by these classes on a system is constant as depicted in Fig. 13.2. In the case of background processing, it is assumed that the system always has a backlog of jobs waiting to enter the system. Thus whenever a process leaves the system it is replaced by a new, statistically identical, process. Therefore the number of background processes in the system remains constant. For example, in a database system, typical background processes include a log writer, a checkpointing process, and a session monitor. In an interactive system, each customer (e.g., transaction, process, user, job) alternates between thinking and waiting. The thinking state corresponds

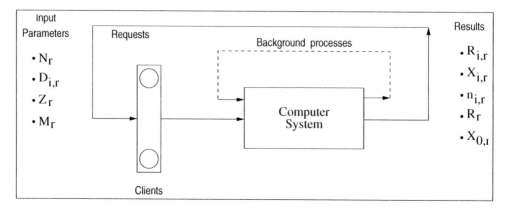

Figure 13.2. Multiple class closed model.

to the period of time that elapses since a customer receives a reply from the system due to the previous request until a new request is issued. After submitting a new request, the customer enters the waiting state while the system executes the request. Each of the M_r terminals is associated with one class r customer. Thus, there exists M_r requests in the system, where each request cycles between spending R_r units of time executing and Z_r time units thinking. A closed model is a combination of interactive and batch classes. The closed system analysis begins with the load intensity vector $\vec{N}$ and the class descriptor parameters $(D_{i,r}, M_r, Z_r)$. The analysis computes the throughputs, response times, and queue lengths of each class.

As with the single-class model, the MVA-based solution of a multiclass system relies on three basic equations applied to each class.

$$X_{0,r}(\vec{N}) = \frac{N_r}{Z_r + \displaystyle\sum_{i=1}^{K} R'_{i,r}(\vec{N})} \qquad (13.5.1)$$

Equation (13.5.1) is obtained by applying Little's Law separately to each class of customers. If r is a batch class, then Z_r is zero. The residence time $(R'_{i,r})$ corresponds to the total time a class r customer spends at server i during its execution. It includes the service demand $(D_{i,r})$ plus the total waiting time at the device. The average response time of class r customers can then be written as $R_r(\vec{N}) = \sum_{i=1}^{K} R'_{i,r}(\vec{N})$.

Applying Little's Law and the Forced Flow Law to each service center yields Eq. (13.5.2).

$$\begin{aligned}
\bar{n}_{i,r}(\vec{N}) &= X_{i,r}(\vec{N})R_{i,r}(\vec{N}) \\
&= X_{0,r}(\vec{N})V_{i,r}R_{i,r}(\vec{N}) \\
&= X_{0,r}(\vec{N})R'_{i,r}(\vec{N})
\end{aligned} \tag{13.5.2}$$

Summing up customers of all classes at device i gives the total number of customers at that device, $\bar{n}_i(\vec{N})$.

$$\begin{aligned}
\bar{n}_i(\vec{N}) &= \sum_{r=1}^{R} \bar{n}_{i,r}(\vec{N}) \\
&= \sum_{r=1}^{R} X_{0,r}(\vec{N})R'_{i,r}(\vec{N})
\end{aligned} \tag{13.5.3}$$

The key equation of the MVA technique can be derived from the observation that the mean response time of a class r customer at service center i equals its own mean service time at that device plus the time to complete the mean backlog seen upon its arrival (i.e., the average number of customers *seen* upon arrival multiplied by each customer's mean service time). Therefore,

$$\begin{aligned}
R_{i,r}(\vec{N}) &= S_{i,r}[1 + \bar{n}^A_{i,r}(\vec{N})] \\
V_{i,r}\,R_{i,r}(\vec{N}) &= V_{i,r}S_{i,r}[1 + \bar{n}^A_{i,r}(\vec{N})] \\
R'_{i,r}(\vec{N}) &= D_{i,r}[1 + \bar{n}^A_{i,r}(\vec{N})]
\end{aligned} \tag{13.5.4}$$

where $\bar{n}^A_{i,r}$ is the average queue length at device i *seen* by an arriving class r customer. As seen in Eq. (13.5.4), the average residence time is a function of the service demand and not of the individual values of the service times and visit ratios.

In the case of a delay server, it follows directly by definition that the backlog is zero, $[\bar{n}^A_{i,r}(\vec{N}) = 0]$, which makes $R'_{i,r}(\vec{N}) = D_{i,r}$. When the scheduling discipline of center i is PS or LCFS-PR, the expression $1 + \bar{n}^A_{i,r}(\vec{N})$ can be viewed as an inflation factor of the service demand due to the congestion by other customers. For FCFS service centers, Eq. (13.5.4) represents the customer's own service demand plus the time to complete the service of all customers in front of it. For practical purposes, scheduling disciplines can be grouped into two categories: delay and queuing. The latter encompasses load-independent servers with the following disciplines: PS, LCFS-PR, and FCFS.

Having as a starting point the fact that the queue length is zero when there are no customers in the network ($\bar{n}_i(\vec{0}) = 0$), Eqs. (13.5.1), (13.5.2), and (13.5.4) can be used iteratively to calculate the performance measures of the model. However, there is a minor problem; no expression for $\bar{n}_{i,r}^A(\vec{N})$ has yet been given. Given that expression it would be easy to solve a multiclass model. Multi-class model solution techniques are grouped into either exact or approximate solutions, depending on the way the backlog *seen* upon arrival [i.e., $\bar{n}_{i,r}^A(\vec{N})$] is calculated.

13.5.1   Exact Solution Algorithm

As pointed out in Chapter 10, an exact solution technique means the exact solution of analytic formulas of approximate models of actual systems. The key to the exact solution of multiclass closed queuing networks is the arrival theorem [16, 17], which states that a class r customer arriving at service center i in a system with population $\vec{N}$ *sees* the distribution of the number of customers in that center as being equal to the steady-state distribution for a network with population $(\vec{N} - \vec{1}_r)$. The vector $\vec{1}_r$ consists of a 1 in the rth position and zeros in the rest of the vector [i.e., $(0, 0, \ldots, 1, \ldots, 0)$]. In other words, it states simply that the arriving customer sees the system in equilibrium with itself removed. In the transaction system example with population $\vec{N} = (1, 3)$, a query transaction that arrives at the CPU sees a queuing distribution equal to that of the system with population $\vec{N} = (1, 2)$. From the arrival theorem, it follows that

$$\bar{n}_{i,r}^A(\vec{N}) = \bar{n}_i(\vec{N} - \vec{1}_r). \qquad (13.5.5)$$

Combining Eqs. (13.5.1), (13.5.2), (13.5.3), (13.5.4), and (13.5.5), the algorithm for the exact solution of closed multiclass models is described in Fig. 13.3.

Input Parameters: $D_{i,r}$ and N_r

Initialization: For $i = 1$ to K do $\bar{n}_i(\vec{0}) = 0$

Iteration Loops:

For $j_1 = 0$ to N_1 do

    For $j_2 = 0$ to N_2 do

    $\ldots$

        For $j_R = 0$ to N_R do

          Begin

           $\vec{N} = (j_1, j_2, \ldots, j_R)$

          If $\vec{N} \neq \vec{0}$

         Then Begin

            For $r = 1$ to R do

              Begin

              If $j_r > 0$

              Then For $i = 1$ to K do

$$R'_{i,r}(\vec{N}) = \begin{cases} D_{i,r} & \text{delay} \\ D_{i,r}[1 + \bar{n}_i(\vec{N} - \vec{1}_r)] & \text{LI} \end{cases}$$

              Else $R'_{i,r}(\vec{N}) = 0$;

$$X_{0,r}(\vec{N}) = \frac{j_r}{Z_r + \sum_{i=1}^{K} R'_{i,r}(\vec{N})}$$

            End;

            For $i = 1$ to K do

$$\bar{n}_i(\vec{N}) = \sum_{r=1}^{R} X_{0,r}(\vec{N}) R'_{i,r}(\vec{N})$$

          End

     End

Figure 13.3. Exact MVA algorithm for multiple classes.

13.5.2 Closed Models: Case Study

Recall the motivating problem of Section 13.3. The algorithm of Fig. 13.3 can be used to obtain the performance measures for each class. The first step is to apply the exact algorithm to the baseline model described in Table 13.1 [i.e., to calculate the results for the population of one update and three query transactions, $\vec{N} = (1, 3)$]. From the arrival theorem, to calculate the residence time at the devices (processor and two disks) for population $(1,3)$, the device queue lengths are required for populations $(0,3)$ and $(1,2)$. These correspond to one less update transaction and one less query transaction, respectively. By continually removing one customer from each class, eventually the performance measures for population $(0,0)$ are calculated, which is the starting point of the algorithm. Fig. 13.4 shows the precedence relationships required to calculate the results of a system with population $(1,3)$ using exact MVA.

Table 13.3 shows for each population of the sequence of Fig. 13.4 the results calculated by the exact MVA algorithm for the baseline model of the transaction system example. It is worth noting that each class can be calculated separately, as indicated in Table 13.3. However, the interaction among the multiple classes is explicitly represented by the term $\bar{n}_i(\vec{N} - \vec{1}_r)$ in the equation $R_{i,r}(\vec{N}) = D_{i,r}[1 + \bar{n}_i(\vec{N} - \vec{1}_r)]$. The average number of customers at device i reflects the contention for common shared resources among the distinct classes of the workload.

From Table 13.3 it is noted that the calculated throughputs for the query and update classes are 4.093 tps and 0.409 tps, respectively, which match the measurement results of Table 13.1. Either using Little's Law, or summing the average device residence times, the average response times are obtained for the two classes: 0.733 sec for queries and 2.444 sec for updates. Once the baseline model has been solved and validated, attention is directed to the prediction phase. To construct a predictive model, the parameters of the predicted system need to be specified. Consider the two questions posed in Section 13.3.

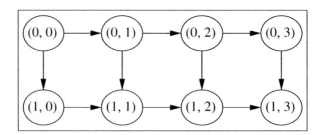

Figure 13.4. Sequence of calculations of MVA.

Table 13.3. Step-by-Step Results of the Two-Class Model Solution

Class	Variable	\multicolumn{8}{c}{Population (Update, Query)}							
		(0,0)	(0,1)	(0,2)	(0,3)	(1,0)	(1,1)	(1,2)	(1,3)
Query	$R'_{1,q}$	-	0.105	0.144	0.174	-	0.141	0.177	0.204
	$R'_{2,q}$	-	0.180	0.294	0.422	-	0.259	0.388	0.529
	$R'_{3,q}$	-	0.000	0.000	0.000	-	0.000	0.000	0.000
	$X_{0,q}$	-	3.509	4.566	5.034	-	2.500	3.540	4.093
	$n_{1,q}$	0	0.368	0.658	0.876	-	0.352	0.627	0.835
	$n_{2,q}$	0	0.632	1.342	2.124	-	0.648	1.373	2.165
	$n_{3,q}$	0	0.000	0.000	0.000	-	0.000	0.000	0.000
Update	$R'_{1,u}$	-	-	-	-	0.375	0.513	0.622	0.704
	$R'_{2,u}$	-	-	-	-	0.480	0.783	1.124	1.500
	$R'_{3,u}$	-	-	-	-	0.240	0.240	0.240	0.240
	$X_{0,u}$	-	-	-	-	0.913	0.651	0.504	0.409
	$n_{1,u}$	0	-	-	-	0.343	0.334	0.313	0.288
	$n_{2,u}$	0	-	-	-	0.438	0.510	0.566	0.614
	$n_{3,u}$	0	-	-	-	0.219	0.156	0.121	0.098

1. What is the predicted increase in the throughput of query transactions if the load of the update class is moved to off-peak hours?

   Answer: Since the update class will be removed, it is reasonable to assume that the number of transaction in the system will remain the same and the system will have a population of 4 query transactions. Solving a single-class model with 4 queries, a throughput of 5.275 tps is obtained. This new value indicates that the removal of the update class increases throughput by 28.87%.

2. Realizing that disk 1 is the bottleneck (i.e., the device with the highest utilization) and disk 2 is lightly loaded, what is the predicted response time if the total I/O load of query transactions is moved to disk 2?

   Answer: To construct the predictive model, it is only necessary to shift the value of $D_{2,q}$ to $D_{3,q}$, to indicate that the I/O load of query transactions will be moved from disk 1 to disk 2. With the new parameters, the model is resolved to give the following results: $X_{0,q} = 4.335$ tps,

$X_{0,u} = 0.517$ tps, $R_q = 0.692$ sec, and $R_u = 1.934$ sec. These results indicate a reduction of 5.6% in the average response time of queries and 20.9% in the mean response time of update transactions. Why does the proposed modification favor the update class? First, consider the system performance measures obtained by the baseline and predictive models, respectively.

From Table 13.4, note that the proposed modification changes the bottleneck from disk 1 to disk 2 and, at the same time, provides a better balance of disk utilization. Now, consider where the two types of transactions spend their time. Let the residence time percentage be the time a transaction spends at device i, expressed as a percentage of the average response time for the transaction [i.e., $(R'_{i,r} / \sum_{i=1}^{K} R'_{i,r}) \times 100$].

From Table 13.5 note that in the baseline model, query transactions spend 72.2% of their average response time at the bottleneck device, whereas update transactions spend 61.4%. When the I/O load of query transactions is moved to disk 2, it becomes the bottleneck. Update transactions benefit more from the modification because they get better disk utilization balance. To confirm this, the results in Table 13.5 show that update transactions spend 24.8% and 38.8% of their time at disk 1 and disk 2, respectively. Moreover, disk 1 has no contention, since it is dedicated to the update transaction class. In contrast, query

Table 13.4. Device Utilization

Model	Class	Utilization (%)		
		Processor	Disk 1	Disk 2
Baseline	Query	42.98	73.67	0
	Update	15.33	19.63	9.81
	Total	58.31	**93.3**	9.81
Modified	Query	45.51	0	78.03
	Update	19.38	24.81	12.40
	Total	64.89	24.81	**90.43**

Table 13.5. Residence Time Percentage

Model	Class	Residence Time (%)		
		Processor	Disk 1	Disk 2
Baseline	Query	27.8	72.2	0
	Update	28.8	61.4	9.8
Modified	Query	31.5	0	68.5
	Update	36.4	24.8	38.8

transactions concentrate their I/O on Disk 2, which is also used by updates.

13.5.3   Approximate Solution Algorithms

Table 13.3 provides a good idea regarding the number of operations required to compute the results of the simple transaction system example that consists of only 2 classes, 4 customers, and 3 devices. Not surprising, the computational effort required to compute performance measures of models of modern systems with several classes, many processes in execution, and hundreds of I/O devices is "significant."

Looking at Fig. 13.4, note that to compute the results of the model with population $(1, 2)$, the results of populations $(1, 1)$ and $(0, 2)$ are needed. Each of these populations requires, as input, queue lengths from two related populations. In the general case, when a system has R classes, each calculation of metrics for a given population demands inputs from R other populations. Due to the precedence relationships in the calculation of performance measures of a multiclass model, the computational complexity of MVA algorithms grows exponentially with the number of classes. The number of multiplications and the number of additions required to solve a multiclass model is proportional to

$$KR \prod_{r=1}^{R} (1 + N_r) \qquad (13.5.6)$$

Modeling distributed systems often involve large queuing networks. For example, consider a multi-tier distributed server environment, modeled as multiclass models [7, 10]. The workload may be viewed as processes running at the front servers, which during their execution require access to a number of files that can be either local or in the back-end servers. Assume that each process visits three back-end servers for file services. Suppose that we have a high speed LAN-based system with 20 front-end servers (processor and disk), 5 back-end servers and 1 process per server. To represent the different routings and service requests, a separate class is used for each process at the front-end servers. Thus, a closed model is constructed with 20 classes, 5 service centers (i.e., processor, disk, and 3 back-end servers), and 1 customer in each class. Substituting these numbers into Eq. (13.5.6), the solution of this hypothetical model would require approximately 104 million operations. So how can one avoid the high computational cost of exact MVA algorithms?

The source of the large number of operations required to compute the exact MVA algorithm is the recursion expressed in the equation

$$\bar{n}_{i,r}^A(\vec{N}) = \bar{n}_{i,r}(\vec{N} - \vec{1}_r) \qquad (13.5.7)$$

With the goal of reducing the time and space complexity of the MVA algorithm, several approximations have been proposed to break up the recursion [18]. The approximate algorithms reduce the complexity by substituting approximations for $\bar{n}_{i,r}^A(\vec{N})$ that are not recursive cite13-Sevcik00. A very simple approximation, due to Bard [4], is as follows:

$$\bar{n}_{i,r}(\vec{N}) \approx \bar{n}_{i,r}(\vec{N} - \vec{1}_r)$$
$$\bar{n}_{i,r}^A(\vec{N}) = \bar{n}_{i,r}(\vec{N}) \qquad (13.5.8)$$

This approximation is attractive when the number of customers becomes large. The most commonly used approximation is one proposed by Schweitzer [19] for BCMP models. It is based on the assumption that the number of class r customers at each service center increases proportionally to the number of class r customers in the network. From this observation, it follows that

$$\frac{\bar{n}_{i,r}(\vec{N} - \vec{1}_r)}{\bar{n}_{i,r}(\vec{N})} \quad = \quad \frac{N_r - 1}{N_r} \qquad\qquad (13.5.9)$$

$$\bar{n}_{i,r}(\vec{N} - \vec{1}_r) \quad = \quad \frac{N_r - 1}{N_r} \; \bar{n}_{i,r}(\vec{N}) \qquad\qquad (13.5.10)$$

Equation (13.5.10) is the basis of an iterative method for calculating performance measures of a closed model, described by the algorithm of Fig. 13.5. The basic idea is to substitute estimates for queue lengths $[\bar{n}_{i,r}(\vec{N})]$ into Eq. (13.5.10) and use the MVA equations to compute the next estimates for $\bar{n}_{i,r}(\vec{N})$. The iterative process starts with an estimate $\bar{n}_{i,r}^e(\vec{N})$ which assumes that class r customers are equally distributed among the K devices of the network. Iteration stops when successive values of $\bar{n}_{i,r}(\vec{N})$ are sufficiently close [i.e., $|[\bar{n}_{i,r}^e(\vec{N}) - \bar{n}_{i,r}(\vec{N})]/\bar{n}_{i,r}^e(\vec{N})| < \epsilon$, where ϵ is a tolerance bound]. Note that in the algorithm, the notation K_r is used to indicate the number of devices for which $D_{i,r} > 0$.

The computational cost of solving the iterative method is proportional to the product $(K \times R)$ per iteration and typical errors are quite small. In several experiments reported in [21], the average errors in throughput and response time for various approximate MVA algorithms are around 2% for relatively small populations and less than 1% for relatively large populations.

For example, the iterative solution of the model of the hypothetical distributed system discussed in Section 13.5.1 would require a number of operations proportional to $(5 \times 20 = 100)$, as opposed to 104 million operations for the exact solution. Although approximate methods provide a cheaper solution for product-form multiclass models, they have a serious drawback. The commonly used approximate methods for solving multiclass models do not provide bounds on the errors introduced by the approximations. Therefore, to assess the approximation's reliability, one has to validate the results against the exact MVA results, which may be impossible in the case of large systems.

To exemplify the accuracy of Schweitzer's approximation, compare the exact results of the transaction system example with those calculated by the iterative process, given that the maximum tolerance for the absolute difference between successive values of the queue lengths is 0.01. Table 13.6

Table 13.6. Exact and Approximate Results

Method	Throughput		Response Time	
	Query	Update	Query	Update
Exact MVA	4.093	0.409	0.733	2.445
Approximate	4.001	0.407	0.749	2.456
Relative error ($|\%|$)	2.25	0.49	0.22	0.45

shows the throughput and response time computed under both methods. As seen, the maximum observed relative error is 2.25%.

Example 13.2

Consider a closed model that represents a packet switching store and forward communication network with flow control mechanism [15]. Consider that each virtual channel is represented by one class. Thus, the number of customers in each class represents the window size (i.e., the maximum number of messages allowed on the virtual channel). To keep the example simple, assume that the devices of the model represent the sink node, the source node, and the virtual channel. All devices are assumed to meet the BCMP requirements. The model to be solved has the following parameters: 2 classes (i.e., 2 virtual channels), $N_1 = 20$, $N_2 = 25$ (window sizes), $\vec{D}_1 = (0.0030, 0.0009, 0.0123)$, and $\vec{D}_2 = (0.0035, 0.0215, 0.0011)$. Table 13.7 shows the iterations required by the Schweitzer's approximation to solve this model. The termination criterion is to have 0.01 as the maximum difference between successive values of $N_{i,r}$. Within 9 iterations, the approximate method obtains results whose maximum error compared to the exact results is 1.59%. Notice that the exact solution requires the computation of queue lengths for 6 (26×21) different populations.

■

13.6   Open Models

Consider a distributed system environment, made up of a collection of clients and servers connected via a high speed local area network (LAN). Servers are placed in the system to provide service upon request. A file server is a key

Table 13.7. Approximate MVA Computation

| | Class 1 | | | | Class 2 | | | |
| | Queue Length | | | | Queue Length | | | |
Iteration	Channel	Source	Sink	TPUT	Channel	Source	Sink	TPUT
1	8.333	8.333	8.333	78.80	6.667	6.667	6.667	61.13
2	3.704	1.111	15.185	81.07	3.352	20.593	1.054	48.34
3	1.914	1.652	16.433	79.73	1.341	22.745	0.915	44.53
4	0.995	1.817	17.189	78.26	0.655	23.448	0.897	43.50
5	0.610	1.843	17.545	77.43	0.399	23.688	0.911	43.22
6	0.459	1.842	17.697	77.05	0.301	23.775	0.923	43.14
7	0.401	1.839	17.758	76.90	0.264	23.806	0.929	43.11
8	0.379	1.837	17.782	76.83	0.249	23.818	0.932	43.10
9	0.371	1.837	17.791	76.83	0.244	23.822	0.933	43.10
Exact	0.377	1.863	17.760	77.43	0.246	23.813	0.942	43.27
Error ($|\%|$)	1.59	1.39	0.17	0.77	0.81	0.03	0.98	0.39

component of this kind of environment. Its purpose is to provide file services for the client processes on the network. Basically, a file server is composed of processors, memory, and a disk subsystem. The workload of a file server can be viewed as a series of file service requests such as read, write, create, and remove, which arrive from the workstations via the LAN. The operation of a file server can be viewed as follows. Requests arrive to the server. A typical request enters the server, possibly queues up while waiting for some resource (processor, memory, disks) to become available, obtains service from the resources, and exits the server. The number of requests being handled concurrently by the server varies over time depending on factors such as the load placed by the clients (i.e., the request arrival rate), the file system capacity, the available memory, and the processor speed.

A file server is a good example of a system suitable to be modeled as an open model. It exhibits the key characteristic of open systems: the variation of the number of customers over time. In practice, the number of customers (transactions, processes, requests) varies dynamically, due to such factors such as process termination, process initiation, and process spawning. An open class is able to represent this variation because it has a potentially unlimited number of customers. Chapter 10 introduces and analyzes the

---

Input Parameters: $D_{i,r}$, N_r, and ϵ

Initialization: $\vec{N} = (N_1, N_2, \ldots, N_R)$

For $r = 1$ to R do For $i = 1$ to K do If $D_{i,r} > 0$ then $\bar{n}_{i,r}^e(\vec{N}) = N_r/K_r$

Iteration Loop

Repeat

    For $r = 1$ to R do

        For $i = 1$ to K do $\bar{n}_{i,r}(\vec{N}) = \bar{n}_{i,r}^e(\vec{N})$

    For $r = 1$ to R do

        For $i = 1$ to K do

            For $t = 1$ to R do

$$\bar{n}_{i,r}(\vec{N} - \vec{1}_t) = \begin{cases} \bar{n}_{i,r}(\vec{N}) & t \neq r \\[2mm] \frac{N_r - 1}{N_r}\, \bar{n}_{i,r}(\vec{N}) & t = r \end{cases}$$

    For $r = 1$ to R do

        Begin

            For $i = 1$ to K do

$$R_{i,r}'(\vec{N}) = \begin{cases} D_{i,r} & \text{delay} \\[2mm] D_{i,r}\left[1 + \sum_{t=1}^{R} n_{i,t}(\vec{N} - \vec{1}_r)\right] & \text{LI} \end{cases}$$

$$X_{0,r}(\vec{N}) = \frac{N_r}{Z_r + \sum_{i=1}^{K} R_{i,r}'(\vec{N})}$$

        End;

    For $r = 1$ to R do

        For $i = 1$ to K do

$$\bar{n}_{i,r}^e(\vec{N}) = X_{0,r}(\vec{N})R_{i,r}'(\vec{N})$$

Until $\max_{i,r} \{|[\bar{n}_{i,r}^e(\vec{N}) - \bar{n}_{i,r}(\vec{N})] / \bar{n}_{i,r}^e(\vec{N})|\} < \epsilon$

Figure 13.5. Approximate MVA algorithm for multiple classes.

birth-death system, which gives the underlying theory for single-class open model. This analysis is extended here to multiclass models.

The load intensity of a multiclass model with R open classes and K devices is represented by the vector $\vec{\lambda} = (\lambda_1, \lambda_2, \ldots, \lambda_R)$, where λ_r indicates the arrival rate of class r customers. As illustrated in Fig. 13.6, the goal of the analysis of multiclass open models is to determine, for each class, perfor-

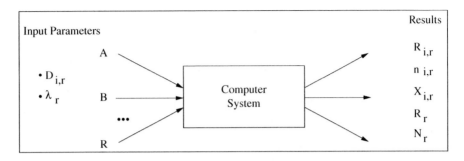

Figure 13.6. Multiple class open models.

mance measures such as average response time, $R_r(\vec{\lambda})$, and queue lengths, $\bar{n}_i(\vec{\lambda})$, as a function of the load intensity, $\vec{\lambda}$.

13.6.1 Analysis of Multiclass Open Models

In steady state, the throughput of class r equals its arrival rate. Thus,

$$X_{0,r} \;=\; \lambda_r. \tag{13.6.11}$$

The application of Little's Law to each device gives

$$\bar{n}_{i,r}(\vec{\lambda}) \;=\; X_{i,r}(\vec{\lambda})R_{i,r}(\vec{\lambda}) \tag{13.6.12}$$

where $R_{i,r}(\vec{\lambda})$ is the average class r customer response time per visit to device i.

The average residence time for the entire execution is $R'_{i,r} = V_{i,r}R_{i,r}$. Using the Forced Flow Law and Eq. (13.6.11), the throughput of class r is

$$X_{i,r}(\vec{\lambda}) \;=\; X_{0,r}(\vec{\lambda})V_{i,r} \;=\; \lambda_r V_{i,r} \tag{13.6.13}$$

Using Eq. (13.6.13) in Eq. (13.6.12) the average queue length per device for each class becomes

$$\bar{n}_{i,r}(\vec{\lambda}) \;=\; \lambda_r R'_{i,r}(\vec{\lambda}) \tag{13.6.14}$$

Combining the Utilization Law and the Forced Flow Law, the utilization of device i by class r customers can be written as

$$U_{i,r}(\vec{\lambda}) \;=\; X_{i,r}(\vec{\lambda})S_{i,r} \;=\; \lambda_r V_{i,r}S_{i,r} \;=\; \lambda_r D_{i,r}. \tag{13.6.15}$$

Thus, to compute the average number of class r customers in service center i, $R'_{i,r}$ is needed as a function of the input parameters (i.e., $\vec{\lambda}$ and the service demands $D_{i,r}$'s). The average time a class r customer spends at a device, from arrival until completion, has two components: the time for receiving service and the time spent in queue. The latter is equal to the time required to service customers that are currently in the device when the customer arrives. Thus,

$$R_{i,r}(\vec{\lambda}) = S_{i,r}[1 + \bar{n}^A_{i,r}(\vec{\lambda})]$$
$$V_{i,r}R_{i,r}(\vec{\lambda}) = V_{i,r}S_{i,r}[1 + \bar{n}^A_{i,r}(\vec{\lambda})]$$
$$R'_{i,r}(\vec{\lambda}) = D_{i,r}[1 + \bar{n}^A_{i,r}(\vec{\lambda})] \tag{13.6.16}$$

where $\bar{n}^A_{i,r}(\vec{\lambda})$ is the average queue length at device i seen by an arriving class r customer when the load on the system is $\vec{\lambda}$. For delay servers, $R'_{i,r}(\vec{\lambda}) = D_{i,r}$.

The arrival theorem [17] states that in an open product-form queuing network, a class r arriving customer at service center i *sees* the steady-state distribution of the device state, which is given by the queue length. (*Note:* This is consistent with the arrival theorem result concerning closed systems. In closed systems, an arriving customer see the steady-state distribution with itself removed. In an open system, since there is an infinite customer population, removing oneself from the network has no effect. Thus, the steady-state distribution seen by an arriving customer is equal to the overall steady-state distribution.) Thus,

$$\bar{n}^A_{i,r}(\vec{\lambda}) = \bar{n}_i(\vec{\lambda}) \tag{13.6.17}$$

From Eqs. (13.6.16) and (13.6.17), we get

$$R'_{i,r}(\vec{\lambda}) = D_{i,r}[1 + \bar{n}_i(\vec{\lambda})] \tag{13.6.18}$$

Substituting Eq. (13.6.18) into Eq. (13.6.14), yields

$$\bar{n}_{i,r}(\vec{\lambda}) = \lambda_r D_{i,r}[1 + \bar{n}_i(\vec{\lambda})] = U_{i,r}(\vec{\lambda})[1 + \bar{n}_i(\vec{\lambda})] \tag{13.6.19}$$

Notice that expression $[1 + \bar{n}_i(\vec{\lambda})]$ in Eq. (13.6.19) does not depend on class r. As a consequence, for any two classes r and s, we have

$$\frac{\bar{n}_{i,r}(\vec{\lambda})}{\bar{n}_{i,s}(\vec{\lambda})} = \frac{U_{i,r}(\vec{\lambda})}{U_{i,s}(\vec{\lambda})} \tag{13.6.20}$$

Using Eq. (13.6.20) and considering the fact that $\bar{n}_i(\vec{\lambda}) = \sum_{s=1}^{R} \bar{n}_{i,s}(\vec{\lambda})$, Eq. (13.6.19) can be rewritten as

$$\bar{n}_{i,r}(\vec{\lambda}) = \frac{U_{i,r}(\vec{\lambda})}{1 - U_i(\vec{\lambda})} \qquad (13.6.21)$$

Applying Little's Law to Eq. (13.6.21), the average residence time for class r customers at device i is

$$R'_{i,r}(\vec{\lambda}) = \frac{D_{i,r}}{1 - U_i(\vec{\lambda})} \qquad (13.6.22)$$

The interaction among the open classes of a multiclass model is explicitly represented by the term $U_i(\vec{\lambda})$ of Eq. (13.6.22), which corresponds to the total utilization of device i by all the classes in the model.

The analysis of a product-form model with multiple open classes begins with the constraint that $U_i(\vec{\lambda}) \le 1$ for all devices of the network and proceeds with the formulas summarized in Fig. 13.7. From Eq. (13.6.15), the stability condition for an open model is

$$U_i \le 1 \ \forall \ i \qquad \text{or} \qquad (13.6.23)$$

$$\sum_{r=1}^{R} \lambda_r D_{i,r} \le 1 \ \forall \ i, r \qquad (13.6.24)$$

13.6.2   Open Models: Case Study

Consider a distributed environment made up of a number of client diskless computers connected via a high-speed LAN to a file server, composed of a single processor and one large disk. The company is planning to double the number of client computers. Because the system performance is critically dependent on the file server, management wishes to assess the impact of the expansion before it is implemented. So, the first question to be answered is: What is the predicted performance of the file server if the number of diskless workstations doubles?

Following the modeling paradigm of Fig. 10.1, the initial step is constructing the baseline model, which begins with the workload characterization. The workload to the file server consists of file service requests, which can be grouped into three classes: *read*, *write*, and *all others*. The latter

Input Parameters: $D_{i,r}$ and λ_r
Formulas:

$$U_{i,r}(\vec{\lambda}) = \lambda_r V_{i,r} S_{i,r} = \lambda_r D_{i,r}$$

$$U_i(\vec{\lambda}) = \sum_{r=1}^{R} U_{i,r}(\vec{\lambda})$$

$$\bar{n}_{i,r}(\vec{\lambda}) = \frac{U_{i,r}(\vec{\lambda})}{1 - U_i(\vec{\lambda})}$$

$$R'_{i,r}(\vec{\lambda}) = \begin{cases} D_{i,r} & \text{delay} \\ \dfrac{D_{i,r}}{1 - U_i(\vec{\lambda})} & \text{LI} \end{cases}$$

$$R_r(\vec{\lambda}) = \sum_{i=1}^{K} R'_{i,r}(\vec{\lambda})$$

$$\bar{n}_i(\vec{\lambda}) = \sum_{r=1}^{R} \bar{n}_{i,r}(\vec{\lambda})$$

Figure 13.7. Formulas for models with multiple open classes.

comprises control requests of the network file system and other file service requests less used. During a period of one hour, the file server was monitored and the following measurement data were collected over one hour: 18,000 reads, 7,200 writes, 3,600 file service requests other than reads and writes, processor utilization at 32%, and disk utilization at 48%.

The measurement data also provide resource utilization on a per-class basis, as shown in Table 13.8. Using the measurement data and the operational relationship $(D_{i,r} = U_{i,r}/X_{0,r})$, each request is characterized in terms of its service demands. Once $D_{i,r}$ has been calculated, it is possible to compute $V_{i,r}$ using the disk service time provided by the manufacturer. For the processor, the parameter $V_{\text{proc},r}$ is calculated using the following expression that relates the visit ratio at the processor to the visit ratios at the I/O

Table 13.8. File Server Workload Characteristics

Class	Arrival Rate	Processor				Disk			
		U (%)	V	S	D (sec)	U (%)	V	S	D (sec)
Read	5 req/sec	9	3	0.006	0.018	20	2	0.020	0.040
Write	2 req/sec	18	6	0.015	0.090	20	5	0.020	0.100
Others	1 req/sec	5	5	0.100	0.050	8	4	0.020	0.080

devices in a central server model

$$V_{\text{proc,r}} = 1 + \sum_{i=2}^{K} V_{i,r} \qquad (13.6.25)$$

where devices 2 through K are the I/O devices. Table 13.8 summarizes the parameters that characterize the file server workload. Motivated by simplicity, the analyst in charge of the capacity planning project decided to construct a single-class model of the file server. The model constructed is an open model where only the file service components (processor and disk) are directly represented. It is assumed that the file server has enough memory so that no request queues for memory. The workstations are implicitly represented in the workload model by the file service requests generated by them. The larger the number of workstations, the larger the request arrival rate. The single-class model equivalent to the three-class model is obtained by calculating the aggregate demands.

$$D_{\text{aggr,proc}} = \frac{0.018 \times 5 + 0.09 \times 2 + 0.05 \times 1}{8} = 0.04$$
$$D_{\text{aggr,disk}} = \frac{0.04 \times 5 + 0.10 \times 2 + 0.08 \times 1}{8} = 0.06$$

By solving the model, the following residence times are obtained: $R'_{\text{proc}} = 0.04/(1 - 0.32) = 0.059$ and $R'_{\text{disk}} = 0.06/(1 - 0.48) = 0.115$. The sum gives an average request response time of 0.174 seconds.

To answer the *"what if"* question, it is necessary to change the baseline model to reflect the effects of doubling the number of workstations. Since this number is not directly specified in the input parameters, some assumptions are necessary. It is assumed that the new workstations will have the same usage as the installed ones. This means they will run the same group of applications and will generate file service requests that follow the current pattern of requests. Thus, by increasing the number of workstations by 100%, the request arrival rate, likewise, is assumed to increase by 100%. Letting $\lambda^{new} = 2 \times 8 = 16$, the model is re-solved to obtain the predicted measures.

$$U_{\text{proc}} = \lambda^{\text{new}} D_{\text{proc,aggr}} = 64\%$$
$$U_{\text{disk}} = \lambda^{\text{new}} D_{\text{disk,aggr}} = 96\%$$
$$R'_{\text{proc}} = D_{\text{proc,aggr}}/(1 - U_{\text{proc}}) = 0.111$$
$$R'_{\text{disk}} = D_{\text{disk,aggr}}/(1 - U_{\text{disk}}) = 1.5$$
$$R_{\text{request}} = R_{\text{proc}} + R_{\text{disk}} = 1.611$$

Therefore, if the number of workstations were doubled, the file server disk would saturate and the average request response time would increase from 0.174 sec to 1.611 sec, an 825% increase! The model clearly indicates that the server would be bogged down and users would suffer with long response times at the workstations.

Now consider some possible alternatives to support system expansion without impairing service levels. The current system performance will be used as a basis for the comparison of the various alternatives under consideration. Each alternative is evaluated by considering the relative change in system performance from the baseline model.

- *Server caching scheme.* A new version of the operating system that provides a cache for the server is available. According to the vendor, read and write cache hit ratios of 70% and 60%, respectively, can be achieved. To reduce the impact of unanticipated failures, every write operation to cache will also be applied to the disk. Thus, the server cache can then be modeled by reducing the visit ratio of read requests [i.e., $V_{\text{disk,read}}^{\text{new}} = (1 - \text{hit ratio})V_{\text{disk,read}}$]. To have a better understanding of the impact of the server cache on the performance of each class of the workload, a three-class model is solved using the predicted arrival rate and letting $D_{\text{disk,read}}^{\text{new}} = (1 - 0.7) \times 0.04 = 0.012$.

- *Client caching scheme.* In this case, when a read is issued at the workstation, the data read are stored in a local buffer pool, called *client cache* [10]. Subsequent remote reads may find the requested data in the local cache. This reduces significantly the number of requests that go to the server. It is assumed that due to reliability reasons, a write operation always goes to the disk in the server after updating the client cache. The introduction of a client cache in the workstations of the environment can be modeled by reducing the arrival rate of read requests. Thus, $\lambda_{\text{read}}^{\text{new}} = (1 - \text{client hit ratio})\lambda_{\text{read}}$. Assuming a client hit ratio of 70%, the new value for the parameter that represents the change is given by $\lambda_{\text{read}}^{\text{new}} = (1 - 0.7) \times 10 = 3$.

- *Upgrade in disk subsystem.* The third alternative considered is to upgrade the storage subsystem and to install a second disk unit in the file server. This change is represented in the model by adding a third service center. The original disk service demand will be equally split between the two disks (i.e., $D_{\text{disk}1,r}^{\text{new}} = D_{\text{disk}2,r}^{\text{new}} = D_{\text{disk},r}/2$).

For each alternative, a three-class model is evaluated according to the formulas of Fig. 13.7. The model inputs consist of parameters from Table 13.8 and those that were calculated to represent each specific change in the baseline model. Table 13.9 summarizes the performance measures obtained for the three alternatives. To obtain a rank of the alternatives in terms of performance, aggregate response time is first calculated for each alternative, which is the average of the individual classes weighted by the class throughput. Table 13.10 displays the aggregate response times as well as the relative change in the response time from the baseline model. The *pure expansion* refers to the alternative that just increases the number of workstations. All alternatives assume that the number of workstations will be doubled.

From the file server perspective, the best alternative is the upgrade in the disk subsystem, because it considerably diminishes the demand on the original disk. The client cache, although seemingly worse than the server cache, may be the best alternative from the system viewpoint. The key issue in this alternative is the reduction in the number of times that a user process

Table 13.9. Results of an Open Three-Class Model

Alternative	Processor		Disk		Extra Disk	
	U (%)	R' (sec)	U (%)	R' (sec)	U (%)	R' (sec)
• Server cache						
Read	18	0.050	12	0.038	-	-
Write	36	0.250	40	0.313	-	-
Other	10	0.139	16	0.250	-	-
• Client cache						
Read	5.4	0.037	12	0.125	-	-
Write	36	0.185	40	0.313	-	-
Other	10	0.103	16	0.250	-	-
• Disk upgrade						
Read	18	0.050	20	0.038	20	0.038
Write	36	0.250	20	0.096	20	0.096
Other	10	0.139	8	0.077	8	0.077

goes to the file server. This reduction implies less overhead of network access, which in many systems has a high cost.

13.7 Mixed Models

A mixed model with R classes of customers has C closed classes and O open classes, where $R = C + O$. In fact, a mixed model can be viewed

Table 13.10. Performance of the Alternatives

Alternative	Response Time (sec)	Variation (%)
Baseline	0.174	-
Pure expansion	1.611	825
Server cache	0.244	40
Client cache	0.354	103
Disk upgrade	0.227	30

as a combination of two separate submodels, a closed model and an open model, that happen to share the common resources of a computer system, as depicted in Fig. 13.8. The load intensity of a mixed queuing network model is defined by a pair of vectors $(\vec{C}, \vec{O})$, where $\vec{C} = (N_1, N_2, \ldots, N_C)$ specifies the customer populations of the closed submodel and $\vec{O} = (\lambda_1, \lambda_2, \ldots, \lambda_O)$ represents the arrival rates of the open submodel.

The basic approach to solve a mixed multiclass model is to solve their submodels independently, but with adjusted service demands to represent the impact on each other. Because the device utilizations do not depend on the closed submodel, the open submodel is solved first and the device utilizations due to the open classes is obtained. The effect of contention at a server due to customers of different submodels is represented by elongating the service demands for the closed submodel. To elongate the service demands appropriately, they are multiplied by a factor that is proportional to the inverse of the idle time remaining from the open submodel [i.e., $1/(1 - U_{i,\text{open}})$] [1]). The closed submodel with the elongated service demands is then solved using the MVA algorithm. Response times of the open submodels are affected by the closed submodel. To account for this interference, the average queue lengths of closed customers is used in the calculation of response times of open customers (i.e., $\bar{n}_{i,\text{closed}}$ is included in the number of customers seen by an arriving open customer). See the mixed class algorithm in Fig. 13.9.

Example 13.3

Reconsider the simple two-class model described in Section 13.3. Suppose now that the way of viewing the system has been changed by deciding to

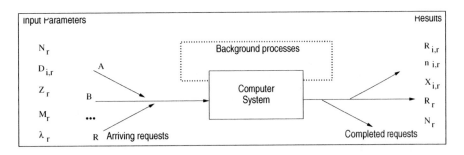

Figure 13.8. Multiclass mixed models.

Input Parameters

$D_{i,r}$, N_r, and λ_r

Steps

1. Solve the open submodel and obtain $U_{i,r}(\vec{O}) = \lambda_r D_{i,r} \ \forall \ r \ \in \ \{1,2,\ldots,O\}$

2. Determine $U_{i,\text{open}} = \sum_{r=1}^{O} U_{i,r}$.

3. Elongate the service demands of the closed classes:
$$D_{i,r}^e = \frac{D_{i,r}}{1 - U_{i,\text{open}}}, \forall \ r \ \in \ \{1,2,\ldots,C\}$$

4. Using the MVA algorithm, compute performance results for the closed model:
$$R_{i,r}'(\vec{C}), \ \bar{n}_{i,r}(\vec{C}), \ X_{0,r}(\vec{C}) \ \forall \ r \ \in \ \{1,2,\ldots,C\}$$

5. Determine $\bar{n}_{i,\text{closed}}(\vec{C}) = \sum_{r=1}^{C} \bar{n}_{i,r}(\vec{C})$.

6. Compute the average residence time for the open submodel:
$$R_{i,r}'(\vec{O}) = \frac{D_{i,r}[1 + \bar{n}_{i,\text{closed}}(\vec{C})]}{1 - U_{i,\text{open}}(\vec{O})}$$
$$\bar{n}_{i,\text{open}}(\vec{O}) = \lambda_r R_{i,r}'(\vec{O})$$

Figure 13.9. Algorithm for mixed multiclass models.

represent the query class as a transaction class, with arrival rate equal to 4.09 tps. Table 13.11 shows the input parameters of the mixed model.

By following the algorithm of Fig. 13.9, the first step is to calculate the utilization due to the open class with $\lambda_1 = 4.09$ tps.

Table 13.11. Measurement Data for the Transaction Processing System

Class	Type	Service Demand			Transactions in the System	Arrival Rate
		Processor	Disk 1	Disk 2		
Query	Open	0.105	0.180	0	-	4.09
Update	Closed	0.375	0.480	0.240	1	-

- Open submodel

$$
\begin{aligned}
U_{\text{processor,query}} &= 0.105 \times 4.09 = 42.95\% \\
U_{\text{disk1,query}} &= 0.180 \times 4.09 = 73.62\% \\
U_{\text{disk2,query}} &= 0 \times 4.09 = 0.0\%
\end{aligned}
$$

Using the utilizations due to the open class, the adjusted service demands are calculated for the closed submodel. By applying the MVA algorithm to solve the closed submodel with $N_1 = (1)$, the following are obtained:

- Closed submodel

$$
\begin{aligned}
D_{\text{processor,update}} &= 0.375/(1 - 0.4295) = 0.657 \\
D_{\text{disk1,update}} &= 0.480/(1 - 0.7362) = 1.820 \\
D_{\text{disk2,update}} &= 0.240/(1 - 0.0) = 0.240 \\
R_{\text{update}} &= 2.717 \\
X_{\text{update}} &= 0.368 \\
n_{\text{processor,update}} &= 0.242 \\
n_{\text{disk1,update}} &= 0.67 \\
n_{\text{disk2,update}} &= 0.088
\end{aligned}
$$

To compute the average response time of the open submodel, the queue lengths of the closed submodel are used to reflect the contention in the servers.

1. Open submodel

$$
R'_{\text{processor,query}} = \frac{0.105}{1 - 0.4295}(1 + 0.242) = 0.229
$$

$$
R'_{\text{disk1,query}} = \frac{0.180}{1 - 0.7362}(1 + 0.67) = 1.140
$$

$$
R_{\text{query}} = 1.369
$$

As with the other types of models, mixed queuing networks can be used easily for predicting purposes. For example, what is the performance of the query transactions if the load of update jobs is doubled? In this case, it is only necessary to change the number of update transactions in the system from 1 to 2 and re-solve the model. The new value for the response time of query transactions is 1.947, which corresponds to a 42% increase.   ■

13.8   Concluding Remarks

In this chapter queuing network models with multiple classes have been analyzed. These models are appropriate for describing workloads of actual systems. Usually, *"what if"* questions that appear in capacity planning are associated with individual classes of customers. Multi-class models provide performance results for individual class analysis. The discussion has concentrated on techniques for solving a special category of multiclass models, known as product-form, separable, or BCMP networks. The techniques are grouped into sections. One section refers to the exact and approximate solutions of closed models, where the load intensity is assumed to be constant. Another section shows how to solve open multiclass models, where external arrivals and departures of customers are allowed. Mixed models with both closed and open classes are solved by a combination of the two previous techniques.

This chapter focused on queuing models with load-independent (LI) devices. The algorithms for solving open multiclass QNs are in the MS Excel OpenQN.XLS workbook and the approximate multiclass MVA solution technique is implemented in the MS Excel ClosedQN.XLS workbook. Some computer systems may have components that behave as load-dependent devices (LD), at which the service rate varies with the number of customers present in its queue. The next chapter presents techniques to analyze the performance of queuing models with load-dependent devices.

13.9   Exercises

1. Consider the system specified by Table 13.1. Solve the system performance model using Bard's approximation, as shown in Eq. (13.5.8). Compare the results with the exact ones obtained by Schweitzer's approximation. What are your conclusions?

2. Consider the transaction system of Section 13.3. Calculate the performance measures of that model using the approximate MVA algorithm. Assume that the stopping criterion is to have a maximum difference

of 0.001 for successive values of $n_{i,r}$. Suppose now that the number of update transactions in the system is tripled. Recalculate the model's results using the exact and approximate techniques. Compare the computational effort required by the two algorithms.

3. In the example of the transaction system of Section 13.3 it is noted that query transactions only make use of disk 1, which increases its utilization and turns it into the bottleneck. Having observed this problem, the support analyst wants to know what would be the effect on performance if the I/O load due to query transactions were balanced among the two disks. Compare the results obtained with the current situation.

4. A database server has one processor and two disks, D1 and D2. The workload is divided into three classes: query (Q) transactions, update (U) transactions, and interactive (I) users. Table 13.12 gives the input parameters for these classes.

   Use the QN solvers provided with the book to answer the following *"what if"* questions:

   1. What is the average response time for each class?

   2. What is the impact on response time if the arrival rate of query transactions is increased by 95%?

   3. In the scenario with an increased arrival rate of query transactions, consider the following hardware upgrades and compare the performance improvements obtained with each one of them.

Table 13.12. Parameters for Exercise 13.4

Class	D_{cpu}	D_{D1}	D_{D2}	N_r^{max}	λ_r	M_r	Z_r
Q	0.06	0.030	0.06	5	3.0	-	-
U	0.10	0.030	0.09	3	1.5	-	-
I	0.09	0.045	0.00	5	-	50	15

- replace disk D1 by one twice as fast.
- replace the CPU by one twice as fast.

4. With the increased arrival rate for query transactions and with a twice-as-fast processor, draw a graph of response time versus the number of simultaneous clients when this number varies from 50 to 250. What is the maximum number of simultaneous clients that can be supported to keep the response time below 1.5 sec?

5. A database server has one CPU and one disk. The server's workload is composed of trivial queries that arrive at a rate of 10 tps, complex queries that arrive at a rate of 0.1 tps, and of a batch workload that generates a report. When the report generation completes, a new report generation is started in 15 minutes. Table 13.13 provides workload related information. Each physical I/O demands 0.015 msec of CPU time and 9 msec of disk service time. The last row of Table 13.13 indicates how much CPU time is required by transactions of each workload in addition to the CPU time related to I/Os.

- Find the average response time and the average throughput for each of the three workloads.
- Find the utilization of the CPU and of the disk.
- Finds the residence times at the CPU and at the disk for each of the three workloads.

Table 13.13. Data for Exercise 13.5

	Trivial	Complex	Report
Avg. Number of SQL Calls	3.5	20.0	120.0
Avg. Number of I/Os per SQL Call	5.0	15.0	40.0
DB Buffer Hit Ratio (in %)	70.0	80.0	30.0
Non I/O Related CPU Time (msec)	30.0	180.0	1250.0

Bibliography

[1] S. Agrawal, *Metamodeling: A Study of Approximations in Queuing Models*, MIT Press, Cambridge, Massachusetts, 1985.

[2] M. Arlitt, D. Krishnamurthy, and J. Rolia, "Characterizing the scalability of a large Web-based shopping system," ACM Transactions on Internet Technology, vol. 1, no. 1, August 2001, pp. 44–69.

[3] F. Baskett, K. Chandy, R. Muntz, and F. Palacios, "Open, closed, and mixed networks of queues with different classes of customers," *J. ACM*, vol. 22, no. 2, April 1975.

[4] Y. Bard, "Some extensions to multiclass queuing network analysis," in *Performance of Computer Systems*, North-Holland Publishing Co., Amsterdam, 1979.

[5] L. Bertolotti and M. Calzarossa, "Models of mail server workloads," *Performance Evaluation - An International Journal*, vol. 46, no. 2, 2001, pp. 65–76.

[6] J. P. Buzen, "Computational algorithms for closed queuing networks with exponential servers," *Comm. ACM*, vol. 16, no. 9, September 1973.

[7] V. Cardellini, E. Casalicchio, M. Colajanni, and P. Yu, "The state of the art in locally distributed web-server system," *ACM Computing Surveys*, vol. 34, no. 2, June 2002.

[8] A. E. Conway and N. D. Georganas, *Queuing Networks - Exact Computational Algorithms: A Unified Theory Based on Decomposition and Aggregation*, MIT Press, Cambridge, Massachusetts, 1989.

[9] L. W. Dowdy, B. Carlson, A. Krantz, and S. K. Tripathi, "Single-class bounds of multiclass queuing networks," *J. ACM*, vol. 39, no. 1, January 1992.

[10] E. Drakopoulos and M. Merges, "Performance analysis of client-server storage systems," *IEEE Tr. Computers*, vol. 41, no. 11, 1992.

[11] J. Gray and A. Reuter, *Transaction Processing: concepts and techniques*, Morgan Kaufmann Publishers, San Mateo, California, 1993.

[12] K. Kant, "MVA modeling of SJN scheduling," *Performance Evaluation - An International Journal*, vol. 15, no. 1, 1992, pp. 41–61.

[13] E. Lazowska, J. Zahorjan, S. Graham, and K. C. Sevcik, *Quantitative System Performance: Computer System Analysis Using Queueing Network Models*, Prentice Hall, Upper Saddle River, New Jersey, 1984.

[14] D. Krishnamurthy and J. Rolia, "Predicting the QoS of an electronic commerce server: those mean percentiles," ACM Sigmetrics, Performance Evaluation Review, vol. 26, no. 3, December 1998, pp. 16–22.

[15] P. Heidelberger and S. Lavenberg, "Computer performance methodology," *IEEE Tr. Computers*, vol. C-33, no. 12, December 1984.

[16] M. Reiser and S. Lavenberg, "Mean-value analysis of closed multi-chain queuing networks," *J. ACM*, vol. 27, no. 2, 1980.

[17] K. C. Sevcik and I. Mitrani, "The distribution of queuing network states at input and output instants," *J. ACM*, vol. 28, no. 2, April 1981.

[18] E. Souza e Silva, S. Lavenberg, and R. Muntz, "A perspective on iterative methods for the approximate analysis of closed queuing networks," in *Mathematical Computer Performance and Reliability*, North-Holland Publishing Co., Amsterdam, 1984.

[19] P. Schweitzer, "Approximate analysis of multiclass closed network of queues," in *International Conference on Stochastic Control and Optimization*, Amsterdam, 1979.

[20] SPEC (Standard Performance Evaluation Corporation), "SPECmail - Mail Server Benchmark," January 2001.

[21] H. Wang and K. C. Sevcik, "Experiments with improved approximate mean value analysis algorithms," *Performance Evaluation - An International Journal*, vol. 39, 2000, pp. 189–206.

[22] C. M. Woodside and S. K. Tripathi, "Optimal allocation of file servers in a local network environment," *IEEE Tr. Software Engineering*, vol. SE-12, no. 8, August 1986.

Chapter 14

Queuing Models with Load Dependent Devices

14.1 Introduction

Load-dependent devices (LD) are used to model service centers where the service rate varies with the number of customers present in its queue. Examples of servers with variable service times, depending on the current load, abound in modern computer-based systems. For example, multimedia traffic uses variable grades of service to control congestion. In congestion control mechanisms for continuous bit rate (CBR) traffic in broadband networks, bit dropping methods are used to discard certain portion of the traffic, such as the least significant bits, in order to reduce the transmission time (i.e., the service time) [11]. Thus, when a system has a large number of requests queued, new arrivals are forced to receive low-grade service, which shortens the service time. Local area networks (e.g., Ethernet) have been modeled by LD devices [13], representing the fact that Ethernet efficiency depends on the number of computers trying to transmit data. Disk servers may also be modeled by load-dependent devices [15]. When there are multiple requests queued up at the disk, the seek time to the nearest request increases inversely with the number of queued requests. Thus, the effective disk service rate varies with the number of queued requests. Queuing models with load-dependent devices capture the dynamic nature of various components of computer systems.

A queuing model may represent different types of resources, according to whether there is queuing and whether the average service rate, $\mu(n)$, depends on the current queue length n or not. As described in previous chapters, load-independent (LI) devices represent resources where there is queuing but the average service rate does not depend on the load (i.e., $\mu(n) = \mu$ for all values of n). In contrast, load-dependent devices are used to represent resources where there is queuing and the average service rate depends on the load (i.e., $\mu(n)$ is a function of n), as shown in Fig. 14.1.

This chapter focuses on the solution of queuing models with load-dependent service times. The MVA method [16] is extended to handle the existence of load-dependent (LD) devices. A motivating example is presented, followed by single and multiple class LD solution algorithms. Closed and open models are allowed. At the end of the chapter, the *Flow Equivalent Server Method* is introduced. This method is useful for reducing the size of a performance model by replacing an entire subnetwork of a QN by a single equivalent LD device.

14.2   Motivating Example

In the classic client-server (CS) computing paradigm, one or more *clients* and one or more *servers*, along with the underlying operating system, in-

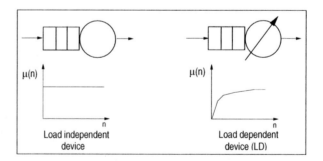

Figure 14.1. Service rate function for LI and LD devices.

terprocess communication system, and network protocols, form a composite system allowing distributed computation [1, 18]. A client is defined as a requester of services and a server as the provider of services. A client is a process that interacts with the user and is responsible for 1) implementing the user interface, 2) generating requests to the server based on user requests, 3) transmitting the requests to the server via a suitable interprocess communication mechanism, and 4) receiving the results from the server and presenting them to the user. A server is a process, or set of processes, that collectively provide services to the clients in a manner that shields the client from the details of the architecture of the server's hardware/software environment. A server does not initiate any dialogue with a client; it only responds to requests [18]. Servers control access to shared resources, such as file systems, databases, gateways to wide area networks (WANs), and mail systems. Remote Procedure Calls (RPCs) or structured query language (SQL) statements are typically used by clients to request services from servers in a client-server system. Usually, clients and servers are located on different machines interconnected by a LAN or WAN. Figure 14.2 shows a request generated at the client and serviced by the server.

For instance, a file service request (e.g., "read block x from file foo") is invoked at the client as an RPC. The RPC obtains service from a file server and returns the result, via the network, to the calling client. Several network messages may be necessary to send the result from the server to the client.

14.2.1 Client-Server Performance

Several factors influence the performance of a client-server application. One of them is the network latency, which directly affects end-user performance. As depicted in Fig. 14.3, the response time of a transaction in a CS system can be decomposed as

$$\text{transaction response time} = \text{client delay} + \text{network delay} + \text{server delay}.$$
$$(14.2.1)$$

The client delay includes processor time at the client workstation plus any disk time at the client workstation. The client processor time accounts for the time necessary to execute the user interface code, plus local preparation of the service request at the application level, plus the time necessary to pro-

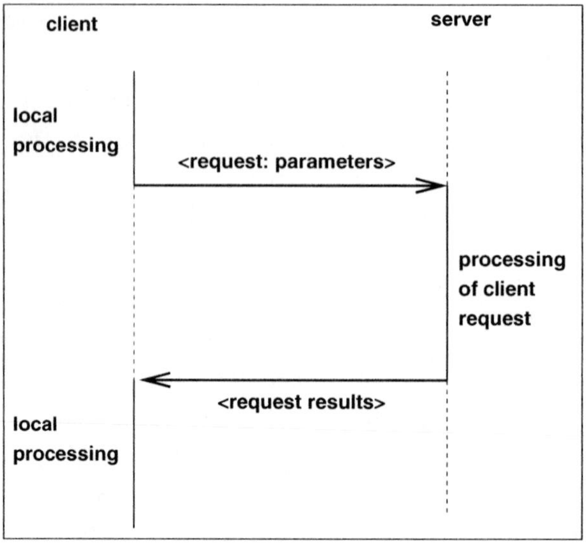

Figure 14.2. Client-server interaction.

cess all protocol levels from the session layer down to the transport/network layer (e.g., TCP/IP [10]). Usually, client workstations have local disks, for operating system purposes, to hold temporary files, and to cache files in order to reduce traffic with the server. The delay at the client is independent of the total system load and consists only of the service demands at the client.

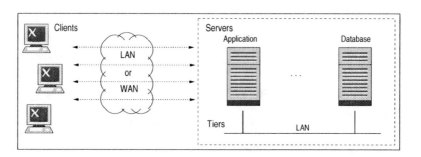

Figure 14.3. Client-server architecture.

The network delay is composed of 1) the time necessary to get access to the network through the appropriate medium access protocol (MAC), such as token-ring or CSMA/CD (Ethernet) [10], and 2) the time necessary to transmit the service request packets through the network. The first component of the network delay (network access time) is clearly dependent on the network load. For instance, the number of collisions in a CSMA/CD network increases as more stations attempt to transmit at the same time. This activity is appropriately modeled using a load-dependent server. Similarly, the time for the token to return to a station, in a token-ring network, increases with the number of stations. Also, the server delay is decomposed into server processor time plus disk service time. Queues may form at these devices since the server is a shared resource being used by all clients. The service demand at the server accounts for the time necessary to process the incoming requests from the clients plus the time necessary to process all the protocol layers at the server side. The service demands at the server disks depend on the type of service provided by the server. For instance, a file server may provide services such as reading or writing a block to a file, while a database server may provide a service such as executing an SQL query involving joining two or more database tables, which could result in numerous physical I/Os. The performance of CS systems is greatly influenced by the congestion levels at the shared resources (e.g.,network, server processor, and server disks).

14.2.2 Design Questions for a CS Application

Consider a company that is designing a data center to process credit inquiries. To support the business, the CS application should provide timely information to its customers. Good performance (e.g., response time) is a necessity for the company to attract customers. The company is planning an architecture that scales to serve several thousands of requests without sacrificing performance. The data center has other QoS goals, such as 24x7 operation, 99% availability, and high reliability. The center consists of a CS system with a relational database. Clients generate financial requests. Each financial request generates SQL requests to the database. Client workstations are connected to the database server via a 100 Mbps LAN network. The queuing model that represents the CS system is depicted in Fig. 14.4.

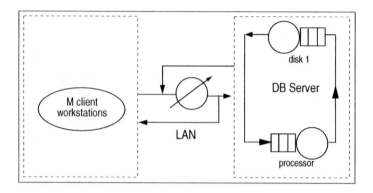

Figure 14.4. Client-server queuing model.

For the sake of simplicity, assume that all financial requests have similar resource demands and can be characterized by a single class. The queuing model has a total of M customers in the population (the number of client workstations) that generate a single class of requests. It is also assumed that each client workstation cannot submit a new SQL request until it receives the response to the previous request. The client workstations are represented by a single delay device with service demand equal to D^{cl}. This represents the time a client spends before submitting the next request to the server. The LAN is modeled by a load-dependent device and the database server by two load independent devices. Typical design questions that could be answered with the help of a performance model are:

- How does the speed of the DB processor influence response times and throughput?

- What is the effect of adding more client workstations to the CS system?

- What is the performance impact of using a faster network to connect clients to servers?

- What is the impact of increasing the level of security of the system through new and stronger authorization mechanisms in the database access or in user authentication procedures?

14.2.3   System and Workload Specification

After building a prototype for the new application, service demands are measured for the various devices. The work unit for the workload characterization is an SQL request generated by financial requests. Consider the following SQL request-related parameters:

- N_{sql}: average number of SQL requests per financial transaction.

- L_{sql}: average size, in bytes, of the result of an SQL request.

- D^{cl}: average time elapsed at the client workstation from when a reply to a previous SQL command is received and a new one is issued.

- $D^{sv}_{processor}$: average processor service demand per SQL request at the database server.

- D^{sv}_d: average disk service demand per SQL request at the database server

Consider the following network-related parameters:

- B: network bandwidth in bits per second (bps).

- S: slot duration (i.e., the round-trip propagation time of the channel, which is also the time required for a collision to be detected by all stations).

- L_p: maximum packet length, in bytes, including header and payload.

- $\overline{L}_p$: average packet length, in bytes.

- L_d: maximum length, in bytes, of the payload of a packet.

The average number of packets, NP_{sql}, generated per SQL request can be computed as follows. Assume that the request from the client to the server consists of a single packet. The number of packets necessary to send the result from the server to the client is given by $\lceil L_{sql}/L_d \rceil$. Thus,

$$NP_{sql} = 1 + \left\lceil \frac{L_{sql}}{L_d} \right\rceil .$$

Table 14.1 shows the values of all measured and computed parameters for the CS model.

Queuing devices represent the processor and disk at the DB server. The service time per packet at the network is dependent on the number of workstations contending for it. As shown in Fig. 14.4, the LAN is represented by a load-dependent device to indicate that, as the load on the network increases, the throughput on the LAN decreases due to the additional number of collisions experienced on the network medium.

14.3   Single Class Models with LD Devices

Chapter 12 presents the three main relationships (repeated below) needed to solve a queuing network using MVA. They assume that service times are load-independent (LI).

$$R_i'(n) = \begin{cases} D_i & \text{if } i \text{ is a Delay device} \\ D_i[1 + \bar{n}_i\,(n-1)] & \text{otherwise} \end{cases} \qquad (14.3.2)$$

Table 14.1. Parameters for the CS Financial Application

SQL-request-related parameters	
N_{sql}	4 SQL commands/request
L_{sql}	10,000 bytes
D^{cl}	0.1 sec
$D^{\text{sv}}_{\text{processor}}$	0.12 sec
D^{sv}_d	0.005 sec
Network Parameters	
B	100 Mbps
S	51.2 μsec
L_p	1,518 bytes
$\overline{L}_p$	1,518 bytes
L_d	1,492 bytes
Computed Parameter	
NP_{sql}	8 packets

$$X_0(n) = \frac{n}{\sum_{i=1}^{K} R'_i(n)} \tag{14.3.3}$$

$$\overline{n}_i(n) = X_0(n)R'_i(n) \tag{14.3.4}$$

For load-dependent (LD) devices, the service rate, and consequently the response time, is a function of the distribution of customers at the device. Therefore, Eqs. (14.3.2) and (14.3.4) need to be adjusted. Instead of simply the mean queue length, the complete queue length distribution at these devices is required. Let

- $P_i(j \mid n)$ = probability that device i has j customers given, that there are n customers in the QN.

- $\mu_i(j)$ = service rate of device i when there are j customers at the device.

An arriving customer who finds $j - 1$ customers at device i will have a response time equal to $j/\mu_i(j)$. The probability that an arrival finds $j - 1$ customers at device i given that there are n customers in the queuing network is $P_i(j - 1 \mid n - 1)$, due to the Arrival Theorem [19]. The average residence time is computed as the product of the average number of visits to the device times the average response time per visit. That is,

$$R'_i(n) = V_i \sum_{j=1}^{n} \text{response time given } j \text{ customers} \times$$

$$\text{probability that an arrival finds } (j - 1) \text{ customers}$$

$$= V_i \sum_{j=1}^{n} \frac{j}{\mu_i(j)} P_i(j - 1 \mid n - 1). \tag{14.3.5}$$

The mean queue length at node i is given by

$$\overline{n}_i(n) = \sum_{j=1}^{n} j P_i(j \mid n). \tag{14.3.6}$$

What remains is the computation of $P_i(j \mid n)$. By definition, $P_i(0 \mid 0) = 1$. If one applies the principle of flow equilibrium to the queuing network states [9], the probability of having j customers at device i for a queuing network with n customers can be expressed in terms of the probability of having $j-1$ customers at device i when there is one less customer in the queuing network. Hence,

$$P_i(j \mid n) = \begin{cases} [D_i X_0(n)/\alpha_i(j)] \, P_i(j-1 \mid n-1) & j = 1, \ldots, n \\ \\ 1 - \sum_{k=1}^{n} P_i(k \mid n) & j = 0 \end{cases}$$

$$(14.3.7)$$

where $\alpha_i(j)$ is a *service-rate multiplier* [12] defined as $\mu_i(j)/\mu_i(1)$. From Eq. (14.3.5) and the definition of the service-rate multipliers it follows that

$$R_i'(n) = \frac{V_i}{\mu_i(1)} \sum_{j=1}^{n} \frac{j}{\alpha_i(j)} \, P_i(j-1 \mid n-1). \qquad (14.3.8)$$

The service time, S_i, when there is no congestion at device i is equal to $1/\mu_i(1)$. Since $D_i = V_i S_i$, it follows that

$$R_i'(n) = D_i \sum_{j=1}^{n} \frac{j}{\alpha_i(j)} \, P_i(j-1 \mid n-1). \qquad (14.3.9)$$

The MVA algorithm for load-dependent devices is given in Fig. 14.5.

Example 14.1

A Web server has two processors and one disk. Benchmarks indicate that a two-processor server is 1.8 times faster than the single-processor model for this type of workload. Thus,

$$\alpha_{\text{processor}}(j) = \begin{cases} 1 & j = 1 \\ 1.8 & j \geq 2 \end{cases}$$

Let the service demand of an HTTP request at the disk and processor be 0.06 sec and 0.1 sec, respectively. For simplicity, let the maximum number of simultaneous connections be 3. Using the algorithm of Fig. 14.5 yields the results shown in Table 14.2. The table also shows conditional probabilities at the load-dependent device that models the 2-processor system. The average response time is 0.24 sec and the average throughput is 12.44 requests/sec. ■

Example 14.2

Consider the financial application described in the motivating example. We want to calculate the database server throughput and response time.

Input Parameters: D_i's, N, K, and service-rate multipliers $[\alpha_i (j)$'s$]$.

Initialization

For $i = 1$ to K do

$$\begin{cases} P_i(0 \mid 0) = 1 & \text{for LD devices} \\ \overline{n}_i(0) = 0 & \text{otherwise} \end{cases}$$

Iteration Loop

For $n = 1$ to N do

   Begin

     For $i = 1$ to K do

$$R'_i(n) = \begin{cases} D_i[1 + \overline{n}_i (n-1)] & \text{LI device} \\\\ D_i & \text{delay device} \\\\ D_i \sum_{j=1}^{n} \frac{j}{\alpha_i(j)} P_i(j-1 \mid n-1) & \text{LD device} \end{cases}$$

   $X_0(n) = n / \sum_{i=1}^{K} R'_i(n)$

     For $i = 1$ to K do

$$\begin{cases} \overline{n}_i(n) = X_0(n) R'_i(n) & \text{LI or delay device} \\ \text{For } j = 1 \text{ to } n \text{ do} \\ \quad P_i(j \mid n) = [D_i X_0(n)/\alpha_i(j)] \, P_i(j-1 \mid n-1) & \text{LD device} \\\\ P_i(0 \mid n) = 1 - \sum_{k=1}^{n} P_i(k \mid n) & \text{LD device} \end{cases}$$

   End

Figure 14.5. Exact single-class MVA algorithm with LD devices.

Suppose that the CS system has 100 workstations. However, the analysts expect that during any given period of time only an average of 30% of the workstations are active. Thus, the number of active client workstations is 30. First, an expression is required for the service rate of the network as a function of the number of client workstations using the network.

Table 14.2. Detailed Results of the Load Dependent MVA

n	$R'_{\text{processor}}$	R'_{disk}	R_0	X_0	$\overline{n}_{\text{processor}}$	$\overline{n}_{\text{disk}}$
0	-	-	-	0.00	0.00	0.00
\multicolumn{7}{c}{$p_{\text{processor}}(0 \mid 0) = 1.0$}						
1	0.10	0.06	0.16	6.25	0.63	0.37
\multicolumn{7}{c}{$p_{\text{processor}}(0 \mid 1) = 0.375$; $p_{\text{processor}}(1 \mid 1) = 0.625$}						
\multicolumn{7}{c}{$U_{\text{processor}} = 0.625$; $U_{\text{disk}} = 0.375$}						
2	0.11	0.08	0.19	10.56	1.13	0.87
\multicolumn{7}{c}{$p_{\text{processor}}(0 \mid 2) = 0.238$; $p_{\text{processor}}(1 \mid 2) = 0.396$}						
\multicolumn{7}{c}{$p_{\text{processor}}(2 \mid 2) = 0.367$}						
\multicolumn{7}{c}{$U_{\text{processor}} = 0.763$; $U_{\text{disk}} = 0.633$}						
3	0.13	0.11	0.24	12.44	1.60	1.40
\multicolumn{7}{c}{$p_{\text{processor}}(0 \mid 3) = 0.177$; $p_{\text{processor}}(1 \mid 3) = 0.296$}						
\multicolumn{7}{c}{$p_{\text{processor}}(2 \mid 3) = 0.274$; $p_{\text{processor}}(3 \mid 3) = 0.253$}						
\multicolumn{7}{c}{$U_{\text{processor}} = 0.823$; $U_{\text{disk}} = 0.747$}						

Let $\mu_{\text{net}}(m)$ denote the LAN service rate measured in SQL requests per second as a function of the number of client workstations m.

$$
\mu_{\text{net}}(m) = \begin{cases} \mu_p(1)/\text{NP}_{\text{sql}} & m = 1 \\[2ex] \mu_p(m+1)/\text{NP}_{\text{sql}} & m \geq 2 \end{cases} \tag{14.3.10}
$$

where $\mu_p(n)$ is the network throughput, in packets/sec, for a network with n stations. Note that when $m = 1$, even though there are two stations in the network (the server and the only client), the server transmits only when requested by the client. No collisions occur. For that reason, $\mu_p(1)$ is used in the expression for $\mu_{\text{net}}(1)$. An expression for $\mu_p(n)$ for an Ethernet network is derived in [12] and is given by

$$
\mu_p(n) = \frac{\overline{L}_p/B}{\overline{L}_p/B + S \times C} \times \frac{B}{\overline{L}_p} = \frac{1}{\overline{L}_p/B + S \times C} \tag{14.3.11}
$$

where C is the average number of collisions and is given by $(1 - A)/A$. The parameter A is the probability of a successful transmission and is given by $(1 - 1/n)^{n-1}$.

Using the parameters in Table 14.1, one can obtain the values of the throughput μ_{net} (m) when there are m client workstations. Using these values for μ_{net} (m), for $m = 1, 2, \ldots 30$, the MVA model with LD devices given in Fig. 14.5 yields a throughput of 82.17 SQL requests/sec and a response time equal to 0.265 sec. The network time is equal to 0.00095 sec, which represents only 0.36% of the total response time. In this case, the LAN can be effectively ignored since the network speed of 100 Mbps is such that collisions and packet transmission times become negligible. ∎

Example 14.3

Consider a database server with eight processors and two disk subsystems. The eight processors allow the server to run concurrent server processes. The use of an OLTP benchmark provides the following scaling factor function over a one-processor configuration:

$$\alpha_{processor}(j) = \begin{cases} 0.56 + 0.44 \times j & j \leq 8 \\ 4.08 & j > 8 \end{cases}$$

The system is used for processor intensive transactions, explaining the need for an 8-processor server. Let the service demand of a transaction at the two disk subsystems be 0.008 and 0.011 sec, respectively. The processor service demand is 0.033 sec. What is the impact of increasing the number of concurrent processes at the multiprocessor database server?

The database server is represented by a simplified model, composed of the three devices. One load-independent (LI) device represents disk subsystem 1, another LI device represents disk subsystem 2, and a load-dependent device (LD) models the eight-processor server, as shown in Fig. 14.6. Consider two scenarios: in the first case, the system executes 20 processes simultaneously and in the second case, the database runs 30 processes concurrently. The results obtained with the algorithm of Fig. 14.5 are shown in Table 14.3.

The model's results indicate that eight processors are capable of handling the processor intensive transactions (i.e., $U_{processor} < 40\%$) However, disk 2 is the bottleneck (i.e., $U_{disk2} > 95\%$) of the database server and limits the system throughput. ∎

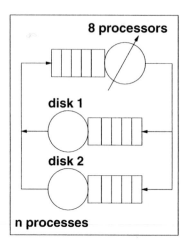

Figure 14.6. Multiprocessor database server model.

14.4   Multiclass Closed Models with LD Devices

The algorithm for solving a multiple-class closed QN with load-dependent devices is given in this section. It is an extension of the approximate algorithm for multiple classes given in Chapter 13 for incorporating load-dependent devices discussed previously in this chapter. It is assumed in this section that the service-rate multiplier of any load-dependent device is class independent (i.e., if device i is load-dependent, then $\alpha_{i,r}(j) = \alpha_i(j)$ for all classes r).

The basis for the algorithm lies in obtaining an appropriate expression for the marginal probability, $P_i(j \mid \vec{N})$, of finding j customers at load-dependent device i given that the QN population vector is $\vec{N}$. This probability can be

Table 14.3. Results for Example 14.3

n	$R'_{\text{processor}}$	R'_{disk1}	R'_{disk2}	R_0	X_0	$U_{\text{processor}}$	U_{disk1}	U_{disk2}
20	0.067	0.024	0.135	0.227	87.96	36.28	70.36	96.75
30	0.069	0.026	0.239	0.334	89.73	37.01	71.78	98.70

obtained from the local balance equations of the network states [9] as

$$P_i(j \mid \vec{N}) = \frac{1}{\alpha_i(j)} \sum_{r=1}^{R} U_{i,r}(\vec{N}) \, P_i(j-1 \mid \vec{N} - \vec{1}_r) \qquad j = 1, \ldots, |\vec{N}|$$

$$(14.4.12)$$

where $|\vec{N}| = \sum_{r=1}^{R} N_r$ is the total number of customers in the network. As in the load-independent case, the dependency on values derived by removing one customer from each class makes an exact MVA solution for even moderate size QNs very expensive. To overcome this problem, it is assumed, as an approximation, that

$$P_i(j \mid \vec{N} - \vec{1}_r) \approx P_i(j \mid \vec{N}) \qquad j = 0, \ldots, |\vec{N}| - 1 \qquad (14.4.13)$$

In other words, it is assumed that the removal from the QN of one customer of class r does not significantly affect the overall queue length distribution at device i [9]. Using Eq. (14.4.13) in Eq. (14.4.12) and the fact that $U_{i,r}(\vec{N}) = D_{i,r} X_{0,r}(\vec{N})$, it follows that

$$P_i(j \mid \vec{N}) \approx \frac{\sum_{r=1}^{R} U_{i,r}(\vec{N})}{\alpha_i(j)} \, P_i(j-1 \mid \vec{N})$$

$$= \frac{\sum_{r=1}^{R} D_{i,r} X_{0,r}(\vec{N})}{\alpha_i(j)} \, P_i(j-1 \mid \vec{N}) \quad j = 1, \ldots, |\vec{N}|$$

$$(14.4.14)$$

Solving Eq. (14.4.14) recursively one can obtain a closed-form expression for $P_i(j \mid \vec{N})$ as a function of $P_i(0 \mid \vec{N})$. $P_i(0 \mid \vec{N})$ can be obtained by requiring all probabilities to sum to 1 (see Exercise 14.5). Thus,

$$P_i(j \mid \vec{N}) = P_i(0 \mid \vec{N}) \prod_{k=1}^{j} \frac{\sum_{r=1}^{R} D_{i,r} X_{0,r}(\vec{N})}{\alpha_i(k)} \qquad j = 1, \ldots, |\vec{N}|$$

$$(14.4.15)$$

$$P_i(0 \mid \vec{N}) = \left[1 + \sum_{j=1}^{|\vec{N}|} \prod_{k=1}^{j} \frac{\sum_{r=1}^{R} D_{i,r} X_{0,r}(\vec{N})}{\alpha_i(k)} \right]^{-1} \qquad (14.4.16)$$

The generalization of Eq. (14.3.9) for the multiple-class case is

$$R'_{i,r}(\vec{N}) = D_{i,r} \sum_{j=1}^{|\vec{N}|} \frac{j}{\alpha_i(j)} \, P_i(j-1 \mid \vec{N} - \vec{1}_r) \qquad (14.4.17)$$

Using the approximation given in Eq. (14.4.13) in Eq. (14.4.17), it follows that

$$R'_{i,r}(\vec{N}) = D_{i,r} \sum_{j=1}^{|\vec{N}|} \frac{j}{\alpha_i(j)} P_i(j-1 \mid \vec{N}) \qquad (14.4.18)$$

The values of the probabilities $P_i(j-1 \mid \vec{N})$ are needed to compute the residence time $R'_{i,r}(\vec{N})$. To compute these probabilities the values of the throughputs $X_{0,r}(\vec{N})$ are needed, which depend back on the residence time values. The following iterative approach is proposed:

1. Estimate initial values for the throughputs $X_{0,r}(\vec{N})$. These estimates can be obtained by approximating the throughput by its asymptotic upper bound, namely $X_{0,r} \leq \min\{N_r / \sum_{i=1}^{K} D_{i,r}, \; 1/\max_i\{D_{i,r}\}\}$. Although this is a loose upper bound, it serves as a starting point for the iteration discussed here.

2. Using Eqs. (14.4.15) and (14.4.16), compute the probabilities $P_i(j \mid \vec{N})$.

3. Compute the residence times using Eq. (14.4.18).

4. Compute new values for the throughputs using Little's result as

$$X_{0,r}(\vec{N}) = N_r / \sum_{i=1}^{K} R'_{i,r}(\vec{N})$$

5. If the relative error between the throughputs obtained in the current iteration and the previous iteration is greater than a certain tolerance ϵ (e.g., 10^{-4}) then go to step 2. Otherwise, compute the final metrics and stop.

This approach is specified in detail in the algorithm of Fig. 14.7. The notation K_r indicates the number of devices for which $D_{i,r} > 0$.

Example 14.4

Consider the client-server architecture shown in Fig. 14.3. Suppose the application layer is designed to support up to 80 running processes simultaneously. Each application process receives a client request, executes the

Input Parameters: $D_{i,r}$'s, $\vec{N}$, K, R, ϵ, $\alpha_i(j)$'s

Initialization

For $r = 1$ to R do For $i = 1$ to K do if $D_{i,r} > 0$ then $\overline{n}_{i,r}(\vec{N}) = N_r/K_r$;

For $r = 1$ to R do $X_{0,r}^{\text{prev}} = \min\{N_r/\sum_{i=1}^{K} D_{i,r},\ 1/\max_i\{D_{i,r}\}\}$;

Error $= \epsilon + 1$; { force entering loop for first time }

While Error $> \epsilon$ do

   Begin

    Compute Queue Lengths for Non-LD Devices

      For all non-LD device i do For $r = 1$ to R do

$$\overline{n}_i(\vec{N} - \vec{1}_r) = \frac{N_r-1}{N_r}\overline{n}_{i,r}(\vec{N}) + \sum_{j=1\ \&\ j\neq r}^{R} \overline{n}_{i,j}(\vec{N})$$

    Compute Probabilities for LD Devices

      For all LD device i do

$$\begin{cases} P_i(0 \mid \vec{N}) = \left[1 + \sum_{j=1}^{|\vec{N}|} \prod_{k=1}^{j}[\sum_{r=1}^{R} D_{i,r} X_{0,r}^{\text{prev}}(\vec{N})]/\alpha_i(k)\right]^{-1} \\ P_i(j \mid \vec{N}) = P_i(0 \mid \vec{N}) \prod_{k=1}^{j} \sum_{r=1}^{R}[D_{i,r} X_{0,r}^{\text{prev}}(\vec{N})]/\alpha_i(k) \qquad j = 1,\dots,|\vec{N}| \end{cases}$$

    Compute Residence Times

      For $i = 1$ to K do For $r = 1$ to R do

$$R'_{i,r}(\vec{N}) = \begin{cases} D_{i,r}[1 + \overline{n}_i(\vec{N} - \vec{1}_r)] & \text{LI queuing device} \\ D_{i,r} & \text{delay device} \\ D_{i,r} \sum_{j=1}^{|\vec{N}|}[j/\alpha_i(j)]P_i(j-1 \mid \vec{N}) & \text{LD device} \end{cases}$$

    Compute Throughputs For $r = 1$ to R do $X_{0,r}^{\text{curr}}(\vec{N}) = N_r/\sum_{i=1}^{K} R'_{i,r}$

    Compute Queue Lengths per Class for Non-LD Devices

    For all non-LD device i do For $r = 1$ to R do $\overline{n}_{i,r}(\vec{N}) = X_{0,r}^{\text{curr}}(\vec{N}) \times R'_{i,r}(\vec{N})$

    Compute Relative Error Error $= \max_r \left|[X_{0,r}^{\text{curr}}(\vec{N}) - X_{0,r}^{\text{prev}}(\vec{N})]/X_{0,r}^{\text{curr}}(\vec{N})\right|$

    Prepare for Next Iteration For $r = 1$ to R do $X_{0,r}^{\text{prev}}(\vec{N}) = X_{0,r}^{\text{curr}}(\vec{N})$

End ; { while }

Figure 14.7. Approximate multiclass MVA algorithm with LD devices.

application logic, and interacts with the database server. After monitoring the application processes, the performance analyst identified three types of processes (i.e., in terms of resource usage) corresponding to the three most common client requests. During the monitoring period, the application had 35 processes running on average. The application architect wants to determine the average database response time in order to understand the impact on the database if the number of application processes is changed. The analyst decides to use a three-class closed model with an LD device to represent the two-tier architecture depicted in Fig. 14.8.

The database server is assumed to have one processor and one disk. The requests are categorized as being of three types: trivial, average, and complex, according to their use of database resources. Ten application processes are responsible for submitting trivial requests, 20 for submitting average requests, and five for complex ones. By measuring the application processes, the analyst parameterizes the behavior of the processes as summarized in Table 14.4. There are various ways of estimating disk service demands. For random data access, as is the case of this example, the service demand could be determined by multiplying the number of I/Os issued by a process by the average disk access time (i.e., average seek time plus the average latency plus the average transfer time, which is a function of the I/O size). However, most modern disk systems have a cache at the controller for caching data recently read or written to the disk [20]. Cache hits are relatively rare for random access, but are higher for sequential access. When estimating service demands from measurement data, all the specific features of the disk architecture are captured by the measuring process. The disk demands reported in Table 14.4 reflect this measurement data. The LAN is assumed to be a 10-Mbps Ethernet with a slot duration S of 51.2 μsec. The average network service demands per transaction class can be computed as

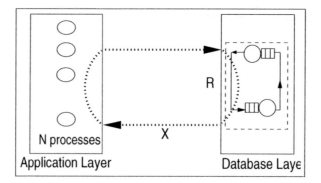

Figure 14.8. Performance model of a two-tier client-server architecture.

Table 14.4. Parameterization Data for the Example of Multiclass Load-Dependent MVA

Req. Type	% of Req.	Think Time sec	Avg. No. Packets/ Req.	Avg. Packet Length per Req. (bits)	Disk Demand (msec)	Processor Demand (msec)
Trivial	16.4	0.1	2	800	8	1.6
Average	63.9	0.2	3	1382	14	10.1
Complex	19.3	0.4	9	1410	25	16.8

the average number of packets × the average packet length divided by the network bandwidth. This gives values 0.16, 0.41, and 1.27 msec for trivial, average, and complex requests, respectively. The network is modeled as a load-dependent device with a class independent service rate function $\mu(n)$. To use Eq. (14.3.11) for the Ethernet throughput, the average packet length $\overline{L}_p$ over all classes is computed from the data in Table 14.4 as follows:

$$\overline{L}_p = 800 \times 0.164 + 1382 \times 0.639 + 1410 \times 0.193 = 1286 \text{ bits.}$$

The average number of packets per request, P_{req}, is given by

$$P_{\text{req}} = 2 \times 0.164 + 3 \times 0.639 + 9 \times 0.193 = 3.98 \text{ packets.}$$

The service rate in requests/sec for the network is equal to its service rate in packets/sec divided by the average number of packets per transaction. The algorithm of Fig 14.7 yields the performance metrics shown in Table 14.5. In this particular example, convergence is achieved after 16 iterations for a tolerance of 10^{-4}. ∎

14.5   Multiclass Open Models with LD Devices

The algorithm presented in this section is an extension of the algorithm presented in Chapter 13 for solving multiple-class open queuing networks. Load-dependent servers are incorporated here. Similar to the closed queuing network case, it is assumed that the service rate-multiplier of any load-dependent device is class independent (i.e., if device i is load-dependent, then $\alpha_{i,r}(j) = \alpha_i(j)$ for all classes r). As discussed in Chapter 13, the

Table 14.5. Metrics for Example of Multiclass Load-Dependent MVA

Req.	Residence Time (sec)			Response Time	Throughput
Type	Network	Processor	Disk	(sec)	(req/s)
Trivial	0.00017	0.0034	0.164	0.167	37.34
Average	0.00044	0.0213	0.288	0.310	39.23
Complex	0.00134	0.0355	0.515	0.552	5.25

solution to an open queuing network exists only if the stability condition is satisfied. In the case of load-dependent multiclass open networks with class-independent service multipliers, the stability condition is

$$\forall i \, \forall j \quad \left[\frac{U_i}{\alpha_i(j)}\right] < 1 \tag{14.5.19}$$

If device i is load-independent, $\alpha_i(j) = 1$ for all j and the stability condition reduces to $\forall i \, U_i < 1$, as shown in Chapter 13.

Let $\vec{L}$ be the vector $(\lambda_1, \ldots, \lambda_R)$ of arrival rates per class. Let $P_i(j \mid \vec{L})$ be the probability that there are j customers, irrespective of their classes, at device i given that the arrival rate vector is $\vec{L}$.

The residence time, $R'_{i,r}(\vec{L})$, of a class r customer at device i is given by

$$R'_{i,r}(\vec{L}) = V_{i,r} R_{i,r}(\vec{L}) \tag{14.5.20}$$

where $R_{i,r}(\vec{L})$ is the average response time per visit to device i of a class r customer. This can be computed from Little's result as

$$R_{i,r}(\vec{L}) = \overline{N}_{i,r}(\vec{L})/\lambda_{i,r} \tag{14.5.21}$$

where $\overline{N}_{i,r}(\vec{L})$ is the average number of class r jobs at device i and $\lambda_{i,r}$ is the average arrival rate of class r jobs at device i. It can be proved (see [9]) that

$$\overline{N}_{i,r}(\vec{L}) = \frac{U_{i,r}}{U_i} \overline{N}_i(\vec{L}) \tag{14.5.22}$$

where $\overline{N}_i(\vec{L})$ is the average total number of customers at device i. $\overline{N}_i(\vec{L})$ can be computed from the device probabilities as

$$\overline{N}_i(\vec{L}) = \sum_{j=1}^{\infty} j P_i(j \mid \vec{L}). \tag{14.5.23}$$

The probability distribution of node i is given by [9]:

$$P_i(j \mid \vec{L}) = P_i(0 \mid \vec{L}) \frac{U_i^j}{\beta(j)} \qquad\qquad j \geq 1 \qquad\qquad (14.5.24)$$

where $\beta(j) = \alpha(1) \times \cdots \times \alpha(j)$. The probability $P_i(0 \mid \vec{L})$ results from requiring that all probabilities sum to 1. Thus,

$$P_i(0 \mid \vec{L}) = \left[\sum_{j=0}^{\infty} \frac{U_i^j}{\beta(j)} \right]^{-1}. \qquad\qquad (14.5.25)$$

Assuming that the service-rate multipliers become constant after some value w_i, as it is true in most practical cases, closed-form expressions are obtained for the probabilities $P_i(j \mid \vec{L})$ and for $\overline{N}_i(\vec{L})$. The stability condition in this case becomes $\forall\, i\; U_i/\alpha_i(w_i) < 1$. Assuming that $\alpha_i(j) = \alpha_i(w_i)$ for $j \geq w_i$ (see Exercise 14.7):

$$P_i(j \mid \vec{L}) = \begin{cases} P_i(0 \mid \vec{L})[U_i^j/\beta_i(j)] & j = 1, \ldots, w_i \\[2mm] P_i(0 \mid \vec{L})U_i^j/\{\beta_i(w_i)[\alpha_i(w_i)]^{j-w}\} & j > w_i \end{cases} \qquad (14.5.26)$$

$$P_i(0 \mid \vec{L}) = \left[\sum_{j=0}^{w_i} \frac{U_i^j}{\beta_i(j)} + \frac{[\alpha_i(w_i)]^{w_i}}{\beta_i(w_i)} \frac{[U_i/\alpha_i(w_i)]^{w_i+1}}{1 - U_i/\alpha_i(w_i)} \right]^{-1} \qquad (14.5.27)$$

and

$$\overline{N}_i(\vec{L}) = P_i(0 \mid \vec{L}) \times$$

$$\left\{ \sum_{j=1}^{w_i} j\, \frac{U_i^j}{\beta_i(j)} + \frac{U_i^{w_i+1}}{\beta_i(w_i)\alpha_i(w_i)} \left[\frac{U_i/\alpha_i(w_i) + (w_i + 1)\left(1 - \frac{U_i}{\alpha_i(w_i)}\right)}{[1 - U_i/\alpha_i(w_i)]^2} \right] \right\}$$

$$(14.5.28)$$

The Service Demand Law implies that $U_{i,r} = \lambda_r D_{i,r}$ and $U_i = \sum_{r=1}^{R} \lambda_r D_{i,r}$ in the above equations. The result is an algorithm to solve multiclass open queuing networks with load-dependent servers as a function of the class service demands and the class arrival rates. Figure 14.9 displays this algorithm. $R_{0,r}(\vec{L})$ denotes the average system response time of class r customers and $\overline{N}_r^s$ denotes the average number of class r customers in the system.

Input Parameters: $D_{i,r}$'s, $\vec{L}$, K, R, α_i (j)'s, w_i's

Compute Utilizations For $i = 1$ to K do For $r = 1$ to R do $U_{i,r} = \lambda_r D_{i,r}$
For $i = 1$ to K do $U_i = \sum_{r=1}^{R} U_{i,r}$

Check Stability Condition If $\exists\, i$ such that $[U_i/\alpha_i(w_i)] \geq 1$ then stop;

Compute Queue Lengths

For $i = 1$ to K do

    Begin

      If device i is LD

      Then Begin

$$P_i(0 \mid \vec{L}) = \left[\sum_{j=0}^{w_i} \frac{U_i^j}{\beta_i(j)} + \frac{[\alpha_i(w_i)]^{w_i}}{\beta_i(w_i)} \frac{[U_i/\alpha_i(w_i)]^{w_i+1}}{1 - U_i/\alpha_i(w_i)} \right]^{-1}$$

$$\overline{N}_i(\vec{L}) = P_i(0 \mid \vec{L}) \times$$
$$\left\{ \sum_{j=1}^{w_i} j\, \frac{U_i^j}{\beta_i(j)} + \frac{U_i^{w_i+1}}{\beta_i(w_i)\,\alpha_i(w_i)} \left[\frac{U_i/\alpha_i(w_i) + (w_i+1)\,(1 - U_i/\alpha_i(w_i))}{(1 - U_i/\alpha_i(w_i))^2} \right] \right\}$$

      End ;

     For $r = 1$ to R do

$$N_{i,r}(\vec{L}) = \begin{cases} U_{i,r} & \text{delay device} \\ U_{i,r}/(1 - U_i) & \text{queuing LI device} \\ (U_{i,r}/U_i)\, \overline{N}_i(\vec{L}) & \text{LD device} \end{cases}$$

    End;

Compute Residence Times per Class

For $i = 1$ to K do For $r = 1$ to R do

$$R'_{i,r}(\vec{L}) = \begin{cases} D_{i,r} & \text{delay device} \\ D_{i,r}/(1 - U_i) & \text{queuing LI device} \\ N_{i,r}/\lambda_r & \text{LD device} \end{cases}$$

Response Times For $r = 1$ to R do For $i = 1$ to K do $R_{0,r}(\vec{a}L) = \sum_{i=1}^{K} R'_{i,r}$
Number in System For $r = 1$ to R do For $i = 1$ to K do $\overline{N}_r^s(\vec{L}) = \sum_{i=1}^{K} N_{i,r}(\vec{L})$

Figure 14.9. Exact multiclass open QN algorithm with LD devices.

Example 14.5

    Peer-to-peer (P2P) networking is viewed as a new paradigm for constructing distributed applications. In contrast to client-server applications, a peer is both a requester and provider of services. In other words, all peers in a P2P system have the ability to function both as a client and as a server depending on the specific context. Peer-to-peer applications have been used mainly for sharing video, audio files and software. P2P architectures can be classified into three basic categories: centralized service location, distributed service location with flooding, and distributed service location with hashing [7].

In client-server computing, clients generate the workload, which is then processed by the servers. Unlike CS computing, peers generate workloads (e.g., requests for downloading files), but also provide the capacity to process workloads. P2P workloads are examined in detail in [17]. There are many issues surrounding the performance of P2P architectures, such as the impact of the size and characteristics of the user population, the influence of different search strategies, and the consequences of P2P traffic on the underlying networks.

Consider a hypothetical P2P file sharing system, composed of a large number of peers. The system has a centralized service location architecture. To locate a file, a peer sends a query to the central server, which performs a directory lookup and identifies the peers where the files are located. The central server maintain directories of the shared files stored on the peers registered in the system. This service is a common service because it serves all requests. Once the desired file has been located, a peer-to-peer interaction is established to download the file. Assume that the system receives λ requests/sec, where a request consists of downloading a file. A QN model is used here to calculate the average time to download a file.

This example presents a simple performance model of a P2P file sharing application based on the modeling technique proposed in [7], which is a novel approach of using QN models to analyze performance. The abstraction presented by the model associates a single server queue with each distinct file in the system. After going through the central server, all requests to download a specific file are required to join the queue associated with the file to be served, as shown in Fig. 14.10. The service rate of the server that represents a given file varies with 1) the number of replicas of the file in the P2P application, 2) the popularity of that particular file, and 3) the total load of the system. Thus, the overall queuing model consists of a load-independent server representing the common service component (i.e., the

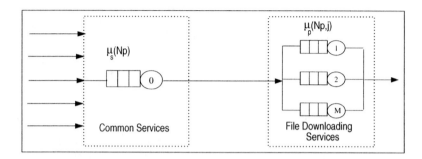

Figure 14.10. Model of a peer-to-peer file sharing system.

central server) and a set of load-dependent servers, representing the files in the system.

The response time of a request is a combination of two factors:

$$\text{response time} \ = \ \text{common service time} \ + \ \text{download service time}.$$
$$(14.5.29)$$

The common service rate (i.e., the file location service) is independent of the number of peers and is given by:

$$\mu_s(N_p) = \frac{1}{\text{common service time at the central server}} \qquad (14.5.30)$$

where N_p denotes the number of active peers in the system.

Studies indicate that Zipf's Law [21] can be used to characterize the access frequency to Internet objects. Zipf's Law was originally applied to the relationship between a word's popularity in terms of rank and its frequency of use. When one ranks the popularity of events, Zipf's Law states that the size y of the rth largest occurrence of the event is inversely proportional to its rank. This means that $y \sim r^{\alpha}$. It can be shown that

$$p_j = \frac{K}{j^{\alpha}}. \qquad (14.5.31)$$

where p_j is the probability associated with event j, K is a constant and α is the scaling parameter of the distribution. The data shown in [2] indicates that Zipf's Law applies to files serviced by Web servers. This means that the n-th most popular document is exactly twice as likely to be accessed as the $2n$-th most popular document, when $\alpha \ = \ 1$, regardless of K.

The service rate for a given file in the system is directly proportional to the number of replicas of that file and to the load of the system (i.e., the number of active peers) [7]. The number of replicas is assumed to be proportional to the popularity of files. Thus, Zipf's Law is used to model the number of replicas providing an estimated download service rate given by:

$$\mu_f(N_p, j) = \frac{N_p \, H \, K}{j^\alpha} \qquad (14.5.32)$$

where H represents the service rate brought to the system by a single peer (i.e., its contribution to the system's capacity).

Consider a small system with three types of files: software, music, and video. A collection of peers generates the three types of requests to the system. Assume that the P2P system has 30 peers connected by links of 200 Kbps. Let H be 1 download/sec, which corresponds to the time needed to download a 0.2 Mb file, using a 200-Kbps link. Assume that all files are equally popular, implying no file replicas and that $K/j^\alpha = 1$. Thus, using Eq. (14.5.32) it follows that the file download rate is $\mu_f(N_p) = N_p \times H = N_p$ downloads/sec. However, as has been observed [8], there are two types of peers, freeloaders and non-freeloaders. Freeloaders are those peers that only download files for themselves without providing files to be further downloaded by others. Thus, using this type of evidence, it is assumed that only 10% of the peers (i.e., 3) contribute to the total capacity of the system. This indicates that the service rate multiplier for the file download queue is given by:

$$\alpha_{\text{file}}(j) = \begin{cases} j & j \le 3 \\ 3 & j > 3 \end{cases}$$

Table 14.6 shows the estimated data for each type of request at the central server. The average file download times, using the algorithm in Fig. 14.9, are 4.12 sec, 6.85 sec, and 10.94 sec, respectively, for software, music, and video files. The average queue length of the load-dependent device is 12.56 requests. ∎

14.6   Flow-Equivalent Server Method

Divide and conquer is a common approach to solving problems in computing. It also applies to solving queuing models. According to this principle, it is of-

Table 14.6. Parameterization Data for Example 14.5

Request Type	Avg. Arrival Rate (req./sec)	Mean File Size (Mb)	Server Demands (sec)	
			Processor	Disk
Software	1.0	0.18	0.005	0.015
Music	0.6	0.30	0.015	0.012
Video	0.4	0.48	0.010	0.008

ten efficient to solve a queuing network by partitioning it into several smaller subnetworks and then combining the solutions of the subnetworks into an approximate solution for the entire network. This approach is referred as *decomposition and aggregation.* The basic idea is to replace each subnetwork of queues by a single load-dependent queue, which is *flow-equivalent* to the subnetwork.

The inspiration for the flow equivalent server (FES) method stems from Norton's Theorem for electrical circuits [5]. For repeated evaluations, the solution of a flow-equivalent server model requires less computation than the original one. This technique is useful in modeling large systems because it allows large queuing networks to be decomposed and reduced to a series of smaller queuing models.

Consider a closed queuing network model composed of a number of queues and a total population size of N. The FES algorithm consists of the following sequence of steps [3, 5, 12].

- *Step 1.* Select a queue or a set of queues, that form the subnetwork β, that will be analyzed in detail.

- *Step 2.* Construct a reduced network by replacing subnetwork β by a "short" (i.e., set the service time of all the servers of the subnetwork β to zero).

- *Step 3.* Solve the reduced network using the MVA algorithm. Determine the throughput of the reduced network when there are n customers in the network, $n = 0, 1, 2, \ldots N$.

- *Step 4.* Replace the reduced network by a load-dependent "Flow Equivalent Server (FES)" whose load-dependent service rate, $\mu(n)$, is equal to the throughput of the shorted network with n customers, $n = 0, 1, 2, \ldots N$.

- *Step 5.* The network formed by subnetwork β and the FES is equivalent to the original network. The behavior of subnetwork β in the equivalent network is the same as in the original network. The equivalent network is solved using MVA techniques with load-dependent servers.

When the flow-equivalent method is applied to closed single-class product-form models, it yields exact results [3]. In non-product form cases, some error is introduced. Courtois [6] has shown that relatively small errors are introduced with this approximation if the rate at which transitions occur within the subnetwork is much greater than the rate at which the subnetwork interacts with the rest of the network (i.e., the reduced FES network).

Example 14.6

Consider the queuing network model of Fig. 14.11(a), representing a server, disks, and with multiple custmomer threads. The system is composed of one processor and three disks. When a thread is executing and issues an

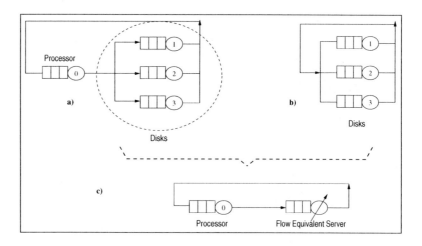

Figure 14.11. Flow-equivalent technique.

I/O request it gets blocked until the request is satisfied. Assume that the server operates with three threads. The model parameters are: $S_0 = 2/15$ sec, $V_0 = 3$, $D_0 = 0.4$ sec, $S_1 = S_2 = S_3 = 1$ sec, $V_1 = V_2 = V_3 = 1$, $D_1 = D_2 = D_3 = 1$ sec, and $n = 3$. The purpose of this example is to analyze the queuing model using the FES method. The original network is shown in Fig. 14.11(a). The subnetwork β in this example consists of the processor. Step 2 sets the processor time to zero and creates a reduced network composed of three disks as indicated in Fig. 14.11(b) (i.e., the disk subsystem). This reduced network is solved for each thread population value ($n = 1, 2, 3$). The MVA algorithm calculates the throughput of the disk subsystem: $X(1) = 0.333$ requests/sec, $X(2) = 0.5$ requests/sec, and $X(3) = 0.6$ requests/sec. The disk subnetwork is then replaced by a load-dependent FES with the mean service rates equal to $X(1)$, $X(2)$, $X(3)$. The original system is then reduced to a network composed of the processor and the load-dependent FES server, as illustrated in Fig. 14.11(c). Since the original model has a product-form solution, the results calculated for the flow-equivalent model exactly match those of the original model. By using the load-independent MVA algorithm om the model of Fig. 14.11(a) and the load-dependent MVA algorithm on the model of Fig. 14.11(c), the same results for throughput and response time, namely 0.569 threads/sec and 5.276 sec, respectively, are obtained. ∎

14.7   Concluding Remarks

The techniques discussed in previous chapters are extended here to allow one to analyze the performance of queuing models with load-dependent devices. Exact algorithms are presented for single class closed QNs with load-dependent servers and for single and multiple class open QNs with load-dependent servers. An approximate algorithm for multiple-class closed QNs is also given. The chapter also introduces a method for analyzing queuing models, called *Flow Equivalent Server Method*, which is the basis for solution techniques for non product-form queuing models, covered in the next chapter.

14.8   Exercises

1. Consider the CS model discussed in Example 14.2. What would be the impact of using a 10-Mbps Ethernet instead of the original 100-Mbps Ethernet. Assume that the 10-Mbps Ethernet has a slot duration $S = 51.2 \ \mu$sec and a maximum packet length, L_p, including header and payload of 1518 bytes.

2. In the the two-tier client-server architecture of Example 14.4, the assumed speed of the LAN is 10 Mbps. What is the response time of the three classes of requests if the LAN were replaced by a faster one, with a bandwidth of 100 Mbps.

3. Consider Example 14.4. Assume that the average number of running processes is to be doubled. The proportion of processes that submit requests of each type (trivial, average, and complex) is kept constant. Thus, the percentage of requests of each type received by the server is unchanged. Compute the new values of the response time and throughput. Make and justify a recommendation to guarantee that the average transaction response time does not exceed 2 seconds.

4. An interactive computer system has M terminals used for a data-entry application. This application presents the user with a screen to be filled out before submitting it to the mainframe for processing. The computing system has one processor and two disks. The results of measurements taken during a 1 hour interval are shown in Table 14.7. Main memory at the mainframe is such that at most 5 transactions may be executed simultaneously. The company intends to redesign the user interface to increase the productivity at each terminal so that the average think time may be reduced to 60% of its original value. Also, the company expects that a change in the economy will boost its business so that more terminals will be needed. Under this new scenario, determine the maximum number of terminals, $M_{\max}$, the system will be able to handle before response time exceeds 3 sec. Plot a response time versus number of terminals curve. When the number of terminals is equal to $M_{\max}$, how much of the transaction response time is spent in the computer system, and how much is spent queuing for

Table 14.7. Data for Exercise 14.4

Number of requests completed	11,808
Number of terminals (M)	100
$U_{\text{processor}}$	0.26
U_{disk1}	0.41
U_{disk2}	0.33
Avg. response time (sec)	0.47

memory? Compute the processor and disk utilizations. Recommend and justify a system upgrade that will be able to handle $1.2 \times M_{\text{max}}$ terminals while keeping the average response time at 3 sec. Use MVA to answer the above questions. To take memory queuing into account, use MVA with load-dependent devices.

5. Show that Eqs. (14.4.15) and (14.4.16) are the solution to Eq. (14.4.14). [*Hint*: Using Eq. (14.4.14), write $P_i(1 \mid \vec{N})$ as a function of $P_i(0 \mid \vec{N})$. Then write $P_i(2 \mid \vec{N})$ in terms of $P_i(1 \mid \vec{N})$. Since $P_i(1 \mid \vec{N})$ is already known to be a function of $P_i(0 \mid \vec{N})$, $P_i(2 \mid \vec{N})$ can be written as a function of $P_i(0 \mid \vec{N})$. Continue this process and observe what the general expression for $P_i(j \mid \vec{N})$ should be. $P_i(0 \mid \vec{N})$ can be computed by requiring that all probabilities sum to 1.]

6. Show that if device i is load-independent, Eqs. (14.5.24) and (14.5.25) reduce, (as expected) to $P_i(j \mid \vec{L}) = (1 - U_i) \, U_i^j$ for $j \geq 0$.

7. Assuming that $\alpha_i(j) = \alpha_i(w_i)$ for $j \geq w_i$ prove Eqs. (14.5.26), (14.5.27), and 14.5.28). (*Hint:* Use the fact that $\sum_{j=a}^{\infty} j\rho^j = \rho^a[\rho + a\,(1 - \rho)]/(1 - \rho)^2$ for $\rho < 1$.)

Bibliography

[1] M. Adler, "Distributed coordination models for client/server computing," *Computer*, vol. 28, no. 4, April 1995, pp. 14–22.

[2] V. A. F. Almeida, A. Bestravos, M. Crovella, and A. Oliveira, "Characterizing reference locality in the WWW," *Proc. Fourth Int. Conf. Parallel Distrib. Inform. Syst. (PDIS)*, IEEE Comp. Soc., December 1996, pp. 92–106.

[3] G. Bolch, S. Greiner, H. de Meer, and K. Trivedi, *Queueing Networks and Markov Chains*, John Wiley & Sons, Inc., 1998.

[4] R. Bodnarchuk and R. Bunt, "A Synthetic workload model for a distributed system file server," *Proc. 1991 ACM SIGMETRICS Conf. Measurement and Modeling of Computer Systems*, San Diego, California, May 1991, pp. 50–59.

[5] K. Chandy, U. Herzog, and L. Woo, "Parametric analysis of queueing networks," *IBM J. Research and Development*, vol. 19, no. 1, January 1975, pp. 36–42.

[6] P. Courtois, *Decomposability: Queuing and Computer System Applications*, Academic Press, 1977.

[7] Z. Ge, D. Figueiredo, S. Jaiswal, J. Kurose, and D. Towsley, "Modeling peer-peer file sharing systems," *Proc. INFOCOM 2003*, San Francisco, California, March 2003.

[8] E. Adar and B. Huberman, "Free riding on gnutella," *First Monday*, vol. 5, no. 10, October 2000.

[9] K. Kant, *Introduction to Computer System Performance Evaluation*, McGraw-Hill, New York, 1992.

[10] J. Kurose and K. Ross, *Computer Networking: A Top-Down Approach Featuring the Internet*, Addison-Wesley, July 2000.

[11] K. Leung, "Load-dependent service queues with application to congestion control in broadband networks", *Performance Evaluation*, vol. 50, no. 1, 2002, pp 27–40.

[12] E. Lazowska, J. Zahorjan, G. Graham, and K. C. Sevcik, *Quantitative System Performance: Computer System Analysis Using Queuing Network Models*, Prentice Hall, Upper Saddle River, New Jersey, 1984.

[13] E. Lazowska, J. Zahorjan, D. Cheriton, and W. Zwaenepoel, "File access performance of diskless workstations," *ACM Tr. Comp. Systems*, vol. 4, no. 3, August 1986, pp. 238–268.

[14] D. A. Menascé, V. A. F. Almeida, and L. W. Dowdy, *Capacity Planning and Performance Modeling: From Mainframes to Client-Server Systems*, Prentice Hall, Upper Saddle River, New Jersey, 1994.

[15] J. Padhye, L. Rahatekar, and L. W. Dowdy, "A simple LAN file placement strategy," *Proc. 1995 Computer Measurement Group Conf.*, Nashville, Tennessee, 1995.

[16] M. Reiser and S. Lavenberg, "Mean-value analysis of closed multi-chain queuing networks," *J. ACM*, vol. 27, no. 2, 1980.

[17] S. Saroiu, P. Gummadi, and S. Gribble, "A measurement study of peer-to-peer file sharing systems," *Proc. Multimedia Computing and Networking (MMCN) 2002*, San Jose, California, January 2002.

[18] A. Sinha, "Client-Server Computing," *Comm. ACM*, vol. 35, no. 7, July 92, pp. 77-98.

[19] K. C. Sevcik and I. Mitrani, "The distribution of queueing network states at input and output instants," *J. ACM 28*, 2, April 1981, pp. 358–371.

[20] E. Shriver, A. Merchant, and J. Wilkes, "An analytic behavior model for disk drives with readahead caches and request reordering," *Proc. 1998 ACM Sigmetrics Conf.*, Madison, Wisconsin, June 22-26, 1998, pp. 182-191.

[21] G. Zipf, *Human Behavior and the Principle of Least Effort.* Addison-Wesley, Cambridge, Massachusetts, 1949.

Chapter 15

Non-Product Form Queuing Models

15.1   Introduction

Most modern computer systems exhibit features that violate the assumptions required by product-form networks. Some system features that violate separable assumptions are: 1) blocking, 2) high service time variability at FCFS centers, 3) simultaneous resource possession, 4) process forking and synchronization, and 5) priority scheduling. These features cannot be modeled directly by product-form models. Thus, many algorithms have been developed to approximate the solution of models that incorporate non product-form features. These algorithms share same basic ideas. They accept a queuing network model that has some nonseparable features and transform it into an approximate network that obeys the BCMP conditions [8]. Some algorithms rely on models that use heuristic extensions to the approximate MVA equations [18, 39]. The approximate QN has a product-form solution and gives approximate measures on the performance of the original model. The input parameters of the original model are either transformed by means of an iterative process or by approximations that resemble the effects of the feature

411

being modeled. Once the new parameters are obtained, an MVA algorithm is used to calculate the performance measures of the approximate network. Some kind of transformation may be required to map the results of the approximate model back to the original one. The following sections present approximate techniques for modeling non product-form queuing models.

15.2   Modeling High Service Time Variability

Examples of high variability abound in computer systems. For instance, the Web shows extreme variability in workload characteristics, including file sizes and file popularity [15]. As another example, it has been shown that network arrivals, measured by packet interarrival times, are not exponentially distributed [28]. The authors also show that Poisson models underestimate the burstiness of TCP traffic. The question one may ask is: what are the sources of variability in computer systems? They are various. Here are some examples: sizes of data objects [27], files stored on Web servers [15], flow lengths traveling through the Internet, files stored in file systems [17], and process lifetimes. It is important to be able to model high service time variability, because increasing variability usually affects the performance of a system. As pointed out in [6], even a small amount of HTTP traffic burstiness degrades the throughput of a Web server. Results shown in Ref. [19] illustrate that the queuing dynamics within IP routers can be qualitatively different depending on whether the network traffic exhibits variability.

The variability of a dataset can be captured by the coefficient of variation (CV), defined as the ratio of standard deviation (σ) to the mean (μ).

$$CV = \frac{\sigma}{\mu}. \tag{15.2.1}$$

The characteristics of the distribution function of a random variable show if the random variable has high variability. For example, the tail of a distribution (i.e., the probability that the random variable is greater than a given value) shows the likelihood of large observations. Distributions whose tail decline with a power law are called heavy-tailed. Power-laws are expressions of the form $y \sim x^{\alpha}$, where α is a constant and x and y are the measures of interest. Measurements of several systems (e.g., Internet, WWW, Ethernet traffic, file systems) show numbers that exhibit a pattern known as "heavy-tailed" [15, 17, 27]. This means that very large numbers could be present in samples of measurements, such as number of bytes transmitted, file sizes and CPU times. These extremely large numbers do affect the performance of a system and should not be ignored. A random variable X follows a heavy-tailed distribution if $P[X > x] = kx^{-a}L(x)$ where $L(x)$ is a slowly varying function. A Pareto distribution is a special case of heavy-tailed distribution where the number of events larger than x is an inverse power of x. Among other implications, a heavy-tailed distribution presents a great degree of variability, and a non-negligible probability of high sample values. Common distributions, such as the exponential distribution, decay much faster than heavy-tailed distributions. In a log-log plot, x^{-a} is a straight line with inclination $-a$. Depending on the value of a, a power law distribution may have infinite mean (if $a < 1$) or infinite variance (if $a < 2$). In practice, these statistics do not occur because values are limited by measured data. Once the importance of variability is recognized, this section presents techniques to analyze models with non-exponential FCFS queues. These techniques were consolidated by Eager, Sorin, and Vernon in [18].

15.2.1   The Decomposition Approach

Consider a closed single-class queuing model with N customers and a FCFS queuing center Γ that has exponentially distributed service time (see Fig. 15.1). Let S_Γ be the average service time at this service center. When the service time of service center Γ is not exponentially distributed and has a coefficient

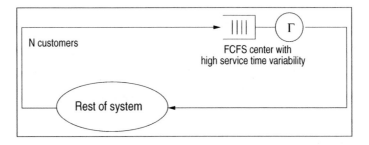

Figure 15.1. FCFS service center with high service time variability.

of variation (CV_Γ), the response time at Γ can be approximated by

$$R_\Gamma(N) = S_\Gamma\left[1 + \frac{N-1}{N}(n_\Gamma(N) - U_\Gamma(N))\right] + \frac{N-1}{N}U_\Gamma(N)\ L \qquad (15.2.2)$$

where $U_\Gamma(N)$ is the utilization of the service center Γ, $n_\Gamma(N)$ is the average queue length at Γ, and L is an estimate [31] (given below) of the mean residual service time of the customer in service at an arrival instant, considering that arrivals do occur at random points in time. Note that Eq. (15.2.2) uses the Schweitzer [35] approximation for the response time equation already discussed in Chapter 13.

$$L = \frac{\tau}{2}(1 + CV_\tau^2) \qquad (15.2.3)$$

The approximation of Eq. (15.2.2) was found to be too pessimistic for centers that have high coefficient of variation for the service time [18].

An alternative approach to solving QN models with high service time variability was proposed in [41]. First of all, the service center Γ with high service time variability is synthesized as having a hyperexponential service time distribution as shown in Fig. 15.2. With probability p_S, customers who visit service center Γ experience a "short" exponentially distributed service time with average S_S. With probability $p_L = 1 - p_S$, customers have a "long" exponentially distributed service time with average S_L. The problem now is given an empirical service time distribution at service center Γ with average service time S_Γ and coefficient of variation CV_Γ find the values of

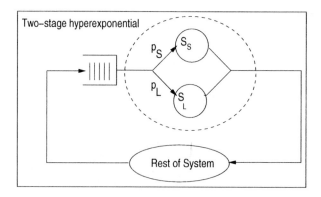

Figure 15.2. Model of a queue with high service time variability.

p_S, p_L, S_S, and S_L that match S_Γ and CV_Γ. It can be easily shown (see Exercise 15.1) that

$$S_\Gamma = p_L S_L + p_S S_S \quad \text{and} \tag{15.2.4}$$

$$CV_\Gamma^2 = 2\frac{p_L {S_L}^2 + p_S {S_S}^2}{(p_L S_L + p_S S_S)^2} - 1. \tag{15.2.5}$$

This system of equations has three unknowns (p_S, S_S, and S_L) and two equations. To solve it, one needs to guess one of the values. A good variable to guess is the probability p_S.

One can now explain, with the help of Fig. 15.3, how the approach proposed in [41] works. The QN on the left of the figure is replaced by two QNs. In each one of them, the hyperexponential service center is replaced by an exponential service center with average service time S_S in one case and S_L in the other. These two QNs are product form QNs and can be solved by the methods discussed previously in the book. Based directly on the theory of near-complete decomposability [14], the performance metrics of the original network (i.e., the one with the hyperexponential service center) can be obtained as the weighted averages of the performance metrics of the two product-form QNs. The weights are the probabilities p_S and p_L. The decomposition approach captures well the behavior of models with high service time variability. This technique yields results within 15% of the exact values over the large region of the parameter space [18]. A disadvantage of this method is its complexity for solving models that contain many centers with high service time variability.

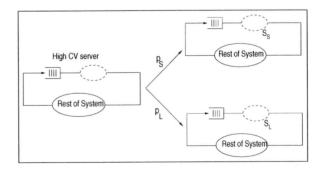

Figure 15.3. Model of a QN with a two-stage hyperexponential service center.

15.2.2   New MVA-based Decomposition Approach

Instead of decomposing the model into two independent QN models, the approach described in this section applies the decomposition principle only to each individual service center with high service time variability [14]. This is done by modifying the MVA equations for these service centers only and keeping the regular MVA equations for the other service centers.

Let Γ be a service center with high service time variability and let D_S and D_L be the service demands at Γ considering the short and long service times discussed earlier. Then, the residence time at Γ can be written as

$$R'_\Gamma(N) = p_L \, R'_{\Gamma_L}(N) + p_S \, R'_{\Gamma_S}(N) \qquad (15.2.6)$$

where p_L and p_S are as before and $R'_{\Gamma_L}(N)$ and $R'_{\Gamma_S}(N)$ are computed as follows

$$R'_{\Gamma_L}(N) = D_L[1 + n_L(N-1)] \qquad (15.2.7)$$

$$R'_{\Gamma_S}(N) = D_S[1 + n_S(N-1)] \qquad (15.2.8)$$

$$n_L(N) = \frac{N}{R'_{\Gamma_L}(N) + R_{\text{rest}}(N)} \, R'_{\Gamma_L}(N) \qquad (15.2.9)$$

$$n_S(N) = \frac{N}{R'_{\Gamma_S}(N) + R_{\text{rest}}(N)} \, R'_{\Gamma_S}(N) \qquad (15.2.10)$$

Eqs. (15.2.7) and (15.2.8) are the well-known MVA residence time equations with the difference that they use the proper service demand (long or short) and the proper expressions for queue length given in Eqs. (15.2.9) and (15.2.10). The queue length equations for $n_L(N)$ and $n_S(N)$ follow the well-known MVA queue length equations with the difference that, in each case, the throughput (i.e., N divided by the response time) includes the short or long residence time plus the residence time, $R_{\text{rest}}(N)$, in the rest of the QN.

Example 15.1

Consider a mail server with a powerful processor and one large disk subsystem. The analyst wants to model the system to analyze the future performance of the server under different workload scenarios . When choosing the abstraction to model the mail server, it was decided to use a closed

QN model because during peak times the mail server has a constant (i.e., maximum) number of processes handling incoming and outgoing messages. A study of mail server workloads [9] shows that message size statistics exhibit a large coefficient of variation. Assuming the processor time to process a message is proportional to the size of the message, it is necessary to include high service time variability at the processor in the model. Assume that the following input parameters were obtained through measurements: $CV_p = 4$, $N = 200$, $D_p = 0.0060$ sec, and $D_d = 0.0071$ sec, where "p" and "d" stand for processor and disk, respectively. The question is: what are the throughput and response time of the mail server?

Consider two solution techniques. The first ignores the high variability for the service time at the processor and the other uses the modeling approach described earlier.

1. *The processor is modeled as an exponential FCFS center.*
   Using the regular MVA equations (see Chapter 12), yields the following results for response time and throughput: 1.42 sec and 141 messages/sec, respectively.

2. *Using the decomposition technique to model processor service time.*
   Assume that $p_S \gg p_L$ and set $p_L = 0.1$. The solution of Eqs. (15.2.4) and (15.2.5) yields $D_L = 0.01436$ sec and $D_S = 0.000136$ sec. Using these values, one solves two MVA models, as shown in Fig. 15.3, yielding the following response times: $R_L = 2.872$ sec and $R_S = 1.42$ sec. Thus, the response time in the QN with high variability is equal to $0.1 \times 2.872 + 0.9 \times 1.42 = 1.57$ and the throughput is equal to 133.7 messages/sec. Note that the exponential service time model overestimates the performance of the mail server.

■

15.3   Modeling Blocking Effects

Blocking is a general phenomenon in computer systems, which occurs when the operation of a system component is suspended because of the unavailability of resources elsewhere in the system [3]. The literature [11] reports three different types of blocking: 1) blocking after service, 2) blocking before service, and 3) repetitive blocking. The latter occurs when a customer at service center j wants to go to center k, whose queue is full. In this case, the customer is rejected at center k and goes to the rear of the queue of center j. This section shows how to model blocking before service, i.e., blocking that occurs when the customer to be served next at center i determines that its next service center is j before entering service at i. If j is already full, the customer cannot enter the service center i and this center is therefore blocked. For example, when the load of a mail server becomes higher than a given threshold, the server queues messages rather than attempting to deliver them. In other words, the send message service is blocked until the load decreases and the system can resume an adequate throughput.

Another example is that of a Web server [5], which typically handles multiple client requests simultaneously. These requests share the the server components (e.g., the processor, disk, memory, and network interface). A common architecture for a Web server consists of a number of processes, where each process handles one request at a time. When the TCP connection is established, the server removes it from the SYN-RCVD queue and places it in the listen sockets queue (i.e., acceptance queue) of connections awaiting acceptance from the Web server [6]. Usually, a Web server imposes a limit on the number of simultaneous processes [5], also called maximum number of clients. Thus, a request may get blocked at the acceptance queue until the server load falls below the maximum number of clients threshold.

The maximum number of processes that may be active simultaneously depends on factors such as available memory, disk subsystem capacity, and the expected load on the server. When the number of requests being served reaches the maximum number of processes, an arriving request must wait in the blocking queue, as illustrated in Fig. 15.4. When a request is completed, another request is selected from the blocking queue to be executed by the system. Figure 15.4 depicts a representation of a system with a blocking queue. The number of available processes is represented by a pool of tokens. If all tokens are occupied, an arriving request must wait. Once a request acquires a process (represented by a token), it becomes ready to use processor and I/O components. After completing execution, a process releases the token, which is immediately assigned to a process in the blocking queue.

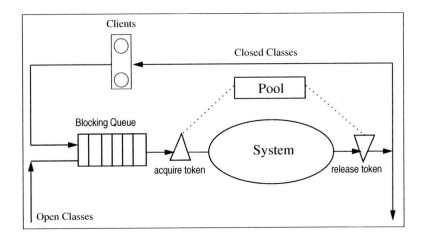

Figure 15.4. A system with a blocking queue.

If the queue is empty, the token returns to the pool of available resources. Given that this model cannot be solved directly by product-form (e.g., MVA) algorithms, an approximate solution is required. Techniques for solving non product-form models rely heavily on the use of the flow-equivalent concept, which was introduced in Chapter 14, as the decomposition/aggregation technique.

15.3.1 Single Class

Let J denote the the maximum number of transactions that may be executed simultaneously in a transaction system. When a transaction arrives and finds J transactions in execution, it has to wait outside the system, in a blocking queue. When a transaction completes execution, another one, from the blocking queue, is admitted into the system. Consider for now that a single-class queuing model is used to represent the computer system with blocking. The workload consists of transactions processed by the system and can be modeled either by an open class (*transaction* type) or by a closed class (*interactive* type). In both cases, the blocking effects appear when the number of transactions to be executed exceeds J. This situation generates a blocking queue, whose length varies with time. The solution of single-class models with blocking queuing is typical of many other non product-form models. It proceeds in five steps.

1. Consider the system in isolation ignoring the external arrivals of transactions.

2. For each feasible customer population (i.e., from 0 to J transactions), solve the model in isolation and obtain the throughput as a function of the population, $X(n)$, $n = 0, 1, 2, \ldots, J$. Use either the exact or the approximate MVA algorithm to solve the model.

3. Define a flow-equivalent (FE) server to replace the system. The service time of the flow-equivalent server depends on the load of the system and is given by:

$$S_{\mathrm{FE}}(n) = \begin{cases} 1/X(n) & n \leq J \\ \\ 1/X(J) & n > J \end{cases}$$

4. Create a reduced model with the flow-equivalent server and the external workload. Fig. 15.5 shows the reduced models for the two representations of the workload. For an interactive workload, the reduced model is closed with population equal to M, the number of clients associated with the class. In addition to the flow-equivalent server, the model has a delay server that represents the average think time (Z). The interactive model can be viewed as having M transactions, which alternate between execution in the flow-equivalent server and thinking in the delay server. The reduced model of the transaction class is an open model with a flow-equivalent server and arrival rate λ.

5. Solve the reduced model. The closed model can be solved using the single-class MVA algorithm with load-dependent devices, described in Chapter 14. The solution of the open model follows that of the birth-death model provided in Chapter 10.

Figure 15.5. Reduced models of a system with blocking queuing.

Example 15.2

A database server has a processor and two disks (D1 and D2) and is responsible for processing transactions that access the database. For workload characterization purposes, the transactions are grouped into a single class, which means that they are somehow similar. A typical transaction is characterized by the following service demands: $D_{cpu} = 0.1$ sec and $D_{D1} = D_{D2} = 0.45$ sec. The arrival rate is $\lambda = 1$ tps. With the purpose of keeping the example simple, the maximum number of transactions was set to three (i.e., $J = 3$). The performance analyst wants to evaluate the effect of the blocking queue (bq) on the transaction response time. In other words, the model should be able to calculate the percentage of the response time that a transaction spends waiting in the blocking queue, before being admitted for execution ($\%bq$).

To answer the question, the analyst needs to calculate the average response time (R_s) and the average waiting time (R_{bq}) in the blocking queue. From Little's Law, it follows that

$$R_s = N_s/\lambda \qquad\qquad\qquad (15.3.11)$$
$$R_{bq} = N_{bq}/\lambda$$
$$\%bq = (R_{bq} \times 100)/R_s = (N_{bq} \times 100)/N_s$$

where N_s is the average number of transactions in the system and N_{bq} is the average number of transactions waiting for execution.

Following the steps to solve a non product-form model, one first calculates the server throughput in isolation for all possible populations. In this case, because of the memory constraint, the server can have at most three transactions in execution ($n = 1, 2, 3$). The single-class MVA algorithm of

Chapter 12 yields $X(1) = 1$ tps, $X(2) = 1.413$ tps, and $X(3) = 1.623$ tps. With these results one can define a flow-equivalent server for the database system. The reduced model is an open system with a load-dependent server and arrival rate λ. Using the results introduced in Chapter 10 for birth-death models one is able to calculate P_k, the probability that there are k transactions in the system. Thus, letting $\lambda_i = \lambda$ and $\mu_i = X(i)$, the probabilities $P_0 = 0.260$, $P_1 = 0.260$, $P_2 = 0.184$, and $P_3 = 0.113$ are obtained. The value of N_{bq} can be obtained from the probabilities P_k as

$$N_{bq} = \sum_{k=1}^{\infty} k \ P_{k+3} \qquad (15.3.12)$$

since when there are k $(k > 1)$ transactions in the blocking queue there are $k + 3$ in execution. Using the probability values in Eq. (15.3.12) yields $N_{bq} = 0.474$. The average number of transactions in the system is given by

$$N_s = N_{bq} + N_e \qquad (15.3.13)$$

where N_e is the average number of transactions in execution given by

$$N_e = \sum_{k=1}^{J} kP_k + J\sum_{k>J} P_k = \sum_{k=1}^{J} kP_k + J\left(1 - \sum_{k=0}^{J} P_k\right) \qquad (15.3.14)$$

Substituting the values of P_k and J into Eq. (15.3.14), yields $N_e = 1.516$. Thus, the average number of transactions in the system is 1.99 and the percentage of time that a typical transaction spends in the blocking queue is $(0.474 \times 100)/1.99 = 23.8\%$.   ∎

15.3.2   Multiple Classes

Chapter 13 showed the importance of multiple-class models for performance engineering. Therefore, one needs to generalize the solution of blocking models to multiple classes. The queuing network models considered here contain K service centers and a number R of different classes of customers. Among the customer classes, C classes $(C \leq R)$ have blocking queues, specified by the maximum number of transactions of each class, J_c, $c = 1, 2, \ldots, C$. For example, consider a simple two-class model with a processor and two disks.

The workload consists of two classes of transactions: queries (q) and updates (u). The execution mix can have at most four queries and one update simultaneously (i.e., $J_q = 4$ and $J_u = 1$). The two classes are characterized by their arrival rates, $\lambda_q = 4.20$ tps and $\lambda_u = 0.20$ tps. Typical capacity planning questions are: What is the effect on the system performance of the doubling the maximum number of transactions in execution at the same time? To answer these questions, one needs to introduce first approximate solution techniques for the blocking queuing problem.

Brandwajn [10] and Menascé and Almeida [24] independently developed a noniterative solution technique for multiple-class models with memory constraints, i.e., blocking characteristics. Basically, the technique requires the calculation of throughputs for all possible combinations of customer populations. These throughputs feed a series of single-class models, whose results are then combined into the solution of the original problem. Although accurate, the technique has a high computational cost. An iterative approximation, developed by Brandwajn [10] and Lazowska and Zahorjan [23], circumvents the problem of computing throughputs for all populations. However, as pointed out in Ref. [37], the iterative algorithm tends to be less accurate than the first technique. The basic approach of the iterative technique developed in Ref. [23] is to reduce a multiclass model to a set of single-class models. To achieve this goal, two assumptions are introduced.

- *Independence.* It is assumed that the average class i population in the blocking model is independent of class j $(i \neq j)$ population.

- *Average Population.* It is assumed that the throughput of class i given n_i customers in the model depends only on the average population of the other classes.

The first assumption allows the creation of flow-equivalent servers for each blocking class c $(c = 1, 2, \ldots, C)$. The second assumption avoids the calculation of throughputs for all possible population configurations. The throughput of a given class i with population n_i, $X_i(n_i)$, is obtained from the evaluation of the multiclass model with n_i class i customers and with other class populations fixed at their average values, $n_j = \bar{n}_j$, $j \neq i$. The average customer population can be obtained by an iterative process that evaluates the single-class model of each blocking class. The full description of the algorithm proposed by Lazowska and Zahorjan [23] blocking models with multiple classes is as follows.

1. Initialize the average population of each blocking class. To obtain an initial estimate for the average population of each blocking class, solve the original multiclass models without blocking. If class c is of type *transaction* it should be modeled as an open class. If class c is of type *interactive* it should be modeled as a closed class. The techniques for solving the unconstrained model are given in Chapter 13 for closed, open, and mixed multiclass queuing networks. For each blocking class, set the estimate $\bar{n}_c$ to the minimum between J_c and the average class c population obtained by solving the unconstrained model. Thus, the outcome of this step is a set of estimates for $\bar{n}_c$.

2. Create a transformed multiclass model. The type of a blocking class is either *transaction* or *interactive*. Change the original type to a *closed*, with population equal to $\bar{n}_c$. The unconstrained classes remain unchanged.

3. For each blocking class $c = 1, \ldots, C$ do:

    (a) Calculate the throughputs $X_c(n_c)$ for $n_c = 1, \ldots, J_c$. These throughputs are obtained through the solution of the transformed multiclass model when $\bar{n}_c$ is substituted for $1, 2, \ldots, J_c$. The population for class s ($s \neq c$) remains fixed at $\bar{n}_s$. The model has to be solved J_c times.

    (b) Define a single-class model with memory queuing and throughputs $X_c(n_c)$.

    (c) Using the FESC-based algorithm of Section 15.3.1, solve the single-class model.

    (d) Using Eq. (15.3.14), calculate $N_{m,c}$, the average number of class c customers in execution. Let $\bar{n}_c = N_{m,c}$.

4. Repeat step 3 until successive values of $\bar{n}_c$ are sufficiently close (i.e., the percentage difference between successive iterations is smaller than a set tolerance).

5. Obtain performance results for the C constrained classes from the solution of the C single-class models of step 3.

6. Obtain performance results for the $(R-C)$ unconstrained classes from the solution of the transformed multiclass model (step 2), which take as input parameter for the blocking classes the final values for $\bar{n}_c$, obtained in step 3.

Example 15.3

Consider again the simple two-class model described in the beginning of this section. Table 15.1 displays the parameters that characterize the model.

Step 1 of the algorithm requires that one solves an open multiclass unconstrained model as given in Chapter 13. The resulting values of the average population are 6.0192 and 0.8540 transactions for classes query and update, respectively. So $\bar{n}_Q$ and $\bar{n}_U$ are initialized as $\bar{n}_Q = \min\{4, 6.0192\} = 4$ and $\bar{n}_U = \min\{1, 0.8540\} = 0.8540$. Table 15.2 shows the first four iterations of step 3 of the algorithm. The columns labeled $X_Q(1)$ through $X_Q(4)$ display the throughputs obtained in step 3a for class *query*, and the column labeled $X_U(1)$ shows the throughput obtained in the same step for class *update*. The columns labeled $\bar{n}_Q$ and $\bar{n}_U$ display the values obtained in step 3 (d) derived from the solution of a FESC model for classes *query* and *update*, respectively. For instance, if one wanted to stop at iteration 4, the response time for *update* transactions would be obtained by dividing the average number of transactions in the system (N_s) obtained by solving the FESC model (1.077 in this case) by the average arrival rate (0.2 tps). The resulting response time would then be 5.83 sec. Table 15.3 shows the solution of this example for a tolerance of 10^{-2}. This table shows that an update transaction spends,

Table 15.1. Input Parameters for the Two-Class Model

Class	Service Demand (sec)			Arrival Rate, λ	J
	Processor	Disk 1	Disk 2		
Query	0.105	0.180	0	4.20	4
Update	0.375	0.480	0.240	0.20	1

Table 15.2. First Four Iterations for Multiclass Example

Iteration	Query					Update	
	$X_Q(1)$	$X_Q(2)$	$X_Q(3)$	$X_Q(4)$	$\bar{n}_Q$	$X_U(1)$	$\bar{n}_U$
1	2.542	3.577	4.115	4.434	3.648	0.342	0.585
2	2.789	3.835	4.350	4.645	3.355	0.381	0.525
3	2.850	3.897	4.407	4.695	3.289	0.386	0.518
4	2.857	3.904	4.412	4.700	3.282	0.386	0.518

on average, 51.74% of the response time waiting for execution. It is clear that the system needs more processes to execute the transactions. The same model can be used to investigate the effect on the performance of update transactions of an increase in the maximum number of processes. Assume that the maximum number of update transactions in execution is doubled. Thus, letting $J_u = 2$ and solving the model again, one obtains 3.09 sec and 2.33 sec for the average response times of updates and queries, respectively. In this case, an update transaction would spend only 0.29 sec waiting for execution.   ∎

15.4   Modeling Priority Scheduling

Priority scheduling schemes have been used for managing and controlling resource allocation in many types of computer systems, such as database management systems [12], Web servers [1], operating systems [23] and in utility grid environments. In Web servers, priority-based request scheduling at both user and kernel level has been used to provide different levels of

Table 15.3. Response Time Profile per Service Center

Class	Response Time (sec)				
	Average	Blocking	Processor	Disk 1	Disk 2
Query	2.17	1.39	0.19	0.59	-
Update	5.36	2.77	0.68	1.67	0.24

quality of service among clients [1]. Most operating systems use priorities as a way to implement a processor scheduling policy. Newly arriving high-priority processes are given the processor, even though processes of lower priority may have been waiting longer for the processor. Priority scheduling may be preemptive or non-preemptive. In the preemptive case, processes lose control of the resource when processes of higher priority arrive. The suspended processes resume their execution when there are no processes of higher priority waiting for the processor. This is called *preemptive resume priority scheduling*. This is the type of priority scheduling that is considered in this section. In the nonpreemptive case, low-priority processes are never interrupted by processes of higher priority while being served. Unfortunately, the use of priority as a scheduling discipline violates the conditions given in Chapter 13 for the existence of a product-form solution for QNs. This means that an approximate solution is needed. The motivation for the approximation is shown through an example. Then, the general algorithm is presented.

15.4.1 Two-Priority Example

Consider a server composed of a powerful processor and two disks (D1 and D2) used to support an interactive service with 500 simultaneous clients. The total workload may be further decomposed into two workloads: corporate partners and consumers. Table 15.4 presents the service demands and workload intensity parameters for the two workloads. Since corporate partners have a more strict response time requirement, one would like to answer the following questions. How would the response time of the corporate partner and consumer workloads classes change if one assigned a higher CPU scheduling priority to the corporate partners? Would the response time for the consumer class be increased significantly?

Before answering these questions, one must use the models to obtain the average response time of both classes when both of them have the same priority. The model is composed of four devices: a delay device to represent the think time at the clients, three queuing load-independent devices to represent the processor, and the two disks. The following response times are obtained with the multiclass MVA algorithm (see Chapter 13): 3.74 sec and 1.75 sec for corporate and customer classes, respectively.

Table 15.4. Input Parameters for Priority Example

Parameter	Class	
	Consumers	Corporate
Service Demand (sec)		
Processor	0.015	0.033
D1	0.011	0.018
D2	0.015	0.022
Number of clients	400	100
Think time (sec)	8	5

The modeling of priorities is considered now. For that matter, the approach called *stepwise inclusion of classes* (SWIC) is used [2]. Note that the consumer class does not interfere at all with corporate requests at the CPU since the latter have preemptive priority at the CPU over the former. Thus, in this respect, corporate requests see the CPU as if it were dedicated to them. On the other hand, consumer requests see the portion of the CPU that is left after corporate requests have used it. On the remaining part of the computer system (i.e., the I/O subsystem), both classes have the same priority.

Start by obtaining an estimate of the CPU utilization due to the corporate class only. This can be done by building a model with the corporate class as the only class. Now, build a model with both the corporate and consumer classes and an additional processor, called *shadow processor* (see Fig. 15.6).

The use of the original and shadow processors by corporate and consumer classes is governed by the following rules:

- corporate requests use only the original CPU.

- consumer requests use only the shadow CPU.

The problem now is how to compute the service demands of the original and shadow CPUs, $D_{\text{cpu},r}^{\text{org}}$ and $D_{\text{cpu},r}^{\text{shw}}$ respectively, for class r, where r may be p (for corporate) or c (for consumer). Since each class uses only its own

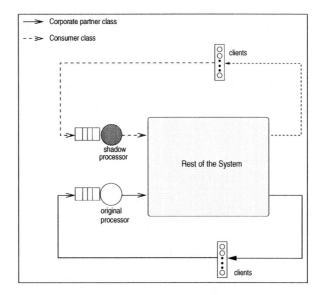

Figure 15.6. Shadow CPU for priority modeling.

dedicated CPU, it follows that

$$D_{\text{cpu},c}^{\text{org}} = 0 \qquad \text{and} \qquad D_{\text{cpu},p}^{\text{shw}} = 0$$

Since the corporate class has higher priority over the consumer class, its service demand at the original CPU is equal to its CPU service demand $D_{\text{cpu},p}$. Hence,

$$D_{\text{cpu},p}^{\text{org}} = D_{\text{cpu},p}.$$

The CPU service demand of consumer requests at the shadow CPU has to be inflated to reflect the fact that it will take these requests longer to go through the CPU due to the presence of higher-priority requests. The higher the CPU utilization due to corporate requests, the more the service demand of consumer requests has to be inflated. The inflation factor $1/(1 - U_{\text{cpu},p})$ has the desired properties. Thus,

$$D_{\text{cpu},c}^{\text{shw}} = \frac{D_{\text{cpu},c}}{1 - U_{\text{cpu},p}}$$

The steps necessary to solve the priority model are:

1. *Build a single-class model.* This model includes the corporate class only, the original CPU, the terminals, and the disks. Using the parameters of Table 15.4 in the MVA algorithm yields the throughput of the corporate class as 11.44 request/sec. Therefore, the CPU utilization can be computed as $U_{\text{cpu},p} = D_{\text{cpu},p} \times X_{0,p} = 0.033 \times 11.44 = 0.378$.

2. *Add the shadow CPU and the consumer class.* Compute the service demands at the shadow and original CPUs as follows:

$$D_{\text{cpu},c}^{\text{org}} = 0 \qquad \text{and} \qquad D_{\text{cpu},p}^{\text{shw}} = 0$$

$$D_{\text{cpu},p}^{\text{org}} = D_{\text{cpu},p} = 0.033 \ \text{sec}$$

$$D_{\text{cpu},c}^{\text{shw}} = \frac{D_{\text{cpu},c}}{1 - U_{\text{cpu},p}} = \frac{0.015}{1 - 0.378} = 0.024 \ \text{sec}$$

Using the MVA algorithm, the response time for the corporate class is computed as 1.04 sec and as 1.78 sec for the consumer class. So there is a significant improvement in the response time of the corporate class (from 3.74 sec to 1.04 sec) with very little increase in the response time of the consumer class (2% increase). The reason is that the consumer class has a much smaller service demand at the processor than that of the corporate class. So, giving priority to the corporate class at the processor does not hurt the lower-priority class too much.

The next section generalizes the algorithm presented in this example to the case of more than two priorities.

15.4.2   SWIC Priority Algorithm

Using the notation introduced in Chapter 2, consider that there are P priority groups numbered from 1 to P. Let $\text{Prior}(r)$ denote the priority of class r customers. Classes in priority group 1 have the highest priority, while those in group P have the lowest one. The SWIC algorithm builds P different models. The first model contains all classes of the highest priority (priority 1) only. The second model contains all classes of priority 1 and 2 and a shadow CPU to be used exclusively by customers of priority 2. As in the previous example, the service demand at this shadow CPU has to be inflated by dividing the original service demand by (1 - CPU utilization of higher-priority customers). In general, each step introduces an additional priority, an additional shadow CPU, and the service demands of the classes just included in the model are inflated. The P different QN models considered by the SWIC algorithm are denoted $\mathcal{Q}_1, \ldots, \mathcal{Q}_P$. Figure 15.7 shows the SWIC algorithm. Let $D_{\mathrm{cpu},r}^p$ indicate the service demand of a class r job of priority p at shadow CPU p. The notation $D_{\mathrm{cpu},r}$ stands, as usual, for the service demand of class r jobs at the CPU. Denote by $\Omega(p)$ the set of classes of priority p. Thus, $\Omega(p) = \{r \mid \mathrm{Prior}(r) = p\}$.

Input Parameters: service demands ($D_{i,r}$'s) and $\mathrm{Prior}(r)$'s
Iteration Loop
For $p := 1$ to P do
    Begin
        Build a QN model $\mathcal{Q}_p$ containing classes r such that $\mathrm{Prior}(r) \leq p$.
        Model $\mathcal{Q}_p$ should contain p shadow CPUs.
        Compute Inflated Service Demands for Shadow CPUs
        For r such that $\mathrm{Prior}(r) \leq p$ do

$$D_{\mathrm{cpu},r}^p = \begin{cases} 0 & r \notin \Omega(p) \\[2mm] D_{cpu,r}/(1 - \sum_{q=1}^{p-1} \sum_{s \in \Omega(q)} U_{\mathrm{cpu},s}) & \text{otherwise} \end{cases}$$

        Solve model $\mathcal{Q}_p$ and obtain the throughputs $X_{0,r}$ for all classes r
        such that $\mathrm{Prior}(r) \leq p$.
        Compute Utilizations
        For all r such that $\mathrm{Prior}(r) \leq p$ do $U_{\mathrm{cpu},r} = D_{\mathrm{cpu},r} X_{0,r}$
    End ;
Compute Final Metrics
The residence times for the I/O devices are obtained from model $\mathcal{Q}_P$.
The residence times at the CPU per class are obtained from the corresponding shadow CPU in model $\mathcal{Q}_P$.

Figure 15.7. SWIC algorithm for priority modeling.

The SWIC algorithm was shown to be very accurate. In Ref. [2], the authors compare the results obtained with SWIC with exact results obtained by solving global balance equations and with results from other approximations. The global balance equation method (explained in Chapter 10) can only be used in very small examples since the number of states grows very fast with the degree of multiprogramming. Other approximations have been proposed. Agrawal presents a nice treatment of various approximation methods for modeling priorities [3]. Lazowska et al. propose another method, which is also based on the notion of shadow CPUs and service demand inflation, but is iterative in nature [23]. A discussion of this method is left as an exercise.

Example 15.4

Table 15.5 contains parameters for an example of the execution of the SWIC algorithm. The example has four classes and three priorities. The assignment of priorities to classes is reflected in the following Ω function: $\Omega(1) = \{1, 2\}$, $\Omega(2) = \{3\}$, and $\Omega(3) = \{4\}$. The system in question has one CPU and only one disk.

Table 15.6 shows the results of the execution of the algorithm. The response times per class are 4.03 sec, 2.93 sec, 3.34 sec, and 4.08 sec, for classes 1 through 4, respectively.   ∎

15.5   Modeling Software Contention

The response time of a transaction or request submitted to a computer system can be broken down into three components. The first is the total

Table 15.5. Input Parameters for SWIC Algorithm Example

Class	Priority	$D_{\text{cpu},r}$ (sec)	$D_{\text{disk},r}$ (sec)	Number of Processes
1	1	0.10	0.50	3
2	1	0.15	0.35	4
3	2	0.80	0.20	2
4	3	0.90	0.06	1

Table 15.6. Results for the SWIC Algorithm Example

	Model		
	$\mathcal{Q}_1$	$\mathcal{Q}_2$	$\mathcal{Q}_3$
$D^1_{\text{cpu},1}$	0.10	0.10	0.10
$D^1_{\text{cpu},2}$	0.15	0.15	0.15
$D^2_{\text{cpu},3}$	-	$0.8/(1-0.324) = 1.18$	$0.8/(1-0.287) = 1.12$
$D^3_{\text{cpu},4}$	-	-	$0.9/(1-0.751) = 3.61$
$U_{\text{cpu},1}$	$0.87 \times 0.1 = 0.087$	$0.77 \times 0.1 = 0.077$	$0.75 \times 0.1 = 0.075$
$U_{\text{cpu},2}$	$1.58 \times 0.15 = 0.237$	$1.40 \times 0.15 = 0.210$	$1.36 \times 0.15 = 0.204$
$U_{\text{cpu},3}$	-	$0.58 \times 0.8 = 0.464$	$0.60 \times 0.8 = 0.480$
$U_{\text{cpu},4}$	-	-	$0.25 \times 0.9 = 0.225$
$\sum_r U_{\text{cpu},r}$	0.324	0.751	0.984

service time, i.e., the total time spent by transactions obtaining service from the various physical resources such as processors, disks, and networks. The second component is the total time spent waiting to use a physical resource. Finally, the third component (*software contention*) is the time spent to access a software resource such as a non-reentrant software module, a software thread, or a database lock. It is important to take into account the effect of software contention when estimating the total response time.

This section provides a simple analytical modeling technique for estimating software contention delays. The technique, first presented in [25], is called SQN-HQN and consists of a two-layer queuing network model. Software resources are modeled by a software queuing network (SQN) and physical resources by a hardware queuing network (HQN). The effect of software contention on the physical QN and the effect of physical resource contention on the software QN requires an iterative technique to solve this dependency. The technique relies on existing solution techniques for open, closed, multiclass queuing networks and can be used with both product-form QNs and approximations [3] used to handle situations such as simultaneous resource possession [3, 21, 26] and priorities [2, 3, 33] as discussed in this chapter. Multi-servers can be handled by using load-dependent servers (see Chapter 14) or approximations [34].

15.5.1 Single Class Algorithm

Consider the case of N processes $P_1, \cdots, P_N$ that alternate between executing non-critical section and critical section code. Any number of processes can be concurrently executing their non-critical code. However, only one of them can be executing the critical section code. If a process attempts to enter its critical section code while another process is inside the critical section, the attempting process is put to sleep at the queue associated with the semaphore that controls access to the critical section. Assume in this simple example that the only physical device used by all processes during the execution of the critical and non-critical section code is the CPU and that the CPU scheduling discipline is processor-sharing.

The software phases of a process execution can be depicted by a *software queuing network* (SQN) as in the top part of Fig. 15.8. The SQN has two resources (software modules). One is a delay-resource (illustrated as a rectangle) that corresponds to the non-critical section code; there is no queuing for a software resource during this phase. The other software resource is a queuing resource, which corresponds to the critical section code.

While a process—a customer in the SQN—is using the software resources in the SQN, it is also using or waiting to use physical resources (e.g., CPUs and disks). Delay resources are used in the SQN to represent software resources for which there is no software contention. The queuing network asso-

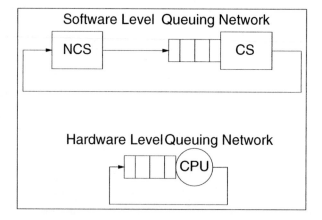

Figure 15.8. Software and hardware QNs for the critical section exampl e.

ciated with the physical resources, the *hardware queuing network* (HQN), is shown in the bottom part of Fig. 15.8. Customers in the HQN are processes using the physical resources as a result of the execution of software modules. The time spent at the NCS and CS resources in the SQN depends on the contention for access to the physical resources, the CPU in this case. Also, the number of processes contending for the CPU, i.e., the number of processes in the HQN, is equal to the number of concurrent processes that are not blocked waiting for entry to the critical section. The blocked processes are sleeping and are therefore not present in any HQN queue. Therefore, the customer population in the HQN is equal to $N - B$ where B is the number of processes blocked for a software resource.

Some notation needs to be defined before proceeding with an explanation on how contention for access to software resources can be computed in the single class case.

- $D^{\text{sh}}_{j,i}$: software-hardware service demand, i.e., total service time of a process executing software module j when using physical resource i in the HQN. The superscript "sh" indicates that these service demands are related to the mapping between the software and hardware QNs. For example, $D^{\text{sh}}_{\text{ncs,cpu}}$ is the total CPU time for the execution of the non-critical section code. This time does not include the time spent waiting to use the CPU while executing non-critical section code.

- D^{s}_j: software service demand, i.e., total service time to execute module j in the SQN. The superscript "s" indicates that this service demand relates to the software QN. For example, $D^{\text{s}}_{\text{ncs}}$ is the total service time to execute the non-critical section code. The service demand D^{s}_j is the sum of all service times at all physical devices during the execution of module j. Thus,

$$D^{\text{s}}_j = \sum_{\forall\, i} D^{\text{sh}}_{j,i}. \tag{15.5.15}$$

- D^{h}_i: hardware service demand, i.e., total service time of a process at physical resource i in the hardware QN. For example, $D^{\text{h}}_{\text{cpu}}$ is the total service time of a process at the CPU. This time is the sum of the service demands due to the execution of all modules of the process.

Thus,

$$D_i^h = \sum_{\forall j} D_{j,i}^{sh}. \tag{15.5.16}$$

For example, $D_{cpu}^h = D_{ncs,cpu}^{sh} + D_{cs,cpu}^{sh}$.

- $R_i'(n)$: residence time, i.e., total time spent by a process at physical resource i, waiting for or receiving service, when there are n processes at the HQN.

An iterative algorithm, the SQN-HQN algorithm, can then be used to estimate software contention time and to compute all performance metrics (e.g., response time and throughput). The inputs to the algorithm are the service demands $D_{j,i}^{sh}$ and the number N of processes. The algorithm iterates between solving the SQN and the HQN. Figure 15.9 illustrates the relationship between the SQN and HQN models. The SQN model receives as input the number of processes N and the software service demands and produces the number B of processes blocked for software resources as output. The HQN model takes as input a number of customers N^h, which is the original number of processes minus the number of processes blocked for software resources, and the hardware service demands. The output of the HQN model is the set of residence times at each physical device. These residence times are used to adjust (see step 5 of the algorithm) the software service demands for the SQN model. The iteration starts by solving the SQN assuming zero contention for physical resources. The algorithm iterates until successive values of the number, B, of processes blocked for software contention are sufficiently close.

- Step 1 - Initialization:

$$D_j^s \leftarrow \sum_{\forall i} D_{j,i}^{sh} \tag{15.5.17}$$

$$D_i^h \leftarrow \sum_{\forall j} D_{j,i}^{sh} \tag{15.5.18}$$

$$B^0 \leftarrow 0 \quad \text{initial value for } B \tag{15.5.19}$$

$$k \leftarrow 1 \quad \text{iteration counter} \tag{15.5.20}$$

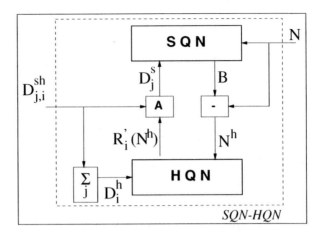

Figure 15.9. SQN-HQN scheme.

- Step 2 - Solve the SQN with D_j^{s} as service demands and N as customer population.

- Step 3 - Compute the average number of blocked processes B^k. In the case of our example, this is equal to the average number of processes waiting in the queue for the CS resource. Thus, $B^k = \overline{n}_{\text{cs}} - U_{\text{cs}}$, where $\overline{n}_{\text{cs}}$ is the average number of processes at resource CS in the SQN and U_{cs} is the utilization of resource CS. In general,

$$B^k = \sum_{\forall j} L_j \qquad (15.5.21)$$

where L_j is the average number of processes in the waiting line for software resource j.

- Step 4 - Solve the HQN with D_i^{h} as service demands and $N^h = N - B^k$ as customer population. Note that the solution to a QN with a non-integer customer population can be obtained using Schweitzer's approximation [35].

- Step 5 - Adjust the service demands at the SQN to account for contention at the physical resources as follows

$$D_j^{\text{s}} \leftarrow \sum_{\forall i} \frac{D_{j,i}^{\text{sh}}}{D_i^{\text{h}}} \times R_i'(N^h). \qquad (15.5.22)$$

Thus, for the critical section example these equations become

$$D_{\text{ncs}}^{\text{s}} \leftarrow \frac{D_{\text{ncs,cpu}}^{\text{sh}}}{D_{\text{cpu}}^{\text{h}}} \times R_{\text{cpu}}'(N^h) \tag{15.5.23}$$

$$D_{\text{cs}}^{\text{s}} \leftarrow \frac{D_{\text{cs,cpu}}^{\text{sh}}}{D_{\text{cpu}}^{\text{h}}} \times R_{\text{cpu}}'(N^h). \tag{15.5.24}$$

- Step 6 (Convergence Test): If $| (B^k - B^{k-1})/B^k | > \xi$ then $k \leftarrow k + 1$ and go to step 2.

Step 5 of the above algorithm can be explained using the critical section example. The residence time equation for MVA applied to the HQN is

$$R_{\text{cpu}}'(N) = D_{\text{cpu}}^{\text{h}}[1 + \overline{n}_{\text{cpu}}(N - 1)]. \tag{15.5.25}$$

But,

$$D_{\text{cpu}}^{\text{h}} = D_{\text{ncs,cpu}}^{\text{sh}} + D_{\text{cs,cpu}}^{\text{sh}}. \tag{15.5.26}$$

Hence, using Eqs. (15.5.25) and (15.5.26), yields

$$\begin{aligned} R_{\text{cpu}}'(N) = {}& D_{\text{ncs,cpu}}^{\text{sh}}[1 + \overline{n}_{\text{cpu}}(N - 1)] + \\ & D_{\text{cs,cpu}}^{\text{sh}}[1 + \overline{n}_{\text{cpu}}(N - 1)]. \end{aligned} \tag{15.5.27}$$

The first term of the right-hand side of Eq. (15.5.27) is the total time (waiting + service) spent at the CPU by a process while executing non-critical section code and the second term is the total time spent at the CPU by a process while executing the critical section code. For example, using Eqs. (15.5.25) and (15.5.27) one can write the total time spent at the CPU while executing the non-critical section code as

$$\frac{D_{\text{ncs,cpu}}^{\text{sh}}}{D_{\text{cpu}}^{\text{h}}} \times R_{\text{cpu}}'(N). \tag{15.5.28}$$

Example 15.5

Consider a computer system with one CPU and three disks (see bottom part of Fig. 15.10). Processes execute non-critical section code and then enter one of two critical sections (see top portion of Fig. 15.10).

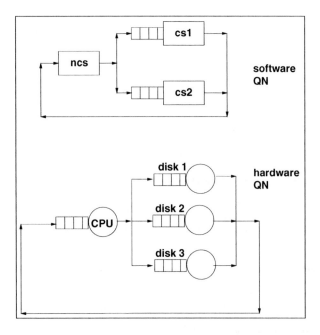

Figure 15.10. Software and hardware queuing networks for Example 15.x

The service demands (i.e, the values of $D_{j,i}^{\text{sh}}$) are given in Table 15.7 and are the same as in [4]. The last row shows the values of D_j^{s} and the last column contains the values of D_i^{h}.

Table 15.7. Service demands (in sec) for the example in [4]

Device	Software Module			Hardware
	NCS	CS 1	CS 2	Demands
CPU	0.2000	0.0600	0.0808	0.3408
Disk 1	0.0560	0.0576	0.000	0.1136
Disk 2	0.0360	0.0000	0.1212	0.1572
Disk 3	0.0360	0.0000	0.0000	0.0360
Software Demands	0.3280	0.1176	0.2020	

Table 15.8 shows the results (i.e., throughputs) obtained with the SQN-HQN algorithm and with global balance equations (i.e., exact solutions), as reported in [4], for eight values of the number of concurrent processes N. The last column of the table shows the absolute percent relative error relative to the global balance equations solution. The error of the SQN-HQN approach is very small and does not exceed 3.05% in this example.   ■

15.5.2   Open QN at the Software Level

The SQN-HQN technique can be extended to include the case in which the SQN is modeled as an open queuing network as illustrated in Fig. 15.11. In that case, processes arrive at a rate of λ requests/sec. The rest of the SQN and the HQN are the same as in the example of Fig. 15.10 and the service demands are as in Table 15.7.

Steps 2 and 4 of the algorithm described in Section 15.5.1 should be replaced by the following to contemplate the case of open SQNs.

- New Step 2 - Solve the SQN with D_j^s as service demands and λ as arrival rate and obtain $\overline{N}$ the average number of customers in the SQN.

Table 15.8. Throughput (processes/sec) for Example 15.x

N	SQN-HQN Solution	Exact Solution	Absolute % Relative Error
1	1.544	1.54	0.27
2	2.088	2.11	1.06
3	2.317	2.37	2.22
4	2.428	2.49	2.49
5	2.487	2.56	2.86
6	2.521	2.60	3.05
7	2.541	2.62	3.00
8	2.555	2.63	2.86

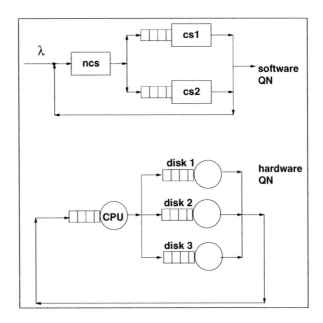

Figure 15.11. Open QN at the software level.

- New Step 4 - Solve the HQN with D_i^h as service demands and $N^h = \overline{N} - B^k$ as customer population. Note that the solution to a QN with a non-integer customer population can be obtained using Schweitzer's approximation [35].

Table 15.9 contains results of running the modified algorithm for the case of $\lambda = 3$ processes/sec. The table shows the results of the first 10 iterations. Column 2 (N^h) is the customer population used to solve the HQN at each iteration. The next column shows the average response time R. Columns 4 and 5 show the average number of requests in the SQN and the average number of blocked requests in the CS1 and CS2 queues, respectively. The last three columns show the modified service demands for the SQN at each step. Note that the values for iteration 0 are the original values of these demands. The relative error in B is 0.123% at the tenth iteration.

Table 15.9. Results of the first 10 iterations for the open SQN example

Iter	N^h	R	N^s	B	Modified SQN Demands		
					NCS	CS1	CS2
0	–				0.3280	0.1176	0.2020
1	1.295	0.821	1.641	0.346	0.3662	0.1302	0.2235
2	1.440	0.946	1.893	0.453	0.3858	0.1365	0.2342
3	1.513	1.014	2.028	0.515	0.3958	0.1397	0.2396
4	1.550	1.050	2.100	0.549	0.4010	0.1414	0.2424
5	1.570	1.069	2.137	0.568	0.4037	0.1423	0.2438
6	1.580	1.079	2.157	0.577	0.4051	0.1427	0.2446
7	1.585	1.084	2.167	0.582	0.4059	0.1430	0.2450
8	1.588	1.086	2.173	0.585	0.4062	0.1431	0.2452
9	1.589	1.088	2.175	0.587	0.4064	0.1432	0.2453
10	1.590	1.088	2.177	0.587			

15.5.3   The Multiclass Algorithm

The algorithm presented in Section 15.5.1 generalizes in a straightforward manner to multiple classes. A generalized notation for the multiple class case is in order. Let

- R: number of classes in the SQN and in the HQN.

- $\vec{N^s} = (N_1, \cdots, N_R)$: population vector for the SQN. N_r is the multi-threading level for class r.

- $\vec{N^h} = (N_1, \cdots, N_R)$: population vector for the HQN. N_r is the number of customers in class r.

- $\vec{B} = (B_1, \cdots, B_R)$: vector of number of processes blocked, i.e., waiting for a software resource. B_r is the number of class r processes blocked for a software resource.

- $D^{\text{sh}}_{j,i;r}$: software-hardware service demand, i.e., total service time at physical resource i of a class r software module j.

- $D^{s}_{j;r}$: software service demand, i.e., total service time to execute module j of class r in the SQN. The service demand $D^{s}_{j;r}$ is the sum of all service times at all physical devices during the execution of module j. Thus

$$D^{s}_{j;r} = \sum_{\forall i} D^{sh}_{j,i;r}. \qquad (15.5.29)$$

- $D^{h}_{i;r}$: hardware service demand, i.e., total service time at physical resource i for class r in the hardware QN. This time is the sum of the service demands due to the execution of all modules of a process. Thus

$$D^{h}_{i;r} = \sum_{\forall j} D^{sh}_{j,i;r}. \qquad (15.5.30)$$

- $R'_{i;r}(\vec{N}^{h})$: residence time, i.e., total time spent by a class r process at resource i, waiting for or receiving service, when the customer population at the HQN is given by the vector $\vec{N}^{h}$.

The iterative algorithm used to estimate the software contention time and to compute all performance metrics (e.g., response time and throughput) is given below. The inputs to the algorithm are the service demands $D^{sh}_{j,i;r}$ and the vector $\vec{N}^{s}$. The algorithm iterates until successive values of $\vec{B}$ are sufficiently close.

- Step 1 - Initialization:

$$D^{s}_{j;r} \leftarrow \sum_{\forall i} D^{sh}_{j,i;r} \quad r = 1, \cdots, R \qquad (15.5.31)$$

$$D^{h}_{i;r} \leftarrow \sum_{\forall j} D^{sh}_{j,i;r} \quad r = 1, \cdots, R \qquad (15.5.32)$$

$$\vec{B} \leftarrow \vec{0} \qquad (15.5.33)$$

$$k \leftarrow 1 \qquad (15.5.34)$$

- Step 2 - Solve the SQN with $D^{s}_{j;r}$ as service demands and $\vec{N}^{s}$ as customer population.

- Step 3 - Compute the average number of blocked processes per class as

$$\vec{B}^k = (\sum_{\forall j} L_{j,1}, \cdots, \sum_{\forall j} L_{j,r}, \cdots, \sum_{\forall j} L_{j,R}) \qquad (15.5.35)$$

where $L_{j,r}$, $r = 1, \cdots, R$, is the average number of class r processes in the waiting line for software resource j.

- Step 4 - Solve the HQN with $D_{i;r}^h$ as service demands and population vector $\vec{N}^h = \vec{N}^s - \vec{B}^k$ as customer population. Note that the solution to a QN with a non-integer customer population can be obtained using Schweitzer's approximation [35]. The solution to the HQN provides the residence time values $R_{i;r}'(\vec{N}^h)$ for all devices i and classes r.

- Step 5 - Adjust the service demands at the SQN to account for contention at the physical resources as follows

$$D_{j;r}^s \leftarrow \sum_{\forall i} \frac{D_{j,i;r}^{sh}}{D_{i;r}^h} \times R_{i;r}'(\vec{N}^h). \qquad (15.5.36)$$

- Step 6 (Convergence Test):
  If $\max_r |(B_r^k - B_r^{k-1})/B_r^k| > \xi$ then $k \leftarrow k + 1$ and go to step 2.

The same considerations discussed in Section 15.5.1 can be applied to the multiclass case. Situations that require modeling a queue for a multi-threaded software server can be considered by including a multi-server queue in the SQN and using approximation techniques [34] to solve QNs with multi-servers or QNs with load-dependent servers as done in Chapter 14. Other approaches to modeling software contention were presented before [4, 20, 22, 32, 29, 36, 42].

15.6   Modeling Fork/Join Queuing Networks

Parallelism and concurrency in computer systems can be modeled by fork-join systems. When entering a concurrent processing stage, an arriving request forks into subtasks that are executed independently either on different service centers or on the same service center. Upon completing execution, each subtask waits at the join point for its sibling tasks to complete execution. The fork operation starts new concurrent subtasks. The join operation forces one subtask to wait for sibling subtasks.

Fork/join models have been analyzed in the context of computer systems and communication networks. Fork/join queuing networks are used to model disk arrays under synchronous workloads [38]. The cache, the array controller, and the disks are represented by individual queuing service centers. The controller is modeled by a fork/join queue. Each disk is modeled by a queuing server of this fork/join queue. A request to the controller is forked into subrequests that are assigned to the disks of the disk array. An I/O request to the disk array is complete when all subrequests are complete, i.e., when they all meet at the join point.

Performance models of modern servers and operating systems typically involve solving a set of non-product form closed QNs with fork/join structures. In these models, fork/join stations model the synchronization constraints between processes at different stages of execution. Obtaining the exact solution for these networks is difficult and may be costly in the case of systems with a large state space. Therefore, approximate methods are needed. This section presents the approximate solution technique proposed in [39, 40] for queuing models with fork/join synchronization.

Consider that the QN consists of one or more interconnected subsystems as illustrated in the example of Fig 15.12. Two types of subsystems are considered:

1. *Serial subsystem:* consists of a single queuing service center like the ones discussed throughout the book.

2. *Parallel subsystem:* consists of k $(k > 1)$ parallel service centers in a fork/join arrangement. That is, a request to a parallel subsystem is split into k independent sub-requests, one for each of the k service centers. The original request completes when all subrequests complete, i.e., when all of them arrive at the join point. Thus, the time spent by a request in a parallel subsystem is the maximum of the times spent in each of the k service centers. The average service time of a request is assumed to be the same at each of the k service centers of a parallel

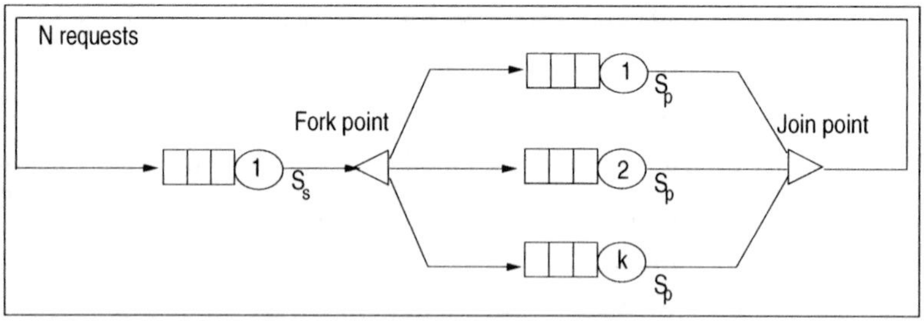

Figure 15.12. Fork and join.

subsystem . Note that a serial subsystem is a special case of a parallel subsystem when $k = 1$.

Consider a closed fork/join queuing network with the following parameters:

- I: number of subsystems in the queuing network model.
- S_i: average service time at subsystem i.
- k_i: number of parallel service centers at subsystem i.
- $R_i(n)$: response time at subsystem i when there are n requests in the queuing network.
- $R'_i(n)$: residence time at subsystem i when there are n requests in the queuing network.
- V_i: average number of visits per request to subsystem i.

The approximate fork/join MVA solution method is based on adapting the response time equation as indicated by Eq. (15.6.37), which is an approximation derived from the arrival theorem [30].

$$R_i = S_i[H_{k_i} + \overline{n}_i(n - 1)] \tag{15.6.37}$$

where $\overline{n}_i(n - 1)$ is the average queue length at subsystem i when there is one less customer in the QN and H_{k_i} is the k_i-th harmonic number defined as $H_{k_i} = \sum_{i=1}^{k_i}(1/i)$. [Note: when $k = 1$, Eq. (15.6.37) becomes the exact

MVA response time equation since $H_1 = 1$.] According to Eq. (15.6.37), when there is only one request in the queuing network the average response time at a parallel subsystem with k_i service centers is $S_i H_{k_i}$. The harmonic number accounts for the synchronization time at the joining point. The rationale for this approximation comes from the fact that the expectation of a random variable defined as the maximum of k exponentially distributed random variables with average S is equal to SH_k. Performance measures for a fork/join queuing network are then obtained through the following approximate MVA equations:

$$R'_i(n) = V_i[S_i(H_{k_i} + \overline{n}_i(n-1))] = D_i[H_{k_i} + \overline{n}_i(n-1)] \quad (15.6.38)$$

$$X_0(n) = n / \sum_{i=1}^{I} R'_i(n) \quad (15.6.39)$$

$$\overline{n}_i(n) = X_0(n) \ R'_i(n) \quad (15.6.40)$$

The relative error of this approximation was shown to be less than 5% for the majority of the cases analyzed [39].

Example 15.6

A database server consists of a powerful processor and two disk array subsystems, 1 and 2. The disk arrays operate under synchronous workload, i.e., transactions are blocked until their I/O requests complete service. A disk array improves I/O performance by striping data across multiple disks [38]. The disk array subsystems consist of k_1 and k_2 disks, respectively. A transaction alternates between using the processor and the I/O subsystem until it completes its execution. Previous measurements indicate that the average response time is 0.34 seconds when 10 transactions are executing concurrently. One of the SLAs for the database server is that the average response time should not exceed 1 second. Before increasing the concurrency level to 50 transactions, the performance analyst wants to predict the new response time to verify whether or not the response time SLA will continue to be satisfied.

The model parameters are as follows. The processor service demand is equal to 0.01 sec and the service demands for each disk of disk arrays 1 and 2 are 0.02 and 0.03, respectively. With the purpose of keeping the example simple, the number of parallel disks in the disk arrays is set to small values, i.e., $k_1 = 2$ and $k_2 = 3$. The queuing model of the database server has three subsystems, the processor and the two storage systems, with two and three disks, respectively. The model is closed with n transactions in execution. Typically a disk array has three components, the cache, the controller and the disks. The disk array in this example is modeled by separate and parallel services centers, such that caching effects as well as controller overheads are implicitly represented in the disk service demands. Each disk array is modeled by parallel subsystem with a fork/join structure, where each disk is a queuing server.

The parameters for the QN model are $n = 50$, $I = 3$ (i.e., three subsystems), $k_0 = 1$ (serial execution at the processor), $k_1 = 2$, $k_2 = 3$ (parallel execution at the disk arrays), $D_{\text{processor}} = 0.01$ sec, $D_{\text{disk array 1}} = 0.02$ sec, and $D_{\text{disk array 2}} = 0.03$ sec. The solution of the algorithm presented in this section provides an average response time of 1.53 seconds, which exceed the SLA of 1 second (see the MS Excel workbook `Ch15-Ex15-6.XLS`).   ■

15.7   Concluding Remarks

Several important aspects of actual computer systems such as service times with high variability, priority scheduling at the CPU, software contention, blocking, and fork and join, are not amenable to modeling with exact queuing network models. Various approximations based on Mean Value Analysis are presented in this chapter in order to deal with these situations.

15.8   Exercises

1. Derive Eqs. (15.2.4) and (15.2.5). (*Hint:* $\sigma^2 = \bar{x}^2 - (\bar{x})^2$ where $\bar{x}^2$ is the second moment of a random variable and $\bar{x}$ its mean.)

2. Consider the example of Section 15.3.2.

   - Use the open multiclass model of Chapter 13 to solve the unconstrained model.
   - Compute the values of line 1 of Table 15.2.

3. Consider the example of Section 15.4.1. Assume that consumer requests have priority at the CPU over corporate requests. Compute the resulting response time.

4. An iterative approach for modeling priorities was presented by Lazowska et al. [23]. In their approach they suggest that one model with P shadow CPUs be built. The service demands have to be inflated properly in the same way as discussed in the algorithm given in Fig. 15.7. However, this requires knowing the values of the utilizations for the various classes. Since the utilization $U_{\text{cpu},r}$ is equal to $X_{0,r} \times D_{\text{cpu},r}$, the algorithm starts by assuming an initial value of zero for all throughputs. MVA can now be used to solve the QN and obtain new values of the throughputs, which are used to compute the utilizations and therefore new values of the service demands for the shadow CPUs. This process continues until the throughput values converge within a given tolerance. Write a program that implements this algorithm and use it to solve the example given in Section 15.4.2.

Bibliography

[1] J. Almeida, M. Dabu, A. Manikutty and P. Cao, "Providing Differentiated Quality-of-Service in Web Hosting Services," *Proc. ACM SIGMETRICS Workshop on Internet Server Performance*, Madison, Wisconsin, June 1998.

[2] V. A. Almeida and D. A. Menascé, "Approximate modeling of CPU preemptive resume priority scheduling using operational analysis," *Proc. 10th European Computer Measurement Association (ECOMA) Conf. Computer Measurement*, Munich, Germany, October 12-15, 1982.

[3] S. Agrawal, *Metamodeling: A Study of Approximations in Queuing Models*, MIT Press, Cambridge, Massachusetts, 1985.

[4] S. Agrawal and J. P. Buzen, "The Aggregate Server Method for Analyzing Serialization Delays in Computer Systems," *ACM Tr. Comp. Sys.*, vol. 1, no. 2, May 1983, pp. 116–143.

[5] B. Krishnamurthy and J. Rexford, *Web protocols and practice: HTTP/1.1, networking protocols, caching and traffic measurement*, Addison Wesley, Boston, Massachusetts, 2001.

[6] G. Banga and P. Druschel, "Measuring the capacity of a web server," *Usenix Symp. Internet Technol. Syst.*, Monterey, California, December 1997, pp. 61–71.

[7] P. Barford and M. Crovella, "Generating representative Web workloads for network and server performance evaluation," *Proc. ACM SIGMETRICS Conf.*, Madison, Wisconsin, November 1998, pp. 151–160.

[8] F. Baskett, K. Chandy, R. Muntz, and F. Palacios, "Open, closed, and mixed networks of queues with different classes of customers," *J. ACM*, vol. 22, no. 2, April 1975, pp. 248–260.

[9] L. Bertolotti and M. Calzarossa, "Models of mail server workloads," *Performance Evaluation*, no. 46, vol. 2, 2001, pp. 65–76.

[10] A. Brandwajn, "Fast approximate solution of multiprogrammed models," *Proc. 1982 SIGMETRICS Conf. Measurement and Modeling of Computer Systems*, Seattle, Washington, 1982, pp. 141-149.

[11] G. Bolch, S. Greiner, H. de Meer, and K. Trivedi, *Queueing Networks and Markov Chains*, John Wiley & Sons, Inc., 1998.

[12] M. Carey, R. Jauhari, M. Livny, "Priority in DBMS resource scheduling," *Proc. VLDB Conf.*, 1989, pp. 397–410.

[13] K. Chandy and E. Sauer, "Approximate methods for analyzing queuing network models of computing systems," *ACM Computing Surveys*, vol. 10, no. 3, September 1978, pp. 281–317.

[14] P. Courtois, "Decomposability, instabilities, and saturation in multiprogramming systems," *Comm. ACM*, vol. 18, no. 7, 1975, pp. 371-377.

[15] M. Crovella and A. Bestravos, "Self-similarity in World Wide Web traffic: evidence and possible causes," in *IEEE/ACM Transactions on Networking*, vol. 5, no. 6, December 1997, pp. 835–846.

[16] L. W. Dowdy, D. Eager, K. Gordon, and L. Saxton, "Throughput concavity and response time convexity," *Information Processing Letters*, no. 19, 1984.

[17] A. Downey, "The structural cause of file size distributions," *Proc. IEEE MASCOTS 2001*, Cincinnati, Ohio, August 2001.

[18] D. Eager, D. Sorin, and M. Vernon, "AMVA techniques for high service time variability," *Proc. 2000 ACM SIGMETRICS Int'l. Conf. on Measurement and Modeling of Computer Systems*, Santa Clara, California, June 2000, pp. 217–228.

[19] A. Feldmann, A. Gilbert, P. Huang, and W. Willinger, "Dynamics of IP traffic: a study of the role of variability and the impact of control," *Proc. ACM SIGCOMM Conf.*, Boston, Massachusetts, September 1999, pp. 301-313.

[20] P. A. Jacobson and E. D. Lazowska, "A reduction technique for evaluating queuing networks with serialization delays," *Performance'83*, eds. A. K. Agrawal and S. K. Tripathi, North-Holland Publishing Co., Amsterdam, 1983, pp. 45–59.

[21] P. A. Jacobson and E. D. Lazowska, "Analyzing queuing networks with simultaneous resource possession," *Comm. ACM*, 25, 2, February 1982, pp. 142–151.

[22] P. Kahkipuro, "Performance modeling framework for CORBA-based distributed systems," Ph.D. Dissertation, Technical Report A-2000-3, Department of Computer Science, University of Helsinki, Finland, 2000.

[23] E. Lazowska, J. Zahorjan, S. Graham, and K. C. Sevcik, *Quantitative System Performance: Computer System Analysis Using Queuing Network Models*, Prentice Hall, Upper Saddle River, New Jersey, 1984.

[24] D. A. Menascé and V. A.F. Almeida, "Operational analysis of multiclass systems with variable multiprogramming level and memory queuing," *Computer Performance*, vol. 3, no. 3, September 1982.

[25] D. A. Menascé, "Two-level iterative queuing modeling of software contention," *Proc. Tenth IEEE/ACM International Symposium on Model-*

ing, Analysis and Simulation of Computer and Telecommunication Systems (MASCOTS 2002), Fort Worth, Texas, October 12-16, 2002.

[26] D. A. Menascé, O. Pentakalos, and Y. Yesha, "An analytic model of hierarchical mass storage systems with network-attached storage devices," *Proc. 1996 ACM Sigmetrics Conf.*, Philadelphia, Pennsylvania, May 1996.

[27] D. Menascé, V. A. F. Almeida, R. Riedi, F. Ribeiro, R. Fonseca, and W. Meira Jr., "A hierarchical and multiscale approach to analyze E-business workloads," *Performance Evaluation*, vol. 54, no. 1, September 2003, pp. 33–57.

[28] V. Paxson and S. Floyd, "Wide area traffic: the failure of Poisson modeling," *IEEE/ACM Tr. Networking*, vol. 3, no. 3, June 1995, pp. 226–244.

[29] S. Ramesh and H. G. Perros, "A multilayer client-server queuing network model with synchronous and asynchronous messages," *IEEE Tr. Software Eng.*, vol. 26, no. 11, November 2000, pp. 1086–1100.

[30] M. Reiser and S. Lavenberg, "Mean-value analysis of closed multi-chain queuing networks," *J. ACM*, vol. 27, no. 2, 1980, pp. 643–673.

[31] M. Reiser, "A queueing network analysis of computer communication networks with window flow control," *IEEE Trans. on Commun.*, vol. 27, no. 8, August 1979.

[32] J. Rolia K. C. Sevcik, "The Method of Layers," *IEEE Tr. Software Eng.*, vol. 21, no. 8, 1995, pp. 689–700.

[33] K. C. Sevcik, "Priority Scheduling Disciplines in Queuing Network Models of Computer Systems," *Proc. IFIP Congress 77*, North-Holland Publishing Co., Amsterdam, 1977, pp. 565–570.

[34] A. Seidmann, P. Schweitzer, and S. Shalev-Oren, "Computerized closed queueing network models of flexible manufacturing systems," *Large Scale Syst. J.*, North-Holland, vol. 12, pp. 91–107, 1987.

[35] P. Schweitzer, "Approximate analysis of multiclass closed network of queues," in *International Conf. Stochastic Control and Optimization*, Amsterdam, 1979.

[36] A. Thomasian, "Queuing network models to estimate serialization delays in computer systems," in *Performance'83*, A. K. Agrawal and S. K. Tripathi (eds.), North-Holland Publishing Co., Amsterdam, 1983, pp. 61–81.

[37] A. Thomasian and P. Bay, "Analysis of queuing network models with population size constraints and delayed blocked customers," *Proc. 1984 ACM SIGMETRICS Conf. Measurement and Modeling of Computer Systems*, Boston, Massachusetts, 1984.

[38] E. Varki, A. Merchant, J. Xu, and X. Qiu, "An integrated performance model of disk arrays," *Proc. IEEE MASCOTS Conf.*, Orlando, Florida, 2003.

[39] E. Varki, "Mean value technique for closed fork-join networks," *Proc. ACM SIGMETRICS Conf. Measurement and Modeling of Computer Systems*, Atlanta, Georgia, May 1999, pp. 103 – 112.

[40] E. Varki and L. W. Dowdy, "Analysis of balanced fork-join systems," *Proc. ACM SIGMETRICS Conf. Measurement and Modeling of Computer Systems*, Philadelphia, Pennsylvania, May 1996.

[41] J. Zahorjan, E. Lazowska, and R. Garner, "A decomposition approach to modelling high service time variability," *Performance Evaluation*, vol. 3, no. 1, pp. 35–53.

[42] C. M. Woodside, "An active-server model for the performance of parallel programs written using rendezvous," *J. Systems and Software*, 1986, pp. 125–131.

Subject Index